Our Catholic Faith

Our Catholic Faith

Living What We Believe

Michael Pennock

ave maria press Notre Dame, Indiana

The Ad Hoc Committee to Oversee the Use of the Catechism, United States Catholic Conference of Catholic Bishops, has found this catechetical text, copyright 2006, to be in conformity with the *Catechism of the Catholic Church.*

Nihil Obstat: The Reverend Michael Heintz

Censor Librorum

Imprimatur: The Most Reverend John M. D'Arcy

Bishop of Diocese of Fort Wayne-South Bend

Given at Fort Wayne, IN on 5 November 2004

The *Nihil Obstat* and *Imprimatur* are official declarations that a book or pamphlet is free of doctrinal or moral error. No implication is contained therein that those who have granted the *Nihil Obstat* or *Imprimatur* agree with its contents, opinions, or statements expressed.

Other references cited as notes on page 280.

Theological Consultant:

Edward P. Hahnenberg, Ph.D.
Professor of Theology
Xavier University
Cincinnati, OH

Religious Education Consultant:

Michael Horan, Ph.D.
Professor of Theological Studies
Loyola Marymount University
Los Angeles, CA

Founded in 1865, Ave Maria Press is a ministry of the Indiana Province of Holy Cross.

www.avemariapress.com

ISBN-10 1-59471-022-8 ISBN-13 978-1-59471-022-3

Project Editor: Michael Amodei

Cover, typesetting, photo research and text design: Katherine Robinson Coleman

Printed and bound in the United States of America.

Cover photo: Tony Gentile/Reuters/Corbis.

Photograpy credits:

Art Resource: p. 57 Erich Lessing/Art Resource, NY; p. 111 Erich Lessing/Art Resource, NY; p. 224 Scala/Art Resource, NY.

Corbis: 10 Behann, 11 Tim Graham, Francis G. Mayer by Raphael, 22 Reuters, 27 National Gallery, 34 Alinari Archives, 75, 207 Reuters, 216 Bettmann, 229 Stepahnie Maze, 238 Historical Picture Archive, 243, 247 Kimbell Art Museum, 268 Kai Pfafenback/Reuters.

Getty Image: 230 Roberto Schmidt/APF

The Crosiers/Gene Plaisted 14, 17, 47, 51, 59, 65, 79, 86, 87, 94, 97, 99, 126, 211, 215, 220, 221, 226.

Bill Wittman 12, 91, 93, 105, 152, 155, 158, 169, 173, 177, 178, 193, 202, 209, 225.

Dedication

To Ken and Luanne Lashutka. Their generosity to Catholic education provided me with a sabbatical year from my teaching to work on this and other writing projects. This remarkable and exemplary Catholic couple has raised a wonderful, faith-filled family. It was my great honor to teach three of their brilliant sons—Matt, Ken, and Phil. Their talented daughters Ann, Lauren, Amy, and Kay are a beautiful embodiment of their love. May God continue to bless Ken and Luanne, their children, and their grandchildren. I am deeply grateful to them for their friendship and Christian witness.

Engaging Minds, Hearts, and Hands

An education that is complete is one in which the hands and heart are engaged as much as the mind. We want to let our students try their learning in the world and so make prayers of their education.

Fr. Basil Moreau,
Founder of the Congregation of Holy Cross

In this text, you will find:

intellectually challenging exercises and projects designed to stimulate you to learn more about the Catholic faith

presentations and activities that promote a prayerful study of the Scripture and connect you to the Church's liturgy

stimulating applications that encourage you in service learning and ministry.

Introduction

Our Catholic Faith

Faith is the realization of what is hoped for and evidence of things not seen.

Hebrews 11:1

We are made up of our faith. Whatever our faith is, so are we.

adapted from an Indian proverb

You Are Wonderful

This true story happened a few years ago at the Paris opera house. It seems that a famous singer had packed the house for the evening's performance but had to bow out at the last moment because of illness. The house manager announced to the tune of audible groans that a stand-in had to replace the ailing star for that evening's performance. The crowd murmured its disappointment so loudly that it failed to hear the replacement's name.

The substitute performer sang brilliantly, but when he finished there was total silence. No one applauded the great performance. Then, from way up in the balcony, a little boy stood up and shouted with glee, "Daddy, I think you are wonderful." Only then did the crowd recognize the superlative performance it had witnessed as it burst into a thunderous standing ovation.[1]

Contents

This story teaches an important lesson. Everyone needs someone in their lives to shout out once in a while, "I think you are wonderful."

The good news of our Catholic faith is that someone is indeed proclaiming that truth to you each day of your life. And that person is Jesus. Picture him hanging from the cross, looking into your eyes, and saying "I think you are wonderful. This is why I am giving my life for you. I love you."

The gift of faith allows us to believe with all our hearts the truth of the Lord's proclamation: "You are wonderful." Unfortunately, like the singer in the story, you may not hear this message often enough or by more than a few people. In fact, contemporary culture may say that you are wonderful only *if* you are good looking, wealthy, live in a certain neighborhood, have a high IQ, are a superior athlete, have a great sense of humor, or (you fill in the blank). All too often, your great God-given worth and value are only acknowledged if you fulfill certain conditions or live up to certain expectations. Rarely will you hear the message that you are wonderful simply because you are you.

The message Christ proclaims is that we have value, dignity, and worth simply because God has made us in his image and likeness. God has destined us for an eternal life of happiness with the Blessed Trinity and our loved ones in heaven. In the words of the great St. Augustine (AD 354–430) in his *Confessions*, "You have created us for yourself, O God, and our hearts are restless until they rest in you."

Life is filled with many deep questions that humans living before Christ had trouble answering: Why am I here? What is my destiny? What is the meaning of life and of death? Does God exist? If so, what is God like? How should I act? The life, death, and resurrection of Christ answers these and other difficult questions. With Christ, human life has great and eternal meaning and dignity.

The Importance of Faith

Which vision of life is correct? The Christian view that holds you are a precious, unique, child of God worth dying for? Or society's view that your worth is tied only to your appearance, what you can do, or how much you own?

How you answer these questions will make all the difference in your life. This textbook will make the point of Christ and his Church, that you have great worth. Faith in Jesus Christ will help you counteract the false message that you are only wonderful if you meet certain conditions. Faith will help give you a true perspective on life and human destiny.

What is faith? Faith is a **virtue.** The *Catechism of the Catholic Church* defines virtue as:

> . . . an habitual and firm disposition to do the good. . . . Human virtues are firm attitudes, stable dispositions, habitual perfections of intellect and will that govern our actions, order our passions, and guide our conduct according to reason and faith. They make possible ease, self-mastery, and joy in leading a morally good life (*CCC*, 1803–4).

virtues—Firm attitudes, stable dispositions, habitual perfections of intellect and will that govern our actions, order our passions, and guide our conduct according to reason and faith (*CCC*, 1804).

theological virtues—Three important virtues bestowed on us at baptism which relate us to God: *faith* (belief in and personal knowledge of God) *hope* (trust in God's salvation and his bestowal of the graces needed to attain it) and *charity* (love of God and love of neighbor).

Discussion Questions

1. Name three qualities you possess that show how "wonderful" you are.
2. List two commercial advertisements that promote a message of conditional acceptance.

Traditionally, there are two categories of virtues: the moral virtues and the **theological virtues.** The four chief moral virtues— prudence, justice, fortitude, and temperance—are known as the cardinal virtues. They get their name from the Latin word *cardo* which means "hinge." Many of the other moral virtues derive from these four, and we will discuss these other virtues in greater detail later in this book.

Faith belongs to the set of virtues known as the theological virtues (*CCC*, 1812–1828). The theological virtues are gifts from God infused into our souls. They enable us to live in relationship to the Blessed Trinity. Their origin, motive, and object is the one, Triune God. The theological virtues are:

1. *Faith.* Faith enables us to believe in God and all that he has said and revealed to us. It also helps us to accept what the Church proposes for our belief, because God is truth himself. Catholics are called not only to cultivate their faith, but also proclaim, bear witness to, and spread it to others.
2. *Hope.* The virtue of hope leads to a desire for heaven and eternal life. It helps us trust in Christ's promises and rely on the help of the Holy Spirit and his graces, not our own strength and abilities. Hope keeps us from getting discouraged as we live the Christian life. Hope makes it possible for us to strive for true happiness and live in imitation of Christ.
3. *Charity (love).* Charity, or love, is the greatest of the virtues. Charity empowers us to love God above all things for his own sake, and our neighbor as ourselves for the love of God (*CCC*, 1822). This key virtue helps us practice all the other virtues. It uplifts our human ability to love, raising it to the perfection of divine love.

Jacopo Tintoretto

England's Prince Harry works in the garden with a little boy at Mants'ase Children's Home, which provides a loving home for destitute children in Lesotho.

Writing Assignment

1. As you begin this semester, write your academic, social, and athletic goals.
2. Write a short essay describing your hopes and dreams for your long-term future.

Reach Out

Be a model of Catholic faith and hospitality. Introduce yourself to a classmate you don't know or don't know well. Make a promise to be friendly to this person and other people you may have ignored in the past throughout the school year.

More about Faith

(*CCC*, 26; 91–100; 142–165; 176–197)

Let's explore the virtue of faith more closely. As noted, faith is a God-given virtue that helps a person firmly embrace the truly good news of our essential goodness and wonderfulness. Faith, in fact, can be thought of as our "lifeline" to God.

Faith is the human response to God's revelation, that is, God's free gift of self-communication. Faith, a gift of the Holy Spirit, enables us to commit ourselves to God totally, both our intellects and our wills. In addition,

1. *Faith makes it possible for us to accept Jesus as Lord.* It endows us with the ability to imitate his life of loving service. Because of faith we can believe God's revealed truths because he has revealed them to us.
2. *Faith in Jesus makes it possible for us to partake of the life of the Holy Spirit who testifies to us who Jesus is.* Thus Christian faith proclaims belief in one God who is a Trinity of Persons: Father, Son, and Holy Spirit.
3. *Faith is a gift, but our response must be free.* No one can be forced to embrace faith against his or her will. Thus, faith is also a free human act in which our hearts and minds cooperate with God's free gift of grace.
4. *Abraham and Mary are two models of faith.* Abraham, the Father of Faith, obeyed God by leaving his homeland to become a pilgrim to a promised land. Because of his faith, God created a people through Abraham and prepared the way for the Messiah. Mary, the Mother of Christ, approached her entire life as a resounding "yes" to God's work. Her fidelity helped fulfill God's plan of salvation through her Son, Jesus Christ.

Faith is an act of the Church. Faith results in **religion** (Latin for "binding into a relationship"). Religion binds us into a relationship with God. Our Catholic religion extends God's invitation to believe in, accept, and dedicate our lives to Christ. Because of God's love for us, at Baptism, Catholics become members of the Church, which is a family of faith who believes that Jesus is Lord.

religion—The relationship between God and humans that results in a body of beliefs and a set of practices: creed, cult, and code. Religion expresses itself in worship and service to God and by extension to all people and all creation.

The faith of the Church comes before the faith of the individual. The faith of the Church gives life to, supports, and nourishes the individual Christian. If we cooperate with faith, we are on the path to eternal life. If we ignore faith, we are subject to God's disapproval:

> "Whoever believes in the Son has eternal life, but whoever disobeys the Son will not see life, but the wrath of God remains upon him" (Jn 3:36).

From the Documents

"The obedience of faith" . . . must be given to God who reveals, an obedience by which man entrusts his whole self freely to God, offering "the full submission of intellect and will to God who reveals," and freely assenting to the truth revealed by Him. If this faith is to be shown, the grace of God and the interior help of the Holy Spirit must precede and assist . . . (*The Constitution on Divine Revelation*, No. 5).

This passage on faith comes from the Second Vatican Council, the twenty-first **ecumenical council** of the Church, held from 1962–1965. This council reformed the Church's liturgy. It also taught on important topics like the Church in today's world, the Church's relationship to other religions, and the role of the laity.

The Constitution on Divine Revelation is one of four Constitutions produced at the Second Vatican Council. The document emphasizes how the Holy Spirit guides the Church by means of Sacred Tradition, Sacred Scripture, and the teaching authority of the Church. The document teaches revelation primarily as God's self-disclosure and secondarily as God's will and intentions. The document also encourages Catholics to read the scriptural word of God.

Read from *The Constitution on Divine Revelation*. Answer: Does a person need God to obtain faith? Explain.

ecumenical council—A worldwide, official assembly of the bishops under the direction of the pope. There have been twenty-one ecumenical councils, the most recent being the Second Vatican Council (1962–1965).

What Catholics Believe

The following are short summaries of Catholic beliefs. These are some of the main beliefs that make us Catholic:

- Jesus Christ is God's Son, the Savior, and the Lord.
- God is a Blessed Trinity, a communion of love, a God worthy of worship and praise.
- The Church is the Body of Christ. Catholics belong to the communion of **saints** and look to saints for inspiration and help. After Jesus himself, Mary, the Mother of God, is the exemplary model of faith.
- The Bible is God's inspired word.
- Faith is conveyed by a living tradition, which is guided by the Holy Spirit and authentically interpreted by the **Magisterium.**
- God can be found in everything. We experience him in a unique and powerful way through the seven sacraments, for example, by experiencing Christ's forgiveness in the sacrament of Penance and by receiving the Risen Lord himself in the sacrament of the Eucharist.
- We are open to truth wherever it is found. We invite all people to grow with the Church in holiness.
- Love and service are hallmarks of our Christian faith. We are fiercely committed to working for peace and justice.

saint—A "holy one" of God who lives in union with God through the grace of Jesus Christ and the power of the Holy Spirit and whom God rewards with eternal life in heaven.

Magisterium—The official teaching authority of the Church. The Lord bestowed the right and power to teach in his name on Peter and the apostles and their successors. The Magisterium is the bishops in communion with the successor of Peter, the Bishop of Rome (pope).

- We are people of hope who see that we have an eternal destiny of union with our God of love.
- We are open to, and strongly defend, the gift of life in all its richness.

Our Catholic Faith is a survey of the Catholic religion. It is divided into three sections: what we believe (the Apostles' Creed); what we hope (celebrating the liturgy and sacraments); and how we live and pray according to Christ's law of love.

Catholic beliefs and teachings are rooted in Sacred Scripture and Sacred Tradition, both of which give us God's revelation. The Magisterium, the Church's official teaching authority comprised of the pope and bishops teaching with him, is responsible for authentically interpreting and passing on divine revelation to us.

In 1992 an official compendium of Catholic Church teaching was published, the ***Catechism of the Catholic Church*** (referenced in this text as *CCC* with the appropriate paragraph cited by number). It is an authoritative, systematic, and comprehensive source of essential beliefs and teachings of the Catholic faith. It is the primary source of reference for this text.

Catechism of the Catholic Church—A compendium of Catholic doctrine on faith and morals published in 1992 that serves Catholics as "a sure norm for teaching the faith" and "an authentic reference text."

The Wedding at Cana

Read John 2:1–12.

Think quietly about the scene. How do you imagine Mary's demeanor as a wedding guest? What lesson does this incident teach about prayer? about service?

Discussion Questions

1. Who models Christian faith for you in an exemplary way? What do you most admire about this person?
2. How is faith like your "lifeline" to God?

Profile of Faith: Mary, the Model Christian

Mary, the Mother of God, is the Queen of the Saints. A saint is a holy person who lives in union with God through the grace of Jesus Christ. Mary is the model of faith.

The biblical account of Mary's life begins in Nazareth, a small town in Galilee of Palestine. Mary was engaged to marry Joseph, a carpenter. While at prayer, the angel Gabriel appeared to her and announced that she would have a child, even though she had not had sexual relations. The angel explained:

> "The holy Spirit will come upon you, and the power of the Most High will overshadow you. Therefore the child to be born will be called holy, the Son of God. And behold, Elizabeth, your relative, has also conceived a son in her old age, and this is the sixth month for her who was called barren; for nothing will be impossible for God" (Lk 1:35–37).

Mary listened carefully to what the angel revealed to her. What the angel said seemed truly impossible—to have a child without having sexual relations with a man. Mary must have been afraid. Still, she trusted and loved God and believed in his power to do anything. Without hesitating, Mary responded:

> "Behold, I am the handmaid of the Lord. May it be done to me according to your word." Then the angel departed from her (Lk 1:38).

Mary's "May it be done to me according to your word" is a powerful symbol of Christian faith. Though she certainly did not fully understand what God had in store for her, Mary said "Yes" to God. Many times we don't fully know every detail of how God is working in our lives. But what God wants from us is not our full understanding. He wants our faith. He leads the way once we surrender to him and allow him into our life.

Luke's gospel reports that the angel left Mary, but God never left her. She instantly conceived God's Son, physically bearing within her womb the Lord who calls each of us his friend. Mary lived the rest of her life in the very presence of God—raising Jesus, teaching him, looking out for his needs, being a good mother.

Mary's original "yes" to God was a demonstration of her faith. She was faithful throughout the rest of her life. She didn't give up when things got tough. She stayed with Jesus to the end, standing beneath the cross at his horrible death. She cried the same tears any loving mother would cry at the death of a son.

Mary was faithful to Jesus in many ways. An incident described in the gospel of Luke reveals one of these ways. When Jesus was twelve years old he became lost from his parents while returning home from a pilgrimage to Jerusalem for the feast of Passover. He had remained in the Temple asking and answering questions of the eminent teachers of the day.

Read Luke 2:41–52.

Imagine Mary's fear and apprehension when she thought she had lost her son. Mary and Joseph did find Jesus. He then returned with them to Nazareth where he lived under their authority. Note Mary's reaction to this incident in Luke 2:51: "His mother kept all these things in her heart." This is the gospel's way of telling us that Mary prayed. She did not fully comprehend everything about her son. But she meditated on the events in his life and the words that he spoke.

Mary teaches us how to be faithful to Jesus Christ; simply to pray and serve. Pray on how God speaks to you in your life. Keep his words close to your heart. And then, like Mary, take the Lord who has been given to you and serve others in his name.

SummaryPoints

- ★ We possess dignity as children of God made in his image and likeness.
- ★ Faith is one of the theological virtues that relate us to the Blessed Trinity. It enables us to believe in God and in all that God has revealed to us.
- ★ A virtue is "an habitual and firm disposition to do the good."
- ★ Faith results in religion which binds us into a relationship with God. Christian faith results in the Christian religion where we believe in, accept, and dedicate our lives to Jesus Christ.
- ★ Faith is a response to God's revelation, that is, his free gift of self-communication. It is a gift and requires free acceptance.
- ★ Abraham, from the Old Testament, is known as the "Father of Faith." The best model of Christian faith is Mary, the Mother of God, who lived a faithful life of service and prayer.
- ★ Faith requires obedience, that is, submission of one's intellect and will to our loving God who has freely given himself to us.
- ★ The Magisterium of the Church is responsible for interpreting and transmitting Catholic beliefs and teachings that are found in Sacred Scripture and Sacred Tradition.

ReviewQuestions

1. How does society grant conditional acceptance to people? What is wrong with this practice?
2. What essential message about the worth of human beings does Jesus Christ give to us?
3. Name the theological virtues.
4. Name the cardinal virtues.
5. Define *virtue*.
6. Discuss three qualities of the virtue of faith.
7. What is religion?
8. Identify *The Constitution on Divine Revelation*.
9. Define *Magisterium*.
10. Identify the *Catechism of the Catholic Church*.
11. How is Mary a model of faith, service, and prayer?
12. Define *saint*.

ApplyingWhatYou HaveLearned

1. Prepare a short report on one of the following:
   - ▶ one of the popular Catholic devotions to Mary (for example, the rosary or a novena)
   - ▶ the meaning of three of the titles of Mary (for example, Immaculate Mother, Our Lady of Perpetual Help, Queen of Peace)
   - ▶ one of the apparitions of Mary (for example, at Lourdes or Fatima)
2. Write a letter to a person who has been a model of faith to you. Tell the person in the letter why he or she has been an inspiration. Mail your letter or deliver it in person.

PrayerReflection

When Mary heard the news that she was to be God's mother, she prayed from her heart the following prayer, the Magnificat, found in Luke 1:46–55:

"My soul proclaims the greatness of the Lord;
my spirit rejoices in God my savior.
For he has looked upon his handmaid's lowliness;
behold, from now on will all ages call me blessed.
The Mighty One has done great things for me,
and holy is his name.
His mercy is from age to age to those who fear him.
He has shown might with his arm,
dispersed the arrogant of mind and heart.
He has thrown down the rulers from their thrones
but lifted up the lowly.
The hungry he has filled with good things;
the rich he has sent away empty.
He has helped Israel his servant, remembering his mercy,
according to the promise to our fathers,
to Abraham and to his descendants forever." Amen.

✣ What does it mean to be humble? How can you practice the gift of humility as represented by Mary?

Our Lady of Guadalupe

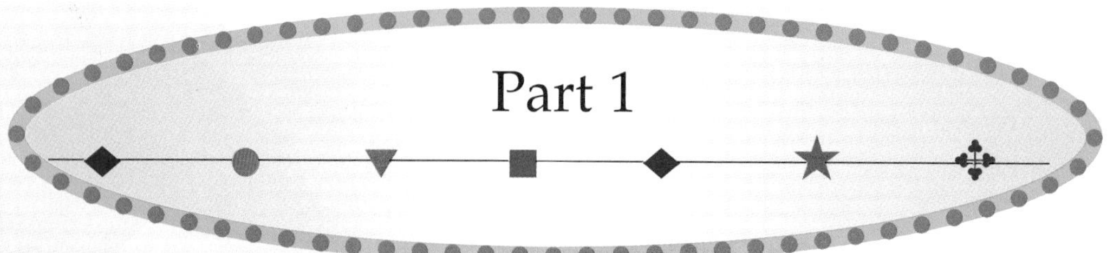

Part 1

We Believe: The Apostles' Creed

Creed: An Expression of Faith

(*CCC*, 166–197)

Faith results in a relationship with Jesus Christ and the Church. Faith brings about the Catholic religion, which has three aspects to it:

1. what we believe,
2. how we worship and pray, and
3. how we live in response to our beliefs.

The *what* of Catholic faith is summarized in its various creeds, including the Church's two most popular creeds—the Nicene Creed, which is recited publicly during Sunday Mass; and the Apostles' Creed, which each believer professes personally at Baptism and at the beginning of each rosary.

A *creed*—from the Latin word *credo* ("I believe")—is a statement of belief. A person who recites a creed makes a personal act of faith. Yet a Christian profession of faith is always made as part of the Church. Our faith comes from God through the Church; it is not something we invent. We believe as a community of believers. Professing our faith in a creed helps unite us to fellow believers. It is similar to the sense of unity and patriotism that results when citizens pledge their allegiance to the flag.

You are probably familiar with the Nicene Creed professed at Mass. It formulates essential Christian doctrines about God the Father, God the

Son, God the Holy Spirit, the Church, salvation, and human destiny. It resulted after decades of controversy begun by Arius, an Egyptian priest. Arius denied that Jesus, the Son, always existed with the Father. Therefore, he rejected the divinity of Christ.

The raging Arian controversy caused extreme dissension in the Church. Due to this, the Emperor Constantine convoked the first general or ecumenical council at Nicaea in 325. One of its major achievements was to reaffirm clearly the divinity of Jesus by issuing the Nicene Creed. The second ecumenical council, the Council of Constantinople (381), endorsed and expanded this creed. The Nicene Creed has served as an excellent summary of Catholic faith ever since.

Based on Part 1 of the *Catechism of the Catholic Church,* chapters 1 to 5 of this text are organized around another faith summary, the Apostles' Creed, which was developed between the second and ninth centuries. The Apostles' Creed is firmly rooted in an early baptismal creed used in Rome in the second century. This is significant because Peter, the first of the apostles and the Christ-appointed leader of the Church, came to Rome to establish the Church there. Thus, the great authority of the Apostles' Creed goes all the way back to the theological formulas that arose during the time of Peter (the first pope) and the apostles.

The Apostles' Creed is simple, short, logically ordered, and prayerful. It highlights the essential Christian doctrine of the Blessed Trinity by proclaiming faith in

- the first divine Person (the almighty and eternal God the Father) and the work of creation;
- the second divine Person (Jesus Christ, God-made-man) and his work of redemption; and
- the third divine Person (the Holy Spirit), who is the origin and source of sanctification that comes to us through Christ's one, holy, catholic, and apostolic Church (CCC, 190).

The Apostles' Creed

I believe in God, the Father almighty,
creator of heaven and earth.
I believe in Jesus Christ, his only Son, our Lord.
He was conceived by the power of the Holy Spirit,
and born of the Virgin Mary.
He suffered under Pontius Pilate,
was crucified, died, and was buried.
He descended into hell.
On the third day he rose again.
He ascended into heaven,
and is seated at the right hand of the Father.
He will come again to judge the living and the dead.
I believe in the Holy Spirit,
the holy catholic Church,
the communion of saints,
the forgiveness of sins,
the resurrection of the body,
and the life everlasting. Amen.

The Lord is true God, he is the living God, the eternal King.

Jeremiah 10:10

Chapter 1 Outline

One, True God

God reveals himself to us through our natural reason.

Beliefs about God

There are no more important questions than those dealing with God's existence.

Divine Revelation

God makes himself known through the mystery of his divine plan.

Who Is God?

God has revealed himself as a Trinity of persons.

Creator of Heaven and Earth

God created out of his wisdom and love in order to share his glory.

Chapter 1

Our Loving God: Father and Creator

Josh Heupel

One, True God

Our culture is certainly overwhelmed by sports. Professional and amateur athletes alike face the constant temptations of money, power, and fame. Many athletes in the public eye disappoint themselves and their fans with poor behavior brought to the public's attention. Religion, faith, and God sometimes seem to come in a distant second to athletics and all of its trappings. But there are exceptions to this generalized premise.

One example is Josh Heupel, the quarterback of the Oklahoma Sooners when they won the 2000 National Championship. In November, before a game with Texas Tech, Josh spearhead a campaign that would eventually collect enough food to feed 250 families on Thanksgiving Day.

Josh's mom described him as always being a caring person, but Josh said a serious football injury while playing for a community college in Utah helped to put his life in perspective. "Things weren't going along the way I planned. My first year in college I allowed other things to become number one. I had to give God complete control over my life."

Shelly Pennefather, the woman's college basketball player of the year in 1987 at Villanova, is another athlete who went to dramatic lengths to put God first in her life. Giving up a lucrative professional basketball career in Japan, Shelly became Sister Rose Marie, a cloistered nun with the Colettine Poor Clares in 1991. The path she chose was not a complete surprise to family members and friends; Shelly had counseled her college coach on the breakup of his marriage and once donated $25,000 she received as a basketball bonus to Mother Teresa's order, the Missionaries of Charity.

Both Josh and Shelly lived in a public way their faith in God, a definite contrast to those who put God on the "backburner" and save thoughts of him for only special times in a day or week. They are certainly apart from many, including **atheists**, who fail to acknowledge God at all.

This chapter discusses the revelation of God as a loving Father and Creator of all that exists. All other aspects of our Catholic faith flow from our belief in the one, true God whom we profess in the Apostles' Creed.

atheist—A person who denies the existence of God.

Beliefs about God

There are many views of God held by people in our world today. Here are some of them. Evaluate each statement according to this scale:

1—I believe this is a correct belief about God.

2—There is some merit to this belief.

3—This is a clearly wrong belief about God.

1. There is a God, and God does indeed make a difference. God made and cares for everything, including me.
2. It is reasonable to conclude that God exists, but I don't see how God could possibly be interested in me. I am like a grain of sand in the immense universe. God is all-powerful, infinite, and much greater than I am.
3. There is no God. God is just an excuse for what cannot be explained. As scientists better explain the "mysteries" of the universe, then we will discover that we simply do not "need" the idea of a God.
4. There is no God. If God did exist why would he allow terrorist attacks on innocent people, senseless wars, helpless fatalities of natural disasters like hurricanes, and ravaging diseases? The best argument against God is the existence of so much evil in the world.
5. Jesus Christ is God. He is my Lord and Savior!
6. Since you can't prove God's existence one way or another, what's the big deal? Best to say, "I don't know."

Discussion Questions

1. Why did you accept or reject any of the statements?
2. Which of the statements must a Catholic believe? Why?
3. Which statements are, in your judgment, clearly false? Why?

Beliefs about God

Few questions are more important than the question of God's existence. Through history, the vast majority of people have worshiped some kind of deity. For example, the ancient Egyptians, Greeks, Romans, Aztecs, and many other civilizations all had involved systems revolving around belief in gods.

Today, it is estimated that well over 90 percent of the world's population believes in God's existence. The number of people who belong to the world's great religions attests to this. Christianity, Judaism, and Islam together claim more than 50 percent of the world's population. They are all **monotheistic** religions, that is, they believe in one (*mono*) God (*theos*). On the other hand, popular Hinduism is **polytheistic**, that is, holding belief in many gods and goddesses. Buddhism, though not believing in a personal god, does hold that there is a sole Ultimate Reality in the Universe.

Some who label themselves as believers take a more philosophical approach to religion. An example is **deism** (illustrated in the second statement in the exercise above). Many of the founding fathers of the United States of America (including George Washington and Thomas Jefferson) were deists who thought of God as a watchmaker or absentee landlord. In other words, the deists believed that God created the universe by "winding it up" and then staying outside his creation while it "worked" on its own. Most deists do not think God destined a special people to know him. Nor do they believe that God performs miracles by becoming involved in his creation.

A recent study found that less than one percent of Americans claim to be atheists.[2] Atheists are people who do not believe in the existence of God, supernatural beings, or heaven and hell. (The third and fourth statements in the exercise above illustrate some of their reasons.) Many atheists are also *secular humanists*. Secular humanists claim that the world can operate without any recourse to God. Humanism makes the human person and human achievement the center of the universe.

monotheistic—Religions that believe that there is only one God. Christianity, Judaism, and Islam are the three great monotheistic world religions.

polytheistic—Religions that believe in multiple gods and goddesses. The ancient Greeks and Romans were polytheistic as is the Hindu faith.

deism—The belief that God did create the universe but that he takes no further interest in it.

agnostics—People who claim that God's existence cannot be known.

Related to atheists are **agnostics** (from a Greek word that translates to "don't know"). Agnostics hold that God's existence cannot be proved or disproved. (The sixth statement in the exercise reflects this view.) Agnostics answer "I don't know" when asked if they believe in God and usually act as though God does not exist. Less than one percent of Americans claim to be agnostics. Divorced from religion, some atheists and agnostics live a hedonistic life where the pursuit of pleasure acts as their god.

Belief in God is reasonable. The fact that so many people through the ages have believed in God and have practiced some kind of religion that involves prayer, ritual, sacrifice, and an ethical code is a strong indicator that humans have a religious nature. Humans intuit that there is some Power in the universe much greater and more awesome than themselves.

But what about the great variety of religions? Does the fact that there are so many varying beliefs about God and differences in worship and doctrine disprove God's existence? Not really. Rather, these differences point out that the human intellect can discover a Supreme Being, but that

A.Buddhist monk in Thailand, **B.** Notre Dame Cathedral in France, **C.** Chiang Mai temple, Thailand **D.** Korean temple, **E.** Asian Buddha statue, **F.** Mormon church.

God's complete identity remains a mystery, only to be discovered with God's direct help or revelation. In fact, the Church teaches "by natural reason man can know God with certainty, on the basis of his works" (*CCC*, 50). St. Paul also understood this to be true:

> For what can be known about God is evident . . . because God made it evident . . . . Ever since the creation of the world, his invisible attributes of eternal power and divinity have been able to be understood and perceived in what he has made (Rom 1:19–20).

There is no ironclad way of proving God's existence. But there *are* signs all around us that point to God. Intelligent people can discover these signs, reflect on them, and reasonably conclude that they point to a Supreme Being. Some of these signs appeal to the intellect, others appeal to the heart or feelings.

Intellectual Proofs for God's Existence

Throughout human history many excellent arguments have been advanced that demonstrate God's existence. St. Thomas Aquinas's (1225–1274) ideas (based on the Greek philosopher, Aristotle) provide us with five "proofs" for the existence of God:

1. *The Unmoved Mover.* There is motion in the world (for example, neutrons, electrons, protons, atoms, etc.). Whatever is in motion had to be moved by something else. This "something else" also must have been moved by Something or Someone. Continue imagining back to the beginning of time and we must conclude there was a "First Mover," an "Unmoved Mover," which is God.
2. *First Cause.* Nothing causes itself. For example, a painting comes about from an artist who was brought into existence by her parents. Who caused these parents? Keep going back to the beginning and you must conclude there was a First Cause or Uncaused Cause which was eternal. This Being we call God. Today, even those who accept the "big bang" theory of the origin of the universe are forced to ask questions about where the primeval matter that started everything came from. The only logical answer is a Divine Being who made it.
3. *Everything Comes from Something* (i.e., "the cosmological argument"). "Nothing" cannot create "something." Therefore, we are forced to conclude there must be one necessary, eternal Being (God) who always was and brought other beings into existence.
4. *Supreme Model.* Persons and things in this world have different *degrees* of qualities like goodness, truth, beauty, justice, and so forth. But we can only speak of different degrees of these qualities by comparing them to a Supreme Model or reference point. This perfect model of goodness, truth, beauty is the perfect being we call God.
5. *Grand Designer.* There is a beauty, immensity, symmetry, and power in our world that forces us to conclude that a Grand Designer made it all. A simple spider spinning its web, a beaver building its dam, the earth rotating around the sun, the chemical mix that produces life, the awesome process of human reproduction—all these and countless other realities suggest a God who implanted laws in the universe to make it work right. G.K. Chesterton once said, "Show me a watch without a watchmaker, then I'll take a universe without a Universe-Maker."

A good application of St. Thomas's five proofs is to ask the simple question, "How did we humans get here?" First, scientists have yet to explain how life could have evolved from matter. Second, statisticians say it is virtually impossible for intelligent, human life to appear by mere chance. Third, when we look at the course of human development, we can detect a hidden but powerfully present Intelligence that is leading and guiding us. The mystery of human life and history *has* to be rooted in the Mystery at the heart of the universe.

Heartfelt Proofs for God's Existence

"The desire for God is written in the human heart, because man is created by God and for God" (*CCC*, 27). We see this deep yearning for God reveal itself in many ways, including:

1. *An unquenchable thirst for joy and happiness.* We all want to be happy. We spend a lot of our time and energy doing and getting things that we think will make us happy. Yet our happiness fades and we soon find ourselves desiring something else. Are we creatures doomed to be ultimately frustrated? We want happiness, but the more we pursue it, the more it slips away. A possible explanation for this reality is that our Creator God implanted in us a kind of homing device that causes us to be restless until we find him. This restlessness for total happiness points to a God who made us this way. Consider the opposite: If there is no God then there is no meaning to life. Our deep yearning for everlasting happiness and joy becomes a meaningless joke.
2. *An experience of beauty and truth.* So much of the beauty and truth of heaven is found on earth: a starlit sky, a breathtaking sunset, or a beautiful piece of music. When we experience profound joy in the presence of some awesome experience, when we encounter truth and it seems so perfectly right, we are getting a taste of God's beauty and truth. God made us, understands us, loves us, and gives us a taste of heaven on earth.
3. *A sense of personal conscience, moral goodness, and justice.* In the depths of our souls we sense God's voice teaching us that we must always do good (for example, treat others fairly) and always avoid evil (for example, "Do not murder"). We sense that there is an absolute moral authority—God—that teaches the standard of human behavior. We also imagine a God of justice. It seems unfair to us that cheaters, liars, and killers often prosper in this life while some good people suffer and are taken advantage of. We have a fundamental feeling that things will be reversed someday, that there is a Power that will right all wrongs, if not in this life, then in the next.
4. *Love.* Love is a spiritual reality with origins that the material universe cannot explain. In fact, love comes from love itself, the being we call God. (The same argument holds for intelligence; it must ultimately come from intelligence itself, that is, God.)

Given the many signs of head and heart that point to the existence of God, it's easy to see that the French philosopher, Blaise Pascal (1623–1662), is right on. He said it is a good bet to believe in God. "If you win, you win everything." With faith in God comes a big payoff—eternal life. With atheism, you only have everything to lose.

Understanding God

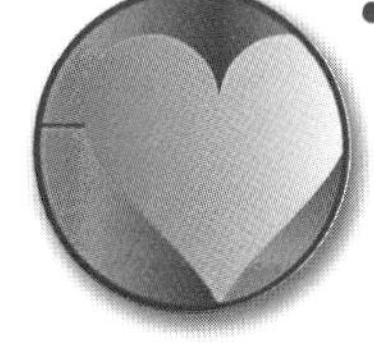

The Scriptures stress both God's **transcendence** and **immanence.** These terms can help us to understand more about God.

- ★ Transcendence is the quality of God's total uniqueness and infinite greatness compared to his creatures. Psalm 102 puts it this way: "They shall perish, but you remain though all of them grow old like a garment; . . . but you are the same, and your years have no end" (27–28).
- ★ God's immanence, on the other hand, refers to God's being in the world, his closeness to, and intimacy with us. In preaching to the Athenians, St. Paul emphasized this quality when he said, "In him we live and move and have our being" (Acts 17:28). A wonderful example of God's immanence is when he allows us mere creatures to receive his very Son, Jesus Christ, in Holy Communion.

1. What kind of God (immanent or transcendent) do you experience when you are happy? worried? guilty? peaceful?
2. Interview two adults and two peers. Ask them for two reasons for believing or not believing in God. Share and compare responses.
3. Choose a piece of *instrumental* music (classical or otherwise) that speaks to you of beauty, truth, or goodness. Listen to the music. Write two or three paragraphs explaining how this music speaks to you of God or other spiritual realities.

Thomas Aquinas

Thomas Aquinas was born in approximately 1225 to a noble family. As a child, his brilliant mind was already asking his Benedictine teachers about God's nature. Against the fierce opposition of his family, at eighteen he joined the relatively new Dominican Order, which had become known for its quality of preachers and teachers.

Thomas studied under the brilliant St. Albert the Great at the University of Cologne. Tradition holds that Thomas merited the nickname "Dumb Ox" for his quiet manner and huge size, but he proved himself to be the most brilliant of all students. Albert reportedly said of him, "This ox will one day fill the world with his bellowing."

After ordination, Thomas received his doctoral degree at the University of Paris. He then embarked on an untiring life of teaching and preaching. But it was his writing that made him a marvel in his own day and the genius theologian of the Catholic Church for all time. A prolific writer of more than sixty works, Thomas's masterpiece is the *Summa Theologica (Summary Treatise of Theology,* 1265–1273). It marks the summit of *scholastic philosophy,* which reconciled Christian faith with human reason and the works of Aristotle with Scripture.

Thomas's contributions to human thought are immeasurable. Besides

Discussion Questions

1. Do you feel that belief in God is reasonable? Explain.
2. Which proof of God's existence leaves you with the most questions? Which proof of God's existence answers more of your questions?
3. Why do you believe in God?

transcendence—A trait of God that refers to God's total otherness and being infinitely beyond and independent of creation.

immanence—A trait of God which refers to God's intimate union with and total presence to his creation.

Doctor of the Çhurch—A Church writer of great learning and holiness whose works the Church has highly recommended for studying and living the faith.

his arguments for the existence of God, Thomas explained how human intellect is necessary to understand the knowledge that humans receive through the five senses and to grasp immaterial realities like God and the human soul. Many truths can be known through human reason—like the nature of the material world and the existence of God—but others can only be grasped through divine revelation (God revealing it to man)—like God taking human form in the person of Christ. Reason and revelation work hand-in-hand and are not opposed to each other. On the one hand, Christian faith can preserve human reason from error. On the other hand, reason can serve the faith, for example, by clearly explaining and defending the truths that God has revealed to us.

Toward the end of his life (December 6, 1273), Thomas had such an ecstatic experience of God that it caused him to stop writing altogether. He said, "I can do no more. Such secrets have been revealed to me that all I have written now appears to be of little value." Thus, he never finished the *Summa;* he died a few months later (March 7, 1274).

Thomas was declared a saint in 1323 and named a **Doctor of the Church,** that is a person of great learning and knowledge whose works the Church has highly recommended for studying and living the faith.

Read more about St. Thomas Aquinas at these websites:
Catholic online: Saints and Angels:
www.catholic.org/saints/saint.php?saint_id=2530
Catholic Forum: Patron Saints:
www.catholic-forum.com/saints/saintt03.htm
New Advent:
www.newadvent.org/cathen/14663b.htm

Divine Revelation *(CCC, 50-73)*

Although human reason can discover that God exists, left to itself it cannot get a true picture of who God really is. God is truly a mystery; his ways are above our ways; his thoughts are not our thoughts (see Is 55:8).

Out of his infinite love and goodness, God freely revealed himself to human beings. Revelation means "unveiling." The God of mystery is beyond human comprehension. Yet, he freely chose to step into history, speak to us through the law and prophets, and invite us into a deeper relationship by sending to us his only divine Son, Jesus Christ. *Divine revelation* refers to this free gift of God's self-communication by which he makes known the mystery of his divine plan.

God's revelation mainly uncovers his saving love. The account of God's saving activity for mankind is known as *salvation history*. Salvation history begins with the creation of the first humans and the beautiful world we live in (told in Genesis 1–2). But this is only the beginning. Adam and Eve disobeyed God and committed the original sin, falling out of friendship with God. God might have abandoned his creatures at this point, but he did not.

Rather, out of his infinite love God established a series of covenants with mankind. A **covenant** is a solemn agreement, an open-ended contract of love in which God commits himself totally to human beings. In the Old Testament, God promised to be faithful to us forever while humans were to remain faithful to him. He promised salvation, redemption, and eternal life. The **Bible** records a number of these covenants, the most of important of which are:

covenant—The open-ended contract of love between God and human beings. Jesus' death and resurrection sealed God's new covenant of love for all time. *Testament* translates to *covenant.*

Bible—The inspired word of God; the written record of revelation.

- ★ *The Covenant with Noah.* After the Flood, God made a covenant with Noah and his descendants and with "every living creature" (Gn 9:10) that was with Noah on the ark. God promised that never again would a flood destroy the earth.
- ★ *The Covenant with Abraham.* A major chapter in salvation history is God's covenant with Abraham, the Father of Faith for the Jewish people and our spiritual father because of our shared ancestry with the Jews. Part of this covenant involved circumcision for Jewish males as a way to set apart the people God would form from Abraham's descendants.
- ★ *The Sinai Covenant.* God formed Israel as his people when he freed them from slavery in Egypt at the time of the Exodus. He gave the Chosen People his law through Moses on Mount Sinai. The Law taught Israel to acknowledge Yahweh as the one, living, and true God. But it did not offer a means of redemption. Through the prophets who came after Moses, God gave Israel hope for salvation. They proclaimed a new covenant to be written on human hearts. They gave hope for a future Messiah who would bring salvation.
- ★ *Jesus Christ, the New Covenant.* The climax of salvation history was the coming of Jesus Christ, God's Son, the fullness of God's revelation. Jesus is God's total Word made flesh, the Son, who lived among us. He taught us in word and deed about God and completed the Father's work of salvation. Since Jesus Christ is God's final word, there will be no further revelation after him. To see Jesus is to see the Father.

Sacred Scripture and Sacred Tradition (*CCC*, 74–141).

God reveals himself through a single "deposit" of faith. Christ entrusted this deposit to the apostles. Inspired by the Holy Spirit, they handed it on through their preaching and their writing to the Church, until Christ will come again. This single deposit is found in Sacred Scripture (Bible) and in the Sacred Tradition of the Church.

Sacred Scripture is like a library of divinely inspired writings (Bible means "books"). God used human authors and their unique talents to put into writing what he wanted written, and nothing more. "The books of Scripture firmly, faithfully, and without error teach that truth which God, for the sake of our salvation, wished to see confided to the Sacred Scriptures" (*Dogmatic Constitution on Divine Revelation*, No. 11, quoted in CCC, 107). This means that the Bible is inerrant; that is, it contains no errors. See pages 262–263 of the Appendix: Catholic Handbook for Faith for more information about the Bible.

Discussion Questions

1. How is a marriage covenant like a covenant between God and mankind?
2. How is Jesus' coming the climax of history?
3. Name three ways that God has revealed himself to you.

A God of Love and Truth (CCC, 218-221; 231)

The Old Testament revealed God as "abounding in steadfast love and faithfulness" (Ex 34:6 as quoted in *CCC*, 214). These qualities are much in evidence in the history of the Jewish nation. For example:

- God chooses the Hebrews and makes them a people (Gn 12:1-2).
- God frees the Israelites from Egypt (Ex 3:8).
- God establishes a covenant with the Israelites, making them a holy nation. God gives them the law through Moses (Ex 19:5-6).
- God gives Israel a land (Jos 1:11).
- God establishes the kingdom of David (2 Sm 7:8-16.)
- God sends prophets to guide Israel (2 Kgs 17:13).
- God sustains the Chosen People in Babylon and restores them to Israel (Is 40:1-2).

Images of God

The Old Testament offers a variety of images for God. Read the following passages. Note the image of God highlighted in the passages.

1. Isaiah 49:15
2. Psalm 24:8, 10
3. Deuteronomy 32:11
4. Hosea 11:1-4

Compose your own prayer of praise using a personally meaningful image for God.

Sacred Tradition—The living transmission of the Church's gospel message found in the Church's teaching, life, and worship. It is faithfully preserved, handed on, and interpreted by the Church's Magisterium.

dogma—A central truth of revelation that Catholics are obliged to believe.

Sacred Tradition is the living transmission or "handing on" of the Church's gospel message. We find this Tradition in the Church's teaching, life, and worship. The apostles, inspired by the Spirit, were the first to receive the gift of faith. They in turn gave it to the care of their successors—the pope and bishops—to "faithfully preserve, expound, and spread . . . by their preaching" (*Dogmatic Constitution on Divine Revelation*, No. 9, quoted in *CCC*, 81).

Christ commissioned the apostles to interpret authentically God's Word—both Scripture and Tradition. This Christ-appointed teaching authority, which extended to the pope and the bishops in communion with him, is known as the *Magisterium* (from the Latin word for "teacher"). With the help of the Holy Spirit, the Magisterium teaches with Christ's own authority. This is especially so when the Magisterium defines a **dogma**, that is, a central truth of revelation that Catholics are obliged to believe.

Recall that faith (*CCC,* 26, 91–100; 142–171) is the theological virtue that enables us to believe in God and all that he has revealed to us and all that the Church teaches regarding our faith. Through faith we can commit our whole lives to God and say "yes" to the gift of revelation given to us in Christ our Lord. In summary, the free response of faith makes us part of the Church, enables us to accept Jesus as Lord, partake in the life of the Blessed Trinity, and commit ourselves totally to God, both with our intellects and wills.

Who Is God? (*CCC,* 205–237; 268–271)

A name expresses a person's inner identity. When Moses encountered God in the burning bush, God revealed his name to Moses—**Yahweh**, "I Am" (see Ex 3:4–14). This holiest of all names can also mean "I am he who is," "I am who I am," or "I am who am." The name Yahweh shows that God is not some impersonal force, but one who creates everything out of nothing and keeps it in existence. God is *omnipresent*; he is everywhere.

Yahweh—The sacred Hebrew name for God which means "I am who am," "I am," or "I am who I am."

The name Yahweh also acknowledges God's mystery. Moses knew this when he took off his shoes and bowed in reverence. God's omnipotent and eternal nature is beyond human understanding. Yahweh reveals himself to be the Holy One in our midst, a God of truth and love. "God's truth is his wisdom, which commands the whole created order and governs the world" (*CCC,* 216).

In fact, God's only motive for revealing himself and for choosing the Jews from among all people is his totally free gift of love. This love is constant. Despite human sinfulness, the Lord is "a merciful and gracious God, slow to anger and rich in kindness and fidelity, continuing his kindness for a thousand generations, and forgiving wickedness and crime and sin" (Ex 34:6–7).

Attributes of Almighty God

God has revealed for us several of his attributes. The Apostles' Creed identifies only one of God's attributes: *omnipotence.* This means that God is almighty. God's power is unlimited, but it is a loving, merciful, and gracious power.

The almighty God possesses many other qualities that are part of his mysterious nature. These attributes are beyond our comprehension and can only be understood by analogy, that is, by comparing something familiar to something unfamiliar. For example, we examine God's perfection by looking first at a human quality like intelligence. Second, we understand that God's intelligence is not like human intelligence, since human intelligence is limited. Third, we state that God transcends, that is, goes infinitely beyond anything humans can understand. God is a perfect being. God is intelligence itself. God is, thus, all knowing.

St. Thomas Aquinas listed the following nine attributes of God that are evidenced through history and in scriptures:

1. *God is unique.* There is no God like Yahweh (see Is 45:18).
2. *God is infinite and omnipotent.* God is everywhere, unlimited, and all-powerful. God can do everything (see Ps 135:5–6).

Describing God

Decide which attribute of God is being named or described in the following scripture passages:

- Lamentations 5:17–20
- Jeremiah 10:10–12
- Psalm 139:1–6
- Isaiah 55

3. *God is eternal.* God always was and always will be. God is the one being who cannot not be. God is (see Is 40:28).
4. *God is immense.* God is not limited to space (see 1 Kgs 8:27).
5. *God contains all things* (see Wis 8:1).
6. *God is immutable.* God does not change—ever (see Ps 102:25–28).
7. *God is utterly simple—a pure Spirit.* The opposite of simple is complex, which means divisible into parts. In God there are no parts, no divisions. God is not material. God's image cannot be made (see Ex 20:4).
8. *God is personal.* God is alive (the source of all life), knows all things, and loves and cares beyond limit. The saving God manifested personal love through the compassionate acts in the history of the Israelites and most supremely by sending his Son, Jesus Christ, to all people (see Jer 31:3).
9. *God is holy.* Holiness is a quality of being absolutely other than creation (see Is 55:8). God's goodness and love are unlimited. We cannot praise the holy God enough.

Discussion Questions

1. How does your name express who you are?
2. Which attribute of God is hardest for you to understand? Why?
3. Why is it appropriate to call God Father?
4. Tell about a loving human father you know who is like God.

God the Father (CCC, 232–242; 261–262).

God the Father is the first person of the **Blessed Trinity**. God has revealed himself as a Trinity of persons. Jesus addressed God as Father (e.g., Jn 17:1) and taught others to do so. God the Father named Jesus as his son (e.g., Lk 3:22). God the Son revealed that the Father would send the Holy Spirit in his name, a Spirit of truth and love (e.g., Jn 14:16–17).

Blessed Trinity—The central dogma of the Christian faith that there are three divine Persons—Father, Son, and Holy Spirit—in one God.

The Blessed Trinity is the central mystery of faith and the source of all other mysteries. This mystery reveals that Jesus is the visible image of God the Father and that the Holy Spirit is sent by the Father in the name of the Son. The activity of the one true God—who is Father, Son, and Holy Spirit—reveals, reconciles, and unites himself to us. This is the story of salvation history. (The dogma of the Blessed Trinity is presented in more detail in Chapter 3.)

Jesus taught us to pray to **Abba**, our Father. Abba is child's word in Aramaic for father, something like "daddy." It is a word of endearment and love. By addressing God as Abba, Jesus showed that God is a loving Father, one whose children should approach him with love and confidence and treat each other as brothers and sisters.

Abba—An Aramaic term of endearment meaning "Daddy." Jesus used this word to teach that God is a loving Father.

Jesus' relationship to the Father is unique. God is Father in eternal relationship with his only Son, who in turn is eternally in relationship to his Father. Jesus is the Word of God who is with the Father from all time; the Word of God is God. Jesus also taught:

> All things have been handed over to me by my Father. No one knows the Son except the Father, and no one knows the Father except the Son and anyone to whom the Son wishes to reveal him (Mt 11:27).

It is right and proper to call God "Father." Today, however, some have difficulties with the address of God as Father, claiming that it creates the impression that God is male. This is not true. God is beyond the biological distinction of male and female. Both men and women are made "in the image and likeness of God." Therefore, it is also proper to use images of motherhood to emphasize God's closeness to us and care for us. For example, the book of Isaiah describes God in this way: "As a mother comforts her son, so will I comfort you" (Is 66:13). Images of parental love can be helpful in understanding God. However, human parents are weak and imperfect. God goes infinitely beyond any human standard of parenthood. "No one is father as God is Father" (*CCC*, 239).

Catholics continue to address God as Father because this is the language of Jesus, the language of revelation, the language of our faith. We call God "Father" because Jesus teaches us to do just that.

Genesis Creation Accounts

The book of Genesis includes two stories of creation. These stories are interested in the *why* of creation; they do not describe *how* the world began. The Bible is not a scientific textbook. Rather, it is a record of revelation about God's love affair with human beings. What the Biblical authors were interested in was religious truth. For example, regardless of how the created world came to be, God is the source of all that is. They also teach the basic reason for human existence and destiny, the meaning and source of evil, God's saving action in human history, and so forth. Thus, when reading these stories, be on the alert for *religious* truth, not scientific fact.

1. Read the first creation story (Gn 1:1–2:4a). Name something God created each day. What does God do on the seventh day?
2. Read the second creation story (Gn 2:4b–25). Why did God create Eve? What does God forbid?

Creator of Heaven and Earth

(*CCC*, 279–308; 315–323; 337–349; 353–384)

Both Scripture and Tradition firmly teach that the Triune God created out of his wisdom and love to show forth and communicate his glory. Creation is not the result of blind chance or fate. God created out of his love, wisdom, and great desire to share his beauty, truth, goodness, and life, especially by making us his adopted children through Jesus Christ by power of the Holy Spirit.

The opening verse in the Bible proclaims that God alone is the Creator of all that exists outside himself; he alone keeps everything that is in existence. Therefore, everything in the world, including human beings, is entirely dependent on God.

The hand of God is an early Christian symbol for God the Father. It represents God's ownership of and providence for all of creation, and comes from the many references to the "hand of God" in the Bible. For example, "O Sovereign LORD, you have begun to show to your servant your greatness and your strong hand. For what god is there in heaven or on earth who can do the deeds and mighty works you do?" (Dt 3:24, *NIV*).

Divine revelation teaches other truths about God's creation:

- *God freely created an orderly and good world out of nothing.* No one helped God create. No preexisting matter was present at creation. All that God makes is good. Created through the Word of God, the universe is made for human beings who are in God's image and likeness.
- *God is totally beyond us. At the same time, God is present to us, upholding and sustaining creation.* God is infinitely greater than his creation, infinitely beyond that which he has made. But because of the love he freely bestows on us, God is present to our inmost being. God is more present to us that we are to ourselves. He does not abandon his creatures, but sustains every moment of their existence. If he would forget us for an instant, we would cease to exist. We show great wisdom when we recognize through grateful hearts that we are totally dependent on God for all that we have and all that we are.
- *God guides creation through* ***divine providence****.* God guides us on our journey to our final goal of eternal life with the Blessed Trinity. Knowing his Father so well, Jesus taught that we should trust in God's providence with childlike faith. He instructed us to seek God's kingdom first, trusting that our loving Father will take care of our needs (cf. Mt 6:31–33).

divine providence—God's loving and watchful guidance over his creatures on their way to their final goal and perfection.

- *God created humans in his image and likeness.* Each person possesses profound dignity. Despite our differences of gender, national or ethnic origins, religion, race, and the like, God calls us into one family. Every person is lovable and worthy of respect—from the first moment of

Creation of the Animals by Jacopo Tintoretto

conception to natural death. Humans are the crown of God's creation, possessing both a body and soul. God creates immediately our spiritual souls in his image and likeness. The soul empowers us with a spiritual nature that enables us to think, to know the difference between right and wrong, and to love God above all and our neighbors as ourselves. There was a time when we did not exist, but now we live forever; God will always keep us in existence. We have an eternal destiny and an eternal life in store. Our earthly vocation is to be like Christ, that is, to reproduce in our own lives the image of God's Son.

- ★ *God created us male and female out of love and for love.* God made us with the same dignity—male and female, both equally good. Our sexuality encourages us to seek companionship, to depend on, and to love each other.
- ★ *God is the creator of all that is seen and unseen.* This includes belief in angels and devils (CCC, 325–336; 350–352; 391–395; 414). The Nicene Creed proclaims that God created all that is seen and unseen, including angels. Attested to in both Scripture and Tradition, angels are spiritual created beings, "surpassing in perfection all visible creatures" (CCC, 330). Personal and immortal, angels possess intelligence and free will. Angels, like humans, had an opportunity to love and accept their loving Creator or reject him out of prideful self-interest. Created good by God, Satan and the other demons became evil by their own doing. Their fall consisted of a free, radical, and irrevocable rejection of God and his reign. Satan and his demons are creatures, so they cannot prevent God's reign from growing.
- ★ *Though essentially good because God made us, humans are tainted with sin.* Because of **original sin**, the human spirit is often willing, but the flesh is weak.
- ★ *Through Jesus Christ and by the power of the Holy Spirit, God invites us into a personal relationship with him* (see chapter 2).

original sin—The fallen state of human nature into which all generations of people are born. Christ Jesus came to save us from original sin.

Sharing God's Beauty

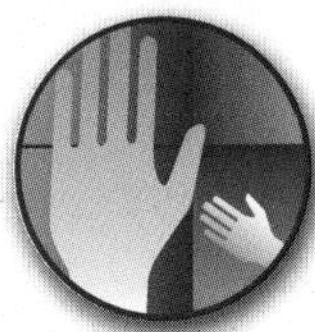

God made you a unique and beautiful creation. He expects that you will share your God-given goodness with others. Write a short essay describing the beauty of creation and what you perceive to be your own goodness. In the essay, develop concrete ways for sharing your and God's goodness with others.

The Fall and Original Sin *(CCC,* 385–421)

While the book of Genesis tells how God created people in his image and likeness, it also uses symbolic language to tell how Adam and Eve rejected God's love, resulting in mankind's loss of his friendship. Adam and Eve's original sin was their misuse of their God-given freedom and their disobedience in not relying on his goodness. Their decision had

original holiness and justice—The state of man and woman before sin. "From their friendship with God flowed the happiness of their existence in paradise" (*CCC*, 384).

concupiscence—An inclination to commit sin that can be found in human desires and appetites as a result of original sin.

serious consequences: the immediate loss of the grace of **original holiness and justice** received from God. Their original sin resulted in disunity between God and all their descendants, caused disharmony between nature and humans, and alienated people from each other.

After the Fall, sin affected all humans. Old Testament stories like Cain's murder of Abel and the many accounts of the Chosen People's failure to keep God's Law attest to this reality. Through the original sin we have inherited a fallen human nature and are deprived of original holiness and justice. Our human nature is also weakened and is subject to ignorance, suffering, the inclination to sin (known as **concupiscence**), and death (*CCC*, 404–405).

Though original sin is inherited by all, it is not an *actual* sin we personally commit. Rather, we are born into a condition where we are inclined to surrender to the powers of evil in the world. Our own efforts cannot liberate us from this condition. Only Jesus Christ has the power to free us from sin. Baptism gives us Christ's life, erases original sin, and restores our relationship with God. However, human nature remains weak, so we need the constant help of the Holy Spirit to fight temptation and choose God's will.

Throughout salvation history, God never abandoned his sinful creatures. He created a Chosen People and was passionately faithful to them through their history. The high point of God's loving concern was his promise to send a Messiah who would restore mankind's proper relationship with God:

> But you, Bethlehem-Ephrathah too small to be among the clans of Judah, From you shall come forth for me one who is to be ruler in Israel; Whose origin is from of old, from ancient times (Mi 5:1).

In God's own time, he was true to his word and sent his only Son, Jesus Christ. His passion, death, resurrection, and ascension overcame the effects of original sin.

> The victory that Christ won over sin has given us greater blessings than those which sin had taken away from us: "where sin increased, grace overflowed all the more" (Rom 5:20) (*CCC*, 420).

There is a tremendous reward for those who believe in the one, true God. The reward is manifested in several ways. Here are three:

1. *We come to knowledge of God's greatness and his love for us.* God loves us unconditionally. He created us out of nothing, gave each of us many gifts and talents, and loves us to the point of sending his Son to redeem us and give us everlasting life.
2. *Our life has meaning.* Belief in God reveals our true identity as brothers and sisters of one another. It reveals our dignity and gives us a mission to care for each other and the precious world God entrusted to us.
3. *God will always care for us.* Salvation history reveals that God will not abandon us when we sin. He will forgive us if we turn back to him. We should always trust him and his love.

Discussion Questions

1. Tell two ways that you recognize God in creation.
2. How can you show your gratitude to God for the many gifts he has given you?
3. Name some ways you can overcome the human inclination to sin.

Explaining Your Faith

If God is all-good, why is there evil in his creation?

This perplexing question has troubled humanity from the very beginning. Since God is all-good, he cannot be the origin of evil. For example, consider the suffering of the innocent Old Testament figure of Job. He discovered that although evil is a great mystery, God's providence is in control; God's ways are not our ways. Only at the end of our journey will we know his plan.

Also note that there are two kinds of evil: moral evil and physical evil. *Moral evil* is much more harmful than physical evil; it is caused by the abuse of human freedom. Out of his great love, God created angels and humans with intelligence and free will. But these creatures whom God wanted to respond freely and lovingly to him have abused their freedom through sin. They have brought about great suffering and evil in the world. Moral evil is caused by the abuse of free will. God permits it because he wants his creatures to be free and because Christ's own suffering and death show that God can bring great good out of it.

Concerning *physical evil,* we can see that God created a world on the way to perfection. It is in a process of becoming. Constructive and destructive forces of nature exist together. The more perfect exists with the incomplete. Physical evil coexists with physical good as long as creation has not reached its end. Just as the great musician must struggle to become excellent, so the world undergoes pain to reach the perfection God intends for it. We do not understand all the reasons why innocent people are caught up in suffering caused by the forces of nature. We simply believe that God has a plan both for us as individuals and as his people as we journey toward perfection.

We look to Jesus as our guide. Though innocent, he unfairly met a very painful death. But God saved him *out* of death. Jesus' suffering, death, *and* resurrection have won for us eternal, joy-filled life. They have conquered the worst evil of all: death and separation from God. This good news of Jesus Christ helps us cope with the mystery of evil and suffering.

Does God know everything ahead of time? If so, how can humans have free will?

God is *omniscient,* that is, all-knowing. God knows all that happens, has happened, and will happen. God also created humans in his image and likeness with an intellect and free will. Free will gives us the power to choose, and our choices are real, not illusions.

God's knowledge does not destroy our freedom. For example, God knows people will sin, which is contrary to God's will and our own good. Nevertheless, God *permits* us to sin because God respects our use of free will. God greatly desires that we choose his will, but God does not force us to love. Love must be freely given or it is not love.

Finally, God has created a world that has its own laws written in the nature of things. Ordinarily, God does not interfere with these laws, even though we can ignore the laws and do ourselves harm.

These examples might help. Say a teen freely chose to drink alcohol at a party, became impaired, and then drove his car into a tree on his way home. Did God *know* this would happen? Yes. Did God *permit* this to happen? Yes, because God respects the young man's free will and ordinarily does not suspend the laws of nature (for example, by moving the tree to avoid the car). Did God *cause* the accident? No, an abuse of human freedom caused it—getting intoxicated, driving under the influence of alcohol, and driving recklessly. God did not foreordain the person to drink. God's knowledge did not take away the young man's power to act freely.

SummaryPoints

- ★ The vast majority of people believe in God. St. Thomas Aquinas offered intellectual proofs. The human heart is also able to discover God. Atheists do not believe God exists. Agnostics claim ignorance on the question. Deists picture God as a watchmaker who does not get involved in the world he made.
- ★ *Transcendence* is a quality of God's total otherness; *immanence* is a quality of God's closeness to us.
- ★ God is an absolute mystery, totally other than humans.
- ★ *Divine revelation* is God's free self-communication of himself by which he makes known the mysteries of his divine plan.
- ★ God entered into *covenant* with mankind. A covenant is a solemn, open-ended agreement of love. God promised to care for humans always while humans were to remain faithful to the one true God. God's greatest and final covenant was the sending of his only Son, Jesus Christ, to save humanity from its sins and rescue it from death and the evil one.
- ★ *Faith* is the human response to divine revelation.
- ★ The deposit of divine revelation is found in Sacred Scripture and the Sacred Tradition of the Church.
- ★ The God of mystery revealed his name to be Yahweh ("I am"). This shows that God is the source of all being, the Holy One in our midst who is pure Spirit, unchangeable, unique, infinite, all-powerful, eternal, immense, merciful, gracious, living, faithful, and true.
- ★ The central dogma about the one true God is that he is a Trinity of Persons—Father, Son, and Holy Spirit.
- ★ Jesus tells us that we can address God as Abba—Father. However, Jesus has a unique relationship to the Father as his eternal Son.
- ★ God made humans in his image and likeness; thus we have incomparable dignity.
- ★ God created an orderly and beautiful world out of nothing. This world includes both visible realities and invisible realities like angels and devils. Humans are the summit of God's creation, are in solidarity with it, and must respect and develop it.
- ★ Adam and Eve, created in God's image with the ability to think and to love, rejected God through an act of disobedience. This is known as *original sin.* All humans have inherited the effects of original sin, including an inclination to sin and a fallen human nature that leads to death.
- ★ Belief in the one true God gives life tremendous meaning by showing that our Creator loves us beyond what we can imagine and revealing our true identity as his children and brothers and sisters in Christ with an eternal destination of happiness in union with the Blessed Trinity.

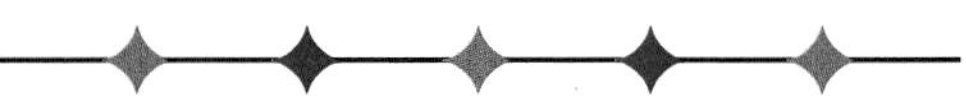

ReviewQuestions

1. Identify: *monotheism, polytheism, atheist, agnostic, secular humanism,* and *deism.*
2. What might the existence of so many religions tell us about God?
3. Explain any five demonstrations for God's existence.
4. What is meant by God's *transcendence*? by God's *immanence*?
5. Write three facts about St. Thomas Aquinas.
6. Define: *divine revelation, salvation history, covenant,* and *faith.*
7. List four covenants that God made with mankind.
8. Where is the single deposit of faith found?
9. What is the meaning of *Yahweh*?
10. List three qualities of Yahweh.
11. What is the central doctrine of Christianity?
12. Why is *Father* an appropriate form of address for God?
13. What is the meaning and significance of *Abba*?

14. Name five things Catholics believe about God as Creator.
15. Define *original sin.*
16. Name two effects of original sin.
17. What is the angel's main function in relation to humans?
18. What is Catholic belief concerning the existence of Satan and demons?
19. How can God be good if there is evil in the world?
20. What difference can believing in God make for your life?

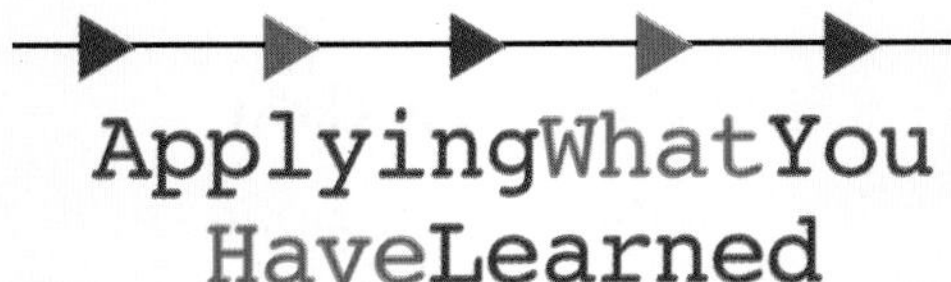

Applying What You Have Learned

1. Write a dialogue between an atheist and a believer who is trying to convince the person that God exists.
2. Read a psalm of praise (e.g., Ps 19, 29, 65, or 104). Create a visual presentation to illustrate the object of the praise.
3. Copy into a notebook or journal ten important quotes from the *Dogmatic Constitution on Divine Revelation.* This document is online at the official Vatican website: www.rc.net/rcchurch/vatican2/dei.ver
4. Research current debates on the teaching of evolution in the public schools. Prepare a short written or oral report.
5. Visit the following websites for further information on some of the topics discussed in this chapter. Write a report on some new information you discovered. Also:

- Test more arguments for the existence of God: www.mb-soft.com/believe/text/argument.htm
- Read more about angels at the EWTN website: www.ewtn.com/library/ANSWERS/ANGELTR.htm

Prayer Reflection

At Baptism, the Holy Spirit endows us with the theological virtues of faith, hope, and charity (love). These virtues enable us to recite with conviction three traditional prayers of the Church. The Act of Faith empowers us to assent to God's revelation. The Act of Hope enables us to proclaim our trust in God's promises. The Act of Love proclaims our love of God above everything and our neighbors as ourselves.

Act of Faith

O my God, I firmly believe that you are one God in three divine Persons, Father, Son, and Holy Spirit. I believe that your divine Son became man and died for our sins, and that he will come to judge the living and the dead. I believe these and all the truths, which the Holy Catholic Church teaches, because you have revealed them, who can neither deceive nor be deceived. Amen.

Act of Hope

O my God, relying on your infinite goodness and promises, I hope to obtain pardon of my sins, the help of your grace, and life everlasting, through the merits of Jesus Christ, my Lord and Redeemer. Amen.

Act of Love

O my God, I love you above all things, with my whole heart and soul, because you are all good and worthy of all my love. I love my neighbor as myself for the love of you. I forgive all who have injured me, and I ask pardon of all whom I have injured. Amen.

1. Compose your own short acts of faith, hope, and love.
2. Perform some "act of love" for a family member, expecting nothing in return.

In the beginning was the Word, and the Word was with God, and the Word was God. He was in the beginning with God. All things came to be through him, and without him nothing came to be. . . . And the Word became flesh and made his dwelling among us.

John 1:1–3; 14

Chapter 2 Outline

Encouraging Words

The good news of Jesus provides encouragement in an often discouraging world.

Beliefs about Jesus Christ

The profession "I believe in Jesus Christ, his only Son, our Lord" reveals much about the Incarnation.

Evidence for Jesus and His Life

The gospels are central for understanding the life of Jesus.

Mysteries of Christ's Life

Learning more about Jesus' hidden life and public life helps us to gain more knowledge of God's saving plan.

Christ Died for Our Sake

Christ won our salvation through his death on the cross. His resurrection proved his divinity.

What We Believe about Jesus

In answering several heresies, the Church formed its beliefs about Jesus.

Chapter 2

Jesus Christ: Lord and Savior

Encouraging Words

Whenever people try to figure out the meaning of life and how they fit into God's large plan, discouragement may set in. The antidote to discouragement is encouragement. The best words of encouragement come from God himself. His loving words appear in the pages of Scripture. Consider God's antidotes of encouragement to the discouraging thoughts we often carry.

You say . . .	**Scripture says . . .**
"It's impossible."	"What is impossible for human beings is possible for God" (Lk 18:27).
"No one loves me."	For God so loved the world that he gave his only Son, so that everyone who believes in him might not perish but might have eternal life (Jn 3:16).
"I can't forgive myself."	If we acknowledge our sins, he is faithful and just and will forgive our sins and cleanse us from every wrongdoing (1 Jn 1:9).
"I am burned out."	"Come to me, all you who labor and are burdened, and I will give you rest" (Mt 11:28).
"I can't do it."	"I have the strength for everything through him who empowers me" (Phil 4:13).
"I feel so alone."	"I will never forsake you or abandon you" (Heb 13:5).

gospel—A term meaning "good news." The term refers to 1) Jesus' own preaching; 2) the preaching about Jesus the Savior (Jesus Christ is the good news proclaimed by the Church); and 3) the four Spirit-inspired written versions of the good news—the gospels of Matthew, Mark, Luke, and John.

This chapter focuses on the encouraging **gospel** or good news of Jesus Christ. It examines in more detail the statements that Catholics profess about Jesus Christ in the Apostles' Creed. Other areas of study include the sources for how the Church has collected knowledge about Jesus and the mysteries surrounding Jesus' public life.

What Do You Know about Jesus?

Before studying this chapter, test some of your knowledge about Jesus. Answer the following questions. (The answers are on page 65.)

1. True or False. The Incarnation refers to God becoming flesh in the person of Jesus.
2. Which of the following is not a book of the New Testament?: a) Daniel; b) Luke; c) James; d) Timothy.
3. True or False. The title *Christ* means Messiah or "anointed one."
4. True or False. The "brothers and sisters" of Jesus referred to in the Bible were other children of Jesus' mother Mary.
5. According to Catholic teaching, Jesus Christ has: a) two natures, two persons; b) one nature, two persons; c) one person, two natures; d) one nature, one person.
6. True or False. Jesus came to abolish the Law of Moses.
7. True or False. The Paschal Mystery refers to the life, death, resurrection, and ascension of Jesus.
8. The following parable of Jesus best illustrates his teaching on love: a) The Mustard Seed; b) The Good Samaritan; c) The Talents; d) The Rich Fool.
9. When Jesus calls God *Abba* in the New Testament, he is calling him: a) Friend; b) Lord; c) Father; d) Spirit.
10. True or False. The Jewish people as a whole are responsible for the death of Jesus.

Discussion Questions

1. Tell three things you believe about Jesus Christ.
2. Who is the person you know who is most like Jesus? Why is this so?
3. How would you like your personal relationship with Jesus to develop?

Beliefs about Jesus Christ *(CCC, 422–463)*

The letter to the Hebrews begins this way:

> In times past, God spoke in partial and various ways to our ancestors through the prophets; in these last days, he spoke to us through a son, whom he made heir of all things and through whom he created the universe (Heb 1:1–2).

Yahweh had gradually revealed himself throughout history, but in Christ, God himself came to the world in the person of his Son. Out of love, God wished to speak his final Word, a word that taught us that he is "the way, the truth and the life" (Jn 14:6).

God's Son, the second person of the Blessed Trinity, took on human flesh in the person of Jesus Christ. The prologue to the gospel of John (see page 40) is a statement of this belief. God took on our human nature, body and soul. This is known as the doctrine of the **Incarnation**. God became man in Jesus Christ who is God incarnate. "Belief in the true Incarnation of the Son of God is the distinctive sign of Christian faith" (CCC, 463). God himself entered human history by becoming one of his creatures, while all the time remaining the Creator of the universe.

Incarnation—The dogma that God's eternal Son assumed a human nature and became man in Jesus Christ to save us from our sins. (The term literally means "taking on human flesh.")

Why did the Word become flesh? (see *CCC*, 456–460). The *Catechism of the Catholic Church* lists four reasons:

1. The Word of God became flesh to save us from sin, death, and eternal separation from God. He did so by reconciling us with God by atoning for our sins. Christ gave his life so we could live.
2. "The Word became flesh *so that thus we might know God's love*" (CCC, 458). Jesus Christ, as truly human, is able to show us the true nature of God.
3. God took on human flesh to be our model of holiness. Jesus shows us how to imitate him: to love one another as he has loved us (Jn 15:12).
4. God became human to make us sharers in his divine nature.

In the Apostles' Creed, Catholics profess belief in the Incarnation saying, "I believe in Jesus Christ, his only Son, our Lord." Each of these words—Jesus, Christ, Son of God, and Lord—reveals unique and profound truths about the Incarnation. The subsections that follow explore these truths based on each of these titles.

Jesus

The personal name Jesus comes from the Hebrew word *Yehoshua* (Joshua) which means "God saves," "God is salvation," or simply, "Savior." Thus God's own name is present in the person of his Son. The angel Gabriel revealed this name to Mary (Lk 1:31), thus signifying Jesus' identity and mission. From his conception, God had destined that Jesus would save the world from sin and death.

The gospels of Matthew and Luke tell us Jesus was born in Bethlehem in Judea during the reign of King Herod the Great, perhaps around the year 4–6 BC. He was raised by his mother Mary and foster father, the carpenter Joseph, in the town of Nazareth in Galilee. According to most scholars, Jesus began his preaching and healing ministry in the "fifteenth year of Tiberius Caesar's reign" (from AD 27–28) after being baptized by John the Baptist in the Jordan River. After a period of trial in the desert, Jesus chose twelve close followers called *apostles* and had many other disciples as well. Jesus proclaimed the coming of God's kingdom (reign). Because of his preaching, deeds, and claims, Jesus ran afoul of the Jewish religious leaders. They claimed he

was committing *blasphemy*, that is claiming to make himself equal to God. Therefore, he was handed over to Roman authorities and ended up "suffering under Pontius Pilate, was crucified, died, and was buried." The story did not end there, however. Jesus Christ is risen from the dead.

Christ

Christ (*Christos* in the Greek) translates the Hebrew title *Messiah*. The Messiah was the "anointed one of Yahweh" through whom all of God's promises to the Chosen People were fulfilled.

Many Jews of Jesus' time were expecting the Messiah to be a political leader who would throw off the yoke of the Romans and restore Israel to its position of glory. Although Jesus accepted the title Christ when he asked his apostles his true identity (Mt 16:13–17), he had to reinterpret the meaning of the title for them. Jesus understood that the Messiah's role was to suffer in accomplishing the Father's will of ushering in the kingdom.

Christ—A title for Jesus meaning "the anointed one." In Greek, the word *Christos* translated the Hebrew *Messiah*.

After the resurrection, Christians took a new look at Jesus' life. They saw that he was anointed with the Spirit of God to accomplish **salvation** through a life of suffering service. He accomplished his task through his threefold office of *prophet*, *priest*, and *king*. A prophet is one who speaks for God; a priest is a mediator between God and humans. A king is a leader and ruler. As prophet, Jesus spoke for his Father and shared the full message of salvation. As priest, Jesus offered his life for all of us on the altar of the cross. Today he continues to fulfill the role of High Priest at each celebration of the Eucharist. As king, Jesus is the rightful ruler of the universe, one who rules gently and compassionately. He uses the power of love and service to attract followers to his way.

salvation—God's forgiveness of sins, accomplished through the mercy of Jesus Christ, resulting in the restoration of friendship with God.

Son of God

The gospels repeatedly make the truth that Jesus was the unique Son of God very clear. For example, at both his baptism and transfiguration, the Father calls Jesus his "beloved Son." Peter proclaims Jesus to be "the Messiah, the Son of the living God" (Mt 16:16). And Jesus himself clearly says that he is the Son of God (Jn 10:36): "The Father and I are one" (Jn 10:30).

Jesus' Father is the first person of the Blessed Trinity. Jesus Christ is the natural son who shares in God's very nature. Human beings, on the other hand, are God's adopted children.

Lord

In the New Testament, *Lord* had various meanings. For example, it could refer to a ruler or someone with great power. It was also used as a polite and respectful form of address, much like "sir."

However, the title Lord when referring to Jesus proclaims his divinity. The Greek translation of the Old Testament used the word *Kyrios* ("Lord") to render the most sacred name YHWH ("I am") which God revealed to Moses. Pious Jews never said the most holy name of God. Therefore, to call Jesus Lord (Kyrios) is to state that he is God!

The simple statement that "Jesus Christ is Lord" is the earliest and shortest Christian creed. Jesus proved he was God during his ministry

Discussion Questions

1. Describe your own analogy for God becoming man.
2. What would Jesus' first disciples have found attractive about him and his message?
3. Which title for Jesus best describes how you understand and relate to him?

through his miracles. "He demonstrated his divine sovereignty by works of power over nature, illnesses, demons, death, and sin" (CCC, 447).

Jesus has the same sovereignty as God and his death and resurrection have won eternal life for humanity, a gift only God can grant. Jesus is the one *true* Lord and the only Lord deserving our total allegiance.

Other Titles and Symbols for Jesus

Besides the titles of Jesus revealed in the Creed, there are other titles and symbols for Christ that come from the New Testament and the early Church that tell more about him.

Jesus upset many of his contemporaries by rejecting their idea of the Messiah as a conquering, earthly ruler. He chose instead to be a *Suffering Servant* who took on the sins of his people and redeemed them. "The Son of Man did not come to be served but to serve and to give his life as a ransom for many" (Mt 20:28).

Jesus often used the title *Son of Man* when he referred to himself. Its Old Testament roots are a vision described in Daniel 7:13: "I saw . . . one like a son of man coming on the clouds of heaven." On the one hand, the title emphasizes Jesus' humanity, one who is like us and will suffer for and serve all people. On the other hand, Son of Man describes Jesus as the judge through whom God will fully establish his kingdom at the end of time.

Several symbols for Jesus developed in the early Church. They also reveal Christian belief about Christ and have roots in Scripture:

"'I am the Alpha and the Omega,' says the Lord God, 'the one who is and who was and who is to come, the almighty'" (Rev 1:8). From the book of Revelation, these are the first and last letters of the Greek alphabet, signifying that Jesus is the beginning and end of our life.

On top of the cross, posted in Hebrew, Latin, and Greek, was the crime for which Jesus was crucified (Jn 19:19–20). *INRI* is an abbreviation of Jesus' crime in the Latin language: **I**=Jesus **N**=of Nazareth **R**=King **I**=of the Jews.

This symbol is a monogram of the first two letters, Chi (X) and Rho (P), of the Greek word for Christ.

More Titles for Jesus

John's gospel has other titles of Jesus. Read the gospel passage for each of the following and explain its meaning. Then, create your own title for Jesus, explain it, and draw a symbol to represent it.

1. Light of the World (Jn 8:12)
2. Good Shepherd (Jn 10:11)
3. Vine (Jn 15:5)

Evidence for Jesus and His Life *(CCC, 124-127)*

Today, few non-believers doubt the existence of Jesus of Nazareth. Although our primary source of knowledge about Jesus comes from the gospels, ancient historians make reference to him and his earliest followers. For example, the Roman historian Tacitus (AD 55–ca. 117) reported on the Great Fire in Rome (AD 64) under the Emperor Nero. Tacitus blamed the fire on Christians, naming them as followers of "Christus" whom Pontius Pilate put to death. Another Roman historian Suetonius (ca. 70–ca. 130) wrote about a riot in a synagogue involving Jews and Christian preachers over a certain "Chrestus." And the Roman writer Pliny the Younger (62–113), the governor of Bithnyia in Asia Minor, wrote to the emperor Trajan (ca. 112) telling him about Christians who worship Christ as a god. Neither he nor the emperor in his return letter ever questioned Jesus' actual existence.

Josephus (37–ca. 101), the famous Jewish historian of the first century, mentions Jesus in two of his writings. In an important passage, he clearly identified Jesus as a wise man, teacher, and wonder-worker who made converts and was killed by Pontius Pilate. Another example from Jewish tradition is the collection of writings known as the *Talmud*, which states that Jesus existed. Had Jesus never lived, undoubtedly rabbis would have tried to disprove the Christian belief in Jesus' existence. But to the contrary, those non-Christians took for granted that he lived.

A most convincing argument against the charge that Christians invented the historical Jesus is simply to ask: "What did they have to gain by doing so?" There was nothing to gain politically or economically. In fact, according to tradition, all the key witnesses of Jesus' public life (the apostles), except John, met martyrdom for their testimony about Jesus.

Centrality of the Gospel

The best source for proving Jesus' existence is the New Testament itself. Its entire focus is Jesus Christ: his acts, teachings, passion, death, and glorification, and the Church he started under the guidance of the Holy Spirit. The heart of the Bible is the gospels, the principal source of the life and teaching of Jesus Christ. The gospels reveal a genius who taught with unique insight. For example, his **parables** are unparalleled stories proclaiming God's kingdom. They are vivid, powerful, life-giving, and original. Also,

parable—A favorite teaching device of Jesus in which he told a short story with a striking, memorable comparison that taught a religious message, usually about some aspect of God's kingdom.

1. Jesus taught that God is Abba/Father and that we can pray to God using this intimate term.
2. He taught that God's reign is in our midst.
3. He taught that we should love our enemies.

These unique teachings, and many others like them, strongly lead us to conclude the historical reality of a remarkable, one-of-a-kind teacher.

For Christians, reading and praying with the gospels is a necessary way to meet and know Christ. St. Jerome, who translated much of the Bible into Latin, said, "Ignorance of scripture is ignorance of Christ."

Contents of the New Testament

(*CCC*, 102; 124–125; 128–130; 134; 140)

Jesus is the New Testament or New Covenant with all humanity. His law is the law of love that requires a change of heart. He is the perfect prophet who fulfilled all prophecies. The New Testament writings show how his words and his actions reveal God's active presence in the world: saving, redeeming, and healing people. Jesus' life and ministry fulfilled all the Old Testament prophecies concerning his birth, his teaching and healing, his rejection by the leaders, his passion, death, and resurrection.

The New Testament continues and fulfills the Old Testament; it does not contradict it. The Old Testament tells us about God's covenant with his Chosen People. The New Testament reveals that our loving God has extended his salvation to all people. A collection of various books, the New Testament's primary purpose is to announce the fulfillment of God's promises in Jesus Christ, his Son. The New Testament consists of:

evangelists—The four evangelists refers to the authors of the four gospels: Matthew, Mark, Luke, and John. The word *evangelist* means "one who proclaims in word and deed the good news of Jesus Christ."

- ★ *The Gospels.* The gospels testify to salvation in Jesus Christ. They contain facts about the historical Jesus and testify to Christian faith about Jesus' passion, death, resurrection, and ascension. Written by **evangelists** ("proclaimers of the good news"), their primary intent is to preach Jesus' miracles and teachings and recount the Paschal mystery of his passion, death, and resurrection that has won for us salvation. The gospels also present some reliable biographical material about Jesus. The gospels are named for the evangelists Matthew, Mark, Luke, and John.

- *Acts of the Apostles.* Written by Luke as a continuation of the gospel, the Acts of the Apostles recounts the history of the Church from Pentecost Sunday until the arrest of St. Paul in Rome around AD 63. It is often grouped with the gospels.
- *The New Testament Letters.* Most of the New Testament letters, or epistles, were written by St. Paul or attributed to him. All of the epistles highlight the importance of faith in Jesus Christ. The New Testament Letters are: Romans, 1 and 2 Corinthians, Galatians, Ephesians, Philippians, Colossians, 1 and 2 Thessalonians, 1 and 2 Timothy, Titus, Philemon, and Hebrews.
- *The Catholic Letters.* These epistles encourage the universal ("catholic") Church to remain faithful to Jesus and to live Christian lives. They are: James; 1 and 2 Peter; 1, 2, and 3 John; and Jude
- *The Revelation to John.* This is a highly symbolic work also known by its Greek name—the Apocalypse. It encourages Christians under persecution to remain faithful to Jesus Christ.

The Formation of the Gospels (CCC: 124–127)

The gospels contain the principal teachings of Jesus and about his life. The Church teaches that there were three stages in their formation.

Stage 1: The Historical Jesus: 4/6 BC–AD 30/33

The first stage of gospel formation was the very life of Jesus. Jesus was born around 4 to 6 BC, lived a typical Jewish life of the time, came onto the public scene probably in AD 28, preached and worked miracles, and was crucified in Jerusalem by the Roman prefect, Pontius Pilate, either in AD 30 or 33.

His early disciples, at first frightened and confused, claimed to have seen Jesus after his death and burial. They were convinced that he was alive and glorified as God's Son and present to them by the power of the Holy Spirit. Their hearts burned with love and joy over his resurrection.

Stage 2: Oral Tradition: AD 30/33–50

The disciples begin to live in light of the resurrection of Jesus. With the help of the Holy Spirit, they now knew that Jesus was the Messiah, the Promised One, the Son of God, and the Lord. The apostles remembered Jesus' command to "Go into the whole world and proclaim the gospel to every creature" (Mk 16:16). Their preaching took three forms and is the centerpiece of the oral tradition:

1. *Kerygma (preaching to unbelievers).* To aid them in this proclamation, the disciples began to assemble collections of material about Jesus—for example, miracle stories, parables, and the passion narrative. Later evangelists drew on these sources to help compose their gospels.
2. *Didache ("teaching").* The *Catechism of the Catholic Church* (425–429) teaches that the center of all catechesis must be Jesus Christ. This is true today and it was also true for early converts to Christ. **Catechesis** literally means to "sound down," that is, to repeat the message and explain it in more depth. "[Catechesis] is to seek to understand the

catechesis—A process of "education in the faith" for young people and adults with the view of making them disciples of Jesus Christ.

meaning of Christ's actions and words and of the signs worked by him" (*Catechesi Tradendae,* No. 5 quoted in *CCC*, 426). To aid in this instruction, lists of sayings of Jesus, for example, the Sermon on the Mount, were probably assembled at this time.

3. *Liturgy ("participation in the work of God").* The celebration of the Eucharist helped shape many of the Jesus stories that the Christian community preserved, for example, Jesus' words at the Last Supper, the Lord's Prayer, and the story of Jesus' passion.

The primary interest of the early preachers and teachers' was to interpret the *meaning* of the key events and sayings of Jesus. They did not set out to offer a complete biography of Jesus. What they remembered, saved, and proclaimed was the heart of Jesus' message—related to the teachings of the Jewish faith and adapted to the audiences who heard it.

The preaching about Jesus based on oral traditions carried on well into the second century, even after the gospels were written.

Stage 3: The New Testament Writings (AD 50–ca.120)

The final stage of gospel formation was the actual writing of the four gospels and the other New Testament writings, the earliest of which were letters of St. Paul. Concerning the gospels, many scholars believe that Mark's was written between 68–73, Matthew's and Luke's perhaps between 80–90, and John's in the 90s. Guided by the Holy Spirit, the four versions of the one gospel of Jesus Christ all tell the truth about our Lord and Savior.

The oral preaching had to be committed to writing because Jesus was not coming back during the lifetimes of the first-generation of Christians, as many of them expected. Eyewitnesses to Christ's life on earth began to die. It became increasingly necessary to preserve in a more accurate manner the apostolic testimony concerning Jesus, especially to combat false teachings that were starting to circulate about Jesus. Christians needed a written record of their beliefs—hence, the New Testament. This written record of the apostles' preaching served both as an aide to worship services and for the instruction of new converts, much in the same way the gospels are used today for the same purposes.

Discussion Questions

1. How do we know about the existence of Jesus?
2. Why are there four gospel accounts?
3. Why was the good news of Christ eventually written down?

Mysteries of Christ's Life (CCC, 512–518; 561–562)

What is meant by the term *mystery* related to the life of Christ? God is a mystery because he is so great, omnipotent, loving, and perfect—the human mind can never totally grasp his infinity, even in heaven. Second, the word mystery (in Greek, *mysterion*) in the New Testament refers to God's saving plan that was gradually revealed in human history.

There is an intimate connection between these two understandings of mystery. The God who is a mystery is the same God who chose to reveal himself in human history. God most fully revealed himself when he became man in Jesus Christ. It follows, therefore, that everything about Jesus—his deeds, works, teachings, passion, death, and resurrection—all reveal a loving, infinite God of mercy.

Several mysteries of Christ's life will be explained in the subsections that follow.

Jesus' Early Life (*CCC*, 512–534; 563–564)

The Infancy Narratives. Each evangelist had a particular audience and theological perspective in mind when he wrote his version of the gospel. For example, Mark wrote for Gentile Christians and stressed Jesus as the Suffering Servant. Matthew wrote for a Jewish Christian audience and emphasized Jesus as the New Lawgiver. Luke highlighted Jesus as the Universal Messiah and his audience, too, were Gentile Christians. John's gospel, written many years later, reflected more developed theology and presented Jesus as God's unique Word who came to be the Way, Truth, and Life.

These different perspectives reflect how Matthew and Luke present the birth of Jesus. For example, Matthew tells us about the visit of the angel to Joseph (Mt 1:18–25); Luke reports an annunciation by the angel Gabriel to Mary, Christ's mother (Lk 1:26–38).

Also, note Jesus' birth stories in Luke 1:1–2:52 and Matthew 1:1–2:23. Each evangelist drew on two very different traditions to record Jesus' birth. However, what is remarkable is on how many basic facts the gospels agree. For example,

1. The principal persons mentioned are Jesus, Mary, and Joseph.
2. Mary was a virgin. By freely consenting to God's action in her life, Mary became the Mother of God and our spiritual mother. She was open to God, serving as a model for all Christians who are to bring Christ into the world.
3. The king reigning at the time of Jesus birth was Herod.
4. Jesus' conception was by the Holy Spirit.
5. Jesus was born in Bethlehem.
6. Jesus received his name before his birth.
7. Jesus was descended from David.
8. The family settled in the town of Nazareth.

The mysteries of Jesus' life in these chapters of Matthew and Luke reveal much about Jesus and his mission.

First of all, Jesus was born in poverty. He came to the world as one of the lowly and poor. He allowed the shepherds to see him first. Pious Jews like the Pharisees derisively referred to shepherds as "people of the land." Their occupation would not allow them to keep faithfully the religious rituals demanded by the Law. Yet, Jesus came to call people such as these.

Epiphany—The feast that celebrates the mystery of Christ's manifestation as the Savior of the world.

Next, Jesus' *circumcision* incorporated him into the Chosen People. He submitted to the Jewish law as a model of humility. At the **Epiphany**, when the Magi from the East visited him, Jesus manifested himself as the savior of all people. Likewise, Jesus' *presentation in the Temple* revealed him to be the firstborn son who belongs to God. The old prophets Simeon and Anna recognize him as the long-expected Messiah, bless God for being allowed to see him, and predict the perfect sacrifice on the cross that the adult Jesus will endure for our salvation ("the sword of sorrow that will pierce Mary's heart").

Two other mysteries from Jesus' infancy—the *flight into Egypt* and the *slaughter of the innocents*—show how the forces of evil war against Jesus, but also reveal how God protects the Son who will save all people.

Jesus lived a hidden life of humble obedience in Nazareth. His obedience to his family contrasts with Adam's disobedience to God. It points to Jesus' obedience to his heavenly Father. He learned a trade from Joseph and grew in knowledge about his Jewish religion. He also regularly attended the religious festivals in Jerusalem. At one of them, he astounded the teachers with his keen knowledge. The finding in the Temple represents Jesus' total consecration to his mission as the Father's Son. Luke's gospel reports that Jesus grew quietly in wisdom, age, and favor with God and with people (Lk 2:52). Truly, his humility during his "hidden years" shows us how to pray, live, and suffer for our faith.

ExplainingYourFaith

Did Jesus have brothers and sisters?

In a few places, the gospels mention so-called "brothers and sisters" of Jesus. For example, Mark 6:3 mentions by name four brothers of Jesus and some sisters. Does this mean that Jesus had blood siblings, and that Mary had other children?

Since the first-century, Catholics have believed that Mary was always a virgin and that Jesus did not have other siblings. Both Scripture and Tradition support this teaching. The gospels share that Mary was a virgin when she miraculously conceived Jesus by the power of the Holy Spirit (Mt 1:20 and Lk 1:34–35). This is the dogma of the **virgin birth.** The Tradition of the Church has always held that Mary was a perpetual virgin. The Fathers of the Church, early influential Church theologians whose writings give us great insights into truths of the faith, taught that the virginal conception was God's work, a mystery of salvation. The virgin birth reveals that Jesus is truly God Incarnate; thus, he is both divine and human. The gospels make no mention that Mary herself had children after the birth of Jesus.

The gospel passages that refer to Jesus' so-called brothers and sisters use a word that also means *cousins* or some other distant relation of the same generation. Even in our day, some cultures refer to cousins and close relatives as brothers and sisters. Interestingly, the gospels identify two "brothers" of Jesus—namely, James and Joseph—as the sons of another Mary, a follower of Christ (Mt 27:56).

virgin birth—A Church dogma that teaches that Jesus was conceived through the Virgin Mary by the power of the Holy Spirit without the cooperation of a human father.

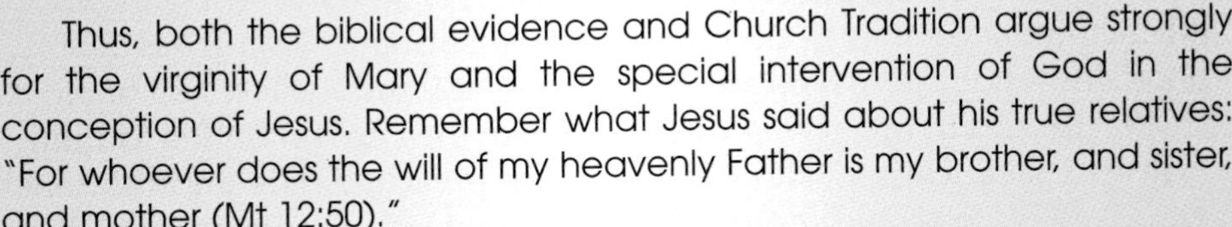

Thus, both the biblical evidence and Church Tradition argue strongly for the virginity of Mary and the special intervention of God in the conception of Jesus. Remember what Jesus said about his true relatives: "For whoever does the will of my heavenly Father is my brother, and sister, and mother (Mt 12:50)."

Jesus' Public Life

As God-made-flesh, everything about Jesus' life on earth reveals the Father. Reflecting on Jesus' teachings and the events of his life teaches us much about God and his love for us. Jesus is the model for human living. His humility, his way of dealing with suffering and persecution, his love of all (including enemies), his compassion, and his other human qualities can teach us how to live. Jesus' public life begins with his baptism by John the Baptist, whom God sent to prepare the way for him.

By submitting to John's baptism, Jesus accepted and launched his mission to be God's Suffering Servant. At his baptism the Holy Spirit descended on Jesus in the form of a dove. A heavenly voice proclaimed Jesus to be the beloved Son, thus revealing him as the Messiah and God's only Son. At his baptism, Jesus

1. showed perfect submission to the Father's will,
2. foreshadowed the baptism of his death for the remission of our sins, and
3. served as the model for our own baptism.

According to Luke's gospel, after Jesus' baptism, the Holy Spirit led him into the desert to pray, fast, and prepare himself for his difficult mission ahead. During this forty-day retreat, Jesus was tempted by Satan. The letter to the Hebrews reveals that Jesus' temptations help him identify with humanity:

> For we do not have a high priest who is unable to sympathize with our weaknesses, but one who has similarly been tested in every way, yet without sin. So let us confidently approach the throne of grace to receive mercy and to find grace for timely help (Heb 4:15–16).

Like us, Jesus was tempted; though he never gave in to his temptations or sinned. Jesus' response to temptations are the opposite of Adam's and show him to be the New Adam. By repudiating Satan, Jesus remained faithful to God. Unlike the Chosen People, who turned from God many times during their history, Jesus was God's obedient servant. He showed that he would be a Suffering Servant Messiah, not a typical earthly ruler.

When he emerged from the desert, Jesus began to preach the good news of God's kingdom. The essence of his message is found in Mark 1:15: "This is the time of fulfillment. The kingdom of God is at hand. Repent, and believe in the gospel." The heart of Jesus' message was that God's

Read&Compare

Note the similarities and differences in how each gospel reports Jesus' baptism. Read:

Matthew 3:13–17

Mark 1:9–11

Luke 3:21–22

John 1:29–34

Answer the following questions below related to each passage:

1. Who sees the sky open?
2. Who sees the Holy Spirit descending in the form of a dove?
3. Who hears the Father's voice?

kingdom was coming in Jesus' very person. This message requires an immediate response: repentance and faith in him. Jesus taught using vivid and memorable parables like the Good Samaritan; in short, and pithy aphorisms ("But many who are first will be last, and the last will be first" [Mt 19:30]); and in life-giving discourses like the Sermon on the Mount.

Jesus was a teacher who lived what he preached. His unconditional love for the poor and needy, the sick, women, foreigners, children, sinners, enemies, and the marginalized showed that God's kingdom was indeed present in him.

Paschal mystery—The saving love of God most fully revealed in the life and especially the passion, death, resurrection, and glorious ascension of his Son Jesus Christ.

Most dramatically, Jesus proclaimed the gospel through the **Paschal mystery**—his passion, death, resurrection, and ascension. This mystery of total love reveals to us that Jesus Christ is the way to salvation. If we allow the Holy Spirit to join us to the Lord, the Blessed Trinity will adopt us into the divine family. Jesus teaches an important lesson: "I am the vine, you are the branches. Whoever remains in me and I in him will bear much fruit, because without me you can do nothing" (Jn 15:5).

The main points of Jesus' proclamation of the good news include:

kingdom of God—The reign of God proclaimed by Jesus and begun in his life, death, and resurrection. It refers to the process of God reconciling and renewing all things through his Son, to the fact of his will being done on earth as it is in heaven.

- *God's kingdom is here.* The **kingdom of God** is God's power and active presence, his saving activity in the entire universe, in heaven and on earth. We can see God's presence in love, forgiveness, healing, compassion, works of justice, and creative goodness. Jesus himself is the divine agent of the kingdom that is present in him. His miracles of healing the spiritual, physical, and psychological illnesses of people are a principal sign of the kingdom. Jesus taught that the kingdom's presence might appear small now and that the forces of evil will resist it, but its growth is inevitable. One day it will transform all of humanity.

- *God is a loving Father.* The Father's love reveals itself in sending his Son to live with and die for us. We can approach our loving Father with simple childlike confidence and trust that he will answer our prayers. This loving Father is incredibly merciful, like the generous father of the parable of the Prodigal Son (Lk 15:11–32) who accepted back his wayward son and forgave his judgmental one.

- *God is merciful.* Jesus is the very image of the compassionate God. "The Father and I are one. . . . [T]he Father is in me and I am in the Father (Jn 10:30, 38)." We must be other Christs, by spreading his good news. We do this by forgiving others—even our enemies—and caring for all, especially the poor and outcast. To allow God's salvation to touch our own hearts means we must turn from our sins and put on Jesus Christ.
- *Jesus is present in his Church.* With God the Father, he has sent the Holy Spirit to empower us to live lovingly. Jesus promised that he would remain with us until the end of time. One way he does this is through his body, the Church, which he established through the apostles. He gave special authority to Peter and his successors (the bishops in communion with the pope) to guide the Church and the truth. The bishops and their co-worker priests continue Jesus' saving activity, for example, by forgiving sin in his name, and by celebrating the Eucharist. They also serve as teachers and leaders who govern the Church.

  Jesus also remains present in the members of the Church who become incorporated into his Body at Baptism. Furthermore, he gives to us his very self—body and blood—in the Eucharist. Finally, he lives in us through the gift of the Holy Spirit who dispenses many gifts that empower us to live a Christian life. The Church continues to preach and exemplify God's kingdom. It is the seed of the kingdom.
- *To accept Jesus is to accept the cross.* To follow Jesus requires living a moral and loving life of serving others. We must turn our backs on sin and the world's false values that promise an empty happiness. A Christian life requires self-denial and sacrifice. We must imitate Jesus: "Whoever wishes to come after me must deny himself, take up his cross, and follow me" (Mt 16: 24). Christ promises we will never be alone when we sacrifice for him:

> Come to me, all you who labor and are burdened, and I will give you rest. Take my yoke upon you and learn from me, for I am meek and humble of heart; and you will find rest for your selves. For my yoke is easy, and my burden light (Mt 11:28–30).

A life of service means dying to selfishness, but it leads to an eternal life of happiness.

Living the Teaching of Jesus

Read the following teachings of Jesus. Determine which teachings are a) most difficult for you to live and b) most difficult for contemporary society to live. Explain why.

Self-denial. "If anyone wishes to come after me, he must deny himself and take up his cross daily and follow me" (Lk 9:23).

Love. "Do to others whatever you would have them do to you" (Mt 7:12).

Peace. "But seek first the kingdom (of God) and his righteousness, and all these things will be given you besides. Do not worry about tomorrow; tomorrow will take care of itself" (Mt 6:33–34).

Humility. "But many that are first will be last, and (the) last will be first" (Mk 10:31).

Simplicity. "Take care to guard against all greed, for though one may be rich, one's life does not consist of possessions" (Lk 12:15).

Prayer. "Ask and it will be given to you; seek and you will find; knock and the door will be opened to you" (Mt 7:7).

Miracles of Jesus *(CCC, 547–550)*

Jesus performed many miracles to accompany his words. These mighty works, wonders, and signs revealed that God's kingdom was present in his very person. They prove that he is the Messiah, the Son of God.

Jesus' miracles were signs of the Messianic age. These signs freed some people from earthly problems and evils, but they did not abolish all human sufferings. Their purpose was to show Jesus' power over sin. His exorcisms demonstrated his control over demons. All of his mighty works foreshadowed his great victory won by his death and resurrection. This victory over the power of sin, Satan, and death won us eternal life.

Miracles

Jesus' miracles can be divided into four categories: healings, exorcisms, nature miracles, and raisings from the dead. Report on the following for each: 1) the problem; 2) how Jesus solved it; 3) the meaning (what the miracle meant for the person involved or those who witnessed it).

Healings:

Cure of the leper (Mt 8:1–4)

Blind man of Jericho (Mk 10:46–52)

Exorcisms:

Cure of demoniac (Lk 4:33–37)

Expulsion of demons in Gardara (Mt 8:28–34)

Nature miracles:

Calming of the storm (Mk 4:35–41)

Feeding of the 5,000 (Lk 9:10–17)

Raisings from the dead:

Lazarus (Jn 11:1–44)

Jairus's daughter (Lk 8:41–42, 49–56)

Transfiguration of Jesus

(*CCC*, 554-556)

Jesus revealed his divine glory before Peter, James, and John up on a high mountain. His face "shone like the sun and his clothes became white as light" (Mt 17:2). By doing so, he was giving a foretaste of the kingdom. In this special revelation, two Old Testament figures—Moses and Elijah—also appear. Their presence recalls how the Law (given to Israel through Moses) and the prophets (Elijah was a great prophet) had announced the sufferings of the Messiah. This vision also reveals all three persons of the Blessed Trinity: the Father (in the voice); the Son; and the Holy Spirit (in the shining cloud).

Discussion Questions

1. Why do you think God the Father allowed Jesus to be born into poverty?
2. How do you imagine Jesus' hidden years in Nazareth? What kind of teenager do you think he was?
3. What do you find most unique about Jesus' gospel message?

Christ Died for Our Sake

(CCC, 456–463; 599–623)

Shortly after the revelation of Jesus' true identity in the Transfiguration, he went to Jerusalem where he was handed over by Jewish authorities to the Romans and put to death. The sacrifice that Jesus made through his life, death, and resurrection repairs the broken relationship between God and man. It bestows God's blessings, grace, and life on mankind and adopts us into God's family. The salvation won by Jesus on the cross brings forgiveness for our sins and redeems us from sin, evil, and death.

Jesus alone is our Savior. As Peter proclaimed, "There is no salvation through anyone else, nor is there any other name under heaven given to the human race by which we are to be saved" (Acts 4:12).

Jesus Suffered under Pontius Pilate (CCC, 624–637)

Jesus shared human nature by undergoing the perfect sacrifice for us. The New Testament explains that Jesus' death was a *redemption*, that is, a "ransom" that defeated the powers of evil. He took on our guilt by substituting for us, by dying a death we deserve. He did so to buy our freedom with his eternal, divine love.

Jesus' death was for all people in all ages. He took our sins to the cross and became the New Adam before the Father. The life he freely surrendered became a perfect instrument of God's love, a gift that opened eternal life to us. His obedient acceptance of suffering and death gave people the hope of an eternal life where there will be no suffering or death.

The Apostles' Creed proclaims the reality of Jesus' death by crucifixion, perhaps the most painful form of capital punishment ever devised. The executioner was the Roman official, Pontius Pilate.

Joseph of Arimathea, a member of the Jewish ruling body known as the Sanhedrin, received permission to bury Jesus. A prominent disciple, Nicodemus, Jesus' mother, Mary, and Mary Magdalene witnessed the place of burial, thus signifying that Jesus was truly dead. According to Matthew's gospel, Pilate even stationed a guard at the tomb to prevent the disciples from stealing Jesus' body.

While in the grave, Jesus' corpse was preserved from corruption because his human soul and body were still linked to the divine person of the Son. The Apostles' Creed professes that the dead Christ went to the abode of the dead (*Sheol* in Hebrew, *Hades* in Greek) to proclaim the good news to the just who were awaiting the Messiah.

The most important event in salvation history took place on the third day following death, the first day of the week. That event was the resurrection of Jesus.

Explaining Your Faith

What were the events leading to Jesus' death?

Jesus offended certain Jewish teachers and leaders because of how and what he taught and who he was. In addition, Jesus associated with sinners and extended God's forgiveness to them. In doing so, he was claiming to be God himself. His forgiving of sins, expelling of devils, curing on the sabbath, and teaching on certain ritual purity laws brought him the charge of being a blasphemer and a false prophet. Finally, he predicted that the temple of his body would be destroyed and rebuilt in three days (see Jn 2:14–23). This was to be a sign of the last days. Certain witnesses who heard this teaching interpreted Jesus' prediction as an attack on the Jerusalem Temple, claiming that he was involved in revolutionary activity. Such a misrepresentation of Jesus' intent was threatening to some Jews who had an economic and religious interest in the Temple.

Under Jewish law, death was the penalty for religious crimes like these. At the time, however, the Romans occupied Palestine. Under Roman law only the Roman prefect could inflict the death penalty. Therefore, some Jewish authorities, acting out of ignorance and a lack of faith, turned Jesus over to the Roman prefect, Pontius Pilate, for execution as a political criminal and potential threat to Caesar's authority.

Thus, Pontius Pilate, the Roman prefect of Judea, Samaria, and Idumea from AD 26–36, sentenced Jesus to death, perhaps in April of the year AD 30 (or 33). Reading the gospel accounts leaves one with the impression that Pilate thought Jesus was innocent. By condemning Jesus, Pilate took the easy route of avoiding the truth.

A tragic historical reality has been to blame the Jewish people as a whole for the death of Jesus. The complex trial of Jesus shows that only a *few* Jewish leaders and Pilate put Jesus to death. Jesus even offered forgiveness to those who condemned him while on the cross. The real authors and instruments of Jesus' crucifixion are sinners, that is, each of us, because it was for our sins that Jesus died.

Jesus freely offered his life to liberate us from our sins and bestow eternal life on us. He underwent the excruciating torments of the most painful form of death devised by human beings out of his immense love for us.

Today, blaming the Jews for Jesus' death—a form of anti-Semitism—is wrong and contrary to the love of Christ. The Second Vatican Council teaches:

> (W)hat happened in His passion cannot be charged against all the Jews, without distinction, then alive, nor against the Jews of today. . . . (T)he Jews should not be presented as rejected or accursed by God, as if this followed from the Holy Scriptures. . . .
>
> Furthermore, in her rejection of every persecution against any man, the Church . . . decries hatred, persecutions, displays of anti-Semitism, directed against Jews at any time and by anyone.
>
> Besides, as the Church has always held and holds now, Christ underwent His passion and death freely, because of the sins of men and out of infinite love, in order that all may reach salvation. . . .
>
> We cannot truly call on God, the Father of all, if we refuse to treat in a brotherly way any man, created as he is in the image of God. Man's relation to God the Father and his relation to men his brothers are so linked together that Scripture says: "He who does not love does not know God" (1 Jn 4:8 *RSV*) (*Declaration on the Relationship of the Church to Non-Christian Religions,* No. 4–5).

On the Third Day He Rose Again

(*CCC*, 638–653; 656–667)

The resurrection of Jesus was a real event. The disciples did not expect anything to occur. In fact, they hid in Jerusalem, fearful that they themselves might be arrested. When the women reported they had seen the empty tomb and the Risen Lord, the apostles at first did not believe. (The empty tomb does not of itself produce faith, but it is a concrete historical sign, a pointer toward belief that the Father brought his Son back to life.)

The apostles and other disciples believed in the resurrection when they actually *saw* Jesus. The New Testament lists many witnesses: Simon Peter, the head of the apostles; the other apostles; more than five hundred men and women and St. Paul himself as he reported in 1 Corinthians 15:5–8; James, the leader of the Jerusalem Church; disciples on the road to Emmaus; and various women, including Mary Magdalene at the tomb and his mother in the Upper Room. These real meetings of the Risen One completely transformed the disciples from frightened and disillusioned followers of the historical Jesus into bold eyewitnesses who proclaimed the good news that "Jesus is Lord!" Their testimony, aided by the Holy Spirit's gifts of faith and fortitude, led many of them to die for their belief that Jesus Christ rose from the dead.

Death was defeated for all time at Jesus' resurrection. Salvation for mankind has been won. Christ conquered Satan and destroyed the power of death. We no longer fear death. Jesus is the gateway to heaven and eternal life.

In his resurrection, Jesus was fully restored to life. As the *Catechism* teaches: "In his risen body he passes from the state of death to another life beyond time and space" (CCC, 646). Jesus' human body was gloriously transfigured, filled with the Holy Spirit, into an incorrupt, glorious, immortal body "seated at the right hand of the Father."

Through the ages, some have tried to explain away Jesus' resurrection by arguing against Jesus' resurrection in some way. Some of the misconceptions of the resurrection were that it was a

- *reanimated corpse*, that is, a body like Lazarus' come back to life that would eventually die again;
- *metaphor*, a poetic way of saying that Jesus' soul was immortal;
- *reincarnation*, a belief that the human soul is reborn time and again into new bodies;
- *psychological explanation* made up by the apostles who were trying to say that the *cause* of their teacher would live on.

Rather, an accurate view of the resurrection follows:

> Faith in the Resurrection has as its object an event which is historically attested to by the disciples, who really encountered the Risen One. At the same time, this event is mysteriously transcendent insofar as it is the entry of Christ's humanity into the glory of God (CCC, 656).

Writing Assignment

Imagine a young child asks you "Who killed Jesus?" Write what you would say and how you would say it.

The resurrection is proof of Jesus' divinity. The resurrection of the crucified Christ shows that he was truly the Son of God and God himself. The resurrection further reveals the unending communion of God as Trinity: the Father who glorifies the Son, the Son whose sacrifice merits his exaltation, and the Holy Spirit who is the Spirit of life and resurrection. Raised to a glorious body and filled with the power of the Holy Spirit, Jesus Christ has definitively conquered sin and death.

What effect does Christ's resurrection have on humanity? Jesus' passion, death, and resurrection repairs our friendship with God. It restores humanity, freeing us from our slavery to sin, death, and suffering. Jesus' resurrection gives us hope for our own rising after death and eternal life with the Blessed Trinity.

No longer limited by space and time, Christ lives and reigns forever. He lives in his Body, the Church, and in a special way in the powerful signs of love he has given his Church—the sacraments. For example, by the power of the Holy Spirit, the Lord comes to us at Baptism, forming us into his own image. In the sacrament of Confirmation, the Holy Spirit strengthens us with spiritual gifts to live like Christ. And we experience the Lord's forgiveness in the sacrament of Penance, experience his healing touch in the Anointing of the Sick, and receive his help to live loving lives of service in Holy Orders and holy Matrimony.

In a special way, Jesus is alive in the Eucharist. There the Risen Lord comes to us under the forms of bread and wine. We receive Christ to become Christ for others. The Lord meets us in each other and, in a special way, in the least of those in our midst—the poor, victims of discrimination, the powerless, the suffering, the lonely.

He Ascended into Heaven and Will Come Again
(*CCC*, 668–670)

The resurrection forms part of the Paschal mystery, the saving event that includes Jesus' death (Good Friday), his descent to the dead (Holy Saturday), and his glorification. Jesus' glorification consists of the resurrection (Easter Sunday), the ascension into heaven (forty days after Easter), and Pentecost (fifty days after Easter).

The Ascension of Jesus refers to the time when Jesus stopped appearing to the disciples in visible, human form. The Ascension indicates a difference between the way the glory of the risen Christ was revealed and that of "Christ exalted to his Father's right hand" (*CCC*, 660). Being seated at his right hand means that Christ now glorifies the Father as the incarnate Son of God, that he continually intercedes for us with the Father, and that it is the beginning of the Messiah's kingdom, one that will have no end.

Parousia—The second coming of Christ when the Lord will judge the living and the dead.

Pentecost is the day on which the Holy Spirit descended on the apostles and gave them the power to preach with conviction the message that Jesus is risen and is Lord of the universe. The feast of Pentecost is often known as the "birthday of the Church."

The Creed proclaims with great confidence the **Parousia**, that is, Jesus' arrival in glory at his Second Coming. The world we know will end at that time. All of God's creatures everywhere will acknowledge that Jesus is

Lord. The glorious Lord Jesus will then fully bring about the Father's kingdom of justice, love, and peace. Jesus told us that the exact time this will take place is hidden in God's almighty plan. However, we are always to be ready. "Be watchful! Be alert! You do not know when the time will come" (Mk 13:33).

He Will Judge the Living and the Dead (*CCC*, 678–679)

According to Matthew 25:31–46, at the Parousia the Son of Man will judge the living and the dead based on how loving we were toward others. Did we feed the hungry and give drink to the thirsty? Did we welcome strangers and minister to the poor, the sick, the imprisoned? If we can answer "yes" to his questions, then our reward will be beyond what we can possibly imagine. Jesus' instructions to us are simple:

> I give you a new commandment: love one another. As I have loved you, so you also should love one another. This is how all will know that you are my disciples, if you have love for one another (Jn 13:34–35).

The second to last verse of the Bible is a prayer to the Lord that he might return right away: "Amen! Come, Lord Jesus!" (Rv 22:20). This is a most appropriate prayer for Christians. In faith, we know who Jesus really is and what he has done for us. Who would not want him to come soon?

Discussion Questions

1. Who were the witnesses to the empty tomb? What is significant about their being the first witnesses to the fact that Jesus is risen?
2. Imagine that Christ is going to return tomorrow. What would you do differently today? Which people would you absolutely want to see? What would you tell them?

What We Believe about Jesus

(*CCC*, 464–483)

The Church defined several of its beliefs about Christ in response to heresies ("false teachings") that arose about Jesus in the early years. The first major **heresy** concerning Jesus—*Gnostic Docetism*—held that God could not have actually taken on human flesh and that Jesus only *appeared* to be a man. It would follow, then, under this belief, that Jesus only *appeared* to suffer and die for us. If that were so, then it would only *appear* that we are saved!

heresy—An obstinate denial after Baptism to believe a truth that must be believed with divine and Catholic faith, or an obstinate doubt about such truth.

Another heresy, promoted by a priest named Arius, denied the true divinity of Jesus. *Arianism* taught that God the Father created Jesus as the greatest of creatures but that Jesus was not equal to God (not of the same "substance"). Once again, if Arius were correct, then our salvation would be void since only God can save us.

A later heresy—*Nestorianism*—taught that Christ was *two* persons and that Mary was the mother of the human Jesus, not the divine Jesus. *Monophysitism* held that Christ's divine nature absorbed his human nature, thus in effect destroying Jesus' true humanity.

Answering the Heresies

To respond to these false ideas, Church leaders, under the guidance of the Holy Spirit, convened a series of ecumenical (worldwide) councils to define carefully the nature of Jesus Christ. These councils were Nicaea (325), Constantinople I (381), Ephesus (431), Chalcedon (451), Constantinople II (553), Constantinople III (680–681), and Nicaea II (787).

They provide the following foundational dogmatic teachings about Jesus Christ:

- *Jesus is the only Son of God.* Mary was Jesus' human mother, but the First Person of the Blessed Trinity is Jesus' Father. Jesus is God the Father's natural son; we humans are adopted children.
- *Jesus Christ is true God, "God from God, Light from Light."* Like the Father, the Son possesses a divine nature. Proceeding from the Father, the Son is of one substance with the Father. Just as light is identical to the light from which it comes, Jesus Christ is true God.
- *Jesus is "begotten, not made, one in Being with the Father."* The always-existing Son "proceeds" from the Father. Forever he proceeded, and he always will proceed. The Son was not generated by God the Father, the way human fathers generate their children. In other words, the Son was not created, that is, made by the Father.

  To underscore this point, the Council of Nicaea distinguished between *begotten* and *created.* The Father begets the Son and creates the world. In other words, the Son *always* existed. He always was in relationship to the Father from whom he proceeds. The Father was always the Father; the Son was always the Son. The prologue to John's Gospel states this: "In the beginning was the Word [the Son], and the Word was with God, and the Word was God" (Jn 1:1).
- *All things were made through the Son.* The Son always existed with the Father and shares his nature. Thus, he also shares in the creation of the world (cf. Jn 1:2–4).
- *There is only one person in Christ, the divine person.* This person is the Second Person of the Blessed Trinity. Because this is so, we attribute everything in Christ's human nature to his divine person, including his miracles and even his suffering and death.
- *Mary is truly the Mother of God. She truly conceived God's Son.*
- *There are two distinct natures in the one person of Christ.* Jesus has a divine nature and a human nature. He is perfect in divinity and perfect in humanity. Jesus Christ is true God and true man.
- *Jesus has a human intellect and a human will.* However, Jesus' human intellect and will are perfectly attuned and subject to his divine intellect and will, which he has in common with the Father and the Holy Spirit.
- *In Jesus, God truly shared our humanity.* The human and divine natures in the one person of Jesus are so perfectly united that it is right to say that the incarnate Son of God truly suffered, died, and rose from the dead for us.

One of the most important professions of faith concerning Jesus comes from the Council of Chalcedon in 451. It reads:

> We all with one voice teach the confession of one and the same Son, our Lord Jesus Christ: the same perfect in divinity and perfect in humanity, the same truly God and truly man, of a rational soul and a body; consubstantial with the Father as regards his divinity, and the same consubstantial with us as regards his humanity; like us in all respects except for sin; begotten before the ages from the Father as regards his divinity, and in the last days the same for us and for our salvation from Mary, the virgin God-bearer as regards his humanity; one and the same Christ, Son, Lord, only-begotten, acknowledged in two natures which undergo no confusion, no change, no division, no separation; at no point was the difference between the natures taken away through the union, but rather the property of both natures is preserved and comes together into a single person and a single subsistent being; he is not parted or divided into two persons, but is one and the same only-begotten Son, God, Word, Lord Jesus Christ, just as the prophets taught from the beginning about him,

and as the Lord Jesus Christ himself instructed us, and as the creed of the fathers handed it down to us.[3]

Other Beliefs about Jesus (Islam)

In this day and age, it is important to understand how other faiths besides Christianity understand Jesus. The Islamic faith acknowledges the existence of Jesus. Moslems hold Jesus to be one of the great prophets, a miracle-worker who cured people of sickness and brought them back to life. However, Moslems do not believe that Jesus is God and the savior of humanity. They claim he did not die during the crucifixion or rise from the dead. Moslems have high regard for Jesus' mother, Mary, even holding that his birth was miraculous. However, they do not consider Mary to be the Mother of God.

Moslems believe that both Jews and Christians are people of the scriptures—the Torah and Gospels. They believe Allah's final revelation was given in their sacred scripture, the Koran. The name *Islam* means "surrender." Moslems hold that Mohammed (570–632) was the last in the line of a series of prophets and was, in fact, God's greatest prophet. The five pillars of the Islamic religion are:

1. *Shahadah:* the profession of faith—"There is no God but Allah and Mohammed is his messenger."
2. *Salat:* prayer five times a day.
3. *Zakat:* the giving of alms to the poor.
4. *Fasting* during the month of Ramadan
5. *Hajj:* a holy pilgrimage to Mecca during one's life.

The Second Vatican Council document, *Declaration on the Relation of the Church to Non-Christian Religions*, No. 3, addresses the Church's attitudes toward Islam:

> The Church regards with esteem also the Moslems. They adore the one God, living and subsisting in Himself; merciful and all-powerful, the Creator of heaven and earth, who has spoken to men; they take pains to submit wholeheartedly to even His inscrutable decrees, just as Abraham, with whom the faith of Islam takes pleasure in linking itself, submitted to God. Though they do not acknowledge Jesus as God, they revere Him as a prophet. They also honor Mary, His virgin Mother; at times they even call on her with devotion. In addition, they await the day of judgment when God will render their deserts to all those who have been raised up from the dead. Finally, they value the moral life and worship God especially through prayer, almsgiving and fasting.
>
> Since in the course of centuries not a few quarrels and hostilities have arisen between Christians and Moslems, this sacred synod urges all to forget the past and to work sincerely for mutual understanding and to preserve as well as to promote together for the benefit of all mankind social justice and moral welfare, as well as peace and freedom.

Discussion Questions

1. What do you think are the three most essential teachings about Jesus Christ?
2. Which teaching about Jesus do you have the most trouble understanding? believing?
3. Who is an experienced Catholic you can go to for help in understanding your questions about Jesus? Why did you choose this person?

Summary Points

- ★ The distinctive sign of Christian faith is belief in the Incarnation, God's Son taking on human flesh in Jesus Christ.
- ★ The name *Jesus* means "Savior" or "God saves." Jesus' titles reveal his identity and the meaning of his coming.
- ★ Ancient Roman and Jewish writers attest to Jesus' existence, while the gospels provide unshakeable evidence of a remarkable person behind them—Jesus of Nazareth.
- ★ *Gospel* means good news. It refers to Jesus' preaching of the kingdom, to the good news about Jesus himself, and to the four written gospels which are our primary source of knowledge about Jesus. These inspired documents resulted from a three-stage process that included the life of Jesus (4–6 BC to AD 30/33), a period of oral tradition, and the written gospels themselves, which were composed between AD 68–100.
- ★ Reflecting on the mysteries of Jesus' life will help us better understand his meaning for us.
- ★ The doctrine of the virgin birth holds that Jesus was conceived by the power of the Holy Spirit and born of the Virgin Mary. We further believe that Mary was perpetually a virgin.
- ★ Jesus taught that God's kingdom is in our midst and that it requires faith and repentance on our part. The principal sign of God's reign is his limitless mercy.
- ★ To follow Jesus means to pick up a cross, to die to self for love of him and others.
- ★ Jesus promised he would always remain with us by power of the Holy Spirit. Thus, we can meet Jesus today through the Church, the sacraments, prayer, the Bible, and each other, especially the "least" of our brothers and sisters.
- ★ Jesus saved us through his Paschal mystery of love. He freely chose to sacrifice his life to redeem us and to allow us to participate in God's own life.
- ★ Jesus really died, was laid in a new tomb, and on Holy Saturday went to the abode of the dead to proclaim the gospel to the righteous ones awaiting the arrival of the Savior.
- ★ Jesus really rose from the dead. Jesus' resurrection is the basis of our Christian faith.
- ★ At the Parousia Jesus will come again to establish God's kingdom fully and to judge the living and the dead.
- ★ Various early heresies like Docetism, Arianism, Nestorianism, and Monophysitism in one way or another denied either Jesus' humanity or divinity. Early ecumenical councils were convoked to combat these false teachings and taught foundational dogmatic statements about Jesus.

Review Questions

1. Define *Incarnation.*
2. List four reasons God became man.
3. What does the name Jesus mean? Why is it appropriate that he was given this name?
4. Discuss the meaning of these titles of Jesus: *Christ, Son of God, Lord, Son of Man, Suffering Servant.*
5. What is our primary source of knowledge of Jesus Christ?
6. What kinds of writing appear in the New Testament? Give examples of each.
7. Name the three stages of gospel formation.
8. What are two religious lessons about Jesus learned from his birth and infancy?
9. Did Jesus have blood brothers and sisters?
10. Why did Jesus submit to the baptism of John?
11. What is meant by the term *gospel*?
12. What did Jesus teach was the meaning of the "kingdom of God"?

13. Name and explain two of Jesus' key teachings.
14. Why did Jesus perform miracles?
15. Define *salvation.*
16. Who is responsible for the death of Jesus?
17. Why is belief in the resurrection essential for Christians?
18. Define *Paschal mystery.*
19. What is the *Parousia*? What should we do to prepare for it?
20. List and discuss several Church doctrines that counteract the heresies of Docetism and Arianism.

Applying What You Have Learned

1. Interview three Catholics of different ages, genders, cultures, and the like. Ask them about their faith in Jesus Christ. For example, how they pray to Jesus, how they meet Jesus in others, their favorite gospel stories, and how they have personally experienced Jesus.
2. After researching on the Internet, create a PowerPoint® presentation on one of the following topics or on another topic of your own choosing:
   - the mysteries of Jesus' life
   - Stations of the Cross: traditional and updated
   - Jesus in art through the ages
   - a tour of important places in the Holy Land.
3. Devise a mini-service project to aid the hungry, thus responding to one of the corporal works of mercy in Matthew 25:35–36. The project can involve direct service (e.g., preparing a meal yourself) or indirect service (e.g., collecting food to deliver to the community food bank).
4. Read the Gospel of Mark in one sitting. Design prayer cards or another art medium using ten of your favorite passages from the Gospel.
5. Depict in any art form your image of what you think Jesus may have looked like.

Prayer Reflection

Recite the famous Jesus Prayer in front of an icon of Christ. One version of the Jesus Prayer goes this way: "Lord, Jesus Christ, Son of the Living God, have mercy on me, a sinner." Note how it includes all the titles discussed in this chapter. It also emphasizes Jesus' role as our Savior.

The word *icon* in Greek means image. When we pray before icons we are putting ourselves in the presence of the holy person or entering into the religious mystery that is portrayed.

This icon of Jesus points to a famous passage from John's gospel: "I am the light of the world. Whoever follows me will not walk in darkness, but will have the light of life" (Jn 8:12).

How has Christ brought light to your life? List five ways you bring light to those around you.

How do you find God's goodness in our world?

Answers to "What Do You Know about Jesus?" (page 43): 1-T, 2-a, 3-T, 4-F, 5-c, 6-F, 7-T, 8-b, 9-c, 10-F.

"Go, therefore, and make disciples of all nations, baptizing them in the name of the Father, and of the Son, and of the holy Spirit, teaching them to observe all that I have commanded you. And behold, I am with you always, until the end of the age."

Matthew 28:19–20

Chapter 3 Outline

The Holy Spirit Is God

The Holy Spirit is worshiped and glorified with the Father and Son.

The Holy Spirit in the Bible

The Spirit is present in both the Old Testament and New Testament.

Name, Titles, and Symbols of the Holy Spirit

Many scriptural and traditional symbols reveal more about the Holy Spirit, called the "Paraclete" by Jesus.

The Holy Spirit in the Life of Christians

The Holy Spirit is present in the Church, gifting us with grace.

The Mystery of the Trinity

We believe that God is in three divine persons: Father Son, and Holy Spirit.

Understanding More about the Trinity

The immanent Trinity is a way to describe God's inner life. The economic or salvific Trinity refers to how God acts in our lives and in our world.

Chapter 3

The Holy Spirit and Blessed Trinity

The Holy Spirit Is God

(*CCC* 243–248; 689–690)

Norwegian explorer Roald Amundsen was the first to discover the South Pole and the magnetic meridian of the North Pole. It is reported that on one of his trips to the North Pole, he took along a homing pigeon and set it free once he reached the top of the world. When the pigeon made it back to his home in Norway before he did, his wife shouted out with joy, "My husband is alive. He's still alive."

The joy of the wife notwithstanding, there is no greater joy than for believers to shout out "Jesus is risen!" The pangs of death were removed once and for all. This feeling of joy was only multiplied when the Holy Spirit descended on Jesus' disciples on Pentecost Sunday. Jesus promised the Holy Spirit to console his disciples just before he began his way of the cross—the road that led to his suffering, death, and finally his resurrection:

> And I will ask the Father, and he will give you another Advocate to be with you always, the Spirit of truth, which the world cannot accept, because it neither sees nor knows it. But you know it, because it remains with you, and will be in you. . . . The Advocate, the holy Spirit that the Father will send in my name—he will teach you everything and remind you of all that [I] told you" (Jn 14:16–17, 26).

After his resurrection and ascension, Jesus' glorified body is no longer visible, but he remains present to us through the power of the Holy Spirit. The Holy Spirit is the very presence of the risen, glorified Lord, the Spirit of love who *always* existed with the Father and Son.

In the Nicene Creed, Catholics profess that the Holy Spirit is "Lord and giver of life." The Council of Constantinople (381) taught as a point of dogma: "With the Father and Son, he is worshiped and glorified." The Holy Spirit is neither a creature (like an angel) nor an impersonal force. He is the Lord God. The Spirit's primary mission is to adopt us into the divine family and to unite us to Christ Jesus. By uniting us to the Son, we are drawn to the Father. This formula says it well: "To the Father through the Son in the Holy Spirit." The Holy Spirit is our interior teacher who keeps us united in Christ: "And no one can say, 'Jesus is Lord,' except by the holy Spirit" (1 Cor 12:3).

This chapter will also explain the central mystery of our faith—the doctrine of the Blessed Trinity and how the Holy Spirit relates to the other persons in the Trinity.

Gifts of the Holy Spirit

The Holy Spirit offers the gifts we need to live Christ-like lives. Traditionally, the Church lists seven **gifts of the Holy Spirit**, qualities that the Old Testament prophet Isaiah (see Is 11:2–3) said would identify the Messiah. Jesus Christ lived each of these gifts perfectly.

Showered on us by the Holy Spirit at Baptism and Confirmation, Catholics are given the grace to use these same gifts to draw others to Christ. The traditional seven gifts of the Holy Spirit are: *wisdom, understanding, counsel, fortitude, knowledge, piety*, and *fear of the Lord*.

Read the following definitions of the gifts of the Holy Spirit. Write about how one of the gifts is particularly evidenced in your life. Also write about how another of the gifts of the Spirit needs more work in your life.

- *Wisdom* is looking at reality from God's point of view. Having wisdom involves praying before making decisions and seeking guidance from those with more experience.
- *Understanding* involves taking the time to uncover the deeper meaning of faith and the mysteries of God's magnificent creation.
- *Knowledge* is the grace to see how God is working in our lives, especially in the areas of great moral decisions.
- *Counsel (right judgment)* helps us to form our conscience in light of Church teaching. We do this by praying and consulting other people before deciding on moral issues.
- *Fortitude (courage)* is the strength to follow our own convictions in the face of peer pressure. It also involves openness to suffering for the Lord.
- *Piety (reverence)* is respect we show to the Lord through praise and worship. Respecting the dignity and worth of others is another important expression of this gift.
- *Fear of the Lord (wonder and awe)* is the gift of the Spirit that helps us to show concern about the reality of sin in our life and to avoid anything that might alienate us from God and others.

gifts of the Holy Spirit—An outpouring of God's gifts that enable us to live a Christian life. The traditional gifts of the Holy Spirit are wisdom, understanding, knowledge, counsel (right judgment), fortitude (courage), piety (reverence), and fear of the Lord (wonder and awe).

Discussion Questions

1. Name the greatest joy you have ever experienced.
2. What does it mean to say that the Holy Spirit is the "giver of life"?

The Holy Spirit in the Bible

The Holy Spirit "spoke through the prophets." He guided the biblical authors to reveal God's Word and gives us the gifts that we need to accept God's revelation and live a Christ-filled life. In salvation history, the Holy Spirit seems hidden, but this is only because the Holy Spirit does not speak of himself. He is like the mysterious power of electricity, always present but out of sight to provide the power to operate electrical appliances.

The Holy Spirit in the Old Testament

(*CCC*, 103–108; 687; 702–730)

Before the coming of Christ and the Holy Spirit's descent on Pentecost Sunday, the Father and the Holy Spirit had a joint, hidden mission. Today, with the light of faith and the Spirit's help, the Church searches the Old Testament to discover the Spirit's active presence in salvation history where he prepared for and promised us the Messiah. The Old Testament biblical authors often use the Hebrew word *ruah* (wind or breath) to speak of God's mysterious, powerful, and life-giving presence in creation and at work among the Chosen People. Over time, the Old Testament gradually came to reveal the Holy Spirit in more personal terms.

The Church discovers the active presence of the Holy Spirit in several ways.

In creation (Gn 1:2) and in giving the breath of life to Adam and Eve (Gn 2:7), the Spirit brings life to the world and keeps the world in existence. By the power of the Holy Spirit, God forged a covenant with the Chosen People through Abraham. Eventually, a Messiah was born among Abraham's descendants.

To Moses, God showed himself by the power of the Holy Spirit, for example, in the **theophany** that revealed God's presence as in the burning bush and in the clouds that led the people through the desert. God's Spirit helped the Israelites keep the Law. The Law served as a teacher to lead people to Christ, but it could not save them. It made people aware of how sinful they were and how impossible it is to obey God's law without the help of the Holy Spirit.

theophany—An appearance or manifestation of God to humans.

The Spirit inspired kings like David to rule in Yahweh's name. But after David's time, the Chosen People drifted away from the Law and ignored God's covenant. God's spirit "anointed" Israel's prophets, like Elijah (2 Kgs 2:9) and Elisha (2 Kgs 2:15), who spoke on God's behalf by instructing people to remain faithful to the covenant. The sinfulness of the Israelites eventually led them to exile in Babylonia. It was then that the Holy Spirit sustained them until they could return to the Promised Land. He continually spoke through the prophets, who promised that one day the Messiah would come to rule them.

The Suffering Servant Songs of Isaiah reveal the Messiah's qualities. They also prophesy the Lord's Passion and his death, the necessary prelude for his unleashing the Spirit of life on all humans:

Yet it was our infirmities that he
bore,
our sufferings that he endured. . . .
But he was pierced for our
offenses,
crushed for our sins,

Upon him was the chastisement
that makes us whole,
by his stripes we
were healed. . . .
Though he was harshly treated, he submitted
and opened not his mouth;
Like a lamb led to the slaughter or a sheep
before the shearers,
he was silent and opened not his
mouth. . . .
Because of his affliction
he shall see the light in fullness of days;
Through his suffering, my servant shall justify
many,
and their guilt he shall bear.
Therefore I will give him his portion among
the great,
and he shall divide the spoils with
the mighty,
Because he surrendered himself to death
and was counted among the wicked;
And he shall take away the sins of many,
and win pardon for their offenses
(Is 53:4–5, 7, 11–12).

Not until Jesus Christ came was the Holy Spirit fully revealed as a separate, distinct Person of the Blessed Trinity.

Scripture Search

Read the following Old Testament passages. Summarize briefly the main point about God's Spirit that the passage expresses.

1. Genesis 1:1–2; 2:7
2. Isaiah 11:1–3
3. Isaiah 61:1–2
4. Ezekiel 36:26–28
5. Ezekiel 37:1–14

The Holy Spirit in the New Testament

(*CCC*, 689–693; 717–732; 743; 745–746)

Pentecost, originally a Jewish harvest festival celebrated fifty days after Passover, was the day the Holy Spirit descended on Christ's disciples hiding in the Upper Room in Jerusalem, the place of the Last Supper. The Acts of the Apostles, written by the evangelist Luke, records how on that day the Holy Spirit came down with power on the early Christians. The Spirit's presence gave the early Church the courage to proclaim the gospel of Jesus Christ to the ends of the earth.

The apostles, the Blessed Mother, and some women were praying, trying to make sense of the events leading to our Lord's death and resurrection:

> Suddenly there came from the sky a noise like a strong driving wind, and it filled the entire house in which they were. Then there appeared to them tongues as of fire, which parted and came to rest on each one of them. And they were all filled with the holy Spirit and began to speak in different tongues, as the Spirit enabled them to proclaim (Acts 2:2–4).

Immediately afterward the apostles went to proclaim the gospel to the crowds in *tongues*, that is, the many languages of the various people who were gathered there. Remarkably, Jewish pilgrims from all around the Roman Empire understood them. At first the crowds were skeptical; in fact, they thought the apostles were drunk. But Peter assured them that they were quite sober—after all, it was only nine in the morning. Peter explained that what was happening was clearly promised by the prophet Joel:

"It will come to pass in the last days," God
says,
"that I will pour out a portion of my spirit
upon on all flesh.
Your sons and daughters shall prophesy,
Your young men shall see visions,
your old men shall dream dreams. . . .
And it shall be that everyone shall be saved
who calls on the name of the Lord" (Acts 2:17, 21).

Pentecost fulfilled Jesus' promise to send the Holy Spirit. On that day, 3,000 people were baptized. By the end of the first century, the gospel had been preached to every corner of the Roman Empire. Today, the same Holy Spirit remains alive in the world and in the Church, bringing Christ's salvation to all people everywhere.

John's gospel tells how Jesus sent the Holy Spirit to the apostles on Easter Sunday. Jesus greeted his apostles with peace and then commissioned them by saying: "As the Father has sent me, so I send you. . . . Receive the holy Spirit. Whose sins you forgive are forgiven them, and whose sins you retain are retained" (Jn 20:21–23).

God breathed life into Adam and Eve at the beginning of human history. After his resurrection, Jesus recreated his disciples by giving them the life of the Holy Spirit, a life as God's children. A major emphasis of John's gospel is to show how the Church is to continue Jesus' work of salvation.

Jesus Is Filled with the Holy Spirit

The Holy Spirit accompanied Jesus through his whole life. The Church was able to recognize this through the eyes of faith. For example:

- The Holy Spirit enabled Mary to conceive Jesus, thus bringing God's Son into our midst. He is *Emmanuel*—"God-with-us."
- The Holy Spirit helped John the Baptist to prepare people for the "way of the Lord."
- The Holy Spirit was at Jesus' baptism, led him into the desert for prayer and fasting, and sustained him there in his battle with Satan.
- Jesus began his preaching ministry in Nazareth filled with the Spirit's power (Lk 4:14). Jesus testified that the Spirit was upon him, anointing him to preach good news to the afflicted, proclaim liberty to captives, give sight to the blind, and let the oppressed go free (Lk 4:16–21). Jesus' miracles of healing, driving out demons, raising from the dead, and showing power over the forces of creation were all done through the power of the Holy Spirit.
- In his public ministry, Jesus gradually revealed the mystery of the Holy Spirit. Examples include his instructions to Nicodemus (Jn 3:5–8), conversations with the Samaritan woman (Jn 4:10, 14, 23–24), and his teaching about the Eucharist (Jn 6:27, 51, 62–63).
- Jesus promised to send the Holy Spirit (Jn 14:16–17, quoted on page 68). In this promise, Jesus referred to the Holy Spirit by the name Advocate or **Paraclete**. A "paraclete" is a helper who will give aid and comfort. Jesus is all of these, but he promised to send *another* Paraclete—"the Spirit of truth" who will live in us and guide us to the truth.
- Finally, the Holy Spirit remained with Jesus even up to his death and resurrection. When the soldier stabbed Jesus with a spear, blood and water gushed out of the wound (Jn 19:34). This symbolizes the life and waters of the Holy Spirit flowing out to the world. Through the Spirit, God raised Jesus from the dead. Our Risen Lord has a spiritual,

Paraclete—Another name for the Holy Spirit that means advocate, defender, or consoler.

glorified body. As resurrected Lord, Jesus is, through the power and presence of the Holy Spirit, the invisible head of his body, the Church. The Holy Spirit gives the Church life and directs it in Christ's continuing work of salvation.

When the Father sends the Son, he also sends the Holy Spirit. The Son and Holy Spirit have a joint, but distinct mission. It is Christ Jesus who is visible, the image of God; however, it is the Holy Spirit who reveals him to us.

Name, Titles, and Symbols of the Holy Spirit

(CCC, 691–701)

You are probably familiar with the terms that go into the proper name of the third person of the Blessed Trinity—"holy" and "spirit." Holy refers to God's total uniqueness from his creatures; he alone is "totally other"; he is awesome and beyond what we can grasp. God is the only all-holy one. Spirit is also an interesting word. Teams or student bodies are sometimes spoken of as having "spirit." The word spirit also refers to the real sense of something, as in the expressions "keeping to the spirit of the law" or "living the spirit of '76." Many religions refer to God as the "Great Spirit" because they recognize that he is the source of life and the one who keeps everything in existence.

Recall the Hebrew word ruah which is translated as spirit. Ruah means "breath, life, wind, air." The biblical authors use ruah 379 times to depict God's actions in salvation history. For example, the "spirit" (ruah) in the image of driving wind hovers over the dark, chaotic waters at creation. In the first creation account (Gn 1:1–2:4a), the Spirit is linked with God's word; it brings light, order, and life into existence. In the second creation account (see Gn 2:4b–25), God breathes the "breath of life" into Adam after making him from clay (Gn 2:7). This "breath of life" is God's gift to us, God's Spirit in us that enables us to live and to communicate with and love God.

When Christians join the terms "Holy" and "Spirit" together. They are clearly following Jesus' revelation about the Third Person of the Blessed Trinity. The Holy Spirit is of the same "substance" (nature) as the Father and the Son. The Holy Spirit is the breath (Spirit) of the Father with whom Jesus is totally filled. The Spirit is active in the Word. He is the gift given by the Father and Son to all of Jesus' followers to do in us what he did in Jesus. He is what St. Paul also refers to as the Spirit of the promise, the Spirit of adoption, the Spirit of Christ, the Spirit of the Lord, and the Spirit of God.

As we saw above, Jesus gives the Holy Spirit the titles of Paraclete and the "Spirit of truth." The Paraclete reveals the Holy Spirit's role in our lives. He consoles, acts as an advocate, and defends us.

Symbols of the Holy Spirit

Some other scriptural and traditional symbols for the Holy Spirit are explained below:

Discussion Questions

1. How would you describe the Holy Spirit in one or two sentences based on the scripture passages in this section?
2. Why do you think the disciples gathered again at the Upper Room following Jesus' death?
3. How is the Holy Spirit a "Spirit of truth"?

Writing Assignment

Read Luke 4:14–30. Answer the following questions.

1. Where does this take place?
2. Which Old Testament prophet is Jesus quoting?
3. What is he claiming when he comments on this passage?
4. How do the people first react?
5. Why do they change?
6. What do they wish to do to Jesus?

Write about a time when speaking the truth got you in trouble.

Fire

God appeared to Moses in a burning bush—a symbol of divine holiness. He led the Israelites through the desert by pillars of fire, helping to purify the people and make them holy. Fire also punishes the wicked, as in the destruction of Sodom. Fire in both cases represents the transforming energy of the Holy Spirit.

Fire also gives light. Jesus calls himself the "Light of the World." His followers are to be light as well, leading others to him and to the gospel truth. Thus, he gives the Holy Spirit to his disciples to empower them to enlighten the world. The Holy Spirit is our inner light to help us see Jesus and burn with love for him and others.

Tongues of Fire

The tongue enables us to speak. Jesus spoke God's truth because he was filled with the Holy Spirit. His words forgave sin, brought about cures, controlled the forces of nature, and brought the dead back to life.

The Spirit whom Jesus gives to his disciples enables us to reverse the prideful confusion brought to humanity at the time of the Tower of Babel (Gn 11:9). The Holy Spirit makes its possible for us to proclaim Christ Jesus, to speak the truth, and to create community in the Lord's name.

Anointing with Oil

The New Testament associates anointing with oil with being anointed with the Holy Spirit. The title Christ means "anointed one." The sacraments of Baptism and Confirmation both use oil to express the gift of the Holy Spirit who makes Catholics anointed ones of the Anointed One. Also, those baptized men who receive the sacrament of Holy Orders are anointed with holy Chrism "as a sign of the special anointing of the Holy Spirit who makes their ministry fruitful" (CCC, 1574). The symbol of the *seal*, as in the expression "The Father has set his seal on Christ," is related to the symbol of anointing. Baptism, Confirmation, and Holy Orders bring about an indelible character through the anointing of the Holy Spirit in these sacraments.

Water

Water can represent both death and life. Too much water causes floods which lead to destruction and death, yet we need some water to live. Images of both death and life appear in the Bible in connection with water. For example, God punished humanity in the time of Noah by sending the Flood. But God also created the world out of the watery chaos and sent springs of water to the Chosen People in the desert.

Jesus associated water and the Spirit when he said to Nicodemus: "Amen, amen, I say to you, no one can enter the kingdom of God without being born of water and Spirit" (Jn 3:5). This clearly refers to the sacrament of Baptism, which brings about our death to our old life of sin and our rebirth to eternal life. The waters of Baptism initiate us into Christ's body, the Church, and bestow on us the gift of the Holy Spirit.

Hand

Jesus healed through touch. His apostles healed in his name as well. And they passed on the Holy Spirit through the imposition of hands. This sign is used in the sacraments (at the laying on of hands) to signify the giving of the Holy Spirit.

Dove

In the Old Testament, a dove released by Noah returned to the Ark with an olive tree branch to show that the floodwaters were receding. The dove is a symbol of life. In Biblical times the dove was also used as a purification offering for the poor (for example, Lk 2:24).

In the gospel stories of Jesus' baptism, the Holy Spirit descends on him in the form of a dove. This image of a descending dove brings to mind God's Spirit hovering over the waters at creation. A dove also signifies gentleness, virtue, and peace—gifts that we receive when we are united to the Holy Spirit.

Two other symbols of the Holy Spirit mentioned in the *Catechism of the Catholic Church* are the *finger* of God that writes the divine law on our hearts and the *cloud and light* which reveal the saving God, yet veil the divine glory.

Symbols for the Holy Spirit

Identify which symbol of God's Spirit or presence is depicted in the following passages. Then use any art medium to devise a symbol for the Holy Spirit based on one or more of the passages.

1. Exodus 19:18
2. Psalm 104:30
3. Ephesians 5:6–20
4. Revelation 21:6

Native American Religion: The Sioux Concept of God

The Native American tribes known as the Sioux typically refer to themselves as Lakota or Dakota, meaning "allies." In the Lakota religion, God is called *Wakan Tanka,* often translated as Great Spirit. This term communicates the idea of one God who is personal, holy, and great, but also mysterious and beyond human understanding.

In the sacred rituals of the Lakota, the drum is often the only instrument used. A holy man, Black Elk, says the drum represents the whole universe for it is round. The strong steady beat of the drum is like a heartbeat; it represents the voice of Wakan Tanka.

Lakota religion associates this Great Spirit with the Grandfather, an impersonal energy that is at work in the universe, and the Father, the creative force that both preserves and destroys.[4] Note the similarity to the Holy Spirit of the "Great Spirit" in this prayer attributed to Chief Yellow Lark of the Lakota tribe.[5]

Oh, Great Spirit,
whose voice I hear in the winds
and whose breath gives life to all the world, hear me.
I am small and weak.
I need your strength and wisdom.

Let me walk in beauty and make my eyes
ever behold the red and purple sunset.
Make my hands respect the things you have made
and my ears sharp to hear your voice.
Make me wise so that I may understand
the things you have taught my people.
Let me learn the lessons you have hidden
in every leaf and rock.

I seek strength, not to be superior to my brother,
but to fight my greatest enemy—myself.
Make me always ready to come to you
with clean hands and straight eyes,
so when life fades, as the fading sunset,
my spirit will come to you
without shame.

Discussion Questions

1. The Paraclete "consoles, acts as an advocate, and defends us." How has this statement been true in your life?
2. Describe examples of both the life-giving and destructive elements of fire and water. How does the Holy Spirit connect with your examples?

The Holy Spirit in the Life of Christians

(CCC, 733–742; 747; 976; 1485; 1830–1832; 1845)

The Holy Spirit makes us Christians: "No one can say 'Jesus is Lord,' except by the Holy Spirit" (1 Cor 12:4). The Holy Spirit also makes a difference in our lives as Christians. How? First, the Holy Spirit is the great Life Giver. He teaches, directs, and strengthens the Church through the Magisterium so we may serve as compassionate and wise servants of the gospel. He lives in each believer, too, as our internal teacher. He inspires us to recognize Christ, and he showers on us many gifts to lead Christ-like lives.

As a Life Giver, the Holy Spirit is God's **grace** to us. Grace is a traditional theological term that means "good will, benevolence, or gift given." When we are baptized, the Holy Spirit comes to us. Filled with the Holy Spirit, we are justified before God. Justification means our sins are forgiven and we are able to enter into a right relationship with God through faith in Jesus Christ. This justification begins a lifelong healing process, a conversion or turning to God that leads to eternal life and makes it possible to share in God's own life.

grace—God's gift of friendship and life that enables us to share his life and love.

Think about this miracle of God's gift to us—sharing his own life, a life of perfect love. The Holy Spirit actually adopts us into the divine family. We become children of God and brothers and sisters to Jesus. We share in Christ's own eternal life because the Spirit of God lives in and loves through us:

> As proof that you are children, God sent the spirit of his Son into our hearts, crying out, "Abba, Father!" So you are no longer a slave but a child, and if a child then also an heir, through God (Gal 4:6–7).

By living in Christians, the Holy Spirit forms the Church, which is the very Body of Christ and Temple of the Holy Spirit. His presence gives life to the Church, builds it up, and sanctifies it. The Holy Spirit uses the Church to draw us to Christ, to reveal the good things the Lord has done for us, and to make present the Paschal mystery of Christ's love. This is done most wonderfully through the holy Eucharist in which we share God's own life. The liturgy is a unique sign of the Blessed Trinity's close friendship with us.

The Holy Spirit showers on individual Christians, and on the Church, many gifts to help us live like Jesus Christ. These gifts build up the Church. They include:

1. *Gifts that make us holy.* These are the seven gifts of the Holy Spirit listed in the feature on page 69: wisdom, understanding, knowledge, counsel (right judgment), fortitude, piety (reverence), and fear of the Lord. These gifts make it easier for us to respond to the Holy Spirit's promptings.
2. *Gifts that serve the Church.* St. Paul lists other gifts that are meant to build up the body of Christ, the Church, (see 1 Cor 12:4–11). Each of these special gifts is known as a **charism**. The charisms Paul mentions include wisdom, knowledge, faith, healing, miracle-working, prophecy, discernment, speaking in tongues, and interpreting tongues.

charism—A special gift of the Holy Spirit that helps us build up the Church, Christ's body. Some of these gifts are the ability to express wisdom and knowledge, healing, prophecy, and discernment of spirits (1 Cor 12:4–11).

fruits of the Holy Spirit—Perfections that result from living in union with the Holy Spirit.

3. *Gifts that result in spiritual fruit.* St. Paul also names some **fruits of the Holy Spirit**, perfections that result from the Holy Spirit living in us. These are the first fruits of eternal glory (see Gal 5:22–23). Church tradition lists them as: charity, joy, peace, patience, kindness, goodness, generosity, gentleness, faithfulness, modesty, self-control, and chastity.

All these gifts of the Spirit are related to one another. When these gifts are present in our lives, they show that we are one with Christ Jesus, the true vine (Jn 15:1). The Holy Spirit is the Spirit of Love, God's great gift to us through Jesus:

> "God is Love" and love is his first gift, containing all others. "God's love has been poured into our hearts through the Holy Spirit who has been given to us." (Rom 5:5) (*CCC*, 733).

Of all the gifts of the Spirit, love is the greatest of all. Love is given to us freely. We cannot earn it. We do not deserve it. It is pure gift. God does not give love to us because we are good. We are good because God loves us and lives in us. We know love in this way:

> Love is patient, love is kind. It is not jealous, [love] is not pompous, it is not inflated, it is not rude, it does not seek its own interests, it is not quick-tempered, it does not brood over injury, it does not rejoice over wrongdoing but rejoices with the truth. It bears all things, hopes all things, endures all things (1 Cor 13:4–7).

Writing Assignment

Review the fruits of the Holy Spirit (above). Name three fruits you would like the Holy Spirit to increase in your life. Explain why.

Where the Holy Spirit Is Present (*CCC*, 683-690; 742-743)

With the descent of the Holy Spirit on Pentecost Sunday, the Paschal Mystery was completed and the mystery of the Blessed Trinity was fully revealed. The Holy Spirit brings the Church into existence. As the Church's Advocate, he sustains it in many ways. The *Catechism of the Catholic Church* (688) teaches that the Holy Spirit actively works in the Church in:

1. the Scriptures, which he inspired;
2. sacred Tradition, witnessed throughout the ages by the Church Fathers;
3. the Magisterium of the Church, that is, in the Holy Father and the bishops whom the Holy Spirit guides in their roles as teachers and servants of God's people;
4. the sacraments, both words and symbols, which put us in contact with the risen Lord;
5. prayer, where he continually intercedes for us;
6. the many gifts and ministries that build up Christ's body, the Church;
7. the signs that go with the Church's apostolic and missionary life;
8. he saints, whose lives over the centuries witness to the presence of the Holy Spirit, his holiness, and his continuing work of salvation.

The Holy Spirit is for living the Christian life. The Spirit's greatest gifts received in Baptism offer faith to proclaim Jesus as our Lord and Savior, adoption into God's own family, and the privilege of being able to address God as *Abba*, Father.

Blessed Pope John XXIII (1958–1963)

Blessed Pope John XXIII was born in northern Italy on November 25, 1881. The fourth of fourteen children, his baptismal name was Angelo Giuseppe Roncalli. He entered the seminary in 1892 and began a practice of making spiritual notes, which he continued his whole life. They were published in one of the great spiritual classics of the twentieth century, *Journal of a Soul.*

Roncalli was ordained to the priesthood in 1905, pursued further studies, and eventually became a professor of Church history in his home diocese of Bergamo, Italy. He was a popular preacher, known for his profound, but simple spiritual insights. At this time, he also became secretary to his bishop.

During World War I, he served in the medical corps and was chaplain to wounded soldiers. These experiences convinced him that war was one of humanity's greatest evils. After the war, he was ordained a bishop (1925) and sent as the Vatican's delegate to Bulgaria. In 1935, he was appointed apostolic delegate to Turkey and Greece. His thirty-years of service as a Church diplomat taught him an openness to people of different faiths and cultures. His years in the Near East brought him into contact with the separated Eastern Churches, which led to his strong commitment to work for Church unity.

During World War II, Archbishop Roncalli was instrumental in helping thousands of Jews escape Nazi persecution. He also served as a papal ambassador to France. There his gentle and tactful skills helped smooth over relations with French citizens who were at odds with collaborators of the Nazi occupation.

Because Archbishop Angelo Roncalli was good at making all kinds of people friends of the Church, Pope Pius XII made him a cardinal in 1953. The pope soon appointed him head of the important Diocese of Venice, where Cardinal Roncalli was loved and admired by the people of the Church there.

Surprising to most Church observers because of his age, the college of cardinals elected the seventy-seven-year-old Cardinal Angelo Roncalli pope in 1958. He took the name John and soon became one of the most beloved popes of all time. His visits to prisons, hospitals, and Roman parishes; and his down-to-earth, simple, and humble manner won for him the name "Good Pope John."

Remarkably in late 1961, Pope John XXIII called the Second Vatican Council (1962–1965), a major undertaking since cardinals, bishops, and other leading Christians would have to pilgrimage to Rome. This was a surprise because everyone thought Pope John would be a transitional pope who would not have any major achievements during his reign. The Pope attributed inspiration for the council to the Holy Spirit. Its purpose, he said, was *aggiornamento,* that is, to update and to renew the Church, to produce a "new Pentecost" that would revitalize the Church and let it speak its gospel message to today's world. The Second Vatican Council produced sixteen documents that renewed the liturgy, explained the role of the Church in the modern world, and advanced the cause of Christian unity. Unfortunately, Pope John XXIII died of painful stomach cancer in 1963 and was only involved in the first session of the council. (His successor, Pope Paul VI reconvened and completed the council.)

Discussion Questions

1. In what ways has your participation in the Church drawn you closer to Christ?
2. How have you experienced the Holy Spirit working in the Church?
3. Identify someone in your family, parish, or school who you feel has one of the charisms of the Spirit. Explain your choice.

Today, the Church of the twenty-first century is still trying to put the reforms of Vatican II into practice as a way to achieve Christian unity. Pope John was beatified in 2000. Beatification, a major step on the road to being canonized as a saint, declares that a holy person like John XXIII lived a life led by the Holy Spirit.

Explore the following websites for more information on Blessed Pope John XXIII. Write three interesting facts you learned about his life from your reading.

1. "Blessed Pope John XXIII: An 'Ordinary' Holiness," www.americancatholic.org/Messenger/Sep2000/Feature1.asp
2. "'Good Pope' John XXIII Radiated The Peace Of Those Who Trust God," www.petersnet.net/research/retrieve.cfm?RecNum=3094
3. "Pope John XXIII," www.catholic-forum.com/saints/pope0261.htm
4. "Pope John XXIII," www.geocities.com/ganesha_gate/roncalli.html

The Second Vatican Council on the Role of the Holy Spirit

When the work which the Father gave the Son to do on earth (cf. Jn 17:4) was accomplished, the Holy Spirit was sent on the day of Pentecost in order that He might continually sanctify the Church, and thus, all those who believe would have access through Christ in one Spirit to the Father (cf. Eph 2:18). He is the Spirit of Life, a fountain of water springing up to life eternal (cf. Jn 4:14, 7:38–39). . . . The Spirit dwells in the Church and in the hearts of the faithful, as in a temple (cf. 1 Cor 3:16, 6:19). In them He prays on their behalf and bears witness to the fact that they are adopted sons (Gal 4:6; Rom 8:15–16, 26). . . . He both equips and directs (the Church) with hierarchical and charismatic gifts and adorns (it) with His fruits (cf. Eph 4:11–12; 1 Cor 12:4; Gal 5:22) (*Dogmatic Constitution on the Church*, 4).

The Mystery of the Trinity (*CCC*, 235; 237; 261–263; 265)

The dogma of the Blessed Trinity is a mystery in the strictest sense, that is, a mystery of God himself. By *mystery*, the Church is not talking about a problem that can be solved as, for example, a math problem can be.

Rather, mystery is a truth of the faith that is knowable, but inexhaustible. It is knowable only because God revealed it to us. It is, however, a reality beyond our full comprehension. Its significance is so profound that the human mind and human words can never fully plumb its depths.

Jesus Reveals the Trinity

Why do we believe God is a Trinity of Persons? Why do we believe that the one God, with one divine nature, is three divine Persons: Father, Son, and Holy Spirit, with the Son proceeding from the Father and the Holy Spirit proceeding from the Father and the Son? Simply, we believe that God is Trinity because of our knowledge of and relationship with Jesus Christ.

In Jesus we see a person so fully attuned to God, that in faith we say that this one-of-a-kind person is God himself. Jesus' words hold truth: "Whoever has seen me has seen the Father" (Jn 14:9). We also believe God's testimony at Jesus' baptism, "This is my beloved Son, with whom I am well pleased" (Mt 3:17).

The apostles and other believers were certain that the God of their ancestors was at work in a unique way in his Son, Jesus. Later, after Jesus' resurrection, they experienced the same God in the Holy Spirit who lives on in Christ's followers. This Advocate, who was poured out on the disciples on Pentecost Sunday, impelled them to go out and preach the gospel they learned from Jesus. Thus, they preached that God reveals himself as a loving Father whose love for humans is bottomless. At the same time, they announced that God also reveals himself as an incredibly loving Son, Jesus Christ, a Savior who frees us from sin and death. Finally, they spread the good news that God also reveals himself as a Spirit of love, a Holy Spirit who dwells in believers with the fullness of the Risen Christ's life.

Thus, we believe in the Blessed Trinity because of the things Jesus teaches about who God really is. The Father shows his immense love for us by sending his only beloved Son and the Holy Spirit. Through them, he teaches us his own intimate life. However, God not only wants to share information about who he is; he wants to share his very life with us. Through Baptism "in the name of the Father and of the Son and of the Holy Spirit," we are invited to partake in a mysterious way in the life of the divine family here on earth and after death in an eternal life of happiness and love.

New Testament Evidence for God as Father (CCC, 238–242)

Many religions call God "Father" in the sense of a creator who loves his children. The Jewish faith also invoked God as a father in that Yahweh created the world, fathered the covenant with the Chosen People, gave the Law, and served as their ruler. Israel also saw God as the "father of the poor" who cared for and protected the defenseless.

Jesus, however, was unique in his teaching about Abba/Father. He taught that the Father of the Chosen People was *his* Father, an eternal Father to him, the unique Son who shared God's own nature. To stress his unique relationship with God, the Lord spoke of "*My* heavenly Father" (Mt 15:13). In contrast, to us he says, "*Your* Father in heaven" (Mt 5:45). Jesus also taught that God is eternally the Father by his relationship to the Son and vice versa:

> No one knows the Son except the Father, and no one knows the Father except the Son and anyone to whom the Son wishes to reveal him (Mt 11:27).

For this reason, the apostles referred to Jesus as the Word of God, the very image of the invisible God. And the early Church council at Nicaea (AD 325) defined that Jesus was *consubstantial* with the Father, that is, having the same nature as God. *Jesus is God.*

Time and again Jesus revealed that God the Father was incredibly loving. He expressed his own unity with the Father in his use of Abba, a simple term of endearment meaning "daddy." Jesus told his followers to address God as Abba when they pray. Parables like the lost coin, the lost sheep, and the lost son all reveal God to be loving beyond what we can imagine (e.g., Lk 15). Jesus' healing miracles reveal a compassionate God. Most significantly, Jesus reveals a Father who gives us his own selfless Son for our redemption. The Father saves us through this Son, Jesus Christ, in the Holy Spirit. The Father brought his beloved Son back to life, and, through him, he promises resurrection to all who believe. As St. Paul writes:

> Thanks be to God who gives us the victory through our Lord Jesus Christ (1 Cor 15:57).

Writing Assignment

List three traits your mother (or another important woman in your life) possesses that you think are holy. Explain the difference it makes to your image of God to know that he possesses those same traits to an infinite degree.

ExplainingYourFaith

If God is our Father, does this mean that God is male?

Scripture most often talks about God as Father. Jesus taught us to say "Our Father" when he taught us the Lord's Prayer. Still, it is important to remember that God is pure spirit, neither male nor female. Therefore we can be sure that God possesses to an infinite degree the traits we associate with both fathers and mothers—creativity, leadership, nurture, sustenance, compassion, tenderness, availability, acceptance, guidance, and love. There is no limit to God's parental love for us.

It is acceptable to refer to God's parental tenderness using images of motherhood. By doing so, we emphasize God's closeness and gentle love for us.

Jesus himself used feminine images when teaching about God's love, for example, by comparing God to a woman who rejoiced when she found a lost coin (Lk 15:8–10) or when he expressed his own desire to gather the people of Jerusalem "as a hen gathers her young under her wings" (Mt 23:37).

The medieval mystic Julian of Norwich wrote that the notion of God as Mother increases our understanding of God's love for us. Consider, for example, how much a mother suffers to give birth to her child. While we know that no earthly mother is perfect, most mothers love and accept their children, do their best to protect them, and forgive them easily.

The Holy Spirit Reveals the Father and Son
(*CCC*, 243–244)

Every page of the New Testament proves the divinity of Jesus. For example, Jesus' many miracles attest to God working through and in him. His teaching authority is another sign of his divinity. The resurrection of Jesus is the great sign that Jesus is God. Filled with the power of the Holy Spirit, the witnesses to the Risen Jesus proclaim him Lord and God. When Thomas probes Jesus' wounds, he is the first to say aloud: "My Lord and my God" (Jn 20:28).

An earlier gospel reference to Jesus' divinity and that of the Father and the Spirit occurs at Jesus' baptism. The gospel of Mark describes the incident:

> On coming up out of the water he saw the heavens being torn open and the Spirit, like a dove, descending upon him. And a voice came

> from the heavens, "You are my beloved Son; with you I am well pleased" (Mk 1:10–11).

This important passage refers to all three divine Persons of the Blessed Trinity. It also points to how Jesus was filled with the Spirit as he began his public ministry. God's Spirit worked with the Lord as he taught, performed miracles, and underwent the Paschal Mystery for our salvation. The full mystery of the Blessed Trinity was revealed at Pentecost when the Father and Son sent the Holy Spirit. As the *Catechism of the Catholic Church* teaches:

> . . . the Spirit will now be with and in the disciples, to teach them and guide them "into all the truth." The Holy Spirit is thus revealed as another divine person with Jesus and the Father (CCC, 243).

The Holy Spirit *always* existed with the Father and the Son. He attracts us to the Son and enables us to proclaim him our Lord and Savior. The Holy Spirit also helps us adore God the Father, the source of all the good gifts the gracious Triune God showers on us.

More about the Mystery of the Trinity

An ancient Church creed, the Athanasian Creed, teaches the following about the mystery of the Trinity:

> Now this is the Catholic faith: We worship one God in the Trinity and the Trinity in unity, without either confusing the persons or dividing the substance; for the person of the Father is one, the Son's is another, the Holy Spirit's is another; but the Godhead of the Father, Son, and Holy Spirit is one, their glory equal, their majesty coeternal (*Athanasian Creed* quoted in *CCC*, 266).

Devise a symbol for the Holy Trinity that you can use in a short lesson to teach primary age children (grades 1 to 4) about the mystery of the Trinity. Work with a religious education program or Catholic school to be able to present your lesson as part of their regularly scheduled class.

Discussion Questions

1. Explain how you understand a God in three persons, the Blessed Trinity.
2. How do you experience God as Father? as Mother?
3. Why is Jesus' baptism central to understanding the mystery of the Trinity?

Understanding More about the Trinity

(CCC, 232–233; 236)

"In the name of the Father and of the Son and of the Holy Spirit. Amen." Catholics are familiar with the Sign of the Cross, a formula that begins many Catholic prayers and worship. The large Sign of the Cross made with our right hand touching our forehead, chests, and shoulders professes that our minds, hearts, and entire beings are under the power of our holy Redeemer. The small sign of the cross—made with the thumb over the forehead, lips, and heart—petitions the Triune God to bless our thoughts, words, and desires. The Sign of the Cross in each form is a clear profession of faith in the Blessed Trinity.

More detail about the formula: We are baptized in the *name* of the Father and the Son and the Holy Spirit, not in their *names*. There is only *one* God. But there are three divine Persons in this one God. How can this be: three-in-one? Recall again that we are dealing with the strict mystery of God. Trying to understand God's inmost nature is like looking directly into the blinding sun.

To help our understanding, Jesus Christ and the coming of his Holy Spirit have revealed to us that God is a Trinity of Persons. So our human minds, guided by the Spirit, have struggled to explain, if even in a partial way, this profound truth of our faith. Great Church Fathers like St. Augustine, and famous theologians like St. Thomas Aquinas, distinguish between two aspects of God when speaking about the Trinity: *theology* and *economy*. "Theology" (from the Greek word *theos*, meaning God) refers to God's own inner life as Trinity. God's inner life is referred to also as the *immanent Trinity* ("how God exists in God"). "Economy" means the many works God has performed to reveal and communicate his divine life. This understanding is also called the *salvific Trinity*. By reflecting on God's works, we learn something about who God really is. The better we understand who God is, the more clearly we see and understand all of his works.

The Immanent Trinity: God's Own Inner Life (*CCC*, 245-256; 264)

When the Trinity is explained in terms of God alone without any references to human beings, this is known as the immanent Trinity, meaning "existing completely within." Early Church councils and Church Fathers considered how best to address the mystery of the Trinity. Three important terms that developed were:

1. *Substance* is a word that means "nature" or "essence." When we say that the Father has the same substance or nature as the Son and the Holy Spirit, we are proclaiming that God is *one* divine being.
2. *Person* refers to the distinctions among the Father, Son, and Holy Spirit.
3. *Relation* designates that the Father, Son, and Holy Spirit are distinct because of their relationships.

Using this vocabulary as background, the Church teaches three important truths about God's own inner life:

1. *There is only one God.* The Blessed Trinity is one God, that is, one divine being, possessing a divine substance or nature
2. *There are three distinct Persons—Father, Son, and Holy Spirit—in one God.* "Person" in the Trinity refers to distinctions between the members (and not in the sense of human persons). Thus, there are not three separate consciousnesses in God. There is only one simple divine being. There are not three separate intelligences or wills in the one God. When one person of the Trinity acts, the other two persons also act. Each person is *distinct* but does not act separately from the others. God is one, a community-in-unity. The divine persons are inseparable in both what they do and in what they are, loving us with the same love and knowing us with the same knowledge.
3. *The divine persons have distinct relationships with one another.* Our faith is in one God with three divine persons who are really distinct from one another. In a mysterious way, we can say "God is one but not solitary" (*Fides Damasi* quoted in *CCC*, 254). The divine persons are distinct in their relations of origin. The Church explains the relationships among the three persons of the Trinity this way:

- *The Father.* The First Person of the Trinity is absolutely without origin. From all eternity he "begets" the Son, the Second Person of the Trinity. The Son proceeds from the Father. There was never a time when the Son did not proceed from the Father.
- *The Son.* We can think of the Father's begetting the Son as God knowing himself perfectly. The Father expresses himself perfectly to himself, and this is the Son, the Word of God. Thus, the Son is the Father's perfect, divine expression of himself. They are one, yet distinct.

- ★ *The Holy Spirit.* The relationship of the Father and Son is a perfect relationship. The Father and Son love each other with an eternal, perfect, divine love. The love *proceeds* from the Father and the Son and is the Third Person of the Trinity, the Holy Spirit. The Holy Spirit proceeds from both the Father and the Son as the perfect expression of their divine love for each other. Thus, the Holy Spirit is the Spirit of Love between the Father and the Son; the Spirit binds them into a community of unity.

In a classic expression of faith, the Athanasian Creed expresses the relationships of the three persons of the Trinity this way:

> The Father is not made by anyone, nor created, nor begotten. The Son is from the Father alone, not made, not created, but begotten. The Holy Spirit is from the Father and the Son, not made, not created, not begotten, but proceeding. . . . The entire three Persons are co-eternal with one another and co-equal, so that . . . both Trinity in Unity and Unity in Trinity are to be adored.

The Economic or Salvific Trinity (CCC, 257–260; 267)

In the economic or salvific Trinity we know God by what he does, how he acts in our lives and in the world. God reveals the Trinity to us through his works in salvation history, especially Christ's Incarnation and the gift of the Holy Spirit. Our own Christian living in union with God strengthens our belief that our one God relates to us as Father, Son, and Holy Spirit.

We meet God through creation—its beauty and greatness, its intricate design and awesome power. Jesus teaches us that we can address our Creator God as Abba, Father. He is merciful, filled with love for us, and compassionate beyond what we could possibly hope for.

A second way we experience God is through God-made-flesh, Jesus Christ. He is Emmanuel, which is "God-with-us." Through the teachings, actions, miracles, and Paschal Mystery, we have met God in Jesus Christ. In Christ, we have experienced God with a human face.

Third, we experience God as the Holy Spirit who gives us life and directs us to live Christ-filled lives. He joins us to Jesus Christ who, in turn, takes us to his heavenly Father. "To the Father, through the Son, in the Holy Spirit." The Holy Spirit is the love of God that was promised by Jesus to always remain with the Church.

God has communicated himself to humanity in three distinct ways. It is the same, one, mysterious God who reveals. But he does so through three distinct Persons or relationships—Father, Son, and Holy Spirit—each of whom works as one.

Thus, all three Persons of the Blessed Trinity are involved in the common work of salvation. However, each Person performs this common work according to his unique personal property.

Therefore, we attribute creation, and its continual existence, to God the Father.

Salvation is attributed to the Son, who became human to reveal the Father's merciful love.

divine missions of the Blessed Trinity—The special roles in salvation history attributed to each member of the Trinity: the Father is the Creator, the Son is the Savior, and the Holy Spirit is the Sanctifier. The whole plan of salvation is the common work of the three divine Persons who possess one and the same nature.

And to the Holy Spirit, we attribute sanctification, that is, the work of making us holy and godlike.

Creation, salvation, and sanctification are known as the **divine missions of the Blessed Trinity**. Although we attribute creation to the Father, salvation (redemption) to the Son, and sanctification to the Holy Spirit, we must remember that all three Persons of the Trinity act as one and are fully present in all the missions.

In contemplating the mystery of the Blessed Trinity, we come to know a God of incredible love who draws us into union with him. God is a Father who has lovingly created us, a Son who gave his life so we might have eternal life, and a Spirit of love who enables us to love, that is, to imitate the very nature of God.

God loved us into existence and wants us to love. As the Church has taught for centuries, our goal in life is to get to know, love, and serve the Blessed Trinity in this life and to be united with God for all eternity. Prayer helps us to accomplish our destiny: *to the Father through the Son in the Holy Spirit.*

Jesus and the Holy Spirit reveal that God is a community-in-unity. We allow the Triune God to live in us when we approach him with others and reach out in love to our brothers and sisters. When we love others, we are imitating the Triune God who is Love. An important lesson of Christian living is that we go to God together with other people. It is the Church that we join with on our journey to God. The Church is the prime means the Lord uses to continue his work of salvation in a world that desperately needs it.

Discussion Questions

1. What does it mean to describe God as a "community-in-unity"?
2. To which Person of the Blessed Trinity do you usually address your prayers? Why?
3. Which symbol for the Trinity described in this section best helps you to understand the mystery of the Trinity? Why?

Trinitarian Symbols

Many images to try to express the mystery of the Triune God.

The Shield of the Trinity

The translation reads this way: The Father (*Pater*) is (est) God (*Deus*); the Son (*Filius*) is God; and the Holy Spirit (*Spiritus Sanctus*) is God. Thus, God's unity is professed. Equality among the persons is symbolized by the equilateral triangle. And the distinction between each person of the Trinity is again conveyed by the Latin: the Father is not (*non est*) the Son nor the Holy Spirit; and the Son is not the Father nor the Holy Spirit; and the Holy Spirit is not the Father nor the Son.

The Shamrock

The legendary story is told that when St. Patrick was preaching to the pagans in Ireland he was challenged to prove how God could be one being yet three persons. St. Patrick picked a shamrock and asked whether he held up one leaf or three leaves. "If three, then why one stem? If one stem then why three leaves?" Those who questioned him could not answer. St. Patrick responded, "If you cannot explain such a simple mystery as a shamrock, how can you hope to understand such a profound one as the Blessed Trinity?"

Tree and Sun

St. John Damascene taught two famous images for the Trinity. The first is a tree where the Father is the root, the Son the branches, and the Spirit the fruit. The substance of each (root, branch, and fruit) is all the same—that of a tree, yet there is distinction. So with the Trinity. Each Person has the fullness of the divine nature; yet, there is distinction. One God, three Persons.

His second image was that of the sun. The Father is the sun, the Son is the rays, and the Holy Spirit is heat. Distinction but all the same substance.

Writing Assignment

Read each of the following quotes about the Blessed Trinity. Then write at least two of your own quotations that describe the Trinity.

God is the beginning, the middle, and the end of every good. But the good cannot become active or be believed in otherwise than in Jesus Christ and the Holy Spirit.

—St. Mark the Ascetic

The Trinity is our maker. The Trinity is our keeper. The Trinity is our everlasting lover. The Trinity is our endless joy.

—Blessed Julian of Norwich

The Spirit works, the Son fulfills his ministry, and the Father approves; and man is thus brought to full salvation.

—St. Irenaeus

SummaryPoints

- ★ The seven gifts of the Holy Spirit are wisdom, understanding, knowledge, counsel, fortitude, piety, and fear of the Lord.
- ★ Working in union with God the Father, the Holy Spirit had an active but hidden role in salvation history before the coming of the Messiah.
- ★ The Holy Spirit came in power on the feast of Pentecost, giving the apostles the courage to proclaim that Jesus is Lord and Savior.
- ★ Sharing a joint mission with the Son of God, the Holy Spirit was present throughout the ministry, life, preaching, miracle-working, passion, death, resurrection, and glorification of Jesus Christ.
- ★ Images of the Holy Spirit include *breath, wind, fire, tongues of fire, water,* and the *dove.*
- ★ The Holy Spirit adopts us into God's family, enabling us to call God Abba/Father. He justifies us, forgives our sins, and enables us to love as other Christs.
- ★ The Holy Spirit is the *Paraclete,* our advocate before God, a helper and consoler. He is the Spirit of Truth who testifies to the Lord.
- ★ Jesus is head of the Church, his body. The Holy Spirit is the soul of the Church who gives it life. We can find him in the inspired Sacred Scriptures, Church Tradition, the Fathers and Magisterium of the Church, the sacraments, prayer, various gifts and ministries, the apostolic and missionary life of the Church, and the witness of the saints through the ages.
- ★ The Holy Spirit is God, the third Person of the Blessed Trinity. He is the Giver of Life who is equal in dignity to the Father and Son. Christians should worship and glorify him.
- ★ Jesus revealed to us in the power of the Holy Spirit that God is a Blessed Trinity. This is a strict mystery that could only be revealed by God. Our minds can never fully grasp it.
- ★ Jesus revealed that God the Father is his unique Father.
- ★ Jesus' miracles, teaching, and Paschal mystery show that he is God's unique Son. He and the Father are one.
- ★ The early disciples discovered God's presence in the Holy Spirit (an Advocate and Comforter) who came on Pentecost Sunday as Christ had promised.
- ★ We are baptized in the *name* of the Father, Son, and Holy Spirit, not the *names.* There is only one God.
- ★ Reflecting on God's inmost life ("theology") reveals God's works (the divine "economy"). Reflecting on God's saving works sheds light on his inner nature.
- ★ God is one divine being. The three persons in this one God—Father, Son, and Holy Spirit—are distinct in their relations. From all eternity, the Father generates the Son. The Son is always begotten by the Father. The Holy Spirit proceeds as the love between the Father and the Son.
- ★ The missions of the Blessed Trinity refer to God's saving action for us. This is also known as the divine economy (work) on our behalf. Creation is attributed to the Father, redemption to the Son, and sanctification to the Holy Spirit. However, God is one divine being. Therefore, all three Divine Persons are involved in the common work of God's saving plan.

ReviewQuestions

1. List and briefly describe the seven gifts of the Holy Spirit.
2. Name three ways the Holy Spirit was active in salvation history before the coming of Christ.

3. What happened on the feast of Pentecost?
4. List and briefly discuss four ways the Holy Spirit was active in the life of Jesus.
5. Define *Paraclete.*
6. Define *ruah.* Give an example of how ruah applied to the presence of the Holy Spirit in the Old Testament.
7. List and explain four other scriptural images of the Holy Spirit besides ruah.
8. Define *grace.*
9. How is the Holy Spirit grace to Christians?
10. What is the Holy Spirit's greatest gift to us?
11. List the three categories of gifts of the Holy Spirit.
12. Discuss five ways the Holy Spirit is active in the world today.
13. How does Christ reveal God as Father, as Son, and as Holy Spirit?
14. How were the three Persons of the Trinity present at Jesus' baptism?
15. Explain the meaning of the Sign of the Cross.
16. Why is the doctrine of the Blessed Trinity a mystery?
17. To what do the terms *substance* and *person* refer when talking about the Blessed Trinity?
18. Identify the term *economic* or *salvific Trinity.*
19. Identify the term *immanent Trinity.*
20. What are the missions of the three Persons of the Blessed Trinity?

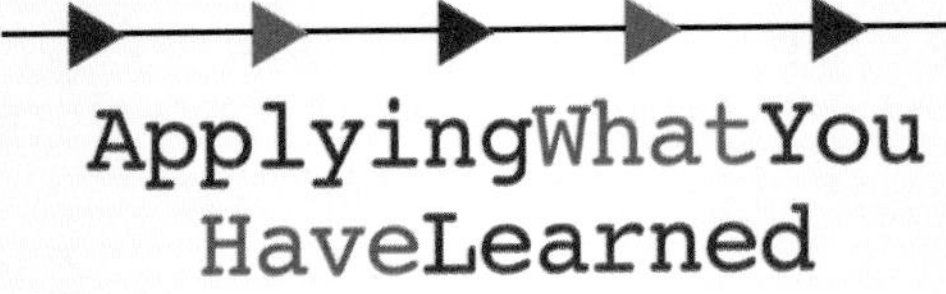

Applying What You Have Learned

1. Make a collage from newspapers and magazines to represent how the Holy Spirit is active in the world today, especially in works of justice and love.
2. Compose a prayer to the Holy Spirit designed to help students who are preparing for a test. Share the prayer with your classmates.
3. Report on the life of a Spirit-inspired person who made a difference in people's lives. For example: Dorothy Day, Archbishop Oscar Romero, or Blessed Mother Teresa.
4. Interview several adults who were brought up in the pre-Vatican II Church. Ask them how the liturgy and parish life were different. Report to the class.
5. Prepare a short report on the Second Vatican Council. Review these websites for more information.

   Documents of Vatican II:
   www.rc.net/rcChurch/vatican2/

   Vatican II:
   www.stjosef.at/council/search
6. Read a passage from one of Blessed Pope John XXIII's writings. Write at least five meaningful quotations from the text. For more information, see:

   Vatican website on John XXIII:
   www.vatican.va/holy_father/john_xxiii/

   The Writings of Pope John XXIII:
   www.intratext.com/IXT/ENG0069/_INDEX.HTM

Prayer Reflection

Write a letter to God. Writing a letter to God can clarify your deepest thoughts and religious feelings. Choose a favorite title for God for your greeting. Then simply write what is on your mind and in your heart. Keep it short. Have faith that our loving God deeply cares for you. He wants to hear about your hurts, how your day or week went, your victories, your angers, your joys.

Next try to imagine how the Lord would respond to the letter you sent to him. First, pray to the Holy Spirit for guidance in answering your letter. Then try to respond to your letter from Jesus' or the Father's viewpoint.

You are the salt of the earth. . . . You are the light of the world. . . . Your light must shine before others, that they may see your good deeds and glorify your Father.

Matthew 5:13, 14, 16.

Chapter 4 Outline

Where Christ Is, There Is the Church

The Church is the living body of believers in Christ.

What Is Church?

Christ established the Church. The Church is a mystery of God's love.

More Descriptions of Church

The Church can also be understood as Sacrament, People of God, Body of Christ, and the Temple of the Holy Spirit.

Membership and Ministries in the Church

Catholics participate in the Church in different states in life and through different ministries.

Marks of the Church

The Church has four distinct marks—one, holy, catholic, and apostolic.

Ecumenism: The Church and Other Religions

The Church of Christ subsists in the Catholic Church. Catholics are called to work to restore the unity of all Christians.

Chapter 4

The Church: The Body of Christ

Church—The Body of Christ, that is, the community of God's people who profess faith in the risen Lord Jesus and love and serve others under the guidance of the Holy Spirit. The Roman Catholic Church is guided by the pope and his bishops.

evangelization—To bring the good news of Jesus Christ to others.

Discussion Questions

1. What would you say to Catholics who get so mad at human failings in the Church, that they decide to leave the Church?
2. How do you find the Church "like a home"?

Where Christ Is, There Is the Church

Reigning from AD 361–363, Roman Emperor Julian renounced the Christian faith. He earned the nickname "Apostate" because anyone who rejects his or her faith bears that name. Julian systematically hunted down and killed Christians in his attempt to reestablish the old pagan religions and their gods. However, in June 363 he lay dying of a stab wound in his gut, either self-inflicted or caused by one of his soldiers who was angry that Julian failed to defeat the enemy Persians.

As the legend surrounding his death is told, in Julian's final moments, he took some of his own blood into his hands and flung it at the sun (which he worshiped as a god), crying out the following words of defeat to Jesus: "Galilean, you won!" (Jesus was from Galilee.)

Julian, like other historical tyrants, failed in his attempt to stamp out Christianity. The followers of Jesus, joined together in his Church, have survived to this very day. In point of fact, Christianity is the largest religion on the face of the earth. About a third of the world's population believes that Jesus Christ is divine. Around half of these Christians are Roman Catholics. Catholics are members of this worldwide community of believers that traces itself back 2,000 years to humble beginnings so long ago.

It is certainly true to say that Jesus has indeed triumphed. Yet the work of proclaiming his gospel has really just begun. Each generation must hear and respond to his good news. The main way this **evangelization** takes place is through the Church. What is the **Church**? The Church is a living body of believers who are grafted onto Jesus Christ as branches are to a vine. As St. Ignatius of Antioch wrote, "Where there is Christ Jesus, there is the Catholic Church."

Like our own family, the Church loves us, accepts us, and contributes to our development. It nurtures and sustains us through life. Because of its human element, the Church sometimes temporarily fails at these tasks. But Jesus' presence in the Church guarantees its ultimate success.

This chapter will focus on several aspects of the Roman Catholic Church: a definition, its images (e.g., Mystery, Sacrament, People of God, Body of Christ, Temple of the Holy Spirit), its requirements for membership, its ministries, its marks (one, holy, catholic, apostolic), and its reaching out to other Christians in its ecumenical efforts.

The Roman Catholic Church is home to many, including, perhaps, you. It is a place where we are treated the best and often grumble the most. As in any family, we are accepted and loved without question. This is the Church.

How Do You Think of Church?

Below are eight brief descriptions of the Church. Read each description. Then determine which two descriptions best fit your idea of Church. Write an explanation for why this is so. Also, write your own definition for Church, explaining each part of your definition.

The Church is:

- a human organization with carefully defined roles that deal with religious affairs;
- a group of people who commit themselves to work wholeheartedly for justice, especially among the poor, the hungry, the sick, the powerless;
- a family that primarily exists to take care of the needs of its members;
- a community of believers whose primary task is to proclaim the good news of Jesus;
- a place where like-minded believers worship God through Jesus Christ.
- Jesus Christ present in the world through those who believe in him and do his will;
- Roman Catholics under the leadership of the pope and the bishops;
- a community of faith committed to loving God above everything and serving fellow humans.

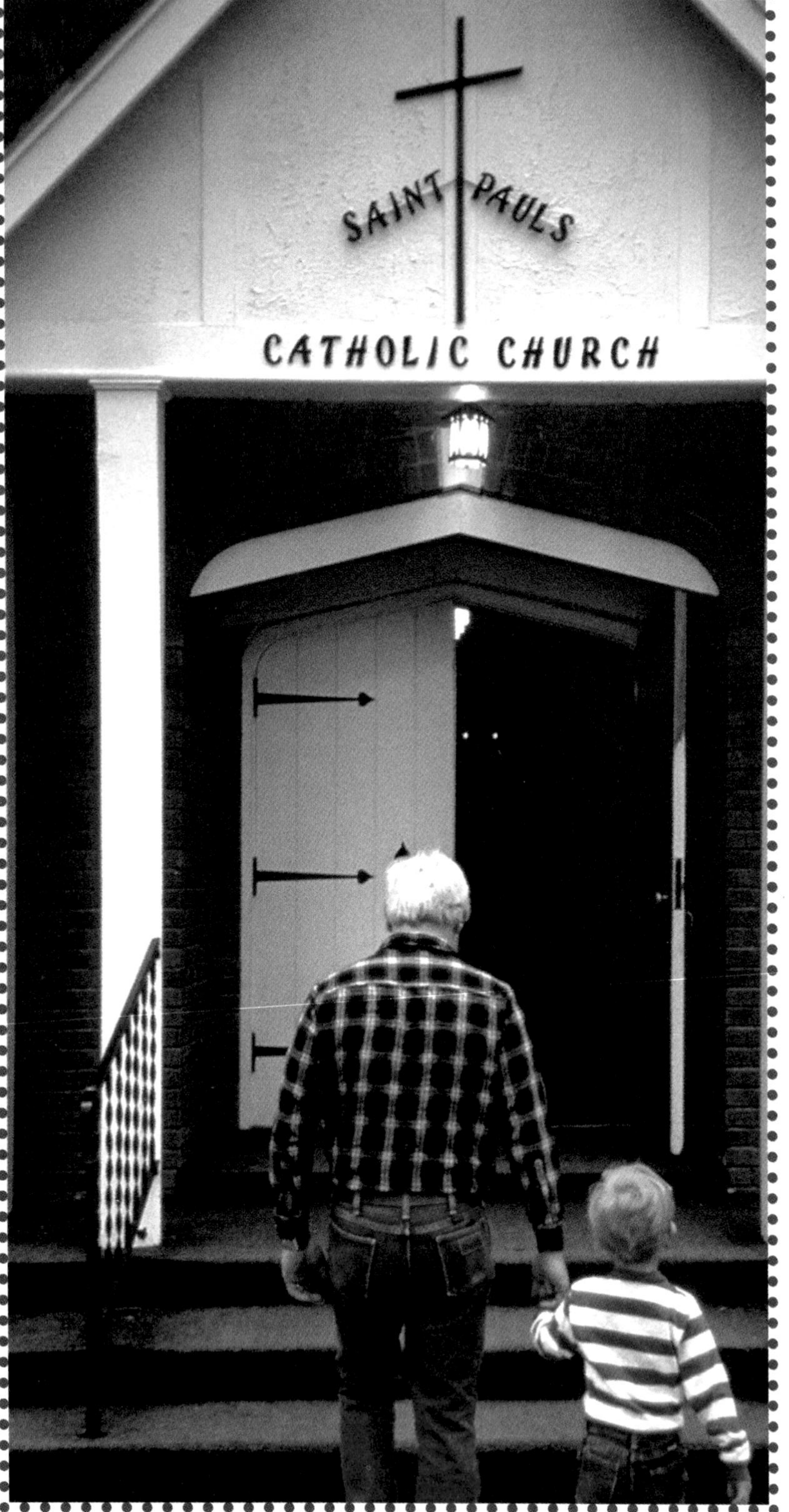

What Is Church?

(CCC, 751–752; 777)

The word *church* means "belonging to the Lord." This is an apt description when we consider that Jesus Christ is the head of his body, the Church, and we are its members. We belong to the Lord because we are attached to him the way an arm is to the body. As the head of the Church, Jesus gives his body direction and vision. The Holy Spirit is the soul of the Church. The Spirit lives in the baptized and showers on them the gifts we need to be holy, alive, and Christ-like. Indeed, without Jesus Christ and the Holy Spirit there would be no Church.

Church is also translated from the Greek word *ekklesia,* meaning "those called out," convocation, or assembly. Old Testament authors used this term for God's Chosen People. Being chosen means having a special task or mission. Christians are chosen to worship and to proclaim Jesus Christ as Lord, to live a sacramental life of holiness, and to join in a life of fellowship and service for the sake of God's kingdom.

"I am going to church." "My church is St. Patrick's." "We are the church." These three expressions reveal how Catholics use the word church today. Each of these expressions has a rightful place:

- The Church is the community of Catholics who assemble to worship. Catholics do this in a superb way when they come together to celebrate the Eucharist. Receiving holy communion, Catholics are united to the Lord so they can become the Lord for others.
- The Church is the local gathering of Catholics in a particular neighborhood. For most of us, this means our parish.
- The Church is also the whole worldwide gathering of those who have faith in Jesus Christ. The Holy Spirit unites people around the world into the People of God, under the leadership of the pope and bishops.

The Church as A Mystery of God's Love (CCC, 758–780; 880)

In the previous chapter, the term **mystery** was used to describe the Blessed Trinity. Divine mysteries, like the Trinity, both reveal and conceal God's ways which are not our ways, yet in these mysteries God has somehow blessed us with the truth of his divine plan. The Church is another mystery of our faith. It is both a means and a goal of the great mystery of God's love for us. Each divine person of the Blessed Trinity was involved in preparing for the Church and helping it come into existence.

mystery—A reality filled with God's invisible presence. This term applies to the Blessed Trinity's plan of salvation in Jesus Christ, the Church which is his body, and the sacraments.

God the Father created the world so human beings could be united with the Blessed Trinity. Creation, therefore, foreshadowed the Church. The Father prepared for the Church in the Old Testament times when he called Abraham and formed a people. Israel was the sign of the Church that was to come.

In God's own time, he sent the Son to accomplish his plan of salvation. As part of this plan, *Jesus Christ established the Church*—a direct result of preaching the coming of God's reign and his own Paschal mystery of selfless love. The Church celebrates the Paschal mystery of salvation in its sacraments, especially the holy Eucharist. The Church, built by Christ on Peter and the twelve apostles, "is the Reign of Christ already present in mystery" (*The Dogmatic Constitution on the Church*, No. 3 quoted in CCC, 763).

Finally, the Holy Spirit came on Pentecost to make the Church holy and to lead it in its mission of preaching the good news of salvation to all people. The Holy Spirit gives us—both the Magisterium and each Catholic—the gifts we need to do what Christ commanded, that is, to "[proclaim] and [establish] among all peoples the Kingdom of Christ and of God" (*The Dogmatic Constitution on the Church*, No. 5 quoted in CCC, 768). Thus, each person of the Blessed Trinity had a role in the planning of the Church and its coming into historical reality.

St. Augustine defined mystery as "a visible sign of an invisible grace." Pope Paul VI described the Church as a reality filled with God's hidden presence. Both of these definitions point to two essential ingredients in the Church: the human and the divine, the visible reality that we can see along with the spiritual reality that brings us God's life. With the eyes of faith, we proclaim that in the Church heaven and earth come together. The Church is at the same time:

- ★ a visible society and a spiritual community;
- ★ a society organized hierarchically and the mystical body of Christ;
- ★ an earthly community blessed with heavenly riches.

Because the Church is a mystery where the human and divine meet, Scripture uses many vivid images to describe the Church; for example: Bride of Christ, pilgrim, God's building and farm, the flock of Christ, Christ's vineyard, God's family, and our mother. Each of these adds to our understanding and appreciation of the mystery of the Church. For example:

Discussion Questions

1. Tell two common ways you use the word "church" in conversations with peers. What does this context reveal about how you feel about the Church?
2. What does it mean to say that the Church is "a visible sign of invisible grace"?
3. Describe concrete ways the human and divine elements of the Church meet.

- In the imagery of St. Paul, the Church is in a *marriage union with Christ*. In this union, Christ Jesus is the bridegroom; the Church is the Bride of Christ. The purpose of this wedding between Christ and his Church is to bring us to God and thus make us holy. The Bridegroom loves his Bride so much that he gave his life for her. He will care for her (the Church) forever.
- The Church as *pilgrim* teaches us that the Church is a community on its way to a final destination—heaven.
- The *building and farm* images remind us that Jesus Christ has planted his disciples and that he still cultivates the Church like a farmer tending his crops.
- The Church as *flock* calls to mind our sacrificing Good Shepherd. It is his voice we must listen to in order to remain safe from perils.
- The *vineyard* image stresses that Christ alone gives life and fruitfulness to the branches.

More Descriptions of Church

In addition to the images of Church related to mystery, the *Catechism of the Catholic Church* highlights four other descriptions of the Church: Sacrament, People of God, Body of Christ, and Temple of the Holy Spirit. Following is a brief discussion of each of these descriptions. It is important to remember as you examine each of the descriptions that none of them defines the Church. The images we use to describe the Church never completely answer the question of what the Church is, either individually or taken together. Ultimately, the Church remains mystery, never fully explained or defined.

The Church Is a Sacrament *(CCC, 774–776; 780)*

sacrament—An outward (visible) sign of an invisible grace. An "efficacious" symbol that brings about the spiritual reality to which it points. This term applies to Christ Jesus, the great sign of God's love for us; to the Church, his continuing presence in our world; and to the seven sacraments.

Mystery and **sacrament** are intimately connected. The Greek word for mystery translates to the Latin term *sacramentum*. The term *sacrament* refers to a very special kind of sign or symbol. An ordinary symbol is something concrete (something we can perceive with our senses) that points to another reality. For example, a stop sign uses shape, color, and a word to point to the *idea* of stopping. However, the stop sign does not *cause* a driver to stop. Let's say your school mascot is a tiger to *represent* strength, speed, intelligence, and vitality. But your school mascot does not *make* the student body strong, fast, smart, or filled with school spirit.

A sacrament is also a symbol, but one different from those described above. A sacrament is an *efficacious* symbol, which means that it brings about what it points to and embodies the very reality that it represents. Hence, a sacrament is a concrete reality that, in some way, *is what it represents*.

Thus it is accurate to say that *Jesus is the prime sacrament of God's love*. Jesus not only points to God; he is God. He not only symbolizes God's love; he is God's love. He is what he represents. He is the first and most important sacrament of all. "Whoever has seen me has seen the Father" (Jn 14:9). He makes concrete God's love for us. Jesus takes us to the Father by remaining with us in his body, the Church, where he remains hidden but very active by the power of the Holy Spirit.

A sacrament, because it is a mystery, has both visible and invisible aspects to it. This is true of the seven sacraments: each sacrament is a visible or outward sign of God's grace. Sacraments both point to a spiritual reality *and* actually bring it about. For example, the Eucharist not only signifies communion with the Risen Lord and one another, it really accomplishes it. When we receive the consecrated bread and wine—the body and blood of Christ—we come into real union with the Lord and are united in him with one another.

This term *sacrament* also applies to the Church. Because of the presence of Jesus and his Holy Spirit in the Church, it too is a sacrament, a meeting place of heaven and earth. It is a special sign that both contains and communicates the invisible, divine reality to which it points. The Church is a visible sign of Christ Jesus in our world. A famous quote from the Second Vatican Council says it this way:

> The Church, in Christ, is like a sacrament—a sign and instrument, that is, of communion with God and of unity among all men (*Dogmatic Constitution on the Church*, 1, quoted in *CCC*, 775).

Three important truths are revealed here by our understanding of Church as sacrament:

1. People from all over the world come together in the Church to be united to God. In the Holy Spirit, the Church is joined to Jesus who takes us to the Father.
2. Because we come together in the Catholic Church, the Church is also a sign of the unity of all mankind. This fact encourages us to give up hate for love, war for peace. Love and sharing help promote unity. Our final goal in life is to be in union with God and each other. The Church is a sign that points to that final union.
3. God uses the Church as an instrument to bring about salvation to the entire world.

Blessed Mother Teresa of Calcutta once described herself as a pencil in God's hand. The Church is also an instrument God uses to bring about the unity, salvation, and holiness he desires for all his people. Here is where the seven individual sacraments come into play. They are the special signs that help bring God's saving love to us. They not only point to the spiritual realities of salvation—healing, forgiveness, communion with God, and the like—but they also actually bring about these spiritual realities because they are efficacious signs.

People of God

(*CCC*, 781-786; 802-804; 849-854)

People of God is another description of the Church from the *Catechism*. The term People of God is marked by several distinct characteristics:

1. It is of God, not the property of any one people.
2. One becomes a member of this People, not by physical birth, but by baptism "of water and spirit."
3. This Church has Jesus Christ as its head.
4. The People of God have dignity and freedom as children of God.
5. The Law the People of God are obliged to follow is the new law of love: "to love as Christ loved."
6. Its mission is to be salt of the earth and light of the world, a beacon of salvation for all.
7. The destiny of the Church is God's kingdom which will be brought to perfection at the end of time.

Each person in the Church has fundamental dignity. The English word **laity** comes from the Greek word for people—*laos*. The People of God are those who are baptized and acknowledge that Jesus Christ is Lord and Savior. Because we are joined to Christ, we share his priestly, prophetic, and royal office (see page 103). This makes us missionaries, ones sent by Christ armed with the gifts of the Holy Spirit to proclaim the gospel to the ends of the world: "As the Father has sent me, so I send you" (Jn 20:21). As Catholics, we are to be ambassadors of Christ's love, letting his light shine through. Just as salt flavors food, we are to live in such a way that we enhance the world with our Christian love. The tasks and challenges of the Church's mission as People of God include:

laity—All the members of the Church who have been initiated into the Church through Baptism and who are not ordained (the clergy) or in consecrated life. The laity participate in Jesus' prophetic, priestly, and kingly ministries.

- ★ *Message.* We must preach the gospel in word and deed. Even in today's world of mass communications, some people have not heard the good news of God's love in Jesus Christ; others have heard it only in a garbled way. The Church must never cease to proclaim that Jesus is Lord, that the kingdom is present in our midst, that we must repent, believe, and be baptized. This timeless message must always be a central focus of the Church.
- ★ *Community.* To be an effective sign of the gospel, nonbelievers must see it in action: a community that actually lives its faith, hope, and love. A loving Church is like a magnet drawing others to the good news of Jesus Christ. Love is not optional for disciples of Christ. Jesus

commands, "Love one another. As I have loved you, so you also should love one another" (Jn 13:34).

- *Service.* It is often said, "Service is the price we pay for the space we occupy." To occupy a place at Christ's table means Catholics must help one another, especially the least in our midst. Catholics must imitate Christ who washed his disciples' feet at the Last Supper and gave his life for all people on Calvary. Non-Catholics will find the Church believable especially when Catholics walk the road that Jesus walked—a way of obedience, simplicity, poverty, and self-sacrificing love, even unto death.
- *Worship*. Worship is a humble admission that God gives us everything: our very life and all the many gifts he has showered on us. He is worthy of our praise, adoration, and gratitude. When we celebrate **liturgy**, the official public prayers and rituals of the Church, we are engaged in the most important work of the Church. (*Liturgy* in Greek means "work of the public.") God's work of salvation takes place in the liturgy, especially in the Eucharist, which both celebrates and creates the Church. Liturgy is the source of our union with the Lord and each other. It is the wellspring of our love. It inspires us to be other Christs, "to become in deed what we proclaim in creed."

liturgy—The official public worship of the Church. The sacraments and the Divine Office constitute the Church's liturgy. The Mass is the most important liturgical celebration.

The Church Is Like . . .

The Church is like a great ship being pounded by the waves of life's different stresses. Our duty is not to abandon ship, but to keep her on her course.

—St. Boniface (ca. 680–754)

Write five other "The Church is like . . . " similes that describe the Church.

Body of Christ *(CCC, 787–796; 805–808)*

We have all experienced the rewards of a group coming together socially, to work for a common goal, or to support one another after a tragedy. Human solidarity is important. Common and shared efforts by a group of like-minded people can accomplish much; on the other hand, each individual has a role to play with his or her unique talents.

The Church is also a communion of people with God, a "mystical communion," the Body of Christ. At the Last Supper Jesus used this vivid image: "I am the vine, you are the branches. Whoever remains in me and I in him will bear much fruit, because without me you can do nothing" (Jn 15:5). The vine gives life to its branches as Christ gives life to his disciples. By the power of the Holy Spirit, Jesus is united closely with the Church. This unity is achieved in a special way in the holy Eucharist. Through the Eucharist, Christ lives in us and we in him. We receive the body and blood of Christ Jesus to take him into the world to others.

The Body of Christ imagery for the Church was also used by St. Paul. When Paul (who was also known as Saul before his conversion) was on his way to Damascus to persecute Christians, the Risen Lord appeared to him and asked: "Saul, Saul, why are you persecuting me? . . . I am Jesus, whom you are persecuting" (Acts 9:4–5). By hunting down followers of Christ, he had been persecuting the Lord himself. Many years after his conversion, Paul wrote to the Christian converts in Corinth:

> As a body is one though it has many parts, and all parts of the body, though many, are one body, so also Christ. For in one Spirit we were all baptized into one body, whether Jews or Greeks, slaves or free persons, and we were all given to drink of one Spirit (1 Cor 12:12–13).

Christ is the head of this body, the Church. We are its members. Baptism incorporates us into the Body of Christ. The Holy Spirit unites us into a single body where each of us has an important role to play regardless of race, color, nationality, and sex. Being a part of Christ's Body, the Church, stresses the great dignity, value, and worth each of us has. St. Paul also wrote, "Now you are Christ's body, and individually parts of it" (1 Cor 12:27). Because of Christ we are linked to one another, and in a special way to poor, persecuted, and suffering people. "Christ and his Church . . . together make up the 'whole Christ'" (CCC, 795).

Each Catholic is important to the health of the Body of Christ. We each have our role to play as prophets, teachers, healers, assistants, administrators, and so forth. Jesus unites himself and his saving acts to our own actions. Though we are one with Jesus, he is still distinct from us. He is the Bridegroom; the Church is his bride. His love for his bride moves him to send his Holy Spirit to shower us with the gifts we need to be faithful to him, to be effective body-builders, and to be worthy preachers of the gospel. Although we may be endowed with different gifts according to the part we are to play, we all have been given the gift of love. It is the greatest gift of all and puts tremendous responsibility on us to do what Christ wants us to do.

The Teaching of the Documents

The Head of this Body is Christ. He is the image of the invisible God and in Him all things came into being. He is before all creatures and in Him all things hold together. . . . All the members ought to be molded in the likeness of Him, until Christ be formed in them. . . .

—*Dogmatic Constitution on the Church,* No. 7

One way to model Christ is to accept and offer all suffering that comes your way to Christ and his cross. In a notebook or journal, keep a log of the sufferings big and small that you endure each day. Keep the log for one week. At the end of each day write a prayer offering these hardships to God.

Temple of the Holy Spirit

(*CCC,* 747; 797–801; 809–810)

The Holy Spirit dwells in the Church, the Body of Christ, to give it life. He is present in the Risen Lord Jesus, the head of the Body of Christ, and in each individual member. The Holy Spirit is the "soul" of the Church. He builds it up, gives the Church life, and makes each of us holy by uniting us to Christ Jesus. Because of the Spirit's presence, we can call the Church the Temple of the Holy Spirit. This Temple—the Church—is "the sacrament of the Holy Trinity's communion" with us (*CCC,* 747), that is, because the Holy Spirit dwells in the Church, the Church both symbolizes and brings about God's presence and his union with his people. The Church is the place in which God's people are united to God, and become "perfect, just as your heavenly Father is perfect" (Mt 5:48). The Church is "a people brought into unity from the unity of the Father, the Son, and the Holy Spirit" (cf. *CCC,* 810).

The Holy Spirit works through the Church and its members to continue the work of salvation. The Spirit uses the sacraments, holy Scripture, and various graces and virtues to help us do good works for others. The Spirit also gives charisms (special gifts) to individual Christians who are to use them under the direction of the Magisterium to build up the body of Christ.

Your Commitment to Christ's Church

Examine your own commitment to Christ and the Church by evaluating your performance of the action called for by the following additional images of Church.

- *Friend* (I go out of my way to help others in need.)
- *Sheep* (Jesus is my Good Shepherd. I listen to his voice and ignore the enticing voices that try to get me to do wrong things.)
- *Witness* (I'm proud to let others know that I am a Catholic.)
- *Light* (Through my actions, I give a good example of how to live a Christ-like life.)
- *Disciple* (A "disciple" is one who learns. I read the Bible and study my religion to learn more about the Christian life.)
- *Temple* (I respect my body by avoiding harmful substances. I respect my sexuality.)
- *Soldier* (I have willingly endured some hardship to stand by my convictions. "No pain, no gain" in the spiritual life.)

1. Which image best describes you as a follower of Christ? Explain.
2. On which image do you need the most work? Explain.

DiscussionQuestions

1. How does a sacrament differ from a symbol? How is the Church a sacrament?
2. "The Church is of God, not the property of any one people." How does this statement give you comfort about your participation in the Church?
3. Share one practical way you can contribute to the Church's mission in each of the following areas: message, community, service, and worship.
4. What is your favorite image of the Church? Why?

Membership and Ministries in the Church

(CCC, 871–873; 897–900; 914–934; 944–945)

Who is a Catholic? What makes a person a member of the Church? And once a member, what privileges and responsibilities does a person have?

First, members of the Catholic Church are those

- baptized Christians who accept Jesus as their Lord and Savior,
- who accept the entire system and means of salvation Christ left with the Church (including union with the pope and bishops), and
- who devote themselves to continue Christ's work of salvation according to their situation in life.

Second, Catholics minister (serve) God in the Church in different ways. Each person is called to one of the three categories of membership in the Church: the hierarchy, the laity, or the consecrated life.

hierarchy—The official, sacred leadership in the Church made up of the Church's ordained ministers—bishops, priests, and deacons. The symbol of unity and authority in the Church is the pope, the Bishop of Rome, who is the successor of St. Peter.

The **hierarchy** is the order of ministry established by Jesus Christ on the apostles and their successors. It includes the pope and bishops and their co-workers, priests. The hierarchy has three essential roles: to teach the faith truthfully and fully; to sanctify the members of the Church, especially through the celebration of the sacraments; and to govern the Church wisely as loving shepherds who serve humbly in imitation of Christ.

The laity includes any baptized Catholic who has not received Holy Orders and does not belong to a Church-approved religious state. The laity has the special call to be involved in the social, political, and economic affairs of the wider human community and to direct them according to God's will. Laymen and women are to be light of the world and salt of the earth.

Those in *consecrated* or *religious life* can be members of the hierarchy or lay people and include hermits, consecrated virgins, secular institutes, different apostolic societies, and men (brothers) and women (sisters) in religious orders like the Jesuits, Franciscans, Dominicans, Benedictines, and so forth. Those living in religious life serve as a special gift to their fellow Catholics. They are a unique witness to the Lord's union with his Church and thus are a sign to the world that God's salvation is taking place in our midst. Other distinctive traits of those in religious life are their public profession of the **evangelical counsels** of poverty, chastity, and obedience; their commitment to liturgical celebration; and their living a shared life in common.

evangelical counsels—Vows of personal poverty, chastity understood as lifelong celibacy, and obedience to the demands of the community being joined which are professed by those entering the consecrated life.

Third, Baptism into the Church makes each Catholic a child of God with equal dignity. Furthermore, it conveys a share in Christ's roles as priest, prophet, and king. The priestly (sanctifying), prophetic (teaching), and kingly (governing) ministries are all essential for building up Christ's body and extending his saving works to all people. Catholics participate in these three offices in several ways. By Baptism, you share in the priesthood of Christ. You offer yourself with him in his sacrifice to the Father. By the gift of faith, you share in the prophetic ministry by becoming witnesses of Christ's truth to the world. And, in your service to those in need, you share in Christ's kingship. In suffering, you join with the royalty of his suffering on the cross.

Each of these ministries is examined in more detail in the subsections that follow.

Priest *(CCC, 893; 901–903; 941)*

The Church shares in Christ's priesthood, his work of sanctification. Jesus came to invite us into friendship with the Blessed Trinity, to give us a life of love and holiness. When he founded the Church, he formed a priestly people to bring salvation to the ends of the earth. Our vocation as a member of Christ's body is to help bring others to Christ.

What is a priest? A priest is a mediator between God and people. A priest offers sacrifice to God. A priest helps people on the path to holiness. These definitions apply perfectly to Jesus Christ, the High Priest. Jesus brought God to us and takes us to God. It is his sacrifice on the cross, his death and resurrection, his glorification that make us holy by the power of the Holy Spirit. He is the perfect mediator between God and mankind. The letter to Hebrews says of Jesus, the Son of God:

> For we do not have a high priest who is unable to sympathize with our weaknesses, but one who has similarly been tested in every way, yet without sin. So let us confidently approach the throne of grace to receive mercy and to find grace for timely help (Heb 4:15–16).

Though some men have a Christ-given vocation (call) to Holy Orders, by virtue of our Baptism, each of us is called to holiness. We are great in God's eyes not because of the special gifts we have been given, but rather because of how much we love him and other people. While a student, you can share in Christ's priestly ministry by dedicating school work, family life, prayer, involvement in sports and other recreational activities, and even your disappointments to Christ. When offered to God in the Eucharist, the activities of your daily life are united to Christ's Paschal mystery, the source of all holiness. You can also do so on a daily basis simply by making a morning prayer to God, offering all your activities of the coming day to him as a gift of love.

If you should marry, the love you have for your spouse will be united to Jesus in the sacrament of Matrimony. Your marriage can be a great source of holiness. Your mutual love, which is open to the sharing of the great gift of life, will result in the *domestic Church,* the unit called the family. Your family will become a miniature Church, in which moms and dads have a unique ministry to lead their children on the path of holiness.

Laymen and women can also serve God's people in certain ministries. For example, they can read the holy scriptures at Mass or serve as special ministers of the holy Eucharist.

To assist him in leading others to holiness, Jesus established the ministerial or hierarchical priesthood. The ministerial or hierarchical priesthood is received by bishops and priests through the sacrament of Holy Orders. The ministerial priesthood serves the common priesthood and is directed at unfolding the baptismal grace of all Christians. It is the means by which Christ builds up and leads his Church.

The Church's ruling office shows the way to serve Christ with humility and love. However, it is the role of the bishops and their co-worker priests to respond to Jesus' command to baptize, celebrate the Eucharist, pray, help the poor and outcast, and forgive sins in his name.

Prophet

(*CCC*, 874–882; 888–892; 936–939; 904–906; 935; 942)

Because Baptism gives us a share in Christ's teaching (prophetic) ministry, each member of the Church is called to be a prophet, that is, one who proclaims the gospel in both word and deed. Teens fulfill this prophetic call in many ways. For example, an opportunity may present itself when a peer wonders why you do not do drugs or engage in premarital sex. Your good example speaks volumes. Living a Christ-like life is often the best form of gospel preaching. St. Francis of Assisi is credited with saying, "Preach the gospel always. Use words if necessary."

In the future you might serve the Church in a special way by training to be a catechist or religion teacher. If you become a parent, you will have the responsibility to pass on the good news of Jesus to your children. Jesus told his disciples to preach the gospel to the ends of the earth (see Mt 28:19–20). This makes us all missionaries. The history of Christianity has given us many models of how to preach Christ effectively to others. For example, in the twentieth century, Mother Teresa of Calcutta taught others to see Christ in the poor and suffering. Another example is the lay missionary Jean Donovan, who left a comfortable life in America to serve the poor in El Salvador. For her prophetic witness, she and three religious sisters were martyred.

The pope, bishops, and priests have been given a special prophetic role. Their role is deeply connected with Church Tradition. Jesus gave the Church the duty to teach authentically and proclaim truthfully the gospel as it appears in both scripture and tradition. The word *tradition* means "handing on." When he established the Church on Peter, Jesus himself promised to be with his Church in a special way until the end of time. As the founder, Jesus is the source of ministry in the Church. He is the one who gives the Church its authority, mission, orientation, and goal.

At the same time, Christ established a hierarchy of leadership to guarantee that the essential jobs of teaching, governing, and sanctification would take place in his Church. The hierarchy is a sacred leadership that receives its ministry of service from the Lord himself. The pope, bishops, priests, and deacons do not act on their own authority. They continue the service of Peter and the apostles whom Jesus appointed to carry on his work of salvation. Their role is to preserve authentic tradition and spread the true gospel as taught by Jesus Christ.

The pope has a unique role in the Church because he is the successor of Peter. He is a symbol of unity and has primacy over the whole Church. The Holy Father is the Vicar of Christ. We base this belief on Christ's own teaching, given after Peter proclaimed that Jesus is the Messiah, the Son of the Living God:

> Blessed are you, Simon son of Jonah. For flesh and blood has not revealed this to you, but my heavenly Father. And so I say to you, you are Peter, and upon this rock I will build my Church, and the gates of the netherworld shall not prevail against it. I will give you the keys to the kingdom of heaven. Whatever you bind on earth shall be bound in heaven; and whatever you loose on earth shall be loosed in heaven (Mt 16:17–19).

Symbol of the Church: Keys of the Kingdom

The key is a symbol of the authority to forgive sin in the name of Jesus. Two keys signify the authority to open heaven for sinners who repent or lock out sinners who refuse to turn to the Lord.

The pope and bishops exercise their prophetic (teaching) role in the follow ways, through:

1. *Magisterial teaching.* The pope and bishops usually teach through the ordinary magisterium of the Church. Recall that magisterium refers to the teaching office of the Church. The task of the Magisterium is to proclaim the gospel, build up Christian love and service, and see to the proper administration of the sacraments and other spiritual and temporal benefits offered by the Church. The Church's magisterial teaching can be found in encyclicals, pastoral letters, sermons, and the like. Because Christ gave the hierarchy the right to teach, Catholics give religious assent to magisterial teaching through prayerful listening and obedience.
2. *Ecumenical councils.* The pope and bishops together form the college of bishops. The bishops must truthfully preach the gospel in union with the pope and each other. The bishops' authority comes from their union with the pope, since he is Peter's successor and the head of the college of bishops. Ecumenical (worldwide) councils bring the pope and bishops together to offer unified teachings. The pope has a special role as the sign of unity when the bishops speak as one. As the bishop of Rome, Peter's successor must be a living sign of unity in Christ for the universal Church, both for the bishops and all God's People. His voice with the bishops is Christ's own voice teaching the Church today.
3. *Infallibility.* Christ promised that he would remain with the Church until the end of time. Therefore, when it comes to essential matters of faith and morals, the Church is infallible. **Infallibility** means that a certain doctrine (teaching) is free from error.

infallibility—A gift of the Spirit whereby the pope and bishops are preserved from error when proclaiming a doctrine related to Christian faith or morals.

Guided by the Holy Spirit, the college of bishops, in union with the pope, can exercise the gift of infallibility when teaching about or protecting Christ's revelation on matters of belief or morality. They do this in a special way when they gather together and teach with the pope in an ecumenical council. Individual bishops can also proclaim Christ's teaching infallibly when they teach collectively around the world always united to the Holy Father.

Papal infallibility refers to the special gift given to the pope as the supreme teacher and pastor of the universal Church. He exercises this gift when he teaches *ex cathedra* ("from the chair" of St. Peter), that is, using his Christ-given authority as the successor of St. Peter. The Holy Father teaches infallibly when he teaches as pastor of all the faithful, is proclaiming a definitive doctrine pertaining to faith or morals, and does so intending to use his full authority in an unchangeable decision.

While the teaching of the pope is the teaching of the apostolic faith and without error, infallible *definitions* are rare. The most recent occurrence is Pope Pius XII's declaration of the dogma of our Blessed Mother's Assumption into Heaven in 1950. Because Christ promised to remain with his Church through the Holy Spirit and not lead it astray, Catholics owe the obedience of faith to infallible statements. Recall that an obstinate denial or doubt by a baptized Catholic of some divine or Catholic truth is heretical.

Infallibility does not mean that the pope is free from sin or mistakes. He is not infallible on matters not pertaining to faith, for example, if he were to propose a solution to a particular political debate or conflict between two nations. The pope's personal opinions, like anyone else's, can be wrong. Infallibility refers solely to the pope's gift as successor of Peter to teach correctly Christ's revelation. This is especially true when some core belief is under attack, thus causing confusion among believers. The purpose of the gift of infallibility is not to inflate a particular person's self-image. Its purpose is to build up the body of Christ and to give the Church certitude about Christ's revelation.

King (*CCC*, 894–896; 908–913; 943)

Jesus is called Christ, the King, reminding us that he is the source of all authority (Mt 28:18). The definition of a king is one who is a ruler, regent, and person with authority. Christ shares his teaching and ruling authority with the hierarchy to guarantee that the Church is able to accomplish its mission of bringing Christ's salvation to the ends of the earth.

The sole purpose for the Church's ruling office is to help people grow in faith and holiness. **Canon law** is another term for the Church's precepts and rules that help Catholics live as loving members of Christ's body. Catholics give respectful obedience to these Church laws, as well as to the legitimate commands of the pope and bishops.

canon law—The official body of rules (canons) that provides for good order in the Catholic Church.

Jesus, the Good Shepherd, is the model of the kingly role taken on by Church leaders: "I am the good shepherd. A good shepherd lays down his life for the sheep" (Jn 10:11). At the Last Supper he told his apostles: "If I, therefore, the master and teacher, have washed your feet, you ought to wash one another's feet" (Jn 13:14). Humble service, even unto death, is the ideal for those exercising authority in the Church.

Lay people also share in Christ's kingly ministry. Catholics are to engage in works of self-denial (e.g., fasting) to help them become masters of sin in themselves and in the world around them. Lay people are also to engage in works of justice to help extend God's kingdom on earth. When invited by bishops or priests, they can serve on various councils, parish finance committees, advisory boards, and the like, so the organizational Church can function more smoothly.

Explaining Your Faith

Can non-Catholics get to heaven? (CCC, 846–848)

Jesus Christ is present in his Body, the Church. Jesus alone is the one mediator between God and humans. He alone is the Savior and the way to the heavenly Father. The Acts of the Apostles puts it this way: "There is no salvation through anyone else, nor is there any other name under heaven given to the human race by which we are to be saved" (4:12).

Where do we meet the Savior today? We meet him in an *explicit* way only through his Body, the Church. As people search for salvation, Christ will draw them to his Body, the Church, because it is the living sign and sacrament of God's love. It witnesses to the way God has shown his love and achieved the salvation of humans through his beloved Son, Jesus Christ. The Church's Christ-given mission is to show people the way to the Lord.

Jesus himself taught that people need faith and Baptism (Jn 3:5). Because of Jesus' own instruction, the Church teaches that anyone who knows "that the Catholic Church was made necessary by God through Jesus Christ, (and) would refuse to enter her or to remain in her could not be saved" (*Dogmatic Constitution on the Church,* No. 14).

But what about people who have never had the gospel preached to them? Or what about those who have a distorted picture of our Savior because of false teachings they have heard? Can such people be saved?

The Church teaches that honest seekers after God, who through no fault of their own have never heard of Christ or his Church, can attain heaven if they respond to the graces God gives them and live according to the dictates of their consciences. Even atheists who, "without blame on their part, have not reached an explicit knowledge of God, but who strive to live a good life, thanks to his grace," can attain salvation because of God's goodness and love (*Dogmatic Constitution on the Church,* No. 16).

The Holy Spirit can mysteriously draw people into God's kingdom. God's love and grace embrace all people who must seek God's kingdom as they know it. Everyone must live with as much love as they possibly can because God, simply, is love. "God is love, and whoever remains in love remains in God and God in him" (1 Jn 4:16).

Discussion Questions

1. How do you show care for other people? Name three concrete ways.
2. What is your attitude toward personal suffering? How willing are you to offer your sufferings for Christ?
3. In your opinion, what should be the criteria for parents wanting to have their infants baptized?
4. How comfortable would you be sharing your faith in words to a group of peers? your family? people you just met? Explain.

However, a person must be sincere. If someone truly knows the truth of the gospel that has been given to him or her as a gift, then this person should recognize and accept the necessity of the Church for salvation. It would be a serious sin for someone who has received the gift of faith to reject the Body of Christ, the Church, because this person would be rejecting Christ himself. Jesus himself taught, "Whoever listens to you listens to me. Whoever rejects you rejects me. And whoever rejects me rejects the one who sent me" (Lk 10:16).

Marks of the Church (*CCC*, 811–812; 853)

The Church has four characteristics or marks to help us understand more about what the Church is, who it includes, and what its mission is. These marks—one, holy, catholic, and apostolic—build up the faith of Catholics. They can also help attract nonbelievers to the Church.

marks of the Church—Four essential signs or characteristics of Christ's Church that mark it as his true Church. The Church is one, holy, catholic, and apostolic.

The **marks of the Church** are present in the Church, but at the same time they also challenge the Church to live up to its true identity. They point to Christ and the Holy Spirit working in the Church. But because the members of the Church are sinners, the marks are not always visible to the waiting world. For example, the Church is holy because of the Lord, but it is the home of sinners who sometimes betray him. The Church is one because of the Blessed Trinity living in it, but the presence of various Christian denominations show a wounded unity. The Church is catholic and open to all people, yet individual Catholics can at times act superior to others. The Church is apostolic, yet certain Catholics are exclusionary, preferring to keep the gospel to themselves. The Church, individually and collectively, needs to constantly repent of its sins. In this way, the marks of the Church will be bright beacons to help bring others to Christ.

One (*CCC*, 812–818; 820; 866)

The Blessed Trinity is the source of unity in the Church. The Church is one because of its founder and source, Jesus Christ, and its soul, the Holy Spirit. Also, Christ continues to pray for unity in his Church (see Jn 17:20–21).

Love (charity) is the spiritual reality that unites the Church's members into one body. In addition, there are visible bonds of unity in the Church, namely:

- *profession of one faith* which goes back to the time of the apostles (for example, the Apostles' Creed and the Nicene Creed);
- *divine worship celebrated in common*, especially the seven sacraments; and
- the *succession of the bishops* from the time of the apostles to today through the power of the sacrament of Holy Orders.

Just because the Church is one does not mean that there is a rigid sameness in the Church. The Lord has blessed the different members of his Body with many different gifts. Because of the differences in God's

People, the Church allows for various local and cultural expressions of the faith, for example, celebrating Mass in the language of the people. As another example, various nationality groups have customs and devotions that appeal to their history, for example, the strong devotion to Our Lady of Guadalupe in Mexico or to the Black Madonna in Poland. These practices contribute to the Church's diversity within its unity.

Holy (*CCC*, 823–829; 853; 867)

Again, Christ is the model for the Church's holiness. In addition, Jesus and God the Father have sent the Holy Spirit to sanctify the Church, to unite its members to the Triune God who alone is holy. We profess that the Church is holy because the Holy Spirit lives in it. It is the "holy People of God," and its members are "saints" (meaning, "holy ones").

God uses the Church to bring his life and light into the world, to sanctify it and its members. He has given the Church "the fullness of the means of salvation," that is, all that we need to become holy. These include:

- the scriptural word of God (the Bible), apostolic tradition, the writings of great saints and theologians, and the Church's teaching office;
- the Church's liturgy, which includes the sacraments, especially the holy Eucharist;
- correct and complete confession of faith;
- full sacramental life;
- ordained ministry;
- apostolic succession; and
- the many different ways of praying practiced by Catholics through the ages.

Though the Church is holy, we, the members of the Church, are both holy and sinful. We are always in need of conversion. We are pilgrims, that is, people on the way to meet God in heaven. Holiness is something we must achieve, with God's help and grace.

However, despite the sins of its individual members through the ages, the Church has always had models of holiness. Their Christian witness was heroic, leading Church leaders to canonize some of them as saints worthy of our admiration and imitation. The process of *canonization* declares that certain holy men and women are with the Lord in heaven and can serve as models of holiness. Saints can intercede for us while we are still on our earthly journey. The greatest saint of all is our Blessed Mother, Mary, the Mother of God. "In her, the Church is already the 'all-holy'" (CCC, 829).

What the saints teach us is just what Jesus taught: The way to holiness is to love God above all and to love our neighbor as ourselves for the love of God.

Catholic—From a Greek word meaning "universal" or "general." The Catholic Church is the Christian community that is one, holy, apostolic, and catholic—that is, open to all people everywhere at all times—and preaches the fullness of God's revelation in Jesus Christ.

Catholic (*CCC*, 830–835; 868)

Catholic means "general" or "universal," a word first applied to the Church by St. Ignatius of Antioch, a bishop who was martyred around 110. The Church is catholic or universal in four ways:

1. As the head of the Church, Christ's presence gives the Church the *fullness* of the means of salvation: a complete and correct confession of faith, an ordained ministry that goes back to the apostles, and a full sacramental life, especially the gift of the Eucharist.
2. The Church follows Jesus' command to go out to all nations, preaching to all people at all places in all times. No matter who a person is, the Church invites everyone to become a member.
3. The Church teaches everything that Christ taught. Therefore, throughout its history, people from every geographical, ethnic, racial, and cultural group have professed the same faith and worshiped the same Lord.
4. Each local diocese, united under its bishop, is also catholic because of its union with the Holy Father in Rome. The worldwide Church shows its catholicity in many different cultures, liturgical rites, and spiritual disciplines and traditions.

Christ's presence in the Church guarantees that the Church will always be catholic. But Catholics must continue to preach the gospel in all times and places for it to remain a universal Church. This means the Church, of its nature, is *missionary*. A missionary is one who is sent to accomplish a certain task. The task is Christ-given: to bring the gospel in word and deed to all people. We do so best when we allow the love of Christ to shine through us, when we work and pray to restore Christian unity, and when we respectfully engage in dialogue with those who have not accepted Christ's salvation.

Apostolic (*CCC*, 857–865; 869)

The Church is apostolic because it continues the faith of the apostles, those Christ especially chose and sent forth to proclaim the gospel to all people. The Church remains apostolic in three ways:

1. It is the Church that Christ founded on the apostles.
2. With the guidance of the Holy Spirit, the Church continues to hand on the teaching of the apostles, without changing anything essential through the ages.
3. The Church continues to be taught, made holy, sanctified, and led by the college of bishops, whom Christ appointed to be the successors of the apostles. The Holy Father and the bishops can trace themselves in an unbroken line of succession to the twelve apostles.

apostle—"One sent" to be Christ's ambassador, to continue his work. In its widest sense, the term refers to all of Christ's disciples whose mission is to preach his gospel in word and deed. Originally, it referred to the Twelve whom Jesus chose to help him in his earthly ministry. The successors of the twelve apostles are the bishops.

By definition, an **apostle** is an "ambassador," or "one who is sent." The pope and bishops are sent to continue to preach, govern, and sanctify. But all members of Christ's body share in the *apostolate* of preaching and living Christ's gospel. The success of our Christ-given mission depends on our wise use of the gifts and talents that the Holy Spirit has given to us. It also depends on our remaining close to the Lord by our participation in the Eucharist.

St. Teresa of Avila (1515–1582)

St. Teresa of Avila was a woman who made the most of her call and individual gifts to build up the Body of Christ. A woman of enormous intellectual ability, Teresa entered the Carmelite Incarnation convent in Avila, Spain when she was twenty. At this time in Church history, convents were almost like finishing schools for young ladies, allowing a lot of freedom, for example, visiting, dancing, entertaining, wearing jewelry, and eating fine foods. At first, Teresa joined in the casual routine of her fellow nuns.

However, Teresa also prayed regularly and performed penance. Gradually, over the course of years, she deepened her spiritual life. She began to experience a close, mystical relationship with Jesus, one which gave her deep spiritual experiences. She developed an intimate friendship with the Lord. Later, she would teach that an excellent way to pray is to imagine talking to Jesus as to a close friend. Her familiarity with Jesus allowed her to scold him. One day, her cart turned over on the road while she was engaging in a good deed. She said to the Lord: "No wonder you have so few friends! Look how you treat them!"

Teresa's friendship with Jesus Christ moved her to reform her Carmelite order of nuns. She left her original convent and set up a reformed convent of thirteen nuns who wanted a simple, austere life. Eventually, her experiment was so successful that she traveled throughout Spain and set up scores of convents that adopted her strict rule. Her Discalced (shoeless) Carmelites lived an austere life of poverty, withdrawal from the world, and intense prayer. Eventually her reforms resulted in a separate order. Her good example encouraged a Carmelite priest, St. John of the Cross, to initiate similar reforms in his own order.

Teresa's profound writings on the spiritual life have been a major gift to the Church. Notable are her *Autobiography;* her *Way of Perfection,* which describes the Christian life; and her *Interior Castle,* which outlines the various steps involved in contemplative prayer.

St. Teresa of Avila is a Doctor of the Church. Read these famous words of St. Teresa:

You Are Christ's Hands

> Christ has no body now on earth but yours, no hands but yours, no feet but yours, Yours are the eyes through which must look out Christ's compassion on the world; Yours are the feet with which he is to go about doing good; Yours are the hands with which he is to bless men now.

On Self-criticism: Be kind to others, but severe on yourself.

On Flexibility: Never be obstinate, especially in unimportant matters.

On Prayer: All the beginner has to do . . . is to labor and be resolute and prepare himself with all possible diligence to bring his will into conformity with the will of God.

> Don't imagine that if you had a great deal of time you would spend more of it in prayer. Get rid of that idea! Again and again God gives more in a moment than in a long period of time, for his actions are not measured by any time at all.

On Jesus: If we never look at him or think of what we owe him and of the death which he suffered for our sakes, I do not see how we can get to know him or do good works in his service.

Read more about St. Teresa at these websites:
www.karmel.at/eng/teresa.htm
www.catholic.org/saints/saint.php?saint_id=208
www.newadvent.org/cathen/14515b.htm
Write a one-page reflection essay about St. Teresa of Avila and her teaching.

Ecumenism: The Church and Other Religions

(*CCC*, 813–819; 866)

The true Church of Jesus Christ *subsists* in the Catholic Church. This means that in the Catholic Church can be found the *fullness* of the means of sanctification that Christ left with us. Also, in the Catholic Church (with the Orthodox Churches) is the apostolic succession traceable to St. Peter. The Pope is the symbol and servant of unity who provides leadership and direction when troublesome conflicts and disruptive differences arise in the Church.

Because of human sin, the Church historically has not always shown perfectly the various marks that set her off as Christ's Bride: one, holy, catholic, and apostolic. For example, a study of Christianity reveals that there is a lack of perfect unity in the Church, the unity Christ willed for it. The various Christian denominations resulted from *heresy*, that is, false teaching that denied essential truths of the Catholic faith; *apostasy*, that is, the denial of the faith; or *schism*, that is, a break in Church unity resulting from the failure to accept the pope as the Vicar of Christ. Historically, there is enough blame to assign to all sides of the controversies that resulted in the various ruptures in Christ's body. It is wrong to blame people living today for these divisions. Unity among Christians is rooted in Baptism, even among those who are not professed Catholics. As the fathers of the Second Vatican Council taught: "Justified by faith in Baptism, [they] are incorporated into Christ; they therefore have a right to be called Christians, and with good reason are accepted as brothers by the children of the Catholic Church" (*Unitatis redintegratio*, 3).

Although we affirm that the Catholic Church possesses all the means of sanctification that Jesus Christ intended for us to have, there are also many means of holiness that can be found *outside* of the Catholic Church. These include:

1. Scripture, the written word of God;
2. the life of grace; and
3. faith, hope, charity, and other gifts of the Holy Spirit.

In the words of the Second Vatican Council:

> The brethren divided from us also carry out many of the sacred actions of the Christian religion. . . . [T]hese actions can truly engender a life of grace. . . (*Decree on Ecumenism*, No. 3).

Role of Ecumenism

(*CCC*, 820–822)

Every Catholic is called to be involved in some way in the work of **ecumenism**, that is, the movement that works to restore the unity of Christ's Church.

The Holy Spirit is working among all Christians today helping them to achieve a closer unity to our Lord and Savior. Catholics are invited as individuals and communities to join in ecumenical efforts. An important first step is to live a holy life of love as taught in the gospels. Catholics can

Discussion Questions

1. How is your local parish "diverse within its unity"?
2. Who is your favorite saint? How does he or she model holiness to you?
3. What can you do to welcome someone different than you into your friendship group or parish youth group?
4. How do you understand the apostles to be the foundation of the Church through the ages?

ecumenism—The movement, inspired and led by the Holy Spirit, that seeks the union of all Christian religions and eventually the unity of all peoples throughout the world.

pray with our Christian brothers and sisters that the Holy Spirit may guide our efforts for Christian unity. Catholics can also study the truths of the Church so they can share with others without prejudice or the negative judgment of others. In addition, Catholics can learn about other Christian denominations from personal research and talking with their members with the goal of promoting unity through increased understanding. Finally, working with other Christians in service and social justice projects can be a major step in furthering ecumenical understanding.

In recent history, Catholic and other Christian scholars have engaged in ecumenical dialogues at the highest levels. These efforts have fostered mutual understanding and produced common professions of faith. The Church is committed to continuing these dialogues.

The Church and Non-Catholic Christians: Protestant and Orthodox Churches

Protestant and Orthodox faith communities "have a certain, although imperfect union" with the Catholic Church. We have much in common with them that is to be respected and praised, namely:

- faith in the Blessed Trinity;
- acceptance of the Bible;
- prayer and grace;
- the theological virtues of faith, hope, and love;
- the gifts of the Holy Spirit;
- the sacrament of Baptism; and
- a commitment to God's kingdom and the desire to live a moral life.

Protestant—A baptized Christian who believes in Christ but who does not accept all the teachings of the Catholic Church. Protestant communities first came into existence during the Reformation in the sixteenth century.

The Catholic Church and the Orthodox churches have a deep communion. Our basic beliefs and traditions up to the **Great Schism** (1054) are the same. Catholics accept as valid all seven of their sacraments and recognize that they have a legitimate hierarchy and priesthood. Our major difference involves the role of the pope, whom Orthodox Christians do not accept as having primacy over the whole Church. However, major ecumenical strides have been made in recent years. Orthodox Christianity is covered in more detail in chapter 7.

Great Schism—A major break between the churches of the West (centered in Rome) and the East (centered in the Greek city of Constantinople). The Roman Church had added the expression "and the Son" to the article of the Nicene Creed, referring to the Holy Spirit ("he proceeds from the Father and the Son), without seeking approval from a Church-wide council of bishops.

The Catholic Church and Non-Christians

(*CCC*, 836–845; 870)

Jesus Christ invites everyone to belong to the one, holy, catholic, and apostolic Church. Catholics, other Christians, and all people to whom God extends the gift of salvation, belong to or are ordered to the unity found in the Catholic Church in different ways. However, full membership in the Catholic Church belongs to

> . . . those who, possessing Christ's Spirit, accept her entire system and all the means of salvation given to her, and through union with her visible structure are joined to Christ, who rules her through the Supreme Pontiff and the bishops. This joining is effected by the bonds of professed faith, of the sacraments, of ecclesiastical government, and of communion (*Dogmatic Constitution on the Church*, No. 14).

However, even baptized Catholics are not *guaranteed* salvation. Catholics must live loving, Christ-like lives to be members of Christ's Church, not only in body, but in heart and soul as well.

For its part, the Church finds much to admire in other religions, finding in them elements of holiness and truth. For example, the Catholic Church esteems the Jewish faith as the spiritual parent of Christianity (see pages 261–262 of the Catholic Handbook of Faith). Also, the Islamic faith is monotheistic, honors Jesus as a great prophet, and recognizes Mary, his mother (see page 63).

There are many other non-Christian religions, including Hinduism and Buddhism. God's grace extends to all people, since God made everyone and destined all for eternal life with the Blessed Trinity. Therefore, the Church accepts whatever is true and holy in each person. The Church

> looks with sincere respect upon those ways of conduct and life, those rules and teachings which, though differing in many particulars from what she holds and sets forth, nevertheless often reflect a ray of that Truth which enlightens all men (*Declaration on the Relationship of the Church to Non-Christian Religions*, No. 2).

The Church respects non-believers since they too are made in God's image and likeness. In a way known to God alone, he offers his grace to them.

A traditional image of the Church is that of an ark, a seaworthy vessel. Christ, the captain of the ship, and the Holy Spirit, who provides the friendly breezes, help us navigate the rough seas that we encounter on our earthly pilgrimage on the way to our eternal destiny. The Church must respectfully listen to and learn from people of other faiths. However, Christ has sent us on a mission to proclaim in deed and word his gospel to a world that seeks the meaning to life. If we do so faithfully and with loving hearts, the members of Christ's body can help all God's children to see the truth and goodness that God has placed in their hearts. It can help lead them to the greatest adventure of all: eternal happiness with our loving God, won for us by our Lord and Savior, Christ Jesus.

Baptists in America

Making up about sixteen percent of the total population, the Baptists are the largest Protestant group in America. There are more than twenty different Baptist denominations in the United States today; the Southern Baptist Convention is the largest of these.

Historically, Baptists find their roots in the Puritan reform movement in the Church of England. Puritans wished to "purify" (hence, the name *Puritan*), or renew church life. To bring this about, some left the official state church and set up separate communities. These groups were called "Separatists." Because of their reform efforts, both Puritans and Separatists met persecution. Many of these congregations came to the new colonies in America to seek religious freedom. The Baptists are offshoots of these groups.

The millions of Baptists worldwide share many beliefs in common with other Christians: a belief in the Trinity, redemption by Jesus Christ, our future resurrection in Christ, and the Lord's final triumph over sin and death. In addition to these fundamental beliefs, Baptists stress the following:

- ★ The Bible is the final authority for faith and conduct. (Tradition is not considered to have authority, nor is there an authentic Magisterium or hierarchy to guide believers in their search for truth.)
- ★ Priesthood of all believers with direct access to God. (Baptists do not have ordained priests.)
- ★ Baptism by total immersion of adult believers who have professed their faith. (There is no infant baptism. Baptism is considered a symbolic act only, not having any power in itself.)
- ★ Local rule of each congregation with voluntary fellowship with other churches. (There is no central authority or symbol of

unity for Baptists. There is no bishop or pope. Local congregations select their own ministers.)

- ★ Freedom of religion protected by the state with the total separation of Church and state. (Baptists believe that the state should favor no particular religion.)
- ★ Each Church member is responsible to put into practice Christ's great commission to go and make disciples of all nations. (Missionary effort at home and abroad is a top priority.)

Do a short report on one of the following Protestant denominations: Lutherans, Presbyterians, or Methodists. Construct a list of beliefs Catholics share in common with the religion. Make another list to indicate differences.

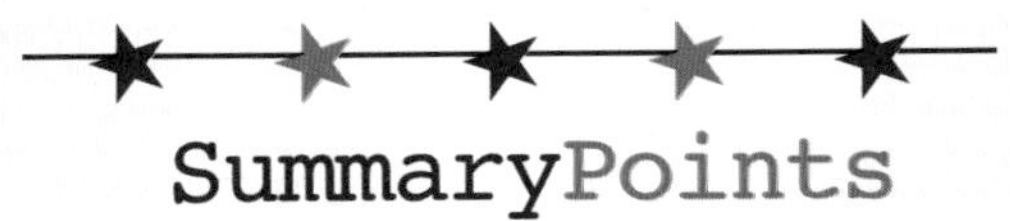

SummaryPoints

- ★ The Church is a mystery of God's love that the Blessed Trinity uses as a means and goal in the plan of salvation.
- ★ Jesus is the first sacrament of God's love, the visible image of God who *is* God. The resurrected Lord lives on in the Church to continue his work of salvation. It is correct to call the Church a sacrament, a special sign that points to and brings about our union with God, through Jesus Christ, in the Holy Spirit.
- ★ Scripture gives us many images of the Church, including these: People of God, Body of Christ, Bride of Christ, and the Temple of the Holy Spirit.
- ★ All members of the Church—hierarchy, laity, and those in consecrated life—share in Christ's prophetic, priestly, and kingly ministries.
- ★ Christ established a special role in the Church for the hierarchy, those in Holy Orders. He endows this sacred leadership with the offices of teaching, sanctifying, and governing the Church. He also blesses the Church with the gift of infallibility, which safeguards the truth when the pope, and the bishops united to him, teach in matters of faith and morals. Catholics owe the obedience of faith to infallible teachings of the Magisterium.
- ★ The four marks of the Church—one, holy, catholic, and apostolic—help us recognize its nature and attract nonbelievers to it.
- ★ God wills the salvation of everyone and invites everyone to belong to the one, Catholic Church. Rejecting the truth of the Church would be seriously wrong for a person who knows that Christ intended the Church as the sacrament of salvation. The true Church of Jesus Christ "subsists in" the Catholic Church, governed by the pope and bishops in union with him.
- ★ In cooperation with the Holy Spirit, ecumenism works for unity among Christians. A spirit of repentance and self-renewal, prayer, study, communication, and shared service help foster Christian unity.
- ★ Out of respect, the Catholic Church acknowledges what is good, holy, and true in other religions. However, blessed with the gospel of salvation, the Church must continue its missionary role of proclaiming the good news of Jesus Christ to nonbelievers.

ReviewQuestions

1. What is the meaning of the word *Church?*
2. In what sense is the Church a mystery?
3. Define *sacrament.* How is Christ a sacrament? How is the Church a sacrament?
4. Name four tasks that the Church as the People of God must perform to fulfill its Christ-given commission.
5. Explain the image of the Church as the Body of Christ.

6. How is the Church the Temple of the Holy Spirit?
7. List the three categories of membership in the Church. Briefly describe each.
8. How do Catholics share in Christ's prophetic, priestly, and kingly ministries?
9. Name the scriptural passage that shows that Christ intended a sacred leadership in his Church.
10. Define *infallibility*. Under what conditions does the Church teach infallibility?
11. Is it possible for a non-Catholic to be saved? Explain your answer.
12. Name the marks of the Church.
13. List the visible bonds of unity in the Church.
14. How is the Church *holy*?
15. In what sense is the Church *catholic*?
16. How is the Church *apostolic*?
17. What is meant by the *Great Schism*?
18. Define *ecumenism*. What part can individual Catholics play in the ecumenical effort?
19. What does the Church teach about Protestant and Orthodox Christians?
20. What does the Church teach about non-Christian religions?

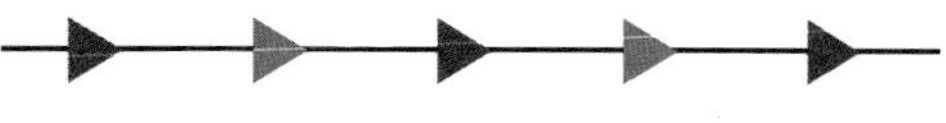

Applying What You Have Learned

1. In today's world, on which issues should the Church take a prophetic stand? Name the issue and a focused plan for what you think the Church should do.
2. Use any art medium to create a new, modern image of the Church. Be sure to include both a divine and human dimension in this image.
3. Research the mission of a Church-sponsored organization (e.g., school, hospital) and how it is fulfilled. Interview the director of this organization or invite a representative to speak to your class.
4. Read and report on Chapter 2 of the *Dogmatic Constitution on the Church*. You can find this document using its Latin title, *Lumen Gentium*, online at: www.rc.net/rcChurch/vatican2/lumen.gen. This chapter takes up the theme of the Church as the People of God.
5. Jesus reminded his disciples that they are light of the world and salt of the earth. Christians should make a difference. With other students in your class, devise a small service project. Here are some examples:
   - Collect food for the needy.
   - Begin a tutoring program for younger students.
   - Help old people with household chores in your neighborhood.
   - Volunteer to help organize receptions to celebrate sacramental celebrations in your parish.
   - Participate in a pro-life awareness day.
   - Visit shut-ins or those in nursing homes.
6. Browse these websites and prepare a report on a topic of interest:
   - Report on something important happening in your diocese: www.nccbuscc.org/dioceses.htm
   - Do a biographical sketch of a cardinal: www.aquinasmultimedia.com/cards/cards.html
   - Learn more about the Church at the official Vatican website: www.vatican.va/
   - Read and report on one of the Pope John Paul II's World Youth Day speeches: www.vatican.va/holy_father/john_paul_ii/messages/youth/
   - Check out this website dedicated to American Catholic Youth: www.disciplesnow.com/
   - Read about the Church around the world: www.shc.edu/theolibrary/around.htm at Theology Library website.

PrayerReflection

The following prayer was written by St. Ignatius of Loyola.

Prayer for Generosity

Lord, teach me to be generous,

Teach me to serve you as you deserve,

To give and not to count the cost,

To fight and not to heed the wounds,

To toil and not to seek for rest,

To labor and not to ask for any reward,

Save that of knowing that I am doing your will. Amen.

Answer these three questions.

1. What have you done for Christ?
2. What are you doing for Christ?
3. What will you do for Christ?

For since death came through a human being, the resurrection of the dead came also through a human being. For just as in Adam all die, so too in Christ shall all be brought to life, but each one in proper order: Christ the first fruits; then, at his coming, those who belong to Christ. . . . The last enemy to be destroyed is death.

1 Corinthians 15:21–23; 26

Chapter 5 Outline

Life Goal

The communion of saints, Christ's judgment, and eschatology are among areas that we discuss when speaking of our eternal destiny.

Communion of Saints

The communion of saints refers to unity among the pilgrim Church, the Church suffering, and the Church triumphant.

One Baptism for the Forgiveness of Sins

Baptism is the primary sacrament of forgiveness because it wipes away sin and unites us to Christ.

The Last Things: Eschatology

Jesus accepted death and taught us that with death comes a new kind of life.

Chapter 5

Communion of Saints, Forgiveness of Sins, Eternal Life

Life Goal

A wise person once predicted that when you get to heaven, there will be three great wonders to observe:

1. Who is there.
2. Who is not there.
3. The fact that you are there!

heaven—A perfect life of supreme happiness with God and the communion of saints for all eternity.

communion of saints—The unity in Christ of all those he has redeemed—the Church on earth, in heaven, and in purgatory.

eschatology—A study of and teaching about the "last things" (death, judgment, heaven, hell, purgatory, the Second Coming of Christ, and the resurrection of the body).

Hopefully at least one of these great wonders is right—that you will make it to your heavenly reward! And would it not be wonderful if all your loved ones were there with you, enjoying the company of Jesus and all the holy women and men who have ever lived?

The single most important goal in life is to get to **heaven**. Thanks to Jesus and the salvation he has won for us, it is possible for this to happen with his help and the help of the Holy Spirit. This chapter will look at three interrelated topics that, in one way or another, deal with our eternal destiny. The doctrine of the **communion of saints** will be explored, including what the Church teaches about Mary, the Queen of Saints and the Mother of God. This chapter also addresses Christ's judgment at the end of time and its relationship with the doctrine of the forgiveness of sins, as well as Christ's forgiveness that makes it possible for us to inherit eternal life. Finally, topics that deal with **eschatology**, a Greek word that means "study of the last things," will be covered. The area of eschatology includes death; judgment (both particular and general); Christ's Second Coming; heaven, hell, and purgatory; and the resurrection of the body and eternal life.

Thinking about the End

What do you think about death? Read each statement. Then write about one statement that most closely explains your feelings about death (and life). Explain.

- ★ Some people are so afraid of death that they never begin to live.
- ★ Death does not scare me; dying does.
- ★ Death is the golden key that opens the palace of eternity.
- ★ Let death be daily before your eyes, and you will never entertain any object thought, nor too eagerly covet anything.
- ★ Since death ends it all, grab everything with gusto while you are alive.
- ★ Live each day as though it were your last.
- ★ "Whoever keeps my word will never see death" (Jn 8:51).
- ★ Italian proverb: "A good death does honor to a whole life."

Communion of Saints (CCC, 946–962)

Think about how you feel just after you have eaten a good meal. The food was delicious and you didn't overeat. Likely, your whole body is satisfied. Conversely, think of how miserable you feel when you have a bad toothache. Your whole body seems in pain due to one small tooth. It is like this with Christ's Body, the Church. Jesus is the head and we are the members. When something good happens to one member, it is communicated and shared with the others. You may have experienced this in your own family. If your parent or sibling is rewarded for something they did, the whole family shares in the glory. In God's family, each person also shares in the spiritual benefits of the other members. How true this is, especially with Christ. He freely shares his goodness and graces with each person.

These ideas form the basis of the doctrine of the communion of saints, that is, unity in holy things and unity among holy persons.

Members of the Church share many "holy things" in common:

- ★ the Catholic faith;
- ★ the graces of the sacraments, especially the Eucharist (also known as *Holy Communion*);
- ★ the spiritual benefits that come from the special gifts (charisms) the Holy Spirit has given to us;
- ★ material goods shared among all people and especially poor people in our midst;
- ★ the fruits that come from working together for a just society; and
- ★ the communion that results from charity, the power of love that unites Catholics to Jesus Christ and each other bythe power of the Holy Spirit.

Communion of saints also refers to the unity among these three groups of people:

- ★ the *pilgrim Church* (those of us who are living on earth today, also known as the "Church militant");
- ★ the *Church suffering* (those undergoing purification in **purgatory**); and
- ★ the *Church triumphant* (the blessed in heaven).

The Catholic doctrine of the communion of saints is an extension of the belief that Church is a community of faith united by the Holy Spirit at Eucharist. The risen Lord is present in his word proclaimed at Mass and in the liturgy of the Eucharist under the forms of bread and wine. By the power of the Holy Spirit, the risen Lord, the source of all holiness, binds and sanctifies the Church into a communion of the faithful.

All members of the Church—those alive today and those who have died—make up one big family united in the Spirit of Christ Jesus. Family members depend on each other. Such is the case in God's family bound together in love. Family members must communicate to grow and thrive. In God's family, prayer is the supreme way to keep alive a relationship with our Christian brothers and sisters.

Discussion Questions

1. Complete these sentences:

   Heaven is . . .

   Hell is . . .
2. Suppose you knew that you only had a week to live. What would you do in the next seven days?
3. What do you think your best friend would say about you at your funeral Mass?

purgatory—The state of purification that takes place after death for those who need to be made clean and holy before meeting the all-holy God in heaven.

Jesus taught, "Whatever you ask for in prayer with faith, you will receive" (Mt 21:22). This is why the Church encourages us to pray and offer up our good works for each other, both for those on earth and those souls in purgatory. The prayers of the faithful on earth help those in purgatory reach the goal of heaven as their prayers can help us here on earth. We also derive great benefit from the saints in heaven, who continue to pray for us to our heavenly Father. We believe that they can offer the merits of their good works for us through Christ, who alone is the one Mediator and Savior.

Once we get to heaven, we will be amazed at how much good others have done for us through their prayers, love, and good works. The Catholic doctrine of the communion of saints really stresses how we are related to all members of God's family. With Jesus, we are never alone.

Life Before Death

Read the following quotations about life and death. With a classmate, enact a plan for making life better for someone else (e.g., young children, elderly, infirm). Enact your plan and report on it to the class.

The best way to prepare for death is to spend every day of life as though it were the last. Think of the end of worldly honor, wealth and pleasure and ask yourself: And then? And then?

—St. Philip Neri[6]

The value of life does not depend upon the place we occupy. It depends upon the way we occupy that place.

—St. Thérèse of Lisieux[7]

Devotion to the Saints
(CCC, 828; 956–957; 963)

The early Church called itself a community of saints. The word *saint* comes from the Latin word *sanctus*, which means "holy." Every member of Christ's body has a call to holiness. Christ has given his Church all the means necessary to attain holiness: the Holy Spirit; the many gifts and graces of the Spirit; and the sacraments, especially the Eucharist.

The example of canonized saints can help all friends of Christ on the path to holiness. Canonized saints are those whose lives have been meticulously examined by Church authorities and declared to be heroic and exemplary. By imitating their virtues and honoring them through prayerful devotion, we are praising God's own holiness and love. It is important to note that Catholic devotion to saints involves *veneration*, not *worship*. Catholics worship God alone. Out of respect and honor, Catholics pray to the saints to petition to God the Father, to be go-betweens on our behalf. Because of their extraordinary goodness, saints have a deep, personal, and loving relationship with God.

Many saints in heaven have not made the official list of canonized saints. Undoubtedly many of them include your own relatives. The feast day of this great multitude of saints is All Saints Day, November 1, a holy day of obligation. It is exciting to know that those living on earth are still in communion with their relatives and friends who have gone before them. In the distant future you might have great, great grandchildren who will pray for *your* heavenly help as they try to live Christ-like lives here on earth. It is our fervent hope to be among that number of countless heroic good women and men who are with God in heaven.

True devotion to the saints involves studying their lives and imitating their virtues. They were flesh-and-blood people who proved their worth by rising to the challenge of the Christian life. They are worthy of imitation. St. John Bosco said, "The history of the Church teaches us that the greatest saints are those who professed the greatest devotion to Mary." This is so because she is the greatest saint of all, the Mother of God. On the cross, Jesus gave her to the Church. He told his beloved disciple, John, "Behold, your mother" (Jn 19:27). This makes Mary the Mother of the Church. A mother's love is very special. When you stay close to Mary, you will inevitably stay close to her Son.

Patron Saints

Generally, the Church approves or appoints a certain saint to be a *patron,* that is, a special intercessor with God on behalf of people in a certain locale or having a special role, vocation, or career. Match the saint in Column B with the description in Column A. Check your answers at the end of the chapter.

Column A		**Column B**
___ 1.	Air travelers	A. St. Martin de Porres
___ 2.	The Internet	B. St. Francis of Assisi
___ 3.	Musicians	C. St. Isidore of Seville
___ 4.	Racial harmony	D. St. Lucy
___ 5.	Repentant sinners	E. St. Brigit of Ireland
___ 6.	Scholars	F. St. Maria Goretti
___ 7.	Animals	G. St. Sebastian
___ 8.	Teenagers (girls)	H. St. Mary Magdalene
___ 9.	Blind people	I. St. Joseph Cupertino
___ 10.	Athletes	J. St. Cecilia

Read more about patron saints at these websites. Write a short report about a saint you have a special interest in.

Patron saints index:
www.catholic-forum.com/saints/indexsnt.htm

Patron saints (general articles):
www.scborromeo.org/patron_s.htm

Mary, the Greatest Saint

(*CCC,* 511; 964–965; 967–969; 973)

Mary, the Mother of God, plays a special role in salvation history. She said "yes" to God's plan to send his Son to accomplish salvation for mankind. Mary did not understand how she was to conceive a child; however, her faithful response showed that she was willing to work with her Son from the very beginning in his mission of salvation.

She and Joseph then raised Jesus in a loving, prayer-filled home. They taught and cared for him. When Jesus came on the public scene, Mary continued to witness to and support him, even as he experienced his arrest, suffering, and death on the cross. In addition, she was a steadfast disciple who prayed with the apostles in the Upper Room awaiting the descent of the Holy Spirit in power on Pentecost Sunday. Without a doubt,

Mary was the most faithful witness to Jesus. She obeyed God's will; she fully cooperated with our Lord's work of salvation; she generously responded to the graces of the Holy Spirit. All of these qualities make her the perfect model of Christian faith and love.

Because of her example, the Church honors Mary with many titles, all of which tell us something about what we believe about her. Mary is Our Lady, the Mother of God, the Immaculate Conception, the Blessed Mother, the Mother of the Church, Ever Virgin, the Queen of Heaven and Earth. Mary is a loving Mother; she continues to plead for us before her Son. This is why the Church prays to her using these titles: Advocate, Helper, Benefactress, and Mediatrix.

Because of her special role in salvation history, the Church teaches certain truths about Mary. The most important of these truths are explained below.

Immaculate Conception

(CCC, 490–493; 508; 722)

Mary, from the first moment of her conception, was preserved immune from original sin. This also means that from the first moment of her existence, Mary was full of grace, that is, free of any alienation from God caused by original sin. She had a special role in God's work of salvation. Therefore, God graced her with this divine favor in anticipation of her son's death and resurrection. We celebrate this doctrine each year on December 8, the Feast of the **Immaculate Conception**, a holy day of obligation. Many people wrongly believe that this feast day celebrates Jesus' conception, but, in fact, it celebrates the gift of grace of Jesus' salvation offered to Mary from the very beginning of her life.

Immaculate Conception—The Church dogma that holds that the Blessed Mother, by a special grace from God and by virtue of her Son's merits, was preserved immune from all stain of original sin from the very first moment of her human existence. This feast is celebrated on December 8, a holy day of obligation.

In addition, Mary was so close to God that she did not commit any personal sins. She lived a blameless life, the most blessed of all human beings. The angel Gabriel proclaimed to her, "The Lord is with you" (Lk 1:28). As the Mother of God, Mary is all-holy.

Virgin Mary

(CCC, 484–489; 494; 496–499; 502–503; 510; 723)

The Apostles' Creed statement that Jesus was born of the Virgin Mary proclaims that God took the initiative in the Incarnation. God alone is the Father of Jesus Christ. Jesus was conceived by the Holy Spirit and born of the Virgin Mary, who remained a virgin "before, in, and after" the birth of the Lord.

This virginal conception of Jesus is God's work, beyond "all human

understanding and possibility" (*CCC*, 497). We can understand its true meaning only with the gift of faith. From all eternity, God chose Mary to be Jesus' mother. She was a true daughter of Israel, in a line of holy women who helped prepare for her mission of cooperating with God's plan of salvation. Her response of "May it be done to me according to your word" (Lk 1:38) helped God's plan of salvation bear fruit.

Mother of God, Mother of the Church
(CCC, 495; 501; 509; 724–726; 963)

The Holy Spirit inspired the early Church to teach that Jesus is *one* divine person possessing both a divine nature and a human nature. The Church also has consistently taught that Jesus was divine from the very first moment of his conception. This is why the Council of Ephesus (AD 431) proclaimed that Mary is "Mother of God" (*Theo-tokos*="bearer of God"). Because Mary is the mother of Jesus Christ, it is therefore proper to call her the Mother of God. This title for Mary is supreme to any of her other titles.

Jesus' words to his disciples, "Behold, your mother" (Jn 19:27) while hanging on the cross makes Mary our Mother, too. She is a spiritual mother whose love for her Son and for us helps bring birth to believers in the Church. She is also the Mother of the Church. Mary is a new Eve who cooperated fully with the Holy Spirit to bring Christ into the world and people to Christ. Children imitate their mothers. By giving Mary to the Church, Jesus wants Catholics to

1. learn from her—her fidelity, obedience, compassion, love, and prayerfulness;
2. know what great things he does for those he loves;
3. have a perfect model of holiness;
4. see what an image of God's love looks like.

Assumption of Mary *(CCC, 966; 974)*

In his official words defining the doctrine of the **Assumption** in 1950, Pope Pius XII said: "The Immaculate Mother of God, the ever Virgin Mary, having completed the course of her earthly life, was assumed body and soul into heavenly glory." This doctrine is based on Christian belief from the earliest years of the Church. It connects two realities:

1. Mary's unique role as God's mother, preserved from original sin.
2. The reality of our final resurrection in Christ.

Mary was preserved from death's decay. Because she is the mother of the Savior, Mary is the first to share in the Lord's resurrection. We celebrate this feast on August 15 as a holy day of obligation, a celebration that reminds us of our own joyous resurrection if we stay united to Mary's

Assumption—The Church dogma that teaches that the Blessed Mother, because of her unique role in her Son's Resurrection, was taken directly to heaven when her earthly life was over. The feast of the Assumption on August 15 is a holy day of obligation.

Son, Jesus Christ.

Veneration of Mary (CCC, 970–972; 975)

It is a hallmark of our Catholic faith to venerate Mary. Praying to and honoring Mary increases our love for her and helps us imitate her virtues, especially her life of total commitment to Jesus.

Giving Mary special honor is not meant to hide Jesus' role as our one mediator. Her motherly role is to help us pay attention to Jesus, the unique Redeemer. Her good qualities make her a special human being, one who attracts us to her Son. All good Marian art—like Michelangelo's *Pietà*—draws our attention not to her, but to her Son. This points to Mary's role in the mystery of salvation: She gives her Son to humanity. She leads us to him. She shows us how to live in response to him. She intercedes on our behalf, like she did for the young married couple in Jesus' first miracle at the wedding of Cana (see Jn 2:1–12).

There are many devotions to Mary. The most popular is the rosary, which includes vocal prayers and meditation on the mysteries of Christ's life. The most repeated prayer in the rosary is the beloved Hail Mary. Other popular Marian devotions include the Angelus, the First Saturday devotion, the Litany of the Blessed Mother, and various novenas.

Our Lady of Perpetual Help

The picture of Our Lady of Perpetual Help is an icon (or holy image) of Mary. It has been venerated by both Eastern and Western rite Christians for centuries. The Archangels Gabriel and Michael are holding the instruments of the Lord's Passion as the Child Jesus looks on and grasps his Mother's hand. The Mother of God looks at us with quiet sorrow in her face. Like all good Marian art, we are drawn into the picture so that we end up focusing on Jesus. Mary serves this function; she attracts and points us to Jesus, her Son, our Lord and Savior.

Praying with Mary

Read more about the following devotions. Choose one of the devotions and make it part of your own prayer:

1. the Angelus
2. First Friday devotion
3. a novena to Mary

One Baptism for the Forgiveness of Sins

(CCC, 976–987)

Jesus forgave sins. This was at the heart of his ministry. Irish author Alice Carey wrote, "Nothing in this lost world bears the impress of the Son of God so surely as forgiveness." For example, imagine the impression Jesus made on the penitent woman who burst into Simon the Pharisee's house. Her rejoicing must have been great when Jesus said, "Your sins are forgiven" (Lk 7:48).

Or consider the reaction of the paralytic who heard Jesus proclaim, "Child, your sins are forgiven" (Mk 2:5). When some Pharisees heard this announcement, they harshly criticized Jesus, mumbling that only God could forgive sin. To the astonishment of all, Jesus proceeded to cure the paralyzed man. In doing so, Jesus revealed his divine identity and the source of his power to forgive sin.

Jesus' proclamation of the good news of God's forgiveness for sinners even occurs at the height of his crucifixion when Christ forgave his executioners: "Father, forgive them, they know not what they do" (Lk 23:34).

Forgiveness of sins was an essential part of Jesus' earthly ministry and deeply connected to his saving actions. Because of this, Jesus instructed his disciples to continue to forgive sins in his name: "Receive the holy Spirit. Whose sins you forgive are forgiven them, and whose sins you retain are retained" (Jn 20:22–23). The Apostles' Creed recognizes this by linking the forgiveness of sin to three other articles of faith: the Holy Spirit, the Church, and the communion of saints.

In obedience to the Lord, who united forgiveness of sin to faith and Baptism, the early Church preached repentance and the need for faith and Baptism in the name of the Triune God. On Pentecost Sunday, Peter proclaimed:

> Repent and be baptized, every one of you, in the name of Jesus Christ for the forgiveness of your sins; and you will receive the gift of the holy Spirit (Acts 2:38).

Baptism is the primary sacrament of forgiveness because it wipes away **sin** and unites us to Christ Jesus. A major effect of Baptism is the complete forgiveness of both original sin and one's personal offenses. In the rite of Baptism, new Christians renounce sin in their lives. (In the Baptism of infants, the godparents and parents renounce sin for their children.) Though Baptism does indeed forgive all sins, the graces of

Discussion Questions

1. Name some benefits of belonging to the communion of saints.
2. How can you become a saint? Name three concrete things you can do.
3. Who is your favorite saint? Why?
4. Tell something about your patron saint.
5. Which doctrine involving Mary do you have the most difficulty understanding?

sin—An offense against God through a violation of truth, reason, and conscience.

Baptism do not free the person from the weakness of human nature and the inclination to sin in the future. Unfortunately, people do commit sins after Baptism. And some of the sins are serious enough to be mortal, that is, deadly. The effects of mortal sin are terrible: killing the person's relationship with God, separating him or her from the other members of Christ's body, and alienating the person from himself or herself.

ExplainingYourFaith

What is sin?

The Church distinguishes between two kinds of sin: *original sin* and *actual sin.*

Original sin is the term used to describe the prideful disobedience of Adam and Eve and the effects of this disobedience that all humans inherit. Although the "forbidden fruit" story in Genesis 3 is symbolic, the nature of the original sin of the first humans was a deliberate act of disobedience against God. This turning from God's love brought with it alienation from God, self, others, and God's beautiful creation. Separation from God's love and the resulting loss of sanctifying grace are the worst spiritual effects of original sin. Physical suffering and death are the worst physical effects of original sin.

A simple glance at the daily newspaper or a self-examination into one's own heart reveals that we are born into a sinful state. The entire human community bears the wounds of original sin. Violence, terrorism, prejudice, drug addiction, sexual aberration, anger, hatred, exploitation of the poor, and our own weak tendencies to give in to temptation—all these testify to the existence of a condition of sin into which we are all born.

Original sin entered the world through two people, Adam and Eve. But the gospel proclaims that the perfect life and loving sacrificial death of one person, Jesus Christ, the Son of God, have conquered sin. Through Jesus, God has redeemed humanity, offering each person forgiveness and birth into a new life. It is this life of grace that God bestows at Baptism. God frees the baptized from original sin. But this does not make the person perfect. The new Christian remains weak and in need of the support, encouragement, and prayers of fellow Christians. The Church gives Catholics many helps—primarily the sacraments—to fortify us to live a Christian life.

Actual sin is personal, individual sin. It is an act, word, or desire contrary to eternal law. "To commit a sin" is to do something evil, knowingly and willingly. Actual sins diminish us as persons and damage our relationships with God, others, and self. Sin offends reason, truth, and right conscience. The root of all sin is within the human heart.

Actual sins include:

- *freely chosen bad attitudes or inordinate desires.* An example of a "bad attitude" is prejudice, which often causes hateful feelings toward others. Lust is an example of an inordinate desire.
- *failures to act.* Examples include sins of *omission* like failing to help a person who falls sick while we pass by.
- *actions (including words) directed against God, neighbor, or self.* Examples include sins of *commission* like stealing, cheating, lying, or misusing the gift of sexuality.

Sins differ in their degree. **Venial sin** refers to "lesser sins" that are a stumbling block on the path of following Jesus. They typically involve a slight matter. Venial sins also occur when full consent of the will is lacking or ignorance is present in the sinner. Venial sins are *not* deadly sins. Unlike mortal sin, they do not destroy sanctifying grace, friendship with God, charity, or eternal happiness. The theft of a small item, a sarcastic word, and not praying regularly are examples of venial sins.

Venial sin is something Catholics should try to eradicate from their lives. The danger of all sin is that we can become attached to it. Repeating the same sinful acts can give a foothold to **vices,** bad habits that turn a person from love. These vices, especially the so-called deadly or **capital sins**—*pride, envy, anger, sloth, greed, gluttony, and lust*—can lead to mortal sin. Venial sin also weakens love, attaches us to created goods rather than God, and merits temporal punishment.

Mortal sin is the most serious kind of sin. Mortal sins include attitudes, desires, or actions (or failures to act) that kill our relation to God and others. Mortal sins destroy love in the human heart by breaking God's law. To sin mortally, the sin must include:

1. *grave matter.* For example, murder, adultery, and apostasy are serious, gravely wrong actions.
2. *sufficient reflection.* This means that the person knows full well that what he or she proposes to do is seriously wrong, but does it anyhow.
3. *full consent of the will.* This means that the person commits the sinful action with freedom and not under the influence of limiting factors like force, fear, or blinding passion.

The Church teaches that just as it is possible for us to love, human freedom also makes it possible for us to sin mortally. Mortal sin results in the loss of love and deprives the sinner of sanctifying grace. If a person does not repent and receive Christ's forgiveness and dies in a state of mortal sin, he or she will merit eternal separation from God—**hell**. A Christian should do everything possible with God's help to avoid mortal sin or to repent immediately and ask for God's forgiveness if he or she should commit deadly sin.

venial sin—Actual sin that weakens and wounds our relationship with God, but does not destroy divine life in our souls.

vices—Bad habits or dispositions (like pride) that turn us from the good and incline us to commit evil.

capital sins—Sins that are the root of other sins and vices. There are seven capital sins: pride, covetousness, envy, anger, gluttony, lust, and sloth.

mortal sin—A serious violation of God's law of love that results in the loss of God's life (sanctifying grace) in the soul of the sinner. To commit mortal sin there must be grave matter, full knowledge of the evil done, and full consent of the will.

hell—Eternal separation from God that results from a person dying after freely and deliberately choosing to act against God's will (that is, not repenting of mortal sin).

Writing Assignment

Read the account of the adulterous woman in John 8:1-11. Then do each of the following:

1. Rewrite this story from the viewpoint of the woman or one of her accusers whom Jesus challenged.
2. Write of a time when someone forgave you. What did you feel at the time? How did this forgiveness affect your relationship?

Discussion Questions

1. Share your favorite gospel story of Jesus' forgiveness.
2. Among your peer group, what are considered the most serious kinds of sins?
3. What has been your experience with the sacrament of Penance? How do you feel after you celebrate the sacrament?

Forgiveness of Post-Baptismal Actual Sins

Because of their gravity, mortal ("deadly") sins kill a person's relationship with God and others. The Church teaches that Christ forgives these sins through the sacrament of Penance. Jesus knew of our human weakness. This sacrament (also known as confession or reconciliation) is a "second baptism" in which the Church proclaims once again Christ's forgiveness of the contrite sinner. Through this sacrament of forgiveness, the Lord gave the apostles and their successors the power of the keys of the kingdom. This authority enables bishops and priests to forgive sins committed after Baptism in the Lord's name.

Sin is a turning away from God and God's family. To be forgiven, we need to convert once again and renounce our sin with sincere and contrite hearts. Having *contrition* for our sins means that we are truly sorry for them. There are three signs of true contrition. First, we must have a sincere intention to avoid sin in the future. Second, we must also avoid what we know can cause us to sin, that is, the "near occasions" of sin. Third, as far as possible, we must try to repair any harm our sins have caused. For example, a person who has cheated on a test must firmly resolve not to do so again. This means never again making a cheat sheet or sitting next to a classmate who is known to copy answers. Also, the person must own up to the past cheating incident and accept the grade that was truly deserved.

When a repentant sinner approaches a priest in the sacrament of Penance, Christ reaches out to pronounce his forgiveness; he removes the person's sins and brings him or her back into communion with the Church.

The Last Things: Eschatology

(CCC, 1002–1003; 1005–1014; 1016–1019)

Everyone faces death, the separation of the immortal soul from the body. St. Athanasius said that it is natural to fear death, but if we put our faith in the cross of Christ, we can despise what we naturally fear. How so? St. Bernard of Clairvaux said: "Death is the gate of life." The Catholic faith holds that with death comes a new type of life. Jesus taught: "I am the resurrection and the life; whoever believes in me, even if he dies, will live, and everyone who lives and believes in me will never die" (Jn 11:25–26).

It is natural to die: "There is an appointed time for everything, and a time for every affair under the heavens. A time to be born, and a time to die" (Eccl 3:1–2). Scripture also teaches that death is a penalty for sin. God did not originally intend for people to die. St. Paul explained how Adam turned from God, thus infecting humanity with death: "Therefore . . . through one person sin entered the world, and through sin, death, and thus death came to all, inasmuch as all sinned" (Rom 5:12).

Had sin not touched humanity, we would be immune from bodily death. Christ rescued humanity from its natural fate. He has conquered death. The Second Vatican Council teaches:

> Although the mystery of death utterly beggars the imagination, the Church has been taught by divine revelation, and herself firmly teaches, that man has been created by God for a blissful purpose beyond the reach of earthly misery. In addition, that bodily death from which man would have been immune had he not sinned will be vanquished, according to the Christian faith, when man who was ruined by his own doing is restored to wholeness by an almighty and merciful Savior (*The Church in the Modern World*, No. 18).

Jesus' own acceptance of his death is a model for all. In the Garden of Gethsemane, Jesus was anxious about his impending death. He prayed: "Abba, Father, all things are possible to you. Take this cup away from me, but not what I will but what you will" (Mk 14:36). This prayer, and his impending death, were Jesus' final acts of total self-giving to the Father. As his followers, we are called to imitate him. Though it is natural to fear dying, in faith we recite with Jesus, "Father, into your hands I commend my spirit" (Lk 23:46).

Death is a profound mystery. But Christian faith reveals that Jesus Christ has conquered death. Christ has won an awesome victory, giving us hope that death is an entrance into an eternal life of union with the Triune God of love. Baptism unites Catholics with the Risen Lord; in a mysterious way the baptized already participate in his heavenly life. The Eucharist nourishes Catholics with Christ's heavenly life.

The fervent hope of all is that we will rise on the last day with Christ in his glory. But this can only occur if we die in union with him. We only have one life to live and one death to experience; there is no reincarnation. This is why Christ instructed us always to be ready, to live each day as though it were our last. This truth is a powerful motivator to help us live purposeful and loving lives today. St. John Vianney observed, "Life is given us that we may learn to die well, and we never think of it. To die well we must live well."

Thinking about your own death can help you resolve to live more lovingly in the present. What if today were your last day to live? How loving would your thoughts, words, and deeds be if you believed that Christ would judge you in the next few hours? Living this way always, you would not only live an exciting, love-filled Christian life, you would attract many people to the Lord Jesus and his great news of salvation.

If we imitate Jesus in his love of others, then we need not fear death. Jesus Christ wants us to befriend him in this life so we can live joyfully with him in eternity. This is not only the good news of the gospel; this is the greatest news we could possibly want to know.

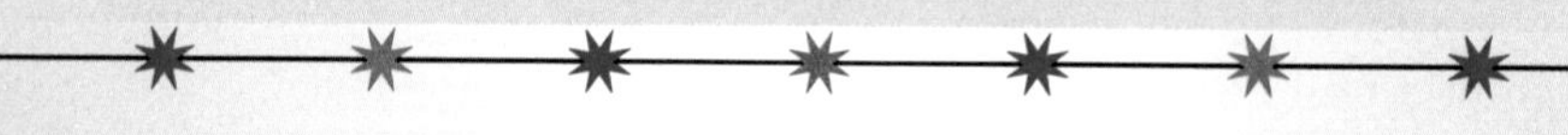

Heaven

For we brought nothing into the world, just as we shall not be able to take anything out of it.

—1 Timothy 6:7

To the good man to die is gain. The foolish fear death as the greatest of evils, the wise desire it as a rest after the labors and the end of ills.

—St. Ambrose

Do one of the following:

- Write a short story about heaven.
- Design your image of heaven using any art medium.

resurrection of the body—The Christian belief that when Christ comes again he will reunite the bodies of every human with their souls.

The Resurrection of the Body

(CCC, 988–1001; 1004; 1015–1017)

God created humans with a body (flesh). God's Son, the Word of God, took on a human body (flesh) to redeem it. Furthermore, the **resurrection of the body** (flesh) completes the creation and redemption of human flesh. These interlocking truths of the resurrection of the body and the gift of everlasting life are fundamental beliefs, based on our faith in the Lord's own resurrection. A hallmark sign of following Jesus is to witness to Christ's resurrection, proclaiming to the world the great news that we will rise with and through him.

At death the human soul separates from the body, which will corrupt. It is immediately after death that God will judge us. Then, when Christ comes again, by the power of his own resurrection, the most Blessed Trinity will raise our bodies. Our resurrected bodies will be made incorrupt and they will join again with our souls. St. Paul uses a vivid image of the Roman triumphal procession to describe the Lord's Second Coming. When the trumpet of God blasts, God will take both living and dead up into the clouds "to meet the Lord in the air" (1 Thes 4:17). Later, good news awaits us: "The one who raised the Lord Jesus will raise us also with Jesus and place us with you in his presence" (2 Cor 4:14).

Our Catholic faith holds that God will raise from the dead all people on the last day. How God will accomplish this is unknown to us, but we trust his Word that he will make our bodies incorruptible when they reunite with our souls. To describe this mysterious transformation, St. Paul used the analogy of the seed:

> But someone may say, "How are the dead raised? With what kind of body will they come back?" You fool! What you sow is not brought to life unless it dies. And what you sow is not the body that is to be but a bare kernel of wheat, perhaps, or of some other kind; but God gives it a body as he chooses, and to each of the seeds its own body. . . . It is sown corruptible; it is raised incorruptible. It is sown dishonorable; it is raised glorious. It is sown weak; it is raised powerful. It is sown a natural body; it is raised a spiritual body. If there is a natural body, there is also a spiritual one (1 Cor 15:35–38; 42–44).

beatific vision—Seeing God "face-to-face" in heaven, the source of our eternal happiness; final union with the Triune God for all eternity.

The most important quality of the resurrected body will be immortality; we will never die again. St. Paul lists other attributes of the resurrected body: imperishable, glorious, powerful, and spiritual. Theologians have interpreted these traits to mean that we will never feel pain. The resurrected body will shine brightly, reflecting the glory of the **beatific vision**, that is, "seeing God." Material creation will not hinder us; for example, we will be able to move about easily and swiftly. Finally, our spirits will control our glorified bodies.

Related to the resurrection of the body is our belief that God will transform material creation in Christ. We simply cannot imagine what God has in store for us. However, it makes sense that he has created a suitable environment where our resurrected, glorified bodies will thrive for eternity.

The belief in the resurrection of the body should encourage a great respect for your own body and for those of other people. Our human existence includes the possession of both a soul and body. They come from God as gifts and will return to glorify him. When we care for and respect our bodies, including those of the most helpless among us (like unborn babies), we are expressing profound respect and gratitude to a loving God who made us as a composite being of body and soul.

The Catholic-held belief in the resurrection of the body contrasts sharply with many other religions that teach an afterlife of the soul alone. Catholic belief goes much deeper in teaching that the whole person—body and soul—will survive death.

Hinduism and Reincarnation

Hinduism, one of the world's oldest religions, has a rich tradition espousing the sacredness of life, prayer, meditation, and spiritual disciplines. It also teaches a belief in *reincarnation*.

Also known as *metempsychosis* (soul migration), reincarnation holds that a person's soul after death is reborn into another body. According to Hindu beliefs, this happens as often as it takes a person's soul (Atman) to reach purification from worldliness. When one achieves perfection, the Atman (innermost soul) will be free of the body and enter a state of bliss known as Nirvana. In Nirvana, the individual soul loses itself in the Brahman, the hidden and impersonal essence of the universe. If a soul does not attain purification and enlightenment (due to sin, materialism, sensuality, false beliefs about the true self), it will rejoin a body that matches its character. Thus, there is a connection between one's actions in this life and the type of body one will get in the new life. This law of *karma*, in its unrefined form, even holds that a particularly evil individual might come back as a lower life form.

Catholic faith opposes this Hindu view of reincarnation. Reincarnation contradicts divine revelation.

1. Scripture reveals that we die only once and then meet God in judgment. This judgment decides our fate for eternity (Heb 9:27). Many other biblical teachings reject reincarnation. (See, for example, Ps 49:19–20, Lk 16:19–31, 20:36, and 2 Cor 5:8.)
2. Reincarnation comes from a philosophy that holds that material creation is either evil or unreal. Christians, on the other hand, know that God's created reality (including the world and human bodies) is both real and very good. Our bodies are imperfect and need Christ's redemption, but the human body is nevertheless a great gift from God.
3. Reincarnation denies the resurrection of the body, a basic truth of the Catholic faith. Jesus' own resurrection has won for us our future resurrection. At that time, our souls will reunite with our transformed and glorified bodies. It is simply impossible to reconcile reincarnation with the doctrine of the resurrection of the body. Consider this very practical problem: What would be the fate of a soul if it had inhabited 100 good bodies and another 100 evil ones?
4. Reincarnation holds that a soul will eventually save itself by finally "getting it right" through purification and enlightenment. Christianity teaches that Jesus alone saves us. "There is no salvation through anyone else, nor is there any other name . . . by which we are to be saved" (Acts 4:12). Salvation is God's pure gift for us, something we cannot earn.

Prepare a more detailed report on some aspect of Hinduism.

Particular Judgment

(*CCC*, 1020–1022; 1051)

An immediate judgment after death is based on divine revelation. This **particular** (individual) **judgment** will determine whether we go to heaven immediately, need purification in purgatory, or must suffer the punishments of hell and eternal damnation. St. Paul writes:

> For we must all appear before the judgment seat of Christ, so that each one may receive recompense, according to what he did in the body, whether good or evil (2 Cor 5:10).

particular judgment—The individual's judgment immediately after death, when Christ will rule on one's eternal destiny to be spent in heaven (after purification in purgatory, if needed) or in hell.

Jesus himself referred to the particular judgment in the parable of the Rich Man and Lazarus (Lk 16:19–31). Because of his selfish lifestyle and neglect of the starving Lazarus, the rich man suffered the fires of Hades (hell). In contrast, good Lazarus went to a peaceful resting place.

If we live a just and loving life, we have nothing to fear when we die. God is a God of justice *and* mercy. God's judgment is based on whether we loved him and our neighbor as ourselves. God is not out to trick us at the particular judgment. There will be no surprises. People know if they have lived loving and God-centered lives or not. The famous poet Dante Alighieri said it well:

> If you insist on having your own way, you will get it. Hell is the enjoyment of your own way forever. If you really want God's way with you, you will get it in heaven.

One way to consider the "day of judgment" is to think of it as our permanent decision to accept or reject Jesus Christ. But Scripture reveals another judgment, at the end of time. It will be a final judgment when there will be final victory over evil.

R.I.P.

R.I.P. is a familiar abbreviation that translates a short prayer asking God to remember the deceased: *Requiescat in pace,* "May he/she rest in peace."

Another Latin phrase, *Sic transit gloria mundi* ("Thus passes the glory of the world"), reminds us that we have only a brief time to make our mark. Time speeds quickly by. What the world holds important may not be so in God's eyes.

Reflect on your own life. Imagine your death for whatever year you choose. Write the following information for an obituary notice to be run in your daily newspaper shortly after you die.

Name:
Age:
Cause of death:
Occupation:
Loved ones left behind:
Major accomplishments:
Epitaph on gravestone:

Also write your responses to the following:

1. Suppose you were to die next week. Note five personal qualities that you could offer to Jesus at your individual judgment that show how you have lived a Christian life.
2. Suppose you were to die at the age of sixty-five. Note five major achievements that you hope you can offer to Jesus to show that you were his faithful disciple during your life.

Heaven, Purgatory, Hell

(*CCC,* 1023–1037; 1052–1058)

At death, all people receive the rewards for their life. Those who have done good merit eternal reward and those who have died while separated from God receive their chosen punishment. Catholic doctrine explains that there is an eternal life which we will spend in heaven or hell. The reward of heaven is eternal life spent in union with God and all those who share in God's life. Hell is eternal separation from God.

The existence of heaven and hell take very seriously the reality of human freedom. If we use our freedom properly, then we will choose our own eternal destiny—a joyous life with our loving, Triune God. On the other hand, if we decide to model ourselves into heartless, unloving, selfish people, then God will respect our decision. When we choose self over God, then we have *chosen* hell. Our God respects our freedom and will give us what we want. But God generously rewards freedom that is used properly. Victor Hugo wrote, "Good actions are the invisible hinges of the doors of heaven."

Many images try to capture the differences between heaven and hell. One comes from a legend that tells of a man who dreamed of both of them. In his first dream he found himself in a magnificent palace where countless millions gathered around eight-foot high tables overflowing with food. However, there was a problem. Although the spoons they had were long enough to reach the food, they were way too long to put the food into their mouths. Despite this, everyone was extremely happy and satisfied because they used their spoons to feed their neighbors and friends. Everyone was feeding others; everyone was being fed.

The man's second dream was like the first. Again, there was a very tall table replete with delicious food. But the people were upset, angry, frustrated, and bitter. Why? They tried to feed themselves. So fixed were they in their selfish mindset, that it never occurred to them to feed those around them.

Heaven

Heaven is the name for our union with the loving Triune God, the Blessed Mother, and all the angels and saints, including our relatives and friends who have lived a God-centered life. Those who reach heaven will live with Christ Jesus forever. They will enjoy the beatific vision, that is, seeing God face-to-face, as he really is, contemplating his heavenly glory. In heaven,

> [God] will wipe every tear from their eyes, and there shall be no more death or

mourning, wailing or pain, (for) the old order has passed away (Rv 21:4).

Jesus' death and resurrection have given us access to heaven. In heaven we will be fully incorporated into Christ. Although we will have perfect communion with him and his loved ones, we will both retain and find our true individual identity as his brother or sister. We will continue to fulfill God's will in heaven and will reign with Christ Jesus forever.

The pleasures and happiness in store for us in heaven are beyond human imagination. Scripture uses many images to help describe them; for example, wedding feast, light, life, peace, paradise, the Father's house, heavenly Jerusalem.

Even these cannot begin to describe heaven. As St. Paul's first letter to the Corinthians explains: "What eye has not seen, and ear has not heard, and what has not entered the human heart, what God has prepared for those who love him" (1 Cor 2:9). There is no goal more worthwhile than getting to heaven. We should always keep it before our eyes and resolve not to do anything foolish enough to jeopardize our attaining it.

Purgatory

Purgatory is the name for the final purification of those who die in God's grace and friendship, but who need purification or cleansing to achieve the holiness necessary to enter heaven. Purgatory is also called the "Church suffering."

The existence of purgatory is rooted in the Bible. For example, Judas Maccabeus and his soldiers prayed for the martyred Jews that they might be released from their sins (see 2 Mc 12:39–46). Church Tradition has interpreted certain New Testament passages as referring to a place of "cleansing fire" after death. From the first centuries, the Church has honored the dead by offering the Eucharist for them and encouraging the faithful to pray for them. In addition, the Church has recommended almsgiving, indulgences, and acts of penance for the "poor souls in purgatory."

The doctrine of "purification," or purgatory, makes sense. To embrace an all-loving God, we must be free of any imperfection in our own capacity to love. Only a clean person can enter heaven to embrace the all-holy God. Not everyone who dies has cleansed himself or herself of his or her venial sins or any punishment due sins that are present at death. To a degree, on our earthly journey we can accomplish this process of purification. However, dying to our attachment to sin and our selfishness is a long and painful process.

Purgatory involves both a joyful and painful process of letting go of sin. Those in purgatory are happy that the Lord has promised them heaven. At the same time, those in purgatory need to leave behind their selfish attachments before meeting the all-holy God. This painful process of "letting go and letting God" may be what is meant by the "fires of purgatory." The process of purgation might be one of "burning" with sorrow and shame over a sinful life, and a profound wish to be united to the loving, good, saving God. To be separated from the Lord whom they love so deeply brings suffering to our brothers and sisters in purgatory. However, when their purgation is complete, their suffering will end as they enter into the bliss of heaven.

We belong to the communion of saints, so we should never forget to pray for those in purgatory and ask for their prayers as well. We can honor our relatives who have gone before us by praying for them and offering our good works and sacrifices on their behalf. Then, when they make it to heaven, they will be sure to remember us before God.

Hell

To die in mortal sin without repenting and accepting God's merciful love means remaining separated from him forever by one's own free choice. This is the meaning of hell. The principal punishment of hell is separation from our loving God who created us for love, life, joy, and happiness—our deepest yearnings that only God can satisfy. Christian tradition speaks of the "fires of hell." These describe the loss of love, self-hatred, and the total loneliness that results from failure to love God above all others and our neighbor as we do ourselves for the love of God. Those in hell grieve over their eternal punishment, suffer spiritually and physically, and give up all hope of salvation.

God does not predestine anyone for hell. God made us to love him. However, for those who freely choose to commit mortal sin by refusing to love God, and die without repenting of their lack of love, their own free choice will forever separate them from God.

Scripture and Church Tradition both affirm the existence of hell. For example, Jesus referred several times to Gehenna (hell). In the parable of the sheep and goats (Mt 25:41–46), Jesus condemned to hell those who fail to respond to those in need. On another occasion, Jesus offered this stern warning:

> "The Son of Man will send his angels, and they will collect out of his kingdom all who cause others to sin and all evildoers. They will throw them into the fiery furnace, where there will be wailing and grinding of teeth" (Mt 13:41–42).

The existence of hell flows from the belief that God is a loving God who made us truly free. God respects our freedom, even if, out of pride, we choose to reject God's love, grace, and mercy. God forever showers his love on us; his mercy is always there for us to embrace. Nevertheless, a person can be hardhearted and stiff-necked, adamantly selfish and unloving. People can and do commit mortal sin. Having created us as free beings, God respects our freedom.

God does not send us to hell; unrepentant mortal sin does. We cannot say for sure who is in hell because we do not know for sure who has defiantly turned their backs on God. Jesus warns us not to judge others lest we be judged ourselves. What we can do is pray to repent and accept God's love and forgiveness.

If we live a life loving God and others, we should not let the existence of hell frighten us unduly. If we have turned from our sins as Christ calls us to do, and struggle to live with love in our hearts, then we should trust and believe that Christ Jesus will save us. He is a merciful, loving Savior who will always forgive us if we repent. His Father is our Abba who loves us more tenderly than any human mother or father possibly could.

However, we should take hell's existence seriously. It challenges us to live responsibly, to repent of our sins, and to reform our lives in the image of Jesus. It reminds us to live a good life *right now* because we never know when we will die.

Differentiating Between Heaven and Hell

Complete each of the following activities:

1. Read the parable of the weeds (Mt 13:24–30, 36–43) and the parable of the net (Mt 13:47–50). Write your own interpretation of these parables based on what they are saying about God's judgment.
2. C.S. Lewis contrasted heaven and hell using images like the ones below. Create at least four more images of your own to contrast heaven and hell.

   Hell is . . .

   an unending Church service without God

   grey and so are its inhabitants

   full of clocks and telephones

   sex without pleasure

   Heaven is . . .

   God without a Church service

   full of colors and all colors of people

   full of only those possessions you gave away on earth

   pleasure without sex.
3. Lewis also wrote, "The safest road to Hell is the gradual one—the gentle slope, soft underfoot, without sudden turnings, without milestones, without signposts." What does Lewis mean? Is he correct? Offer evidence one way or the other.

The Last or General Judgment (*CCC*, 1038–1050; 1059–1060)

last (general) judgment—Jesus Christ's judgment of the living and the dead on the last day when he comes to establish God's kingdom fully.

The events of the last day of human history are known as the **last** or **general judgment**. On that day, the resurrection of the just and unjust will take place and the Risen Glorified Lord will come again (see the Parousia, pages 60–61). Christ, who is Truth itself, will show each person's relationship with God. Finally, everyone will recognize God's saving plan in Christ Jesus. The Son of Man, in the presence of all the angels, will separate the sheep from the goats (Mt 25:31–32).

As to *when* this will take place, only the Father knows. When the day comes, however, everyone will see "that God's justice triumphs over all the injustices committed by his creatures and that God's love is stronger than death" (*CCC*, 1040). Followers of Christ look forward to this day of final judgment because the unity with God that our hearts yearn for will be accomplished. Furthermore, on this day God will transform and restore the entire physical universe. Along with a transformed humanity, "the new heavens and new earth" will share in Christ Jesus' own glory. Since we do not know the exact hour of Christ's return and our final judgment, we should always be ready. The time to live a Christ-like life is now.

Today we have a glimpse of our future life, because Christ has already launched the kingdom of God. Despite the sinful forces at work in the world to undermine God's saving love, his loving grace is very much alive to help attract people to our Triune God. The Spirit gives Catholics the power and the mission of cooperating with Christ's work of freeing people. He strengthens us with virtues like fortitude to work tirelessly as peacemakers. We can work for justice by helping people attain their God-given rights. We also cooperate in Christ's plan when we promote human solidarity and respect the dignity of every human being. In a special way, we promote the kingdom of God when we extend mercy to the weak, poor, and defenseless.

The Holy Spirit gives us the virtue of hope. It helps us look forward to the glorious day of Christ's Second Coming. It helps us pray the prayer that concludes the entire Scriptures: "Amen! Come, Lord Jesus! The grace of the Lord Jesus be with all" (Rv 22:20–21).

A New Earth and a New Heaven

We do not know the time for the consummation of the earth and of humanity. Nor do we know how all things will be transformed. As deformed by sin, the shape of this world will pass away. But we are taught that God is preparing a new dwelling place and a new earth where justice will abide, and whose blessedness will answer and surpass all the longings for peace which spring up in the human heart (*Pastoral Constitution on the Church in the Modern World,* No. 39).

1. What do you fear about God's judgment?
2. What do you look forward to about God's judgment?

Amen—A Hebrew word for "truly" or "it is so," thus signifying agreement with what has been said. New Testament and liturgical prayers, creeds, and other Christian prayers end with "Amen" to show belief in what has just been said.

Discussion Questions

1. Why is death a mystery?
2. How do you imagine your body after its resurrection?
3. How do you feel about Jesus being the judge of your life?

Amen (CCC, 1061–1065)

Amen is the traditional way we end our prayers, including the Apostles' Creed. Amen is also the word that ends the Bible. Amen means "so be it, I agree, certainly, it is firm." Amen comes from the Hebrew word for "believe." Thus, when we say "Amen," we are making an act of faith, proclaiming the truth of what we pray and celebrate. Amen summarizes our heartfelt conviction and expresses our solidarity with it.

Jesus often said "Amen" to stress that what he was about to teach was trustworthy, that it came from his Father. God the Father also said "Amen" when he sent us his Son. The Lord is indeed the "yes" of God's saving love for us.

Finally, death is really an "Amen" to our lives. For Christians who have "fought the good fight," death is a state that readies us for eternity. If we live struggling to do right, trying to love, repenting of our sins, trusting in Jesus—then our death is not something to fear. Rather, it is a fitting end to our lives, a "yes" to the life of a disciple about to enter eternity.

Catholic beliefs about the "last things" assure us that God has the final word. Our end in this life is but the birthday to an eternal life with the Lord. The doctrines of the resurrection of the body, judgment, and life everlasting teach that everything we do, or fail to do, has significance. If we choose Jesus and stay close to him in this life, then we can embrace these comforting words of St. Paul:

> And when this which is corruptible clothes itself with incorruptibility and this which is mortal clothes itself with immortality, then the word that is written shall come about: "Death is swallowed up in victory. Where, O death, is your victory? Where, O death, is your sting?" The sting of death is sin, and the power of sin is the law. But thanks be to God who gives us the victory through our Lord Jesus Christ. Therefore, my beloved brothers, be firm, steadfast, always fully devoted to the work of the Lord, knowing that in the Lord your labor is not in vain (1 Cor 15:54–58).

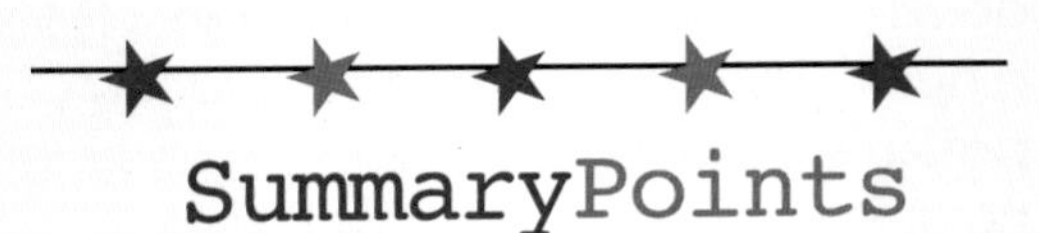

Summary Points

- ★ Those alive on earth ("the Church militant"), those suffering in purgatory ("the Church suffering"), and the blessed ones in heaven ("the Church triumphant") make up the communion of saints.
- ★ Christ calls all of us to be saints, that is, to be holy.
- ★ The Church canonizes some saints to declare that they lived lives of heroic Christian witness. We honor the saints when we imitate their virtues and pray to them, asking them to intercede for us.
- ★ Mary is worthy of our devotion as the holiest of all humans. Her faith in becoming the Mother of God, her loving service of her Son, and her response to the Holy Spirit make her the supreme example of what a Christian should be.
- ★ Mary is the Mother of God and our Blessed Mother, too. She is the Mother of the Church who prays for us always.
- ★ *Original sin* resulted from the prideful disobedience of Adam and Eve. All humans suffer the effects of this first sin, including the loss of God's friendship and physical suffering and death. Jesus has conquered original sin and makes it possible for us to be united once again with our loving God.
- ★ *Actual sin* is personal, individual sin. It can be an act, word, or desire contrary to God's law. *Venial sins* partially reject God. *Mortal sins* kill our relationship with God and others. To sin mortally there must be grave matter, sufficient reflection, and full consent of the will.
- ★ The apostles and their successors have the Christ-given power to forgive sin in his name, a major component of his saving activity. The Church follows Christ's command to forgive sin through the sacraments of Baptism and Penance (reconciliation or confession).
- ★ Baptism forgives all sin. The sacrament of Penance forgives post-baptismal sin of sincere and contrite sinners.
- ★ Death, introduced by Adam's sin, is a great mystery. But Christ Jesus overcame death through the Paschal mystery of his death on the cross and his resurrection. If we die united to Jesus Christ, God will raise us on the last day to share in his glory.
- ★ Our bodies will rise to an incorruptible, eternal life joined to our souls in the resurrection of the dead.
- ★ When we die, we will appear before God for a particular judgment that will determine if we enter heaven, purgatory, or hell.
- ★ Heaven is eternal union with God. Purgatory is a place or state of purification for those who die in God's friendship but need to be cleansed of their attachment to sin before meeting the all-holy God. Hell is eternal separation from God.
- ★ Only the Father knows the day and hour of Christ's Second Coming. On that day of general judgment, Christ will reveal the truth of every person's relationship with God. The just will find their reward in heaven; the unjust will go to hell.
- ★ When we say "Amen," we are professing anew our faith in what has just preceded. Jesus is the great Amen of God's love for us.

Review Questions

1. Define *eschatology.*
2. What three groups does the "communion of saints" embrace?
3. What advantages are there for being devoted to the saints?
4. Briefly explain the following Marian doctrines: Immaculate Conception, Assumption of Mary, Ever Virgin, Mother of God, and Mother of the Church.
5. Why does the Church honor Mary?
6. What role did forgiveness play in Jesus' ministry?

7. Define *original sin.*
8. What are some of effects of original sin?
9. Define *actual sin.* Discuss three general types of actual sin.
10. Distinguish between *venial sin* and *mortal sin.*
11. How does one obtain forgiveness of sins committed after Baptism?
12. What is the meaning of the doctrine of the resurrection of the body?
13. Distinguish between the *general* and the *particular* judgments.
14. Explain why Catholic belief opposes reincarnation.
15. Identify the term *beatific vision.*
16. Describe the nature of purgatory.
17. What is hell?
18. What will happen at the Second Coming of Christ?
19. What is the meaning of the word *Amen*?
20. Why is saying Amen an appropriate way to end the Apostles' Creed?

Applying What You Have Learned

1. Research and report on what one of the following religions teaches about the afterlife: Judaism, Islam, Buddhism, Hinduism, or a Native American religion.
2. Write an essay entitled, "Mary, the First Disciple." Support reasons for stating that Mary is the Christian disciple *par excellence.*
3. Research the process of canonization in the Roman Catholic Church. Briefly summarize the requirements of each step leading to sainthood. *Suggestion:* Begin the research with the article "Canonization Process" at the Catholic-Pages.com website www.catholicpages.com/saints/process.asp.
4. Devise a project to put two of the corporal works of mercy—visit the sick and bury the dead—into practice. For example: (1) visit a nursing home and talk to the lonely patients there; (2) do chores for an elderly neighbor; (3) set up for a luncheon (through your parish's hospitality committee) for the family members and friends of a deceased parishioner after the funeral Mass and burial.

Prayer Reflection

The rosary blends vocal prayers with meditation. The vocal prayers center on the recitation of a number of decades of Hail Marys, each decade introduced by the Lord's Prayer and concluded by a Glory Be. Introductory prayers to the Rosary include the Apostles' Creed, an initial Our Father, three Hail Marys, and a Glory Be. During the recitation of these vocal prayers, we meditate on certain events, or mysteries, from the life of Christ and Mary.

Since the year 2002, when Pope John Paul II added five mysteries, the complete rosary has twenty decades, but we usually recite only five at a time. The purpose of rosary beads is to help us keep track of the prayers.

The repetition of the Hail Marys is a way to occupy our minds as we meditate on the mysteries. Next to the Lord's Prayer, the Hail Mary is a favorite Catholic prayer. The first part of the prayer comes from Luke's gospel where he records the greeting of the angel Gabriel (Lk 1:28) and that of Mary's cousin, Elizabeth (Lk 1:42). The second part of the prayer asks Mary to intercede for us.

Hail Mary, full of grace, the Lord is with thee;
blessed art though among women
and blessed is the fruit of thy womb, Jesus.
Holy Mary, mother of God, pray for us sinners
now and at the hour of our death. Amen.

Here are the mysteries of the rosary, divided into four categories:

Joyful Mysteries

1. The Annunciation
2. The Visitation of Mary to Elizabeth
3. The Birth of Jesus
4. The Presentation of Jesus in the Temple
5. The Finding of Jesus in the Temple

Mysteries of Light

1. Jesus' baptism in the Jordan
2. Wedding Feast at Cana
3. Proclamation of the Kingdom of God and call to conversion
4. Transfiguration of Jesus
5. Institution of the Eucharist

Sorrowful Mysteries

1. The Agony in the Garden
2. The Scourging at the Pillar
3. The Crowning with Thorns
4. The Carrying of the Cross
5. The Crucifixion

Glorious Mysteries

1. The Resurrection
2. The Ascension
3. The Descent of the Holy Spirit on the Apostles
4. The Assumption of Mary into Heaven
5. The Crowning of Mary Queen of Heaven

- Which five of the above twenty mysteries speak most powerfully to your own heart? Why?
- For the next twenty days, recite a decade of the rosary for your daily prayer.

Answers to quiz on patron saints, page123.
1-I; 2-C; 3-J; 4-A; 5-H; 6-E; 7-B; 8-F; 9-D; 10-G

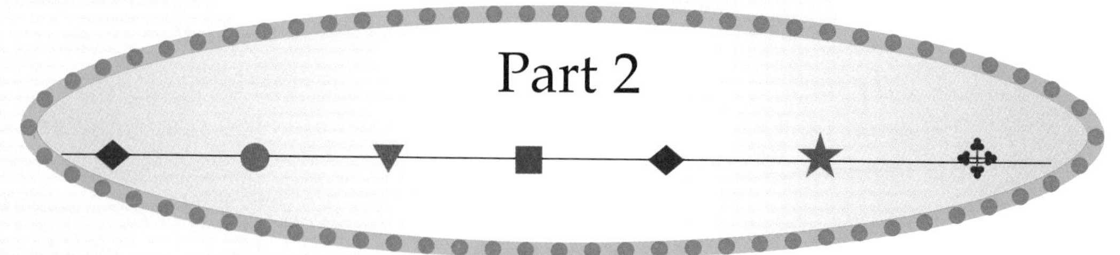

We Hope: Celebrating the Christian Mystery

Our Participation in God's Work

Part 2 of *Our Catholic Faith* discusses how Catholics celebrate our faith in Christ. The liturgy is our participation in God's work of salvation. The seven sacraments are "efficacious" (truly effective) signs of God's grace. Celebrating the liturgy, especially the Eucharist, is central to our membership in the Body of Christ.

By celebrating the sacraments, we are trusting that our Lord continues to do his work. We show confidence that he uses the sacraments to help us on our journey to eternal life. The sacraments also strengthen our faith in God who provides for us and increases in us the virtue of love, God's own life in us.

The Liturgy

(*CCC*, 1066–1069; 1073–1076; 1135–1144; 1187–1188)

The word *liturgy* means a "public work" or "people's work." Today, this term refers to the Church's prayerful participation in and celebration of God's work—our redemption and salvation. Liturgy is the Church's official public worship. Christ continues his work of salvation through, in, and with the liturgy. It is the source of the Church's power.

"Liturgy is the 'action' of the *whole Christ*" (*CCC*, 1136). This means that those of us on earth celebrate the liturgy in union with the saints in worshiping our loving Trinity. Since Baptism gives every Christian a share in Christ's priesthood, all are actively involved when participating in any liturgy. However, through the sacrament of Holy Orders, the Holy Spirit empowers some members to serve as celebrants (leaders) of liturgy. In addition, there are other various special ministries at liturgies, for example, readers, commentators, servers, and choir members.

Through the Holy Spirit, Jesus makes his saving actions present to us in the liturgy. In the liturgy, we join Christ in his own prayer to the Father in the Holy Spirit. Also, especially in the Eucharistic liturgy and the other sacraments, we meet the living God, the source of our life, joy, and happiness. The Holy Spirit uses the liturgy to gather us together as members of Christ's body to celebrate, to pray, to worship God, to proclaim the gospel, and to live out the Paschal mystery in our own lives.

The Liturgy and the Blessed Trinity (*CCC*, 1077-1112)

The Blessed Trinity is at work through the Church's liturgy in the following ways:

1. God's People bless, praise, adore, and thank *God the Father* for all his gifts and blessings given in creation. We especially acknowledge the gift of salvation won for us through his beloved Son and the gift of the Holy Spirit who has adopted us into the divine family.
2. Jesus promised to be with his Church as its head. One way *God the Son* is present to us is through the liturgy, both in the priest who leads the worship and in the assembled community, but especially in the Eucharist, the bread and wine that becomes Christ's body and blood through the action of the Holy Spirit. The Risen Lord continues to speak to the Church through the Scripture, and he dispenses his graces through the sacraments. Christ also joins the Church to the heavenly liturgy celebrated by the angels and saints, giving us a foretaste of our eternal destiny.
3. *God the Holy Spirit* is active in many ways in the liturgy. He prepares the worshiping community to meet Christ by recalling God's work in the Old Testament (for example, the Exodus and Passover) and by helping us to pray the psalms. It is the Spirit who invites us to meet the Lord Jesus in the liturgy and enables us to participate in the Lord's Paschal Mystery. This happens in a special way in the **epiclesis** (invocation prayer) of the Eucharist. In this prayer, the priest petitions God the Father to send the Holy Spirit to transform ordinary bread

epiclesis—The prayer that petitions God to send the Holy Spirit to transform the bread and wine offered at the Eucharistic liturgy into the body and blood of Jesus Christ. This term also applies to the prayer said in every sacrament that asks for the sanctifying power of the Holy Spirit.

and wine into the body and blood of Jesus Christ. Finally, the Holy Spirit is the source of our unity in Christ and each other. He empowers us to bring Jesus' love into the world.

Sacraments

(*CCC*, 1113; 1115–1116; 1118–1124; 1128–1134; 1145–1162; 1189–1192; 1996–1999; 2002–2003; 2023)

The principal liturgical actions in the Church are the sacraments. A *sacrament* is "an efficacious symbol," that is, an "effective" or "powerful" sign that causes what it points to. A sacrament is what it represents. An ordinary symbol like a stop sign points to the *idea* of stopping; it does not cause it. In contrast, a sacrament like Baptism actually brings about the rebirth that the baptismal waters signify. Because Baptism is an "effective" sign, it actually washes away sin and brings about spiritual rebirth into God's family.

We already studied how the term sacrament fits both Jesus and the Church. Jesus points to God's love; at the same time he *is* God's love for us who has reconciled the world to his Father. Jesus' Incarnation is the primary sacrament of our salvation. His death on the cross shows how great God's love is for us. The mysteries of his life serve as the foundations of what he gives to us in the sacraments, through the ministers of the Church. The Church is also a sacrament, an effective sign that continues his work of salvation. The Holy Spirit gives life to the Church, and we can meet Jesus in the Church. The Lord Jesus continues to speak to us through his word proclaimed. And through his Church, he calls each of us to be effective signs of his love. We, too, are to be sacrament people, that is, light to the world. Our faithful lives of love and service point the way to Christ and his Father.

Christ instituted the seven sacraments, special powers that flow from his body, the Church. They are effective, symbolic actions of Christ that not only point to divine life, but actually convey it to the members of Christ's body. Some important truths about the sacraments include the following:

1. *The sacraments are signs.* Comprised of body and soul, humans express and perceive spiritual realities through signs and symbols. God reaches out to us through created, material realities. For example, most people first learned of God's love through the warm affections of their parents. Christ uses many signs and symbols to help us celebrate his Paschal Mystery of love and to communicate God's life to us. The mysteries of Christ's life—from the words and actions during his hidden life and public ministry—already were salvific because they anticipated the power of the Paschal mystery. The saving effects of the Paschal mystery are communicated through the sacraments. Examples include signs from creation, like fire and water (e.g., Baptism); from ordinary human life, like washing, breaking bread, and sharing a cup (e.g., Eucharist); from the Old Testament, like anointing and laying on of hands (e.g., Baptism, Confirmation, Holy Orders, and Anointing of the Sick) and Passover rituals (e.g., especially related to Eucharist);

and from Christ himself, who used physical signs (like anointing of the sick) and ordinary words (the parables) to proclaim God's kingdom.

2. *The sacraments are effective (efficacious).* Christ himself works through the sacraments. Their power comes from God in the Holy Spirit, not by the personal holiness of either the minister or those of us who receive them.
3. *The sacraments convey grace.* All the sacraments convey **sanctifying grace**, that is, God's free and undeserved favor and help and a participation in God's own life. Sanctifying grace makes the Church holy and pleasing to God, adopts us into God's family, and makes us temples of the Holy Spirit and heirs of eternal life.
4. *Each sacrament conveys sacramental graces.* For example, the Eucharist represents the sharing of a common meal in Christ. At the same time, it *actually* and *really* causes union with the risen Lord.
5. *Baptism, Confirmation, and Holy Orders confer a* ***sacramental character.*** This character or "seal" relates a Christian to Christ's priesthood according to a different state or function. We can receive these three sacraments only once, because the Holy Spirit uses them to configure us to Christ and the Church in an indelible way.
6. *Sacraments require proper dispositions on our part.* If we want the sacraments to bear fruit in us, we must receive them worthily. We must have faith and use the gifts God gives to us through the sacraments.

Christ continues his work of preaching the good news and establishing his Father's kingdom through his Church. The Holy Spirit has helped the Church identify the seven sacraments as privileged signs and liturgical actions that build up the kingdom of God in a special way. These signs are "by the Church" because the Church is Christ's sacrament in the world. At the same time, they are also "for the Church" because they help make the Church. They do so by revealing to people the mystery of the Blessed Trinity's union of love with us through Christ. The seven sacraments are: Baptism, Confirmation, Eucharist, Penance, Anointing of the Sick, Matrimony, and Holy Orders.

sanctifying grace—The grace, or gift of God's friendship, that heals fallen human nature and gives us a share in the divine life of the Blessed Trinity. A habitual, supernatural gift, it makes us perfect, holy, and Christlike (*CCC*, 1999).

sacramental character—A lasting effect of Baptism, Confirmation, and Holy Orders that seals and configures the recipient to Christ in a special way. Baptism makes us a child of God; Confirmation makes us a witness of Jesus Christ; Holy Orders permanently designates a man as a bishop, priest, or deacon. These sacraments can be received only once.

I am the bread of life; whoever comes to me will never hunger, and whoever believes in me will never thirst. . . . For my flesh is true food, and my blood is true drink. Whoever eats my flesh and drinks my blood remains in me and I in him.

John 6:35, 55–56

Chapter 6 Outline

Our Need for Symbols and Signs

Humans need signs and symbols to express and deepen the mysteries of life. Baptism, Confirmation, and Eucharist are the three sacraments of initiation.

Baptism

Baptism is the gateway to the Church and the other sacraments.

Confirmation

Confirmation completes the sacramental grace of Baptism.

Eucharist

The Eucharist completes a Catholic's initiation into the Church. It is a memorial of the Lord's passion, death, and resurrection.

The Liturgical Year

Over the course of a year, the Church's liturgy celebrates the various mysteries of our redemption, recalling events in the life of Christ.

Chapter 6

The Sacraments of Initiation

Our Need for Signs and Symbols

In some hospitals where babies remain pending adoption, volunteers are sought to hold, cuddle, caress, and feed the infants. The regular staff simply does not have the time to give the loving attention these infants need. Medical science has dramatically shown how human touch and the interaction of human words help newborns thrive, trust their new world as a safe and warm place, and develop as healthy and well-adjusted human beings.

Because humans are composed of spirits and bodies, we all need signs and symbols to express and deepen mysteries like love. People need smiles, humorous cards, hugs, sympathetic words, kisses, handshakes, gifts, and other signs to communicate love. Jesus understands human nature and the need for signs and symbols that remind us that someone loves and cares for us. That is why he left his Church the *sacraments*, special symbols of God's love and important signs of grace and divine friendship. St. Augustine of Hippo defined sacrament as a "visible sign of an invisible reality, a visible sign of invisible grace." Through the sacraments, we both *perceive* and *receive* the invisible grace of God's own life. Through them, we experience the good news of God's love.

Jesus gave the sacraments to his Church to communicate God's life to us. Their purpose, according to the Second Vatican Council, is:

> to sanctify [people], to build up the body of Christ, and finally, to give worship to God. Because they are signs, they also instruct. They not only presuppose faith, but by words and objects they also nourish, strengthen, and express it (*Constitution on the Sacred Liturgy*, No. 59).

This chapter focuses on three sacraments that initiate us into God's People: Baptism, Confirmation, and the Eucharist. In Chapter 7, the Sacraments of Healing and ministry will be discussed.

Discussion Questions

1. What do you think convinced people in the first three centuries to enter the catechumenate despite its risks?
2. Who has been a model of faith for you?
3. About how many catechumens were initiated at your parish at the last Easter Vigil? About how many will be initiated this year?

Sacraments of Initiation

(*CCC*, 1229–1233; 1247–1249; 1275)

The three sacraments of initiation are Baptism, which brings new life in Christ; Confirmation, which strengthens the new life; and the Eucharist, which nourishes Catholics with Christ's body and blood. Together they "gather in" God's people and make us members of Christ's body, the Church. These sacraments give us the life of Christ and bestow the gift of the Holy Spirit so we can be Christ for others.

In the early Church most converts were adults. Christian initiation was seen as a journey that took place in stages. It was a serious decision to become a Christian, because people had to renounce sin and take on a new life in Christ. There was also a real danger of being persecuted or martyred, as Christianity was illegal through three centuries. A person studying to become a Christian was known as a **catechumen**. This same

catechumen—An unbaptized person who is preparing to receive all of the sacraments of Christian initiation.

term is used today. Catechumens had sponsors who helped them prepare through a three-year period of prayer, fasting, and self-denial before becoming members of the Church. The *catechumenate* ("period of preparation") coincided with the Paschal mystery of Christ's death and resurrection. Finally, after a forty-day period of prayer and formal instruction in the faith during **Lent** when the catechumens learned the creed and the Lord's Prayer, they received all three sacraments of initiation at the Easter Vigil, Holy Saturday.

During the first three centuries, the bishop was the main celebrant of the initiation sacraments. After questioning the candidates to see if they were seriously committed to Christ-like lives, he anointed them with oil. The candidates then disrobed and were plunged into the baptismal waters three times, each time expressing their faith in the Triune God. When they emerged from the water, their five senses were anointed and the Holy Spirit was invoked. This anointing was the sacrament of Confirmation. The new Catholics (called **neophytes**) received white garments to symbolize a new life in Christ. They also received candles to remind them of their new vocation to be the light of Christ. After common prayers and the sharing of a sign of peace, the Eucharist was celebrated. At this liturgy, the neophytes received their first Holy Communion

Following the legalization of Christianity in AD 313, most Catholics were baptized in infancy. Today, Holy Communion is typically received at age seven, the age of reason. However, when adults seek conversion, the Second Vatican Council has restored the ancient way of initiating adults into the Church. Its distinct steps, consisting of four periods and three stages, are found in the *Rite of Christian Initiation of Adults* (RCIA).

Each of the sacraments of initiation are examined in detail throughout the rest of this chapter.

Lent—A season of intensified prayer, fasting, and almsgiving in preparation of Christ's resurrection and our redemption at Easter. The season begins on Ash Wednesday and continues to Holy Thursday, a period of forty weekdays and six Sundays.

neophytes—Those newly received into the Church through the sacraments of initiation at the Easter vigil.

Coat of Arms

Create a personal coat of arms that symbolizes for you some of your goals, values, and dreams. Divide it into five sections. Draw simple pictures or find illustrations that capture your thoughts about the following:

1. Your idea of success.
2. Your concept of love.
3. Your most noteworthy achievement.
4. Your attitude toward Jesus.
5. The biggest obstacle that stands in the way of your growth.

Baptism

(*CCC*, 1214–1228; 1276–1277)

The word *Baptism* comes from a Greek word that means "to plunge" or "to immerse" into water. This symbolic plunging and rising up again from the water reminds us that a new Catholic enters into Christ's death and then rises to a new life of grace.

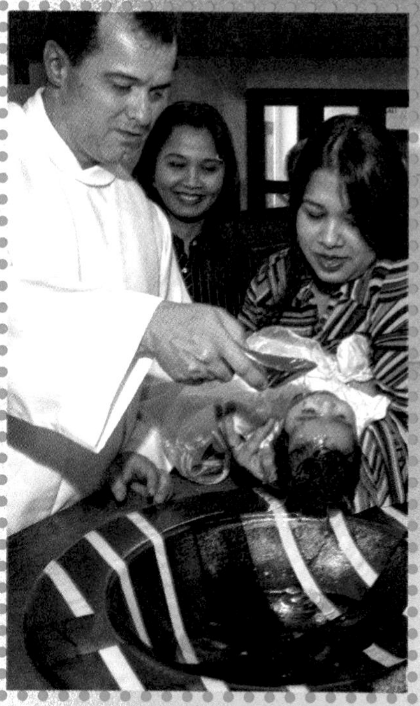

The sacrament of Baptism has its roots in Scripture. The Old Testament foreshadows this sacrament. For example, in the creation account in Genesis the Spirit of God overshadows the waters to bring life to the earth. This prefigures how today the Holy Spirit imparts new life at Baptism. Another Old Testament example comes in the story of the renewal of the earth following the Great Flood (see Gn 9). The New Testament tells how Jesus himself was baptized (see, for example, Mt 3:13–17). Also, before ascending to heaven, Jesus commanded:

> Go, therefore, and make disciples of all nations, baptizing them in the name of the Father, and of the Son, and of the holy Spirit, teaching them to observe all that I have commanded you" (Mt 28:19–20).

Beginning with the day of Pentecost, the Church has preached the need for Baptism. Through Baptism Catholics participate in the death, burial, and resurrection of Christ.

Infant Baptism

(*CCC*, 1234–1245; 1250–1256; 1278; 1282; 1284)

The Church has baptized infants from its earliest days. The practice of infant Baptism shows that salvation is a pure gift of Christ's grace that extends even to children. The practice of infant Baptism makes clear that the Church relies on the faith of the parents, godparents, and all the Church to ensure that the child is baptized in a faith-filled environment where they learn about the faith they have received.

essential rite—That portion of the liturgical celebration of a sacrament that is strictly necessary in order for the sacrament to be valid.

Chrism—Blessed by the bishop, this perfumed oil is used for anointing in the sacraments of Baptism, Confirmation, and Holy Orders. It represents the gift of the Holy Spirit.

Most infant Baptisms take place on Sunday, often as part of the Sunday liturgy. Even when not held as part of Mass, Baptisms should always take place in a company of believers. The rite of Baptism begins with a greeting from the ordinary minister of the sacrament (priest, deacon, or bishop). The baptismal rite includes an instruction to the parents and godparents to raise the child in a Christian home, a welcoming of the child, a proclamation of God's word, and prayers of exorcism to free the child from sin and Satan's power. The child is anointed with the Oil of Catechumens to proclaim that he or she is to be joined to Christ, the Anointed One. After the baptismal waters are blessed, those assembled recite their baptismal vows, and the parents and godparents state that they desire Baptism for their child. Next comes the **essential rite** of Baptism: The minister pours water on the head of the child three times (or immerses the child in water three times) and pronounces the words:

> "N., I baptize you in the name of the Father,
> and of the Son, and of the Holy Spirit.

After the Baptism, the crown of head is anointed a second time with sacred **Chrism** (perfumed oil), a white garment is placed on the child, and a lit candle is held by one of the parents. The celebrant touches the ears and mouth of the child and prays that the child will hear the gospel and proclaim his word. Everyone recites the Lord's Prayer, after which the celebrant concludes the ceremony by blessing the parents and everyone assembled.

The various symbols used in Baptism reveal important spiritual truths about its meaning:

- *Water.* Water represents cleansing. It also symbolizes death to an old life of sin and rebirth into a new life with Christ Jesus. Jesus told Nicodemus that he was living water, the source of all life. In Baptism we are reborn to a new life with Jesus Christ. Original sin is washed away, and we inherit eternal life as adopted children of God.
- *Oil.* In the ancient world, oil was used to anoint kings and queens to show that they were set apart from others. The natural symbol of oil also represents healing and protection. The title *Christ* means "anointed one." The oils of Baptism (Chrism) represent that we have been anointed in Jesus. We belong to him. We share in his life and salvation. We receive the Holy Spirit who protects, guides, and strengthens us. We also share in Christ's priestly and kingly ministries, sent by him to preach the good news of God's kingdom. We also help him in his healing ministry by serving others, especially the poor in our midst, and by working toward the unity of a wounded human community.
- *White garment.* When early Christians came out of the baptismal pool, they donned new white robes to represent rising with Christ. Today, the white cloth symbolizes "putting on Christ" (Gal 3:27). It is a symbol of purity, happiness, and a new identity of living in union with the Lord.
- *Candle.* The baptismal candle, lit from the Easter candle, reminds us how Christ is the light of the world and that his followers should be Christ's light to others.

Effects of Baptism (*CCC*, 1262–1274; 1279–1280)

The sacrament of Baptism is the gateway to the Church and the reception of the other sacraments. Its has many effects, including:

1. Baptism forgives both original and personal sin and remits all punishment due to sin. However, some consequences of sin remain, for example, suffering, weakness of character, inclination to sin (traditionally called *concupiscence*), and death.
2. Baptism gives us birth into a new life in Christ. It makes us a child of God and a temple of the Holy Spirit.
3. Baptism confers sanctifying grace, the grace of justification. This enables us to believe, hope, and love. Baptism also brings the Holy Spirit and the Spirit's gifts that enable us to grow in holiness and goodness.
4. Baptism initiates and incorporates us into Christ's Body, the Church. It empowers us to share in Christ's priestly ministry of worship and service. Baptism joins us to all Christians, even to those who are not yet fully united to the Catholic Church.
5. Baptism seals a Christian with an indelible spiritual *character* that marks us as belonging to Christ. This is why Baptism can be received only once and should never be given to someone who has already been baptized. This baptismal character consecrates us for Christian worship and binds us to the Lord. If we live our baptismal promises, Christ has promised a resurrected body and a life of happiness with God and all his people forever.

Water Symbolism

Read the following passages and note what water symbolizes in the particular context of the passage.

Exodus 17:2–7

Psalm 23:1–4

Ezekiel 47:1–12

Romans 6:1–5

Revelation 22:1

Writing Assignment

1. What would you say to a young couple who told you they were going to let their children decide when they are older whether they want to be baptized or not?
2. If you were the pastor of a parish, would you baptize the child of a mother and father who never came to Church? Why or why not?

Explaining Your Faith

Can unbaptized babies be saved?

Baptism is necessary for salvation because Jesus himself said to the Pharisee Nicodemus: "Amen, amen I say to you, no one can see the kingdom of God without being born from above" (Jn 3:3).

Traditionally the Church has taught that there are three forms of Baptism: baptism of water (through the sacrament of Baptism), baptism of blood (the death of martyrs who died for their faith before being baptized), and baptism of desire. *Baptism of desire* refers to catechumens who die before receiving the sacrament. Their turning from sin, desire to be baptized, and life of charity assure them of the salvation the sacrament conveys. Baptism of desire also applies to all those good people who have not been given the gift of faith, but whose lives show that they would have accepted Jesus Christ had they been given the chance on earth to know him.

The Church trusts that God's infinite and mysterious mercy will touch unbaptized babies because God wants everyone to be saved. Jesus himself showed tender love to children (Mk 10:14). However, since divine revelation does not specifically address the question of unbaptized infants, the Church asks parents to baptize their infants as soon as possible.

Discussion Questions

1. Who are your godparents? Why did your parents choose them?
2. What is the meaning of your Christian name? Why did your parents choose it?

Confirmation

(*CCC*, 1285; 1302–1311; 1316–1317; 1319)

The sacrament of Confirmation completes the sacramental grace of Baptism. Every Catholic who has been baptized, and yet not confirmed, should receive this sacrament. In the Western Church, once a person has reached "the age of discretion" he or she can be confirmed. However, in danger of death, even children should be confirmed. A candidate for this sacrament must profess the faith, be in the state of grace, intend to receive the sacrament, and be prepared to witness to our Lord Jesus Christ.

Today the sacrament of Confirmation is often received in the teen years to help represent a teen's increasing personal commitment to faith. In preparation for the sacrament, teens learn more about the Holy Spirit and how to use the Spirit's many gifts to serve the Church, including their own parish. Prayer and the sacrament of Penance are also part of the preparation for the sacrament. Those to be confirmed also choose a Confirmation sponsor to accompany them in preparation and at the rite. It is most appropriate that this be one of their baptismal godparents. The effects of the sacrament of Confirmation include:

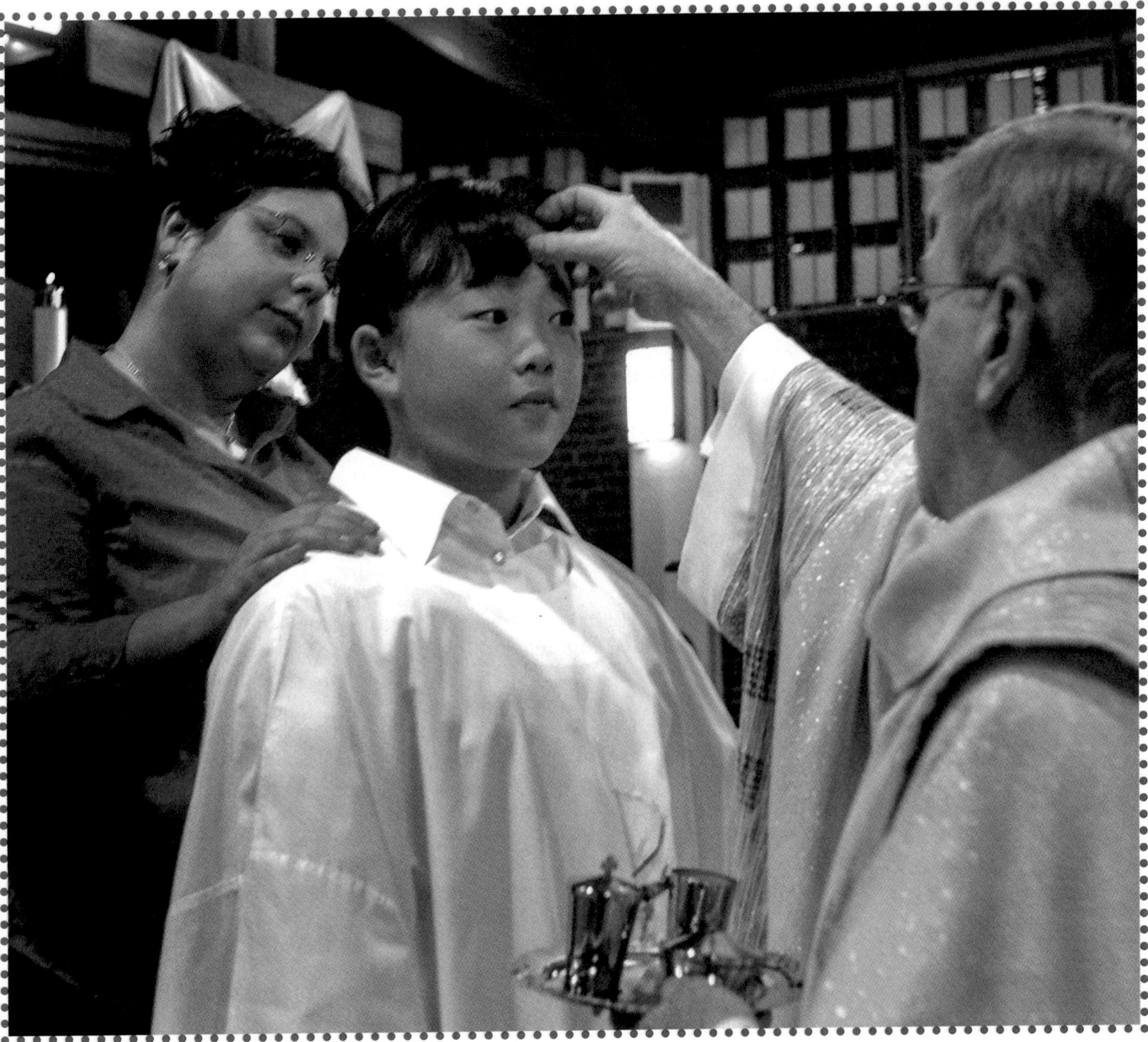

1. the full outpouring of the Holy Spirit, which makes it possible for us to cry out, "Abba! Father!";
2. binding us more closely to the Church and more firmly to Christ; and
3. increasing the gifts of the Holy Spirit in us, especially his strength to spread and defend the Christian faith by word and deed.

Confirmation, like Baptism, imprints an indelible spiritual mark on the soul, and so can be received only once. The sacramental character consists of marking Christians with the seal of the Holy Spirit, giving them the power to witness to the Lord. This completes the common priesthood of the faithful received in Baptism.

Biblical Roots and Historical Dimensions

(*CCC*, 1286–1292; 1297; 1312–1314; 1318)

Like the other sacraments, Confirmation is rooted in the Bible. For example, the Old Testament prophets promised that the Spirit would rest on the coming Messiah. At Jesus' Baptism, the Spirit did indeed rest on him. The Holy Spirit was present throughout Jesus' life. Examples include his conception by power of the Spirit, his public ministry of teaching and healing in union with the Spirit, and his promises to send the Holy Spirit to the Church.

The origin of the sacrament of Confirmation is found in the apostolic laying on of hands. Acts 19:1–6 tells the story of a group of new disciples who have been baptized by John the Baptist. Paul taught them about Jesus and baptized them in Jesus' name. When he laid hands on them, the Holy Spirit came upon them. They received special charisms, or gifts of the Spirit, namely the gifts of tongues and prophecy. An anointing with perfumed oil (Chrism) signifies the gift of the Holy Spirit. Chrism is related to the name *Christian*, meaning "anointed" of Christ, who was himself anointed with the Holy Spirit.

In the early Church, Baptism and Confirmation were part of the adult initiation process, which climaxed at the Easter vigil liturgy with the bishop presiding. In these early years, children probably joined their parents in the initiation process. Whole households became Christians together. As Christianity grew, infant baptisms multiplied. Because it became increasingly difficult for the bishop to be present at every Baptism, priests were allowed to baptize. However, the bishop wished to retain some role in the initiation process.

In the Western Church the custom grew of the bishop at some later date "confirming" the baptismal commitment of Christians baptized as infants. This practice emphasizes that each Christian is in communion with the bishop, who guarantees and serves Church unity, catholicity, and apostolicity. By the thirteenth century the Church saw the wisdom of teaching youngsters more about their baptismal commitment. Therefore, the time of preparation to receive Confirmation became a good time to give them further instruction in the faith.

Therefore, in the Western Church, *the bishop was and is the ordinary minister of Confirmation* for those who were baptized as infants. Confirmation takes place some time after a person reaches the age of reason, generally between seven and sixteen years. For a serious reason, the bishop can delegate priests to confirm. In the case of adult baptism, or Christian converts being accepted into the Catholic Church, the priest who baptizes or receives them also confirms them at the Easter vigil. And any priest can administer Confirmation when there is danger of death.

Eastern rite Churches administer all three initiation sacraments at the same time, including for infants. This stresses the unity of Christian initiation. In the Eastern rites, the priest confirms the new Christian after Baptism and then celebrates the first Eucharist. However, the priest confirms only with *myron* (or Chrism) which has been blessed by a bishop. This signifies the special bond with the bishop resulting from Confirmation.

Confirmation and the Holy Spirit

Read the following Scripture passages that cite the Holy Spirit. Answer the questions that accompany each reading.

Ezekiel 36:24–28 What does Yahweh promise to the Chosen People?

John 14:15–17 What quality of the Holy Spirit does Jesus emphasize in his promise?

Mark 1:9–11 When does the Holy Spirit descend on Jesus?

Romans 8:14–17 What does the Holy Spirit enable us to do?

Galatians 5:22–23 What qualities will a person who lives in the Spirit have?

The Rite of Confirmation (*CCC*, 1293–1296; 1298–1301; 1320–1321)

Like Baptism, Confirmation usually takes place during Eucharist, thus stressing the unity among the sacraments of initiation. The Confirmation liturgy begins with a renewal of baptismal promises and a profession of faith by those to be confirmed (*confirmands*). The bishop then extends his hands over them and invokes the outpouring of the Holy Spirit. The essential rite follows:

> The minister *anoints the forehead of the confirmand with sacred Chrism* (in the Eastern Churches, the other sense-organs as well), *lays on his hand, and recites the words: "Be sealed with the Gift of the Holy Spirit."* (In the Eastern Churches, the minister says, "The seal of the gift that is the Holy Spirit.")

A sign of peace concludes the rite, thus signifying unity with the bishop and the Church.

The anointing with oil in Confirmation represents total consecration to Christ, a sharing in Jesus' mission. The newly confirmed person is charged with bringing forth in word and deed "the aroma of Christ." The Confirmation anointing permanently marks the Christian with the seal of the Holy Spirit. In Confirmation, we are sealed totally to Jesus Christ to be servants of his gospel forever.

Discussion Questions

1. At what age do you think those who were baptized as infants should be confirmed? Why?
2. Name three things a confirmed Catholic can do to exhibit a commitment to his or her faith.
3. Why is Confirmation a sacrament that can be received only once?

Eastern Rite Churches

What do we mean when we refer to Eastern Rite Churches? Eastern Rite Churches are Catholic Churches following one of the six rites derived from the ancient traditions of Christian churches that were centered in Constantinople (modern Turkey). Eastern Rite Churches are in communion with the Pope and the Latin or Western Church.

The term *rite* refers to a special way of doing the liturgy, but it also refers to a variety of traditions, including: married clergy, special sacramental traditions like confirming baptized infants and giving them the Eucharist, and the use of ancient languages in liturgies. Eastern rite Churches have their own version of canon law (Church law) and are governed by a patriarch.

The Eastern Rite Churches are also called "Eastern Catholic Churches" or "Uniate Churches" (meaning, in union with the Roman Catholic Church). There are more than ten million Eastern Catholics. They belong to one of these six rites: Byzantine, Alexandrian or Coptic, Syriac, Armenian, Maronite, and Chaldean. There are subdivisions within each of these rites along national or ethnic lines.

Numerically, the largest group of Eastern Catholics belongs to the Byzantine rite.

Read and report on one of the Eastern Rite Churches listed above. View the following websites:

Eastern Catholic Rites: www.silk.net/RelEd/eastern.htm

Eastern Christianity: www.melkite.org/eastern.htm

Eastern Rites Today: www.catholicculture.org/docs/doc_view.cfm?RecNum=2729

Eucharist

(CCC, 1322–1344; 1356–1397; 1409–1412; 1414–1418)

The Eucharist completes a person's Christian initiation. It unites the new Catholic to Christ's sacrifice on the cross, a sacrifice of praise and thanksgiving to the Father. Through this wondrous gift, Christ continues to pour out his saving graces on the members of his body, the Church.

The Eucharist has its roots in Scripture. The Old Testament foreshadowed the Eucharist when the priest Melchizedek offered God bread and wine (Gn 14:18), when the Jews celebrated Passover to commemorate the Exodus from slavery (Ex 12:1–20), and when God gave manna to the Chosen People in the desert (Ex 16:4–35).

In the gospels, Jesus' multiplication of the loaves and his changing of water into wine at Cana prefigured the institution of the Eucharist. Moreover, Jesus made direct reference to the Eucharist in John's gospel (6:53–59) when he declared the importance of eating his body and drinking his blood, a hard teaching that caused some disciples to leave him. The Lord established the Eucharist at the Last Supper in the context of the Jewish feast of Passover. He took unleavened bread, blessed and broke it, and gave it to his apostles, saying:

> "This is my body, which will be given for you; do this in memory of me." And likewise the cup after they had eaten, saying, "This cup is the new covenant in my blood, which will be shed for you" (Lk 22:19–20).

Various Names for the Eucharist

We can never completely understand the Eucharist, since it is such a rich mystery of God's love for us. But by reflecting on some of its various names, we can begin to appreciate it more.

Eucharist

The term *Eucharist* in Greek means "thanksgiving." In this sacrament, we thank God for his gifts of creation; redemption through our Lord and Savior, Jesus Christ; and sanctification in the Holy Spirit.

Lord's Supper

The term *Lord's Supper* brings to mind the Last Supper. Jesus chose a Passover meal to launch the events of our salvation. A meal is a universal symbol of friendship and life. The Eucharist is Christ coming to us as our greatest friend and Savior and giving us a share in his own divine life.

Breaking the Bread (cf. Acts 2:42)

The apostles recognized Jesus in the *breaking of the bread* (Lk 24:35), a symbol for sacrificing and sharing. We are to be broken like the Lord as we serve others. We receive the bread of life to become the bread of life for others.

Eucharistic Assembly

Eucharistic assembly emphasizes how we celebrate the Eucharist in the midst of the assembled Church. Validly ordained priests are the only ones who can preside at this Eucharistic assembly, to consecrate the bread and wine so that these ordinary species can become the Body and Blood of the Lord (CCC, 1411).

Holy and Divine Liturgy

The Eucharist is the very heart of the Church's liturgical life. The term liturgy means "people's work." The *holy and divine liturgy* of the Eucharist is the supreme worship we can give God, "the source and summit of the Christian life" (*Dogmatic Constitution of the Church*, No. 11). This is why Church law requires Catholics to attend Mass on Sundays and holy days. The Sunday obligation comes from Jesus himself, who told us to break bread in his name. Weekly Mass attendance joins us to our brother and savior Jesus Christ and to one another in worship of the Father.

Most Blessed Sacrament

The Eucharist is the *Most Blessed Sacrament*. The consecrated Eucharistic species reserved in the tabernacle also go by this name. The essential signs of the Eucharistic sacrifice are wheat bread and grape wine. In the Eucharistic liturgy, the priest consecrates bread and wine by invoking the blessing of the Holy Spirit. He does so with the words of Jesus himself: "This is my body which has been given up for you. . . . This is the cup of my blood. . . ."

Holy Sacrifice

The word *sacrifice* means "to make holy." The Eucharist is a memorial of our Lord's passion, death, and resurrection. It makes present Christ's sacrifice and includes the offering of the Church. The shedding of his blood on Calvary was Christ's supreme act of love. It makes us holy and pleasing to God because:

1. Jesus is the High Priest and the victim who offers himself through the celebrant and the assembly in praise, thanksgiving, petition, and atonement to Almighty God.
2. It makes present Christ's sacrifice on the cross by memorializing it and by applying its fruits to the members of Christ's body. Because the Church is the Body of Christ, the Eucharist is also the sacrifice of the Christian faithful, the whole Church, including the pope, bishop of the local diocese, minister of the Eucharist, and the communion of saints. It involves their adoration, prayers, sufferings, and works.
3. It celebrates the presence of Christ by the power of his word and spirit. The Lord is uniquely present in the Eucharistic species, the consecrated blood and wine, which are the body and blood of Christ.

transubstantiation—The term used to describe what happens at the consecration of the bread and wine at Mass when their entire substance is turned into the entire substance of the Body and Blood of Christ, even though the appearances of bread and wine remain. The Eucharistic presence of Christ begins at the moment of consecration and endures as long as the Eucharistic species subsist.

Holy Communion

The Eucharist unites us with Christ and forms us into his body, the Church. In the Eucharist "the body and blood, together with the soul and divinity, of our Lord Jesus Christ and, therefore, *the whole Christ is truly, really, and substantially* contained" (CCC, 1374, quoting the teaching of the Council of Trent). This presence of Christ in the consecrated species of bread and wine is called the "real presence." Exactly how Jesus is present in the consecrated bread and wine is a mystery. The term **transubstantiation** expresses that at the consecration of the Mass the reality (the substance) of the bread and wine change into the reality of Jesus—his risen, glorified body and blood. The Lord is present whole and entire in each species from the moment of consecration for as long as the Eucharistic species subsist (see CCC, 1377).

The Church encourages us to receive *Holy Communion* every time we participate in a Eucharistic liturgy. (The bare minimum, though, is at least once a year, if possible during the Easter season.) However, we must receive Holy Communion worthily, that is, we must be in the state of sanctifying grace.

The Eucharist communicates God's very life to us by giving us the Risen Lord himself, who, by power of the Holy Spirit, binds us together and makes us the Church. Among the many graces of "Holy Communion" are:

1. Spiritual life and nourishment.
2. Cleansing from *past* sins by wiping away venial sin and preservation from *future* mortal sins. (The sacrament of Penance is the proper sacrament to gain forgiveness of mortal sin. The Eucharist is the sacrament for those who are in the state of sanctifying grace, in full communion with the Church.)
3. A greater commitment to the poor, because when we receive Christ in Holy Communion, we must recognize him in the poorest people in our midst.
4. Increase in the theological virtues of faith, hope, and love and strengthening of the gifts and fruits of the Holy Spirit.
5. Spiritual energy for our earthly pilgrimage, a foretaste of heaven, and union with the Blessed Mother and the saints in heaven.

In sum, the Eucharist puts us in touch with the saving effects of the Paschal mystery, the eternal life that Jesus' sacrifice has won for us.

Holy Mass

The term *Holy Mass* derives from the sending forth in the dismissal rite (in Latin, *Ite missa est*). We are to become for others the Christ we receive in the Blessed Sacrament of the Eucharist.

The Celebration of Mass (*CCC*, 1345–1355; 1408)

The Mass consists of two major parts—the *Liturgy of the Word* and the *Liturgy of the Eucharist*. In the Liturgy of the Word we hear God's word and are called to respond to it. The Liturgy of the Eucharist celebrates the Paschal mystery of Jesus Christ's love for us. The order of the Mass is as listed in the following subsections.

Introductory Rites

Entrance and Greeting. The Mass begins with the congregation standing and singing an appropriate song. The celebrant and people make the Sign of the Cross. The priest greets the people.

Penitential Rite. To worship with a pure heart, we acknowledge our sinfulness and ask for God's forgiveness.

Gloria. A prayer of praise and thanksgiving to the Triune God is shared.

Opening Prayer. The priest offers a prayer of supplication, which recalls the mystery of salvation proper to the day or feast.

Liturgy of the Word

The First Reading and *Responsorial Psalm*. Typically, the first reading comes from the Old Testament. Its theme is similar to the message of the gospel. The psalm response, either sung or recited, shows that we plan to take God's word to heart.

Second Reading and *Alleluia* or *Acclamation*. The second reading usually comes from one of St. Paul's letters and often deals with a problem facing followers of Jesus. It is not explicitly connected to the other readings. The Alleluia verse is our resounding "yes" to God's word.

Gospel. The most important reading is from a gospel, thus linking us to the Word of God, Jesus the Lord. Standing is a sign of reverence. Signing ourselves with a small cross on the forehead, lips, and heart symbolizes our commitment to make God's word come alive in what we think, say, and do.

Homily. The celebrant or another priest or deacon preaches the homily to apply Scripture to our lives.

The Creed. Our profession of faith in the Nicene Creed expresses our common belief. It binds us more closely as a community.

General Intercessions. Here we pray with confidence that the Lord will take care of our needs and those of our world.

Liturgy of the Eucharist

Offertory. The bread and wine are brought to the altar in procession. The prayer said over these gifts tells of God's goodness that we now offer back to God. The congregation offers a Sunday collection to support the Church's ministries and those who are in need.

The Eucharistic Prayer. This prayer is the heart of the Eucharistic liturgy. The *preface* (an introductory prayer) reminds us of our duty to thank the Father through Jesus Christ in the Holy Spirit. The entire congregation assents to the preface by singing or reciting a hymn of praise called the *Sanctus* ("Holy, Holy, Holy").

The Church has four standard Eucharistic prayers, used on different occasions. Each of these prayers:

- ★ invokes the power of the Holy Spirit (the *epiclesis*);
- ★ recounts the words of institution spoken by Jesus at the Last Supper, remembers and acknowledges Christ's saving deeds (*anamnesis*), and offers the sacrifice of Jesus to the Father;

Discussion Questions

1. A friend has told you that she stopped going to Mass because she was bored with the repetitious ritual. What could you say to her to help her reconsider?
2. What are some other excuses you have heard that teens (and others) use not to go to Mass on Sunday? Discuss a good response to each of them.
3. Tell about the most memorable liturgy you have ever participated in.

- contains intercessions that petition God for peace and various intentions of the whole community;
- concludes with the Great Amen, in which we respond with a resounding "yes" affirming we agree with what was prayed.

Communion Rite. The communion rite includes the Lord's Prayer, the prayer for deliverance, the prayer for peace, the sharing of a sign of peace, and the breaking of the bread while the *Lamb of God* is sung or recited. The congregation approaches the altar to receive the food of salvation, God's heavenly gift to us—the Risen Lord. The communion rite closes with a prayer of petition on behalf of the community.

Concluding Rite

After any announcements, the Mass concludes when the celebrant blesses and dismisses the people. We are to "go in peace to love and serve the Lord" as the priest and others process out to the singing of an appropriate song.

Preparing A Homily

Locate the readings that will be used at next Sunday's liturgy. (You can find them at the website of the United States Conference of Catholic Bishops: www.usccb.org/nab/index.htm.) Read and summarize the main themes of the readings. Then, prepare a short outline of a talk you could give on these readings to a group of primary school students. *Hint:* Look for a central theme in the first reading and the gospel. Arrange to share your homily in a religious education class for the primary age you chose.

The Liturgical Year

(*CCC*, 1163–1173; 1193–1195)

Sunday is the Lord's Day, the day Christ rose from the dead. Sunday is the day that all Catholics are required to attend Mass. At the Sunday Mass we listen to God's word, and the Paschal mystery is made present to us. We thank God for our Savior Jesus Christ and receive him in Holy Communion. Sunday is also a time for us to celebrate family life and seek rest from work.

Over the course of a year, the Church's liturgy celebrates the various mysteries of our redemption, including the incarnation of Jesus Christ, the major events of his teaching ministry, his ascension, the sending of the Holy Spirit on Pentecost, and the future anticipation of Jesus' Second Coming. The Church's liturgical calendar is organized as follows:

1. ***Advent.*** Advent prepares for Christ's coming. It begins at the end of November and lasts for four Sundays.

2. *Christmas Season.* This period begins with Christmas, a feast that proclaims *Emmanuel,* "God is with us!" This joyful season also celebrates the feasts of the Holy Family, the Solemnity of Mary (January 1), and Jesus' Epiphany or manifestation to the Magi. The season ends with the feast of the Lord's Baptism.

Advent—The four-week season in the liturgical year that prepares for the coming of our Savior on Christmas.

3. *Ordinary Time 1.* Between the Christmas season and Lent, the Church does not celebrate any particular aspect of the Christian mystery. Rather, the readings take the gospels in sequence: Matthew (Cycle A), Mark (Cycle B), and Luke (Cycle C). (John's gospel is read during the Lenten and Easter season and for some of the Ordinary time in Cycle B since Mark's gospel is short.) Participating in the Sunday liturgy over a three-year period exposes us to much of the gospel.
4. *Lent.* The word lent comes from an Anglo-Saxon word for "spring." Beginning on Ash Wednesday, Lent prepares us for the solemn and joyful feast of Easter. Lent lasts six Sundays and forty weekdays, concluding on Holy Thursday with the celebration of the Lord's Last Supper.

   Historically, catechumens prepared for Baptism during Lent. Today's *Rite of Christian Initiation for Adults* continues this tradition by preparing the *elect* for the initiation sacraments of the Church. Lent also calls all baptized Christians to renew their own baptismal commitment through penance and prayer.

Triduum—The three-day long liturgy that is the Church's most solemn celebration of the Paschal mystery. It begins with the Mass of the Lord's Supper on Holy Thursday, continues through the Good Friday service, and ends on Holy Saturday with the conclusion of the Easter vigil. Although it takes place over three days, the Triduum is considered one single liturgy.

5. ***Triduum.*** Easter is the center of the liturgical year and of the Christian faith. Easter celebrates our redemption in Christ and his promise of everlasting life. It consists of a Triduum (three days): 1) sunset of Holy Thursday to sunset of Good Friday, 2) sunset of Good Friday to sunset of Holy Saturday, and 3) sunset of Holy Saturday to the sunset or Evening Prayer of Easter Sunday. Easter is celebrated on the first Sunday after the first full moon of the spring equinox and is thus a moveable feast.
6. *Easter Season.* This joyful season consists of the fifty days from Easter to Pentecost Sunday. Readings focus on the themes of resurrection and living a life of grace. The final ten days of the Easter Season celebrate the promise and gift of the Holy Spirit. Ascension Thursday occurs forty days after Easter. Pentecost Sunday (fifty days after Easter) celebrates the descent of the Holy Spirit, the event in salvation history that inaugurated the Church.
7. *Ordinary Time 2.* Ordinary Time resumes after the Easter season and proceeds to Advent and a new Church Year. Trinity Sunday is celebrated one week after Pentecost, and the feast of Corpus Christi one week later. The other Sundays in Ordinary Time look to the teaching and ministry of Jesus. Near the end of this period, the readings focus on the end of time and Christ's Second Coming. The feast of Christ the King is the last Sunday of the Church Year.

sacramentals—Sacred signs (for example, objects, places, and actions) that resemble the sacraments. Through the prayers of the Church, spiritual effects are signified and obtained.

icons—Religious images or paintings that are traditional among many Eastern Christians.

In addition, during the annual cycle of celebrating Christ's life, the Church honors Mary, Mother of God, with a special love. She is an excellent example of the faithful disciple who took Christ's words to heart. In the same way, the Church honors saints and martyrs as a way to provide us with models of Christian holiness.

Sacramentals *(CCC,* 1667–1679)

Sacramentals are sacred signs that resemble the sacraments. They include objects, actions, and prayers that help us become aware of Christ's presence. Sacramentals prepare us to receive the sacraments. The Church institutes and blesses these holy signs that can gain spiritual benefits for us through the Church's intercession. The spiritual value of sacramentals depends on our personal faith and devotion. This is not the case with the sacraments because our Lord works through them even when our faith is weak.

Examples of sacramentals include *actions* like blessings (for example, persons, meals, objects, and places), genuflections before the Blessed Sacrament, and the sign of the cross; *objects* like candles, holy water, statues and **icons**, blessed palms, rosary beads, relics, vestments, scapulars, Church buildings, crosses, and religious medals; *places* like the Holy Land, Rome, Lourdes, places of pilgrimage, chapels, and retreat centers; *prayers* like grace recited before meals; and *sacred time* like holy days, feasts of saints, and Fridays in Lent.

Besides the sacraments and the sacramentals, many other popular devotions enrich our lives as Catholics. They do not replace the liturgy; rather, they extend it. You are probably familiar with many of these; for example, the recitation of the rosary, Stations of the Cross, and novenas.

Your Favorites

Share two favorite sacramentals with the class. Offer an explanation of their meaning.

- ★ St. Augustine of Hippo defined sacrament as "a visible sign of an invisible reality, a visible sign of invisible grace."
- ★ The sacraments make us holy, build up Christ's body, and give worship to God.
- ★ The sacraments of initiation are Baptism, Confirmation, and the Eucharist.
- ★ In the early Church, new converts entered a three-year period of preparation known as the *catechumenate* before receiving the three sacraments of initiation on Holy Saturday.
- ★ Today, most in the Western Church are baptized as infants. Bishops, priests, and deacons are the ordinary ministers of Baptism.
- ★ The essential rite of Baptism includes the pouring of water (or immersion) and the words, "N., I baptize you in the name of the Father, and of the Son, and of the Holy Spirit." The main symbols of Baptism are water, oil, white garment, and candle.
- ★ Baptism forgives original and personal sin, gives us new life in Christ, adopts us into God's family, and makes us a temple of the Holy Spirit. It confers sanctifying grace, incorporates us into the Church, and seals us with an indelible character that consecrates us in a unique way to our Lord and Savior.
- ★ The effects of the sacrament of Confirmation include the full outpouring of the Holy Spirit, binding more closely to the Church and more firmly to Christ, and increasing the gifts of the Holy Spirit, especially the strength to spread and defend the Christian faith.
- ★ The sacramental character of Confirmation seals the recipient to the Holy Spirit and gives him or her the power to witness to the Lord.
- ★ The bishop is the ordinary minister of Confirmation for those who were baptized as infants. The essential rite of Confirmation includes the minister of the sacrament anointing the forehead of the one being confirmed with Chrism, the laying on of hands, and the recitation of the words, "Be sealed with the Gift of the Holy Spirit."
- ★ Jesus instituted the Eucharist at the Last Supper. Eucharist means "thanksgiving." In this sacrament we thank God for his many gifts, especially for redemption through his Son and sanctification by the Holy Spirit.
- ★ We refer to the Eucharist as the Lord's Supper to recall his Passover that won our salvation.
- ★ The Eucharist is also the holy and divine liturgy, the supreme worship we give God, "the source and summit of Christian life." By calling the Eucharist "the most Blessed Sacrament," we are acknowledging the presence of Christ in the consecrated bread and wine which we receive as Holy Communion and which we worship in the tabernacle. The Eucharist is also the Holy Sacrifice of the Mass. It is the sacrifice offered by Jesus the high Priest and Victim that memorializes his Paschal mystery.
- ★ When we receive Holy Communion, we receive the body and blood of our Lord Jesus Christ who is truly, really, and substantially present under the form of bread and wine.
- ★ The Eucharist gives us spiritual life, cleanses us from venial sin and helps preserve us from mortal sin, increases in us the theological virtues, gives us spiritual energy and a foretaste of heaven, and unites us with the Blessed Mother and saints in heaven.
- ★ Catholics are called to celebrate the Eucharist each Sunday (or the Vigil Mass on Saturday evening) to commemorate the Paschal mystery and to recall the Lord's Day—his resurrection on Easter Sunday.
- ★ The Church Year consists of Advent, Christmas Season, Ordinary Time 1, Lenten Season, Easter, Easter Season, and Ordinary Time 2. The center of the liturgical year and of our Christian faith is Easter.

★ Sacramentals—including objects, actions, and prayers—resemble the sacraments and prepare us to receive them. Their spiritual value depends on our personal faith and devotion.

Review Questions

1. What is the purpose of the sacraments?
2. Name the sacraments of initiation.
3. Explain the initiation process for adults in the early Church.
4. What are some Old and New Testament scriptural roots for Baptism?
5. What is the essential rite of Baptism?
6. List and discuss the meaning of three important symbols used in Baptism.
7. Discuss four effects of receiving the sacrament of Baptism.
8. When is Confirmation ordinarily administered in the Western Church?
9. List three effects of the sacrament of Confirmation.
10. Who is the ordinary minister of the sacrament of Confirmation in the Western Church? in the Eastern Church?
11. List three scriptural roots of Confirmation.
12. Explain the essential rite of Confirmation.
13. Explain three meanings of anointing with the oil of Confirmation.
14. Name some scriptural roots for the Eucharist.
15. When did Jesus institute the Eucharist?
16. What does the term *Eucharist* mean?
17. Briefly note an important truth that we can learn about the Eucharist when we speak of it as:
    - The Lord's Supper
    - Breaking the Bread
    - Holy and Divine Liturgy
    - Blessed Sacrament
    - Holy Sacrifice
    - Holy Communion
    - Mass
18. Name four spiritual effects of the sacrament of the Eucharist.
19. What are the main divisions in the Church Year?
20. Define *sacramental.* Give five examples of sacramentals.

Applying What You Have Learned

1. Prepare a report on the Jewish Passover Meal. Note several ways the Eucharistic liturgy resembles it.
2. Report on a particular aspect of the liturgy (e.g., history, vestments, vessels). Search the Internet using the words "vestments" and "sacred vessels."
3. Make visits to several other Catholic churches. Take pictures of the altar, crucifix, and other appropriate signs and symbols inside the church. Prepare a presentation for your classmates.
4. Read the following passages from the gospels. Summarize what took place when Jesus celebrated meals with others.

   Matthew 9:9–13   Luke 7:36–50
   John 21:9–17   Luke 19:1–10
5. Design an appropriate symbol for one of the sacraments.

PrayerReflection

A good spiritual practice is to visit our Lord in the Blessed Sacrament either in your school chapel or your parish church. Here are a few suggestions on how to approach our Lord:

1. St. Teresa of Avila suggested using a variety of images when praying to Jesus. For example, you can "speak to him as with a father, or a brother, or a lord, or as with a spouse; sometimes in one way, at other times in another" (*The Way of Perfection*, 28:3). Tell the Lord how your day is going.
2. Speak to Jesus as you would to your best friend. Tell him about what is worrying you. Settle down and let his healing presence calm your heart.
3. Simply sit in the presence of the Lord. There is no need to say anything because your friend knows you are there.
4. Recite the following prayer attributed to St. Patrick. Say it slowly, pausing after each line:

I rise up today,
The power of God directing me,
The strength of God supporting me,
The wisdom of God guiding me,
The eye of God looking before me,
The ear of God listening to me,
The hand of God protecting me,
The way of God stretching out before me,
The shield of God defending me,
The angels of God guarding me,
against snares of devils,
against temptations of vices,
against inclinations of nature,
against everyone who will wish evil to me.
Christ with me, Christ before me, Christ behind me,
Christ in me, Christ beneath me, Christ above me,
Christ on my right hand, Christ on my left hand,
Christ where I sit, Christ where I arise,
Christ in the heart of everyone who thinks of me,
Christ in the mouth of everyone who speaks of me,
Christ in every eye that sees me,
Christ in every ear that hears me.

5. Ask yourself: Where is Christ in my life?

Is anyone among you sick? He should summon the presbyters of the Church, and they should pray over him and anoint (him) with oil in the name of the Lord, and the prayer of faith will save the sick person, and the Lord will raise him up. If he has committed any sins, he will be forgiven.

James 5:14–15

Chapter 7 Outline

Christ for One Another
The Sacraments of Healing—Penance and the Anointing of the Sick—continue Jesus' work of healing.

Penance
Christ gave the Church the sacrament of Penance to forgive post-baptismal sins.

Anointing of the Sick
The sacrament of the Anointing of the Sick brings Jesus' healing to those suffering from serious illness, the elderly, those facing major surgery, and the dying.

Holy Orders
Holy orders consecrates certain baptized men to one of the three degrees of a sacred order and makes them bishop, priest, or deacon.

Matrimony
Christ enters into the covenant of love between a man and woman and makes it a sacrament.

Chapter 7

The Sacraments of Healing and Ministry

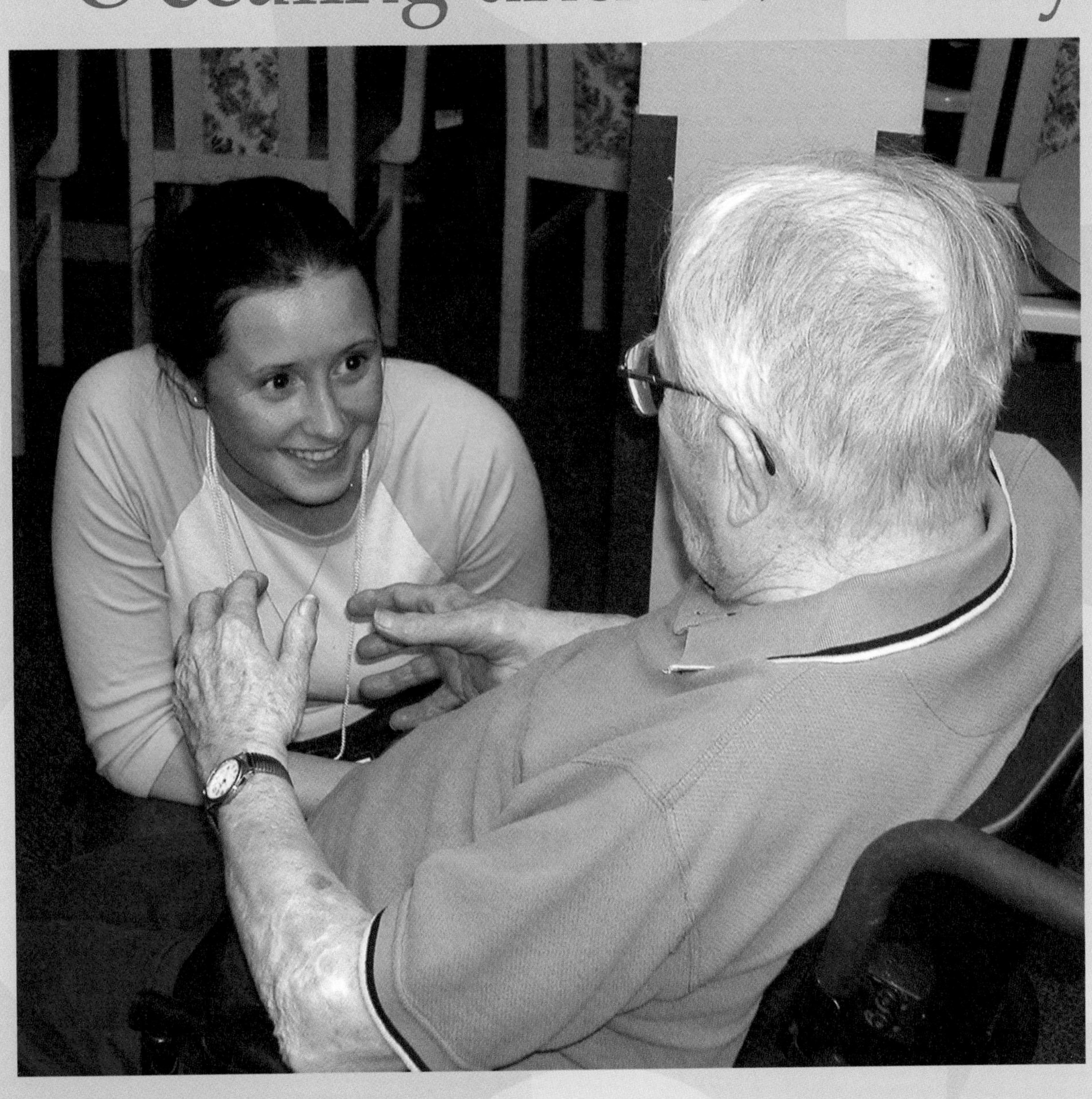

bishop—A successor to the apostles who governs the local Church in a given diocese and governs the worldwide Church in union with the pope and the college of bishops. A bishop receives the fullness of the sacrament of Holy Orders.

Anointing of the Sick—A sacrament of healing, administered by a priest to a baptized person, in which the Lord extends his loving, healing touch through the Church to those who are seriously ill or dying.

Christ for One Another

Once there was a village parish that had fallen upon hard times. Only five members remained, the pastor and four parishioners. They were all more than sixty years old.

Nearby in the mountains lived a retired **bishop**. One day, the pastor went to the bishop for his advice on how to save the parish. After a long conversation, the bishop had only this to say: "The only thing I can tell you is that the Messiah has come back and he is one of *you*."

The pastor returned to his small flock and reported what the bishop had said. In the following months, the elderly parishioners talked and thought about the bishop's words and began to treat each other, including themselves, with great respect, patience, care, and kindness, just in case one of them might really be the Messiah.

Months passed. Soon visitors to the parish noticed how kind and gentle the five old members were to each other and their visitors. Without being able to explain it, more and more people began to come back to the church for Mass. They started to bring their friends, who in turn brought their friends. Before long, the small parish had once again become a thriving faith-filled community.[8]

There is only one Messiah—our Lord Jesus Christ. But Catholics are called to minister to one another in Jesus' name. The sacraments help us live out Jesus' ministry:

1. Christ continues to show his compassion to us through the sacraments of Penance and **Anointing of the Sick**. He forgives our sins in the sacrament of conversion and helps suffering people with his graces in the sacrament of the sick.
2. The **sacrament of Holy Orders** calls men to minister to us in Jesus' place.
3. The **sacrament of Matrimony** helps married couples be Christ to each other and their families.

Our common ministry often involves reaching out to others in times of sin and suffering. As you observe the cruelty and injustice that takes place in this world, you have probably called out with many who have come before you, "Why does God permit suffering?"

Suffering is directly related to sin. Both suffering and sin are tied to God's gift of free will. In order for God to have made people perfectly free, the possibility of humans choosing to do evil has always existed. Suffering is the result of sinful choices.

Jesus was asked the question about why people suffer. He never gave a clear explanation. Rather, when he encountered a person in need of either physical or spiritual healing, all Jesus did was heal the person or forgive his or her sins. In the cure of the paralytic (see Mk 2:1–12) Jesus did both. To show that he had been given the power to forgive sins he said to the man, "I order you: get up, pick up your stretcher, and go home."

The Sacraments of Healing—Penance and the Anointing of the Sick—continue Jesus' work of healing. These sacraments do not provide answers to why people must hurt, why people must suffer. Instead, they seek simply to heal the hurt, heal the suffering that people are feeling.

Undoing much of the suffering of the world and making the world a better place to live are part of the effects of the sacraments of Holy Orders and Matrimony. These are two sacraments that build up Christian life. Both of them involve love and service, two essential features of our living together in the same Body of Christ.

This chapter presents the Sacraments of Healing and the Sacraments at the Service of Communion in more detail.

Talents to Serve

Everyone has a vocation, a calling to bring Christ into the world. Examine your talents and your call to serve others by doing the following:

1. Read the following New Testament passages.

   1 Corinthians 12:4–11
   Matthew 25:31–40
   John 13:1–20

2. Reflect on your gifts. Choose one of your talents. How can you use it in the coming week to help someone at home, school, parish, or work? Write your answers to the following questions:

- What is my talent?
- How can I use it for others?
- Who will benefit from my generosity?
- What is my specific plan of action?
- How can I check the results of my service?

Discussion Questions

1. What concrete things do you imagine the parishioners of the small church did for one another that made their parish so attractive and inviting that visitors returned and brought friends?
2. How have you come to grips with the perennial question, "Why does God permit suffering?"
3. What are some questions you have about the sacraments of Penance, Anointing of the Sick, Holy Orders, and Matrimony as you begin study of this chapter?

sacrament of Holy Orders— The sacrament of apostolic ministry at the service of communion whereby Christ, though the Church, ordains men through the laying on of hands. It includes three degrees: episcopate, presbyterate, and diaconate. Those who exercise these orders are bishops, priests, and deacons.

sacrament of Matrimony— A sacrament at the Service of Communion in which Christ binds a man and woman into a permanent covenant of love and life and bestows his graces on them to help them live as a community and as a loving family, if he blesses them with children.

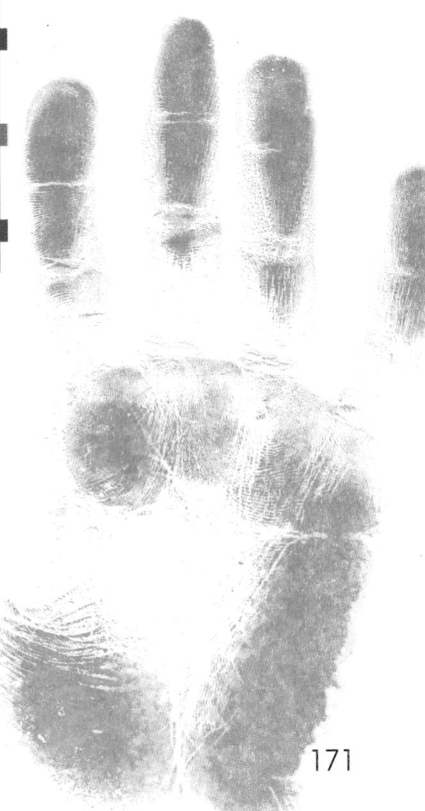

sacrament of Penance—A Sacrament of Healing, also known as reconciliation or confession, through which Christ extends his forgiveness to sinners, bringing about reconciliation with God and the Church. Its essential elements consist of the acts of the penitent (contrition, confession of sins, and satisfaction) and the prayer of absolution of the priest.

absolution—The prayer by which a priest, by the power given to the Church by Christ Jesus, pardons a repentant sinner in the sacrament of Penance.

Penance

(*CCC*, 1422–1438; 1440–1446; 1461–1470; 1486–1495)

Even though we receive new life in the sacraments of initiation, we still have a weakened human nature. We are still tempted to commit sin, a condition known as concupiscence. The Christian life requires lifelong conversion. That is why Christ has given the Church a sacrament of conversion called the **sacrament of Penance,** a great help on our spiritual journey. For Catholics, individual and integral confession of our sins in this sacrament, followed by **absolution,** is the ordinary way of reconciliation with God and the Church. Jesus chose this sign of love to show, in a personal way, his merciful forgiveness to individual sinners.

The sacrament of Penance is also called *conversion*, *confession*, *forgiveness*, and *reconciliation*. Each of these names reveals something important about this sacrament of healing.

As the sacrament of *conversion*, Penance takes seriously Jesus' call to repent, the first step in returning to our loving Father. A gift from the Holy Spirit, conversion or repentance helps us to return to our Lord after we sin and to have the courage to begin anew. Conversion involves changing our lives by rooting out sin, by hating the evil we have committed, by firmly intending to sin no more, and by trusting in God's infinite mercy and grace.

The term *confession* highlights a key element of the sacrament—telling our sins to the priest. In this sacrament we also "confess," that is, praise God for the great mercy God extends to us.

Calling this sacrament the sacrament of *forgiveness* reminds us that God imparts pardon and peace through the priest's words of absolution. Sin is a great evil because it offends God's honor and love, causes a break in our union with God, disfigures the sinner who is made in God's image, and ruptures our relationship with other members of Christ's body, the Church. Only God can forgive sin. He gave us his Son, whose major mission among us was to forgive sin and to associate with sinners, to show how much God loves his wayward children.

Christ also gave the power to absolve, that is, to forgive sin, to the apostles and their successors, a ministry carried on today by our bishops and priests (Mt 16:19). Through the formula of absolution, the bishop or priest proclaims God's forgiveness of the sinner. When the priest holds his hands over the penitent's head and recites the words, "I absolve you from your sins in the name of the Father, and of the Son, and of the Holy Spirit," Christ himself is giving us the sign we need to know that God forgives us.

The sacrament is called the sacrament of *reconciliation* because God's loving forgiveness:

- reconciles (unites) us with God and the Church, whom we have alienated by our sins;
- brings peace of conscience and spiritual comfort;
- strengthens us to live the Christian life;
- takes away some of the temporal punishment due to sin;
- remits fully the eternal punishment that results from mortal sin; and

★ prepares us for our meeting with our Divine Judge when we die by teaching us how to repent, do penance, and have faith in a loving and merciful God.

Finally, the official name, the sacrament of *Penance,* stresses that, when we turn from sin, we must do penance and make satisfaction for the sins we have committed. A sign of inner conversion is being willing to do external actions of penance. Examples are fasting, prayer, and almsgiving—three traditional acts that express conversion in relation to self, God, and others. We can also express interior conversion by being peacemakers, praying for our neighbors, praying to the saints, receiving the Eucharist, doing other acts of charity like showing concern for the poor, and accepting the trials and sufferings that come into our lives.

Rite of Penance

(*CCC,* 1447–1460; 1480–1484; 1491; 1497)

The way the sacrament of Penance is celebrated has changed through the ages. In the earliest centuries it was tied to rigorous public penances and often celebrated only once a lifetime. Around the seventh century, private, individual, devotional confession to a priest became the norm. This is the form we celebrate today. However, two essential elements of the sacrament were always present. They are:

1. The *acts of the penitent,* which include:

★ ***Contrition,*** which is genuine sorrow for one's sins, a detesting of them, and firmly resolving not to sin again. *Perfect* contrition is sorrow that comes from love of God. *Imperfect* contrition comes from other motives, for example, fear of punishment.

contrition—Heartfelt sorrow and aversion for sins committed along with the intention of sinning no more. Contrition is the most important act of penitents, necessary for receiving the sacrament of Penance.

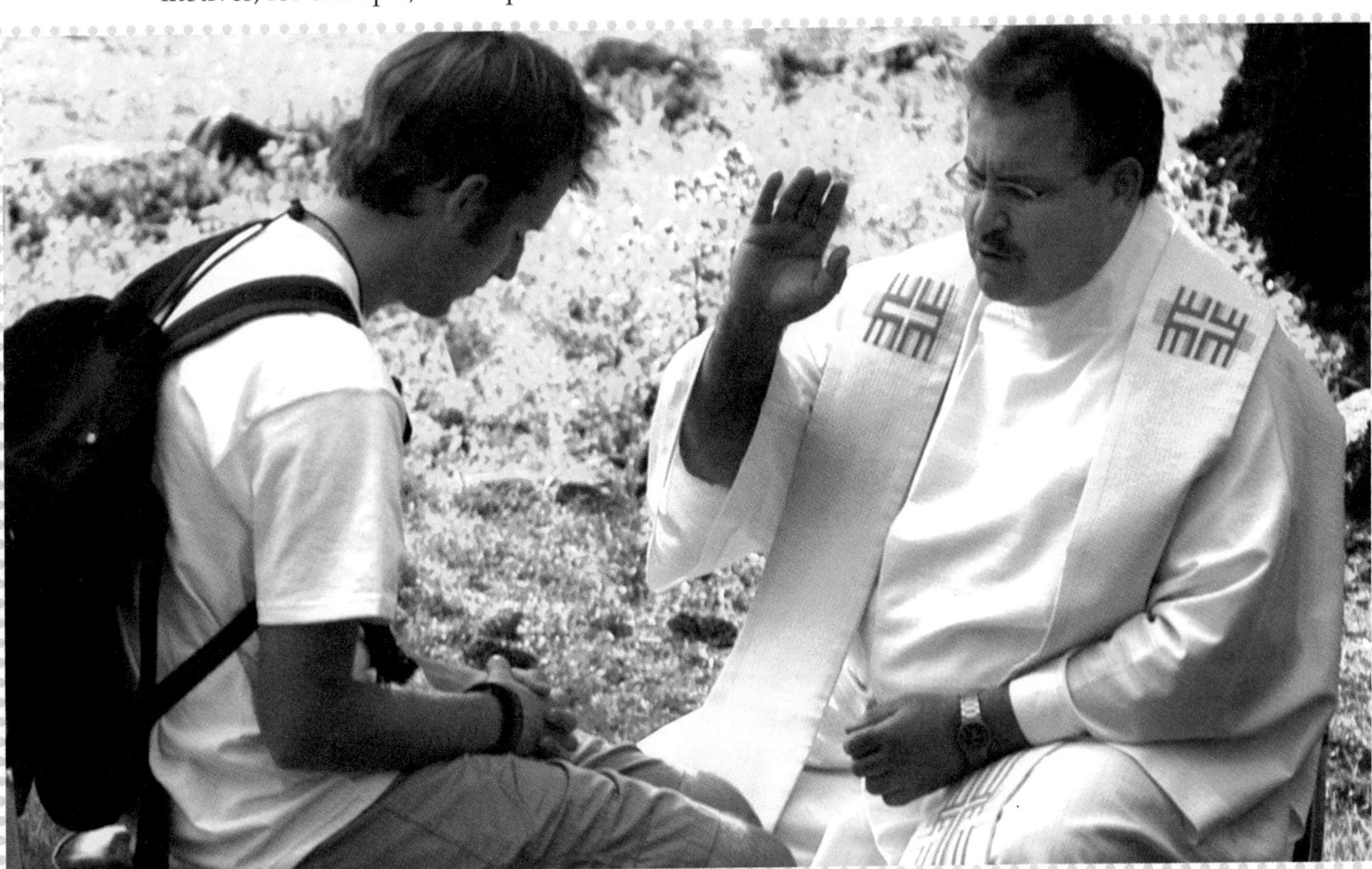

- *Confession* of one's sins, which takes place after examination of one's conscience in light of God's word. Catholics are obligated to confess their mortal sins at least once a year or before receiving Holy Communion, which requires a state of grace. Although we are not required to confess venial sins, doing so helps us grow in the spiritual life.
- *Satisfaction,* also called penance, a part of the reparation sinners need to do. Examples include praying and doing works of mercy, service, and self-denial. We show we are truly sorry when we try to repair the harm our sins caused, for example, by returning stolen goods. Although absolution forgives our sins, it does not repair or make satisfaction for the harm our sins have caused.

2. *God's action,* which works through bishops and their priest co-workers who forgive sin in Jesus' name. Standing in place of the Good Shepherd, they also determine what type of penance to give to penitents.

The ordinary way we celebrate this sacrament today is through the anonymous or face-to-face confession of sins to a priest by an individual penitent. The liturgy involves a greeting and blessing by the confessor and a Scripture reading on God's forgiving love. The penitent then confesses his or her sins, making sure to mention any mortal sins committed since the last confession. The priest assigns a suitable penance, pronounces the words of absolution, and concludes with a prayer of praise and thanksgiving and a dismissal blessing.

A second form of this sacrament often takes place during certain liturgical seasons like Lent and Advent. Parishes then conduct a communal celebration of the sacrament of Penance which includes the opportunity for individual confession of sins to a priest and individual absolution.

In times of serious need, a priest may give general absolution after a general confession of sin by those assembled. However, those in mortal sin must intend to confess their sins individually as soon as possible.

Explaining Your Faith

Why do we have to confess our sins to a priest?

There are many possible answers to this question. But the key reason we should celebrate the sacrament of Penance is to experience the gift of Jesus' forgiveness. Christ meets us in a special way in this sacrament. Confession enables us to experience firsthand the saving love of Christ that reaches out to us through his minister (the priest) and his Church. Other good reasons for confessing our sins to a priest include:

1. *Confession helps us know the truth about ourselves.* Everyone sins. Everyone carries guilt. Everyone needs to be honest. We all yearn to open ourselves to another. When we name our sins aloud to a priest, we own up to our darkest secrets. We accept responsibility for what we have done. Saying our sins aloud is an excellent sign of sincere contrition; it helps us overcome self-deception. Modern psychology tells us "confession is good for the soul." This is especially true in the sacrament of Penance because it lifts burdens, forgives sins, relieves guilt, and gives us a fresh start on our spiritual journey.
2. *The sacrament helps us to hear Christ's forgiveness and reassurance of his love.* It is only human to want assurance of love and forgiveness when we have gone astray, yet repented of our sins. Jesus understood this in his own ministry for he often *spoke* his word of forgiveness. He continues to speak today through his Church's sacraments. A forgiving word spoken and heard brings joy and strengthens us to recommit ourselves to following the Good Shepherd.
3. *We need to celebrate reconciliation with others.* Though we often sin alone and

privately, sin is never a private affair. Sin harms our relationship with God and others. When we confess, we acknowledge that our sins affect others and that we have become estranged from our brothers and sisters in faith. The celebration of the sacrament of Penance is a public declaration that we want to reconcile with the Church. It is also an acknowledgement that our personal sin is linked with the sins of society. The sacrament heals our sinfulness and gives the graces to help transform our heart. It also challenges us to heal and transform the sinful conditions in the world, to become part of the solution and not part of the problem.

4. *The sacrament helps us to grow in holiness.* All the sacraments strengthen friendship with God. Reconciliation sharpens our conscience, prods us out of our spiritual laziness, heals our spiritual weakness, and unites us more closely with God and our neighbors.

Discussion Questions

1. Why is it important for you to go to confession?
2. What are regular times during the year you can make for going to confession?
3. What would be a good penance for a priest to assign for the following sins:

- cheating on tests
- disrespect of one's parents
- racial slurs
- making fun of a handicapped classmate
- missing Sunday Mass
- poor sportsmanship in a game

Writing Assignment

Read the following passages. Then write how each passage involves healing, forgiveness, conversion, and reconciliation.

John 8:2–11 (woman caught in adultery)

Mark 2:1–12 (cure of the paralyzed man)

Luke 15:11–32 (parable of the prodigal son)

Anointing of the Sick

(*CCC*, 1499–1512; 1514–1515; 1526; 1528–1529)

Jesus Christ announced the coming of God's kingdom. One way he showed that the kingdom is present was through his compassionate healing ministry. Jesus cured blind and lame people, cleansed lepers, and brought the dead back to life. Jesus touched suffering people and healed their spiritual, psychological, and physical sicknesses.

After his ascension, Jesus' earliest disciples obeyed his charge to continue his healing ministry by preaching repentance, casting out demons, and anointing and healing the sick. Today, the Lord continues to heal us through the prayers of the Church and through the sacraments, especially the Eucharist, and the sacrament of the Anointing of the Sick. The letter of James shows the roots of the sacrament of Anointing of the Sick (see page 168).

Anointing and praying for the sick were commonplace in the early Church (see, for example, Acts 9:34 and Acts 28:8–9). However, by the

viaticum—Holy Communion received by dying persons to help them pass over to God in the afterlife.

Middle Ages, this sacrament was usually administered only to those who were dying. The term for the sacrament became *extreme unction*, that is, the "last anointing" before death. Penance and **viaticum** ("food for the way"), the reception of a final Eucharist, come before the sacramental anointing of a dying person.

The liturgical reforms of the Second Vatican Council stress that the sacrament of the Anointing of the Sick is for those suffering from serious illness, for the elderly, for those facing major surgery, as well as for the dying. And sick persons may repeat the sacrament if, after recovery, they fall ill again or if the original condition worsens.

WritingAssignment

1. The gospels give many examples of Jesus' power over sickness. Read the following passages. Summarize and comment on the meaning of each:
   - Matthew 9:18–26
   - Luke 7:1–10
   - Luke 17:11–19
   - John 4:46–54
   - John 5:1–9
2. Write your answers to the following questions:
   - What are some of the crosses young teens have to bear in today's world?
   - How have you helped others who were having a tough time cope with their sufferings?
   - Create a list of people known to you who have crosses to carry. Brainstorm ways young people can help them bear their crosses.

Rite of the Sacrament of Anointing

(*CCC*, 1513; 1516–1519; 1524–1525; 1530–1531)

Only priests and bishops may administer the sacrament of the Anointing of the Sick. However, the prayerful support of the entire Church is important because it shows the unity of the family and friends with the sick person. When the sacrament takes place during Mass, the parish community is reminded in a special way to respond in love to those who are suffering. The essential elements of the sacrament include:

1. the priest lays hands on the sick person(s);
2. he prays for them in the faith of the Church; and
3. he anoints their forehead and hands (in the Roman Rite) or other body parts (in the Eastern Rite) with oil ideally blessed previously by a bishop (or, if necessary, by himself).

In the rite of the sacrament, an act of repentance precedes the liturgy of the Word. This awakens the faith of the sick person and of the

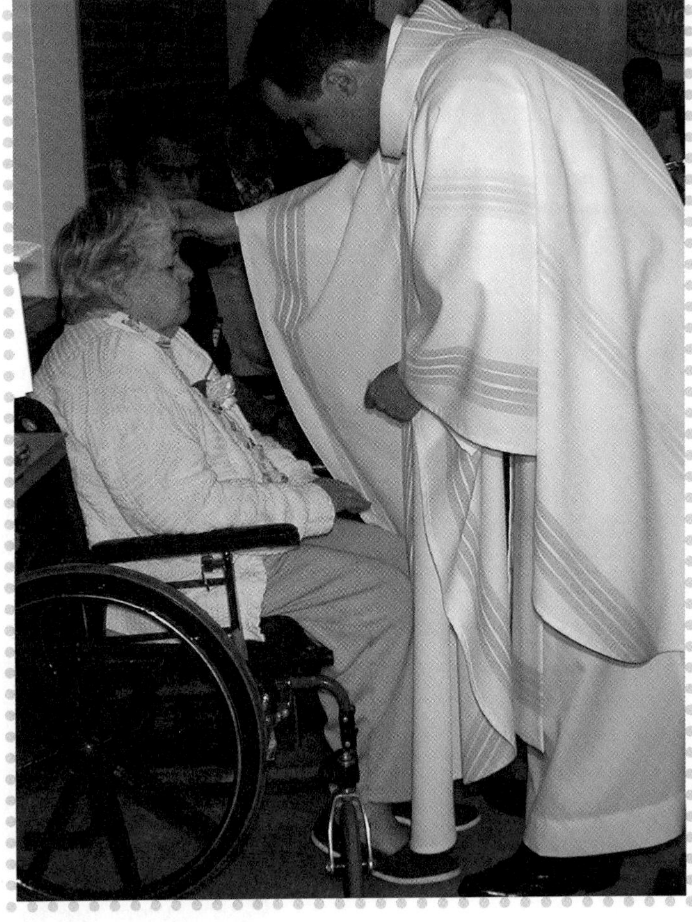

community to pray to the Lord for the Holy Spirit's strength. Next comes the laying on of hands. This is an important biblical sign of Jesus' loving touch and the outpouring of the Spirit of strength, love, and forgiveness. The prayer of the priest over the sick person invokes the grace of the Spirit:

> Through this holy anointing may the Lord in his love and mercy help you with the grace of the Holy Spirit. May the Lord who frees you from sin save you and raise you up.[9]

In the Latin rite, the priest recites this prayer while anointing the forehead and hands of the sick person. Anointing with blessed oil symbolizes healing, strength, and special dedication to God.

This sacrament encourages those who are sick to overcome the alienation caused by sickness, to grow to wholeness through the illness, to identify with the sufferings of Jesus Christ, and to enter more fully into the Paschal mystery.

Effects of the Sacrament of Anointing

(*CCC*, 1520–1523; 1527; 1532)

The effects of the sacrament of the Anointing of the Sick include:

1. the forgiveness of sin, if the sick person has not been able to obtain it through the Sacrament of Penance;
2. spiritual healing, including the comfort, peace, and courage of the Holy Spirit to overcome the difficulties of this particular illness;
3. physical healing, when this will help the person in his or her condition before God;
4. the union of the sick person more closely to Christ's redemptive passion, which will benefit both the individual and the good of all God's people;
5. for dying persons, the strength of the anointing and viaticum in the final struggle before entering eternity and meeting our loving God.

My Prayer for the Sick

Compose a short prayer for a sick or dying person whom you know personally. Recite it daily for their benefit.

Discussion Questions

1. How can you help care for family members and neighbors who are ailing?
2. How do the revisions of the sacrament of the Anointing of the Sick from Vatican II help to take the fear out of receiving the sacrament?
3. Name some appropriate (and inappropriate) times a person should receive the sacrament of the Anointing of the Sick.

diaconate—The third degree in the hierarchy of Holy Orders. The diaconate is not a degree of the ministerial priesthood. Deacons are ordained ministers who assist bishops and priests in the celebration of liturgy, distribute communion, witness and bless marriages, proclaim and preach the Gospel, celebrate funerals, and perform various ministries of Christian charity all under the authority of their bishop.

presbyters—Priests or members of the order of priesthood who are coworkers with the bishop and servants to God's people, especially in celebrating the Eucharist.

Holy Orders

(*CCC*, 1533; 1536–1538; 1544–1553; 1591–1592)

Although all of us are called to serve others, and our Baptism and Confirmation initiate us into the common priesthood of the faithful, the Lord saw a special need for certain members in the Church to "minister to the ministers." The ministerial or hierarchical priesthood is received by bishops and priests through the sacrament of Holy Orders. Sacramental ordination consecrates certain baptized men to one of three degrees of a sacred order: *episcopacy* (bishops), *presbyterate* (priests), and ***diaconate*** (deacons). (Deacons do not participate in the priesthood which Christ exercises through bishops and priests. More information on deacons follows on page 180.) Bishops and their co-worker priests lead the members of Christ's body by helping unfold the graces of Baptism of all Christians. "Those who receive the sacrament of Holy Orders are *consecrated* in Christ's name to feed the Church by the word and grace of God'" (*CCC*, 1535 quoting *Lumen Gentium*, 11 § 2). For this reason Holy Orders (along with Matrimony) is one of the Sacraments at the Service of Communion.

The ministerial priesthood continues the special ministry Jesus entrusted to the apostles. It is essentially different from the common priesthood of the faithful. Through the ministerial priesthood, Christ himself becomes visibly present to the Church as its head and high priest of his redemptive sacrifice.

Holy Orders confers a gift of the Holy Spirit that allows bishops and priests to exercise a "sacred power" on behalf of Christ for his Church. Bishops and priests must:

- proclaim and teach God's word to all people,
- lead the Christian community in worship, and
- guide and rule God's people by imitating Jesus' model of humble service.

Roles of the Ordained Ministers

(*CCC*, 1539–1545; 1550; 1554; 1590; 1593)

The Jews, God's Chosen People, were "a kingdom of priests, a holy nation" (Ex 19:6). From among these special people, Yahweh chose the tribe of Levi to serve the nation at liturgical services. The priesthood of Aaron and Melchizedek and the seventy elders also prefigured the ordained ministry of the New Covenant. Although in Old Testament times there was a special rite to consecrate priests, their sacrifices and prayers could not bring salvation.

Christ fulfilled the Old Testament prefigurements of the priesthood. His unique sacrifice brought about our redemption once and for all. He is the High Priest.

The sacrament of Holy Orders is exercised in different degrees by those who have from the earliest times been called bishops, priests, and deacons. There are various New Testament roots of the sacrament of Holy Orders. Examples include St. Paul writing to Timothy about the laying on of the hands of ordination (2 Tm 1:6) and reference to the office of bishop being a worthy way to serve God's people (1 Tm 3:1).

Just as the Eucharist makes present Jesus' saving sacrifice, so does Holy Orders make present Christ's priesthood. Jesus is really present through the priesthood of bishops and priests; therefore, we be can certain that his graces come to us when the sacraments are administered. Christ works through bishops and priests, despite their human weakness. Deacons help and serve bishops and priests.

Each of the three degrees of ordained ministry has a special role.

Episcopacy (CCC, 1555–1561; 1594)

Bishops receive the fullness of the sacrament of Holy Orders, the "high priesthood." Consecration to the episcopacy confers a sacred character as a successor to the apostles to take Christ's place as teacher (to instruct), as shepherd (to rule), and as priest (to sanctify). The pope must approve the ordination of bishops, who may be consecrated only by other bishops. This practice shows how the order of bishops is a college of bishops united with the pope, the bishop of Rome who is the visible bond of unity in the worldwide Church. Each bishop is the visible head of a local Church (diocese). With the college of bishops, he serves the worldwide Church under the authority of Peter's successor, the pope.

Presbyterate (CCC, 1562–1568; 1595)

Priests work alongside bishops as their helpers and extensions. Ordination to the presbyterate makes them members of the sacerdotal college around the bishop. (This is similar to the bishops forming a college around the pope.) Priests also receive a sacramental character from the Holy Spirit to act in the person of Christ. They do this most fully when they celebrate the Eucharist. Priests represent their bishops to their parishes and are joined to them in an intimate sacramental fellowship.

Diaconate (CCC, 1569–1571; 1596)

Deacons receive a sacramental character from ordination to the diaconate that configures them to Jesus Christ "to serve, not to be served." The bishop of a local diocese commissions deacons to serve. The reforms of the Second Vatican Council in the Latin Church allow married men to be ordained to the permanent diaconate.

Deacons are not priests, so they cannot celebrate the Eucharist, forgive sin in the sacrament of Penance, or anoint the sick. Rather, they help bishops and priests at liturgies, distribute Holy Communion at Mass and to the sick, proclaim and preach the gospel, witness and bless marriages, preside at funerals, and perform many other actions of service for God's People.

Ministries and Graces of the Sacrament

The following is a comparison of the various ministries and graces of the sacrament of Holy Orders in three degrees (cf. *CCC*, 1581–1589):

Ministries of the Bishop

1. Successor to the apostles and in union with the pope and other bishops
2. Responsible for the welfare of the whole Church
3. Spiritual "father" of his diocese
4. Minister of all sacraments (He is the only one who can administer Holy Orders and is the normal minister of Confirmation.)

Graces of the Episcopacy

1. Prudence and love to guide and defend their Churches
2. Strength to reach out to the poor, sick, and needy
3. Courage to proclaim the gospel far and wide
4. Help to live an exemplary life with special devotion to the Eucharist

Ministries of the Priest

1. Helps the bishop and is his extension into the diocese
2. Presides at Eucharist
3. Preaches and teaches God's word
4. Is an active agent for building the Church

Graces of the Presbyterate

1. Gifts necessary to proclaim the gospel truthfully
2. Love to offer spiritual gifts and sacrifices to draw others to the faith through preaching, Baptism, and upright living

Ministries of the Deacon

1. Serves the bishop and the people of God by baptizing, distributing communion, teaching, conducting marriages and funerals, administering sacramentals, doing works of charity, and perhaps doing Church administrative work

Graces of the Diaconate

1. Gifts for the service of the liturgy, gospel, and various works of charity
2. Dedication to serve the Church under the direction of bishops and in cooperation with priests

Finally, Holy Orders confers an indelible spiritual character that configures those ordained to Christ. It helps them to serve Christ in his triple office of priest, prophet, and king.

Rite of Holy Orders (CCC, 1552; 1572–1578; 1597–1598; 1600)

The sacrament of Holy Orders is administered within Mass, ideally on a Sunday and at the diocesan cathedral. It is good for God's people to be present at this sacrament because they are the ones to be served by the newly ordained ministers. Only validly ordained bishops have Christ's authority to ordain, thereby continuing the apostolic line begun from the earliest days of the Church.

The Church has the authority to ordain only baptized men (males). It does not have the authority to ordain women to the priesthood. Although in his earthly ministry Jesus greatly emphasized the dignity of women, Jesus chose only male apostles. Not even the Blessed Mother was chosen to serve as an apostle, bishop, or priest. The apostles followed the example of Jesus when they chose only male collaborators to succeed them in the ordained ministry.

A theological reason for male-only ordination comes from the truth that sacramental signs, including persons and objects, should represent what they signify by natural resemblance. The priest is a sign of Christ, a representative of the Lord when he leads the Church in prayers to God. Because Christ was a male, the priest must also be male.

Priesthood is a gift of Christ to his Church. No one has a *right* to ordination because it is a call by God to serve the Church in a very special way. There are many other ways to serve in the Church for both men and women. Baptism gives us great dignity as God's adopted daughters and sons. The Holy Spirit showers us with many gifts and talents to bring God's love into the world to the millions of people who are desperate for it.

The essential sign for all three orders is the bishop's laying his hands on the head of the one to be ordained, followed by a prayer of consecration. This prayer asks the Holy Spirit to grant the special graces needed for bishops, priests, or deacons to serve God and his people with love and fidelity.

Clerical Celibacy (CCC, 1579–1580; 1599)

In the Latin rite of the Catholic Church, priests and bishops may not marry. Men who are married may be ordained deacons. However, they may not remarry if their wife dies. Nor can men ordained as deacons while single ever marry. Catholic priests observe **celibacy** to express freely their wholehearted commitment to serve both God and God's people. They follow this discipline because:

- By living a loving, celibate life for the sake of the gospel, a priest is a living sign pointing to eternal life when there will be no marriage.
- Jesus himself did not marry. By not marrying, a priest is imitating Jesus who committed himself totally to doing God's will by serving others.
- Celibacy frees a person from family obligations and therefore allows priests or bishops to give themselves totally to the Lord.
- Giving up the blessing of a family witnesses dramatically the call Jesus makes to some of his followers. He said, "And everyone who has given up houses or brothers or sisters or father or mother or children or lands for the sake of my name will receive a hundred times more, and will inherit eternal life" (Mt 19:29).

celibacy—The state of being unmarried that priests and other religious choose in order to dedicate their lives totally to Jesus Christ and God's People.

Discussion Questions

1. What is the name of your local bishop? Where does he live?
2. Name five qualities of a good priest.
3. Who is the best priest you know? What makes him such a good person?
4. Why might it be a good idea for priests and those in religious life to wear distinctive clothing? Explain.

The Eastern Orthodox Church

The Eastern Orthodox Church celebrates seven sacraments and has a valid hierarchy and priesthood. The basic difference is that the Orthodox Church claims the jurisdiction of the pope does not extend over the whole Church.

Orthodox Christians trace themselves back to Pentecost when the Church started under the inspiration of the Holy Spirit with Christ as its head. The early Church was strongly missionary. It preached Christ's gospel all over the known world, including the Eastern parts of the Roman Empire. In various parts of the world, heresies (false teachings) arose that had to be addressed by the bishops (including the Bishop of Rome) at ecumenical councils like Nicaea (AD 325). True teaching about Christ, the Trinity, Blessed Mother, and other aspects of the Christian faith came from these councils under the inspiration of the Holy Spirit. The adjective *orthodox* (meaning "straight teaching") was sometimes applied to Christ's true Church in contrast to those who followed false teaching.

As the Church spread and became a legalized religion under the Emperor Constantine, bishops of certain great cities, especially Rome, Constantinople, Alexandria, Antioch, and Jerusalem emerged as leaders of their particular regions. They assumed titles like *patriarch, archbishop,* or *metropolitan* and presided over their regions without interference from other bishops as long as they did not teach heresy. It was always the bishop of Rome, the pope, who had a preeminent role to play, because he succeeded Peter, to whom Christ entrusted his Church.

In the following centuries there were certain complex cultural, political, and language differences between the Church in eastern and western Europe. For example, the Easterners spoke Greek; the Westerners, Latin. Unfortunately, by the eleventh century, the differences between the East and West became so great that they led to a separation in 1054. The Eastern Church was called the Eastern Orthodox Church, and the Western Church became known as the Roman Catholic Church. Though many factors were involved in this rift in the unity of Christ's body, the major factor was that the Eastern Churches did not recognize the authority of the Holy Father to have jurisdiction over the *entire* Church. From the Catholic point of view, a schism took place, that is, a break in unity with the successor of Peter, the pope.

Eastern Orthodox Christians recognize the authority of the first seven Ecumenical Councils (up to the Second Council of Nicaea in 787). They hold much in common with Roman Catholics including acceptance of the Nicene Creed and seven sacraments. A special feature of Eastern Orthodox Christians is their use of icons (holy images). These were and are used to teach believers about God and to help focus our minds when we pray or meditate. Icons also help remind believers that God is present everywhere in our world.

Since the Second Vatican Council, international commissions of Roman Catholic and Orthodox theologians have made many efforts to reunify. These efforts continue today.

Read and report on an aspect of the Eastern Orthodox Church. One of the following websites may be of help.

Eastern Orthodoxy:
http://ic.net/~erasmus/RAZ23.HTM
Orthodox Church in America:
www.oca.org

Matrimony *(CCC, 1601–1617; 1659–1661)*

Christian marriage is a wonderful sign of God calling a man and woman to holiness through ordinary married life. Christ Jesus enters this covenant of love by making it a sacrament. Through it, he joins the couple to bless, sustain, and rejoice in their union. In this holy union the couple is committed to raise a family responsibly if God should bless them with children.

God is the source of marriage. Out of love, he created men and women in the divine image for the purpose of loving each other. Therefore, marriage is a vocation written into our very nature, because a God of infinite love made us. Because of original sin, however, men and women need God's grace and help to live in the harmony he intends for us.

This understanding of marriage grew gradually throughout salvation history. At first, **polygamy** (men taking more than one wife) and divorce were tolerated. However, in the book of Genesis, several divine truths about marriage were revealed, including:

1. God made us male and female in the divine image. This established both human sexuality and marriage, both of which God declared to be "very good" (Gn 1:31). He commanded us to "Be fertile and multiply; fill the earth and subdue it" (Gn 1:28).
2. The second purpose of marriage is companionship between friends who share the same life and love. This is the meaning of the story where God creates Eve from Adam's rib. Genesis tells us they should cling to each other and become one body (see Gn 2:23–24). This means that from the beginning God intends a permanent, exclusive, monogamous relationship between man and woman who have been created in the divine image. This union helps the married couple overcome self-centeredness and opens them to each other, "to mutual aid and to self-giving" (*CCC*, 1609).

Later in salvation history, prophets like Hosea and Malachi preach about marriage as an image of how Yahweh (the husband) loves his beloved people, Israel. He does so with great faithfulness. Other Old Testament books describe the qualities of an ideal wife, talk about how spouses should be faithful and tender, and see the affection between husband and wife in marriage as good, holy, and joyful.

In the New Testament, the gospels tell us of Jesus' attendance at the wedding feast of Cana, acknowledging his love and support of the married couple and the institution of marriage. He saw that marriage is both natural and good. In his teaching ministry, Jesus also told us what his Father intended for marriage—it should be a permanent, exclusive love relationship. Therefore, he condemned divorce, saying it was equivalent to adultery (Lk 16:18). Jesus also taught that lustful thoughts lead to sexual sins. Jesus stressed purity of heart. For example, men must treat women with respect, as equals, and as persons endowed with great dignity (see Mt 5:27–28).

polygamy—Having more than one wife at the same time. It distorts the unity of marriage between a man and a woman and offends the dignity of women.

The early Church learned from Jesus and thus viewed marriage as sacred. St. Paul, for example, taught that husbands must love their wives as they love their own bodies (Eph 5:28–32). In short, the Church saw in the union of a husband and wife a comparison to the union Christ, the Bridegroom, has with his Church, his Bride. St. Paul calls this a *mystery* (a word translated by St. Augustine as "sacrament"), an outward sign of Christ's love. Marriage, in fact, is a covenant, a total lifelong commitment that mirrors Christ's love for his Church.

Jesus Christ is the Father's gift of love to us. He is the fulfillment of God's promises to humanity. The Lord we receive in the Eucharist makes us one, gives us many gifts, treats us as special individuals, and challenges us to serve others. A Christian marriage is like this open-ended commitment to love that the Father made with us in Jesus Christ. True, committed love brings forth life. So, too, life is brought forth in a marriage where God gives a husband and wife the privilege of procreation. A Christian marriage is a unique way to live a Christ-like life of love and service in the context of family living. Through this sacrament of love, Jesus and his Holy Spirit give the couple the graces they need to love each other with the same love he has for the Church. These graces lift up their human love, strengthen their indissoluble unity, and sanctify them on their journey to eternal life.

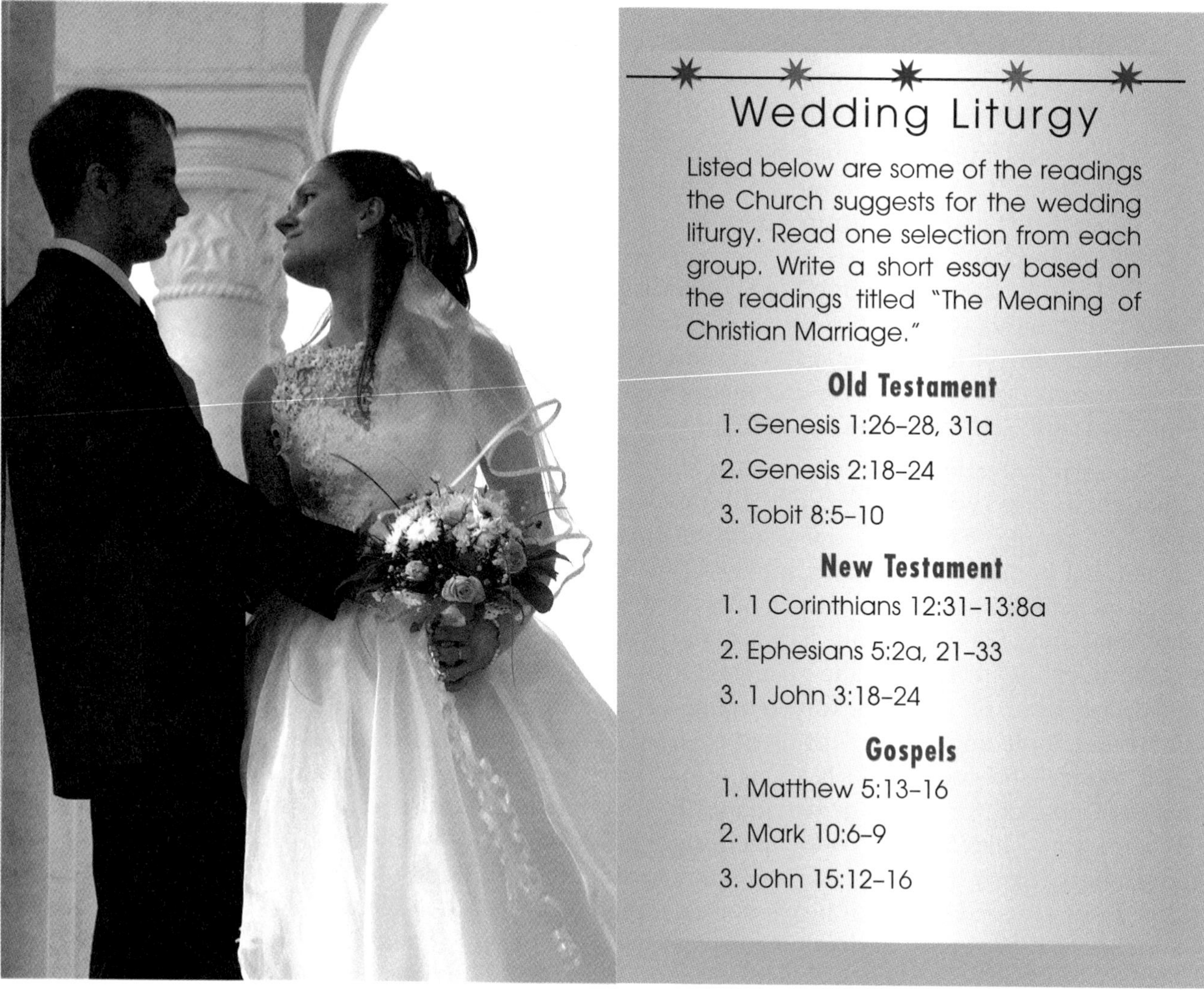

Wedding Liturgy

Listed below are some of the readings the Church suggests for the wedding liturgy. Read one selection from each group. Write a short essay based on the readings titled "The Meaning of Christian Marriage."

Old Testament

1. Genesis 1:26–28, 31a
2. Genesis 2:18–24
3. Tobit 8:5–10

New Testament

1. 1 Corinthians 12:31–13:8a
2. Ephesians 5:2a, 21–33
3. 1 John 3:18–24

Gospels

1. Matthew 5:13–16
2. Mark 10:6–9
3. John 15:12–16

Preparation for Marriage (CCC, 1621–1637; 1662–1663)

The Church can administer the sacrament of Matrimony only to a couple who are baptized, of a mature age, unmarried, not closely related by blood or marriage, and are able to give their free consent to marry. To give free consent, the couple must not be under any constraint (like fear or force) or blocked by any natural or Church law. *The exchange of consent between the partners is the indispensable element that makes for a valid marriage.* If freedom of consent is missing, then a true marriage never really exists.

To have true consent, the man and woman must commit to a lifelong covenant of love; be capable of sexual intercourse, which is the sign of mutual love and union; and be open to raising a family if God should bless them with children.

Because Christian marriage is a serious commitment, the couple should prepare for their future life together. Most dioceses today require engaged couples to attend marriage preparation classes to learn about the spiritual dimensions and practical aspects of married life. Also, if a Catholic is going to marry a non-Catholic Christian (known as a mixed marriage), Church authority must give permission. When a Catholic is going to marry someone who is not baptized, Church authority must give a dispensation for the marriage to be valid. In either case, the Catholic partner must promise to live his or her Catholic faith and have the children baptized and raised in the Catholic faith. The non-Catholic partner is made aware of this pledge, but not required to make any promises. Both partners must know and not exclude the essential purposes and qualities of marriage.

The ministers of the sacrament of Matrimony are the bride and bridegroom themselves. In the Latin Rite, the sacrament of Matrimony usually takes place during Mass. The essential sign of the sacrament takes place after the homily, when the bridal couple exchanges vows in the presence of the priest, two witnesses, and the assembled Church. They promise unconditional love—to be true in good times and bad, in sickness and in health, and to love and honor each other until death. The priest is the official witness of the Church who blesses the wedding rings, which serve as symbols of fidelity and unending love. A nuptial blessing takes place after the Lord's Prayer.

Effects of the Sacrament of Matrimony

(*CCC*, 1638–1645; 1652–1658; 1664; 1666)

Because Christian marriage is a covenant, it is valid for life, until death separates the couple. Christ promises to be with the husband and wife each day of their marriage. He helps them stay united and true to their vows. He gives them the graces they need to live lovingly each day. He sanctifies their sexual sharing and strengthens them to be signs of love to each other, their children, and to all their friends and acquaintances. If he blesses their marriage with children, he helps them to raise and educate them in a Christian family setting.

The covenant of marriage involves a couple's total commitment that results in a deep unity of body, heart, and soul. Therefore, Christian marriage requires the virtues of faithfulness until death and openness to children. Practices like polygamy (having more than one spouse); divorce, which separates what God has joined together; and a refusal to have children are contrary to any Christian marriage.

Married love is one of God's great gifts to us, a profound way a man and a woman express their mutual affection and commitment. Therefore, sexual sharing must take place according to God's twofold plan for it. First, sexual intercourse in marriage must be *unitive* because it is a powerful sign that binds a man and woman together as lifelong partners. Second, it must be *procreative,* that is, open to a share in God's creative activity of bringing new life into the world.

God uses the married love between a couple for the procreation and education of children. Children are God's greatest gift to a married couple. They help make up a family, what is known as the *domestic Church,* in which we live out our faith on a daily basis. The Christian family, supported by a loving marriage, is a prime way to holiness for all its members. Family prayer, regular celebration of the sacraments, and participation in parish programs are helpful means God gave to families to help them grow in holiness together. Like Holy Orders, the sacrament of Matrimony is one of the Sacraments at the Service of Communion. An old saying puts it this way, "The family that prays together stays together."

The parish should always be a welcoming place both for childless couples and single people. The parish is a family for everyone, and in a special way for those who live alone.

Rules for a Successful Marriage

Compose a list of ten rules for preparing for a happy marriage (e.g., "practice patience," "learn to listen," "learn self-control"). Show your list to a recently married couple and to a long-time married couple. Write the reactions of all parties to your list, noting how effective they believe your rules to be.

Divorce and Annulment

(*CCC*, 1629; 1646–1651; 1665)

Jesus taught that marriage must be permanent and exclusive. He commanded, "What God has joined together, no human being must separate" (Mt 19:6). Because of Jesus' direct commandment that tells us of the permanence of marriage, the Church cannot permit divorce and remarriage. Only death can dissolve the marriage covenant of validly married Catholics.

However, in certain circumstances (like the abuse of a wife by a husband), a couple may separate for the good of the wife and children. Though the civil authority may dissolve the legal aspects of a valid marriage (called in civil law a divorce), the state has no authority to dissolve a true Catholic sacramental marriage. Legally separated Catholics (divorced under civil law) may not remarry while their spouses are alive. The Church follows this teaching because it comes from Jesus who said, "Everyone who divorces his wife and marries another commits adultery" (Lk 16:18).

annulment—An official Church declaration that what appeared to be a Christian marriage never existed in the first place.

Annulment is not the same thing as a divorce. Rather, an annulment is an official declaration of the Catholic Church that what appeared to be a valid Christian marriage, in fact, was not. For example, one of the partners might not have given free, true consent to the marriage. Or perhaps one of the partners never intended to have children. Both of these conditions must be present for there to be a true sacramental marriage. In cases like these, the diocesan marriage tribunal (court) might declare that the marriage was not a valid sacramental union from the beginning. If this is the case, then the individuals involved would be free to enter a true Catholic marriage in the future.

Entering a marriage is serious business because it involves love, and love is always serious. It also involves a willingness to stick by one's partner through good times and bad. Like a good mother, the Church wants to make sure that engaged couples prepare adequately for this sacrament. But the Church also announces the good news that it is never two that get married—it is always three. In a Christian marriage, Jesus is always there to befriend the couple. He promised his Spirit and the grace and strength to endure the tough times and to rejoice in the good ones.

Christian marriage reminds us that we are each the flesh-and-blood sacrament of our parents' love. In addition, our Baptism makes us each a special sign of God's grace.

We are all symbols of the Lord's presence in the world. He uses us to bring others to him.

Marriage and Friendship

Friendship is a skill that you can learn now to help you prepare for marriage. A wife and husband should be each other's best friends. Read each of these statements having to do with qualities of friendship. Then develop one of these statements into an essay on the meaning of friendship.

- ★ I am good at sharing ideas and feelings and at listening.
- ★ I have many interests.
- ★ I am patient with others and myself.
- ★ I can forgive and ask for forgiveness.
- ★ I am growing in self-mastery.
- ★ Jesus plays an important role in my life.

Summary Points

- ★ The sacrament of Penance is a sacrament of conversion that enables sinners to begin anew as the Lord extends his forgiving mercy and grace.
- ★ The term *penance* emphasizes that we must make satisfaction for the sins we have committed. This is an external sign of our internal conversion.
- ★ Sin offends God's honor and love, causes a break in our union with God, disfigures the sinner, and ruptures our relationship with members of Christ's body. This is why we need the sacrament of forgiveness.
- ★ Through the formula of absolution, a bishop or priest proclaims God's forgiveness of sinners.
- ★ Penance is also known as the sacrament of reconciliation because it unites us once again with God and his Church; brings peace and spiritual comfort; strengthens us for the Christian life; takes away some temporal punishment due sin; remits eternal punishment resulting from mortal sin; and teaches us how to repent, do penance, and trust a loving and merciful God.
- ★ The acts of the penitent in the sacrament of Penance include contrition (genuine sorrow for sins and firm resolve not to sin again), confession of sins, and doing satisfaction or penance in reparation of sin.
- ★ God's action in the sacrament of Penance works through the bishop or priest to forgive sin in Jesus' name.
- ★ The sacrament of the Anointing of the Sick brings Christ's healing touch to those suffering from serious illness, the elderly, and for dying people.
- ★ Only a priest or bishop may administer the sacrament of the Anointing of the Sick. Its essential features are the laying of hands on the sick person, a prayer recited in the faith of the Church, and a sacramental anointing of the forehead and hands (in the Roman Rite).
- ★ The sacrament of the Anointing of the Sick forgives sin, if the person has not obtained it through the sacrament of Penance; brings spiritual healing and physical healing, if this will help the person before God; unites the person more closely to Christ's redemptive passion; and gives dying persons the strength to endure to the end before meeting our loving God.
- ★ Although all baptized Christians share in Christ's priestly ministry, our Lord desired an ordained ministry comprised of a hierarchy of bishops, priests, and deacons to unfold the graces of Baptism of all Christians. This ordained ministry continues the special ministry he entrusted to the apostles.
- ★ The "sacred power" which ordained men exercise on behalf of Christ and his Church involves proclaiming and teaching God's word, leading the Church in worship, and guiding and ruling God's people.
- ★ Bishops receive the fullness of the sacrament of Holy Orders, making them successors to the apostles. They are spiritual fathers of the local Church. Along with the college of bishops, and in union with the pope, they are responsible for the welfare of the whole Church.
- ★ Priests are the bishop's helpers, his extension into the diocese. They are members of the sacerdotal college around the bishop. They preside at the Eucharist, preach and teach God's word, and actively build up the Christian community.
- ★ Deacons serve bishops and priests. Although they cannot preside at the Eucharist or serve as confessors, they still have a variety of ministries. These include baptizing, distributing Holy Communion, teaching, doing works of charity, and so forth.
- ★ Holy Orders confers an indelible spiritual character that configures those ordained to Christ. The Church has the authority from Christ to ordain men only.

- ★ The essential sign in the rite of ordination for all three orders is the bishop's laying his hands on the head of the person ordained, followed by a prayer of consecration to the Holy Spirit.
- ★ Following the call and example of Jesus himself, priests in the Latin Rite follow a rule of celibacy. This means that they forego marriage for the sake of serving God and his people wholeheartedly.
- ★ The sacrament of Matrimony is a covenant in which a baptized man and woman vow their love in an exclusive, permanent, sexual partnership that is open to the procreation of children.
- ★ Creating us male and female in his divine image, God established our sexual nature and is the source of marriage. From the beginning, God intended men and women to marry, to treat each other with respect and love, and to procreate in a permanent, exclusive, and monogamous relationship.
- ★ Jesus condemned divorce and lust, teaching that men must treat women as equals.
- ★ The exchange of consent between the marriage partners is the indispensable element that makes for a valid marriage. The ministers of the sacrament are the couple themselves, who exchange their vows before a priest and two other witnesses.
- ★ Effects of a Christian marriage include the help the Lord gives the couple to be true to each other and the graces to live lovingly toward each other and to their children and friends. If he blesses them with children, he sends his graces to help raise and educate them in a Christian family, which is known as the *domestic Church.*
- ★ Sexual sharing in marriage has two outcomes: the *unitive,* which is the sharing of love and affection; and the *procreative,* openness to helping God bring new life into the world. Children are God's greatest gift to a married couple.
- ★ Because Jesus taught that marriage is permanent and exclusive, he forbade divorce. Only death can dissolve the marriage of validly married Catholics. The Church may annul a marriage, however, by declaring that what appeared to be a valid Christian marriage was not. This is the case when an essential element (like consent) was missing from the beginning.

ReviewQuestions

1. Explain the meaning of the sacrament of Penance under each of these names: sacrament of conversion, penance, confession, forgiveness, and reconciliation.
2. What are some results of sin?
3. Define *absolution.*
4. What are some of the effects of receiving the sacrament of Penance worthily?
5. Briefly discuss the acts of the penitent and God's action in the sacrament of Penance.
6. Name three good reasons to "go to Confession."
7. Identify these terms: *extreme unction, viaticum.*
8. How is the sacrament of the Anointing of the Sick administered? What are its effects?
9. What is the threefold task of the ordained ministry that Christ established for his Church?
10. What are some sacred roles and graces of each of the ordained orders (bishops, priests, and deacons)?
11. Why does the Church not ordain women?
12. What is the essential sign in the rite of ordination?
13. List some of the factors that led to the Great Schism between Eastern Orthodox Christians and Roman Catholics.
14. Define *icon.*
15. What does the Old Testament teach about marriage?

16. What does Jesus teach about marriage?
17. What is necessary for true consent for a Catholic marriage?
18. Who are the ministers of the sacrament of Matrimony?
19. Name some effects of the sacrament of Matrimony.
20. What is the difference between an annulment and divorce?

ApplyingWhatYou HaveLearned

1. Prepare a PowerPoint® presentation on icons so that you can show some examples of icons to the class.
2. Compose an examination of conscience made up of questions dealing with love of God, love of neighbor, and love of self. If possible, illustrate each category with an appropriate picture or symbol.
3. Report on the activities of any program your parish conducts as part of its ministry to the sick. Offer your services.
4. Write a letter of appreciation to a favorite priest who has inspired you to be a better person.
5. Contrast the wedding and marriage customs of a non-Christian religion to that of a typical Catholic wedding and marriage.
6. Interview your parents, grandparents, or another married couple you are close to asking why they decided to get married and how they planned their life together.

PrayerReflection

Put yourself in the Lord's presence. Thank him for the gift of life and for all the good things that have come your way during the previous day.

Ask the Lord to send the Holy Spirit to help you look back over your day.

Think back to the times that your actions and words hurt others. Honestly look into your heart and discover the missed opportunities to love and to serve.

After this brief examination of conscience, please recite the following traditional Act of Contrition, expressing to God your sorrow for your sins. Do so slowly, reflecting on the meaning of each word.

Act of Contrition

O my God, I am sorry for my sins with all my heart. In choosing to do wrong and failing to do good, I have sinned against you whom I should love above all things. I firmly intend, with your help, to do penance, to sin no more, and to avoid whatever leads me to sin. Our Savior Jesus Christ suffered and died for us. In his name, my God, have mercy. Amen.

1. What area of your life needs the most work *right now*?
2. Think of someone you hurt and resolve to make amends this coming week.

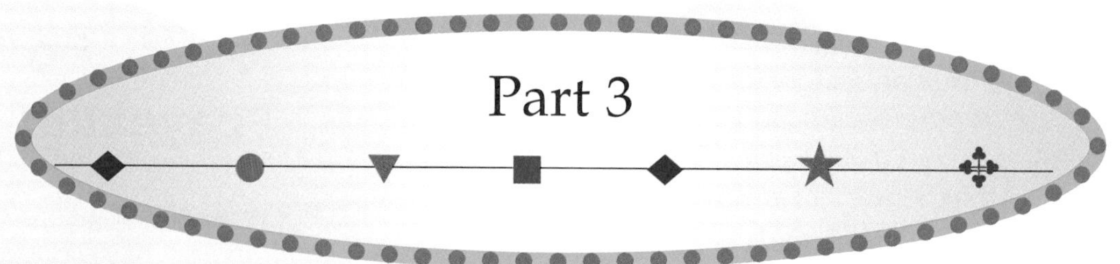

We Love: Our Life in Christ

Living in Love

If you ever take a look at marquees outside of many different churches you might discover some of the following words of wisdom:

"No God—No Peace. Know God—Know Peace."
"Fight truth decay—Study the Bible Daily."
"If You're Headed in the Wrong Direction, God Allows U-turns."
"In the dark? Follow the Son."
"If you can't sleep, don't count sheep. Talk to the Shepherd."

In one way or another, all of these signs are trying to tell us how to live a happier life. For Christians, the essential element is to be a friend of our Lord and Savior, Jesus Christ, and to follow his path.

This section explores what it means to live our lives as Catholics. "Our life in Christ" means that we must live moral lives by acting responsibly according to our dignity. If we do, we will be happier in this life and be rewarded with eternal joy in heaven.

The heart of Christian morality is love. This is what Jesus commanded when he taught:

> You shall love the Lord, your God, with all your heart, with all your soul, and with all your mind. This is the greatest and the first commandment. The second is like it: You shall love your neighbor as yourself (Mt 22:37–39).

To be Catholic means that we must respond to God's own gift of love and salvation in Christ Jesus. The Holy Spirit gives us the graces necessary to follow God's will, to live in conformity to his plan for us. The Spirit gives us the ability to choose Jesus and to love as he commands us to do. And he empowers us with virtues that help us be the persons we are meant to be. Chapter 8 will build on these topics and discuss other basic elements of Catholic morality. Chapter 9 will study the Beatitudes and the Ten Commandments, each which provide guidance on how to live a life in Christ.

This is my commandment: love one another as I love you.

John 15:12

Chapter 8 Outline

Modeling Christ

A moral life is one lived in Christ while practicing the cardinal virtues.

Humans Are Made in God's Image

We have the ability to think and the power to choose. God has destined us for himself.

Conscience and Moral Decisions

A person with a formed conscience can discover three sources of morality—the object chosen, the end or intention, and the circumstances—and make good choices based on these.

Virtues and Other Helps to Live a Moral Life

The theological virtues provide the foundation for a moral life. The moral law, natural law, and precepts of the Church are other helps for a life in Christ.

Sin, Justification, and Grace

God's grace can help us to avoid sin. When we sin God offers his forgiveness and mercy.

Chapter 8

The Basics of Catholic Morality

Modeling Christ

Some years ago, a class of children in a remote mission school in Vietnam was asked to donate blood for a classmate, a sickly girl. Only one boy had her blood type. He volunteered.

The boy bravely underwent what must surely have been an ordeal for one unfamiliar with a blood donation. At one point, the medical team noticed that he was crying. They asked if it hurt him. He said it didn't hurt. "Then what's the matter?" they asked. "It's just that I don't want to die yet." Our little hero mistakenly thought that by donating blood to his sick classmate he would die.

When the nurse inquired why he agreed to go through with the procedure, especially since he thought he was going to die, the boy replied that he did it so his friend could live. She needed his blood or she would die. So he thought he would sacrifice himself for his friend and classmate.

The boy in this true story was a most courageous hero who exemplified love and demonstrated the true meaning of friendship. He certainly modeled a life in Christ.

This chapter examines the foundations of Catholic morality, all of which teach us how to befriend the Lord Jesus. These building blocks of Catholic morality are built on these three rules:

1. Be who you are.
2. Form and follow your conscience. (Use your head to apply the principles.)
3. Respond to God's call to holiness by using the helps he gives to us to live virtuous lives, to avoid sin, and to do good.

Practicing the Cardinal Virtues

cardinal virtues—The "hinge" virtues from which all other virtues come. They are prudence, justice, fortitude, and temperance.

One of the great helps the Holy Spirit has given us to live a life in Christ are the four **cardinal virtues.** *Cardinal* in Latin means "hinge." Other virtues—good habits that enable us to choose the good—hinge on these cardinal virtues: prudence, justice, fortitude, and temperance. Human reason and personal effort help us acquire these virtues; God's grace assists us in developing them.

Listed below is a brief description of each cardinal virtue. Analyze how well you are putting each virtue into practice. Write a short analysis on how you can improve in following the virtues.

1. *Prudence,* according to St. Thomas Aquinas, is "right reason in action." It is spiritual common sense that tells us how we should act.
2. *Justice* is respecting the rights of God and other people. It is treating others with fairness.
3. *Fortitude* is the spiritual strength to do right, even when tempted or afraid.
4. *Temperance* helps control our appetites, especially in the areas of food, drink, sex, and possessions.

Humans Are Made in God's Image

(*CCC*, 1701–1715; 1730–1748; 1762–1775)

Genesis reveals that human beings are fundamentally good because God created us in his image and likeness, conforming us to Jesus Christ who is "the image of the invisible God." Therefore, we have a spiritual and immortal soul. Our souls give us two great gifts: the ability to think (an intellect) and the power to choose and to love (free will). We are one-of-a-kind creatures because God made us for himself and destined us for eternal happiness (or "beatitude"). Because we are made in God's image, several other truths apply:

- ★ *We have dignity and worth.* Each human being, from the very first moment of conception, has tremendous dignity and value that do not have to be earned.
- ★ *We can think.* Because we are rational, we can recognize God's voice in our conscience, understand what is loving or not loving, and distinguish between good and evil.
- ★ *We have freedom.* Being made in God's image also gives us true freedom, that is, "the power, rooted in reason and will, to act or not to act, to do this or that, so to perform deliberate actions on one's own responsibility" (*CCC*, 1731). Free will helps us desire what is good and then choose it. When we choose to do good for other people, then we are loving. When we choose evil by refusing to keep God's law, we commit sin. We abuse our freedom and become slaves to sin.
- ★ *We are responsible.* Freedom to choose between good and evil characterizes human acts. We are responsible (that is, blameworthy) for our actions if they are voluntary, that is, if we directly will them, for example, when we freely spread gossip about someone. We are also responsible for indirectly voluntary actions. An example would be a driver speeding in a school zone and causing an accident. She did not directly intend to hit a pedestrian, but she should have followed the law by slowing down in a school zone.
- ★ Blameworthiness for our actions can be lessened or destroyed by factors like ignorance that is not our fault, inattention, fear, force, habit, and **passions**. Passions are emotions that move us to act or not to act in relation to something we feel or imagine to be either good or evil. The most basic passion is love, which attracts us to the good. Other passions include hate, joy, sadness, desire, fear, and anger. Passions are morally neutral. Morality comes into play when our wills and intellects are involved. If our emotions move us to do good, then they are morally good. If our emotions cause us to perform evil, then they are bad. Consider this example: A teacher believes you cheated

passions—Our emotional response to the good or evil we encounter.

on an exam and insists you take another one to "prove" that your answers were your own. If your anger at the accusation fuels your determination to score even better on the second exam, it is morally good. If, however, you decide to slash the teacher's car tires after school, then the passion of your anger becomes evil.

- *We are wounded by sin.* Though we are fundamentally good, we have inherited the effects of original sin from our first parents who disobeyed God. We have a wounded human nature. We desire what is good, but we are weak, inclined to do evil, and easily make mistakes. Because of our fallen nature, the freedom God gave us is limited and prone to error. An obvious example is the trouble we have controlling our emotions. This is why we need the help of the Holy Spirit to gain mastery over them and channel them to good. The Spirit endows us with gifts, like the cardinal virtues, to help us master our feelings and grow in holiness.
- *We are children of God.* We should not despair over our weak human nature. The good news of our salvation is that Christ's Paschal mystery of salvation has forgiven our sins and rescued us from Satan. Jesus Christ has won for us a new life in the Holy Spirit. God has adopted us into his family through his gifts of grace, faith, and baptism. If we cooperate with Christ's grace, our Lord helps us to live morally, to choose God who is the Supreme Good and the source of our happiness, and to love as he loves according to God's plan.
- *We are friends of the Lord.* Jesus Christ is not only our Savior, he is our friend. "You are my friends if you do what I command you. . . . This I command you: love one another" (John 15:14, 17). This brings great joy. Neither he, nor his loving and merciful Father, will ever let us down. What we must do in return for God's friendship is to love him above all and our neighbor as ourselves.

Humans and Society

(*CCC*, 1877–1948)

By nature, humans live with and for others. God calls us, both individually and as communities, into union with the Blessed Trinity, which is a true communion of love. We fulfill our human vocation when we dialogue with, serve, and love others.

society—Any community of human beings that unites them in a common purpose.

Because we are social beings, we belong to many societies. A **society** is a group of persons united by a principle that goes beyond the individual. Whether a society is personal like the family, voluntary like a social club, or political like the state, it must always make the human person its "principle, subject, and end" (*CCC*, 1881). Each society must treat people as ends (persons of worth) and not as a means (objects to attain a goal). A good society promotes virtue and love among its members and inspires its members to respect and serve others, and to treat them always with justice.

A great deal of moral teaching involves our participation in society. Therefore, the Church gives us many good guidelines on how to live our life with others. Several examples follow, explained in the paragraphs below.

Societies should observe the principle of **subsidiarity**, which holds that a larger social unit should not take over the functions of a smaller group if the smaller unit can achieve for itself the **common good**. For example, the government should not dictate to parents what form of religious education to give their children. This principle safeguards the dignity of the individual person. Therefore, it would outlaw any system of government, like communism, that says the individual person only has value if the state says he or she has value.

subsidiarity—A principle of Catholic social justice that holds that a community of a higher order should not interfere in the internal life of a community of a lower order, depriving it of its functions.

We should respect and obey persons and institutions that possess the rightful authority to make laws. In the final analysis, all authority comes from God. Citizens have the right to choose their leaders who must work to pass laws that promote the common good.

common good—The sum total of social conditions that allow people to reach their fulfillment more fully and more easily.

We should work for the common good, that is, "the sum of those conditions of social life which allows social groups and their individual members relatively thorough and ready access to their own fulfillment" (*CCC*, 1906 quoting *The Church in the Modern World*, No. 26). The common good involves respecting inalienable human rights (for example, the right to life, food, clothing, employment, education, freedom of worship) of every person, promoting the social well-being of various groups, and working for a peaceful society.

Government officials have the duty to promote the worldwide common good of nations around the world as well by supporting human development and acting justly in international relations. Everyone has the right and duty to be involved in his or her social groups. For example, teens can help families thrive by obeying their parents and helping younger siblings. Citizens must keep up with social justice issues and exercise their right to vote in a responsible way. Parishioners should get involved in various parish ministries that help the unfortunate in their midst and that promote the spiritual life of the Church.

social justice doctrine—The teachings of the Magisterium that pertain to the ways in which societies function to promote the common good.

Our social nature is crucial for our life together. This is why, over the centuries, the Church has developed a body of teaching on how we should treat each other. This body of teaching is known as the **social justice doctrine** of the Catholic Church. It is directly related to our being made in God's image and being gifted with adoption into God's family and called into friendship by Jesus Christ. Some of its key points are:

- *Respect each person.* Every human being has basic worth that Jesus Christ elevated when he became man. He taught that *every* person is our neighbor, another self. Therefore, we must respect and love everyone. We must even forgive our enemies. He told us to have a special love for

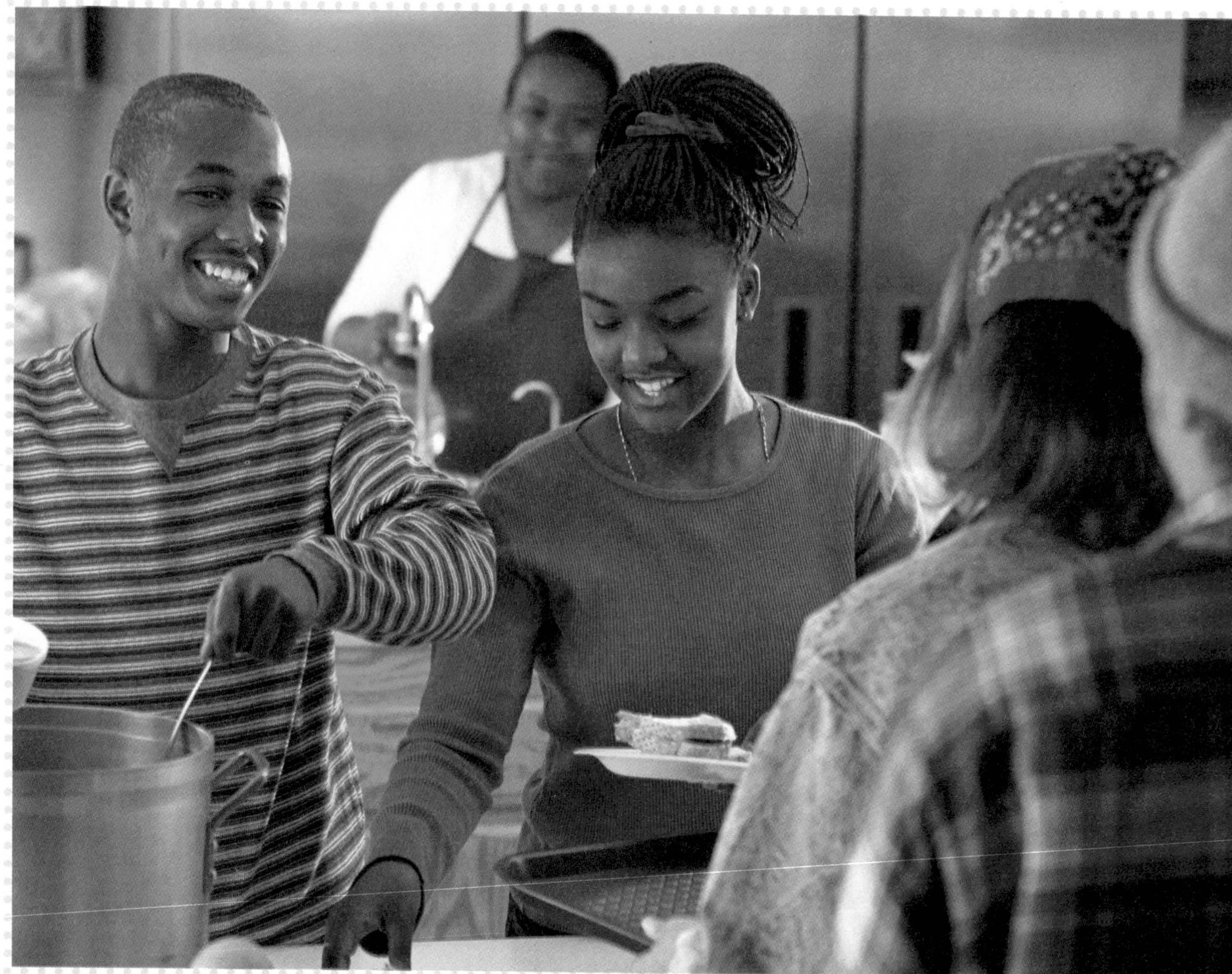

the downtrodden and the poor. When we serve the poor we are directly serving our Lord.

★ *Treat others as equals.* Each person has the same human nature, a common destiny, and fundamental dignity. We have God-given rights that do not have to be earned. Any prejudice or discrimination directed toward others because of their sex, color, race, ethnic background, religious practice, or the like contradicts God's loving plan for us, the special creatures he calls to be united to him.

★ *Develop and share your gifts.* Although we are all equal in dignity, God gave us different talents, all part of his plan. We must develop and use these gifts for others. In a special way, those of us who have been given wealth and education must use our talents to promote peace, fight injustice, and combat economic and social conditions that treat others unfairly.

solidarity—A Christian virtue of charity and friendship whereby material and spiritual goods are shared among members of the human family.

★ *Show* ***solidarity*** *with others.* Solidarity is a Christian virtue of friendship or social charity that works to share both material and, more importantly, spiritual goods with others. We must be one with others, especially the poor.

Considering the above points, we can conclude that we act morally when we

★ responsibly use our God-given intellects and wills;

★ choose good and avoid evil;

★ act as persons of incomparable worth who respect the essential dignity of others;

★ allow the Holy Spirit to live in us;

★ are Christ-like and act as a true son or daughter of a loving Father;

★ act like a true friend of Jesus—showing our love for God by loving our neighbor, live responsibly as members of various communities, always respecting the rights of others, and helping out the weak in our midst.

The Proverbs as A Source for Moral Living

The book of Proverbs provides many helpful maxims and sayings to guide us in living morally upright lives. Choose five proverbs from chapters 20 and 27 of the book of Proverbs that express how to live a good, happy, and moral life. Rewrite them in your own words.

The Dignity of the Human Person

But God did not create man as a solitary. For from the beginning "male and female he created them" (Gn 1:27). Their companionship produces the primary form of interpersonal communion. For by his innermost nature man is a social being, and unless he relates himself to others he can neither live nor develop his potential.

—*Church in the Modern World,* No. 12

How do your relationships with others help you to reach your potential? Write a letter to a person you love telling him or her how the love you share has made you a better person.

Discussion Questions

1. Name several benefits of God's gifts to us to think, choose, and love.
2. Share an example of how the principle of subsidiarity protects one of yours or your family's God-given rights.
3. Why does Catholic moral teaching demand that we respect proper authority?
4. How do the groups you belong to (family, community, parish, school) promote the common good?

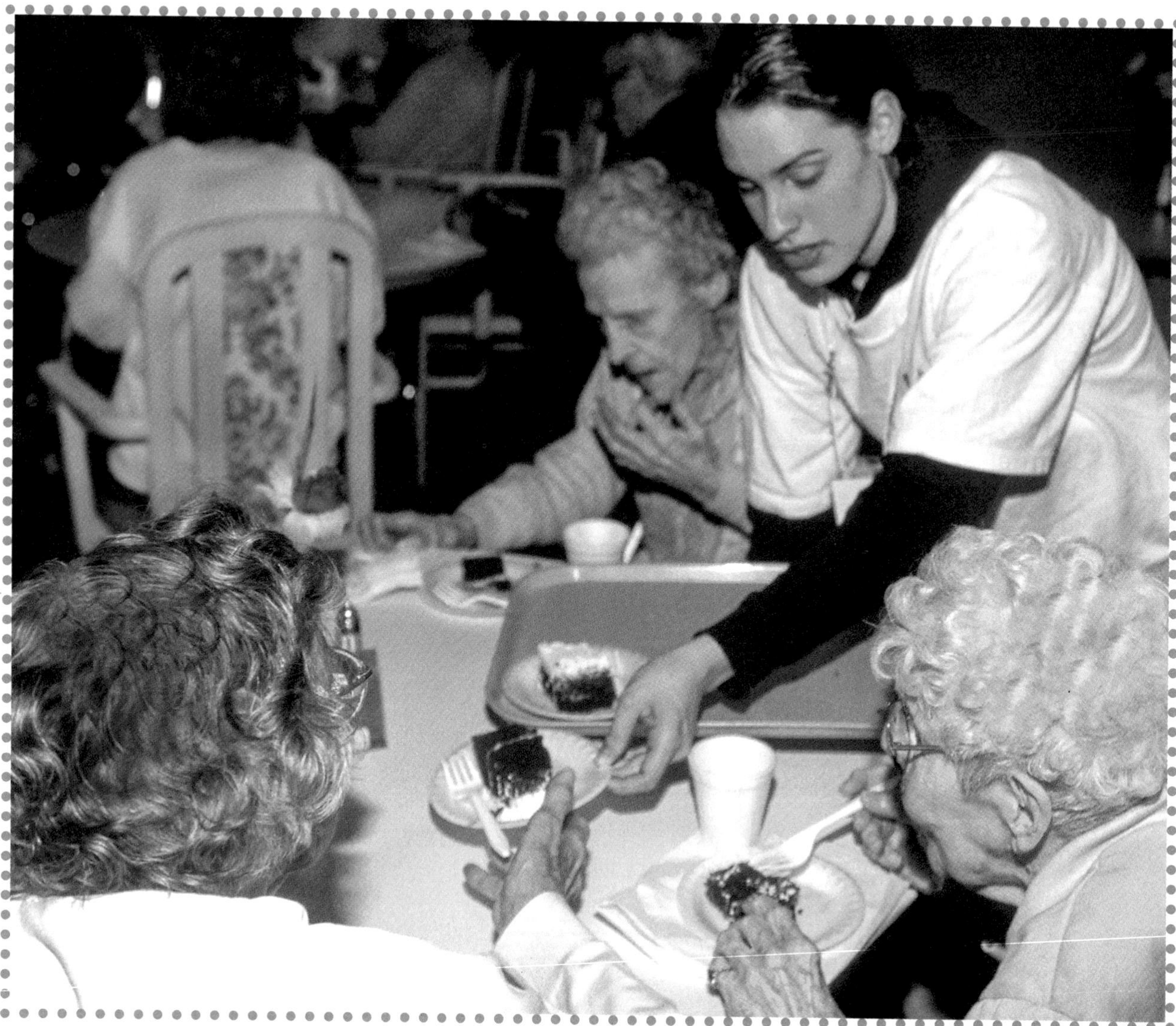

Conscience and Moral Decisions

(*CCC*, 1776–1789; 1795–1800; 1802)

As the *Catechism of the Catholic Church* defines: "Conscience is a judgment of reason whereby the human person recognizes the moral quality of a concrete act that he is going to perform, is in the process of performing, or has already completed"(*CCC*, 1778). God gave each of us a conscience to help us live like Christ.

Our conscience helps us determine if what we are doing is good or evil, whether it is in accord with God's plan or goes against it. Conscience helps us grasp what the moral thing to do is before we act, but it also helps us judge whether we did right after we act. It calls us to responsibility. Also, our conscience calls us to repent if we have sinned by going against it, by turning from our Lord's law of love.

The Second Vatican Council called conscience "the most secret core and sanctuary" of a person. Here we are alone with God, whose voice we can hear calling us to love the good and avoid evil. Every human being has a fundamental right to follow his or her conscience and to act freely on it by making morally responsible judgments. No one should be forced to act contrary to the true dictates of conscience. This is especially true in decisions affecting religion.

Forming Your Conscience

To form a true and upright conscience we need to be sincere and examine our lives before God. As Christians, in order to form a good conscience, we must:

- use our God-given ability to think to discover God's goodness and truth;
- listen to Jesus Christ, who teaches us how to be loving and virtuous;
- look to his death on the cross as the perfect example of how to love and how to obey God the Father;
- obey the teaching of the Magisterium and the example of other wise and holy people;
- use the gifts and graces of the Holy Spirit that help us live virtuous lives.

sources of morality—The three basic elements of every action: the moral object (what we do), the intention (our motive), and the circumstances (context and consequences). All three elements must be good for a proposed action to be good. In addition, some moral objects (like murder and adultery) are always evil and can never be justified. Also, a good intention can never justify an evil act.

An important first step in forming our conscience is to exercise human reason before making any decision. A thoughtful person can discover three **sources of morality**: the object chosen, the end or intention, and the circumstances surrounding the action. By reflecting on these, we can often discover the right course of action.

The *moral object* is the matter of our actions, the "what" we do. Examples of good moral acts are donating money to the missions and babysitting a younger sibling. In contrast, something that involves bad matter does not contribute to our good. For example, hurling racial insults is an evil action.

There are certain objective norms of morality that human reason and conscience can discover. These norms help us judge whether some act or attitude is good or evil, whether it is in harmony with God's will or goes against it. Some of these actions are always seriously wrong because the matter involved is always seriously wrong and involves a disorder of the will. Neither a good intention nor circumstances can turn them into morally good acts. Examples of acts that are always wrong are murder, blasphemy, adultery, child abuse, and perjury. Nothing can ever justify them.

Catholic teaching holds that the most important element for judging the morality of an act is the moral object because it determines "whether it is capable of being ordered to the good and to the ultimate end, which is God" (*Splendor of Truth*, No. 79).

A second source of morality is the *intention,* that is, one's motive or purpose for acting. Rooted in the will, our intention tells us *why* we did something. It looks to the "end," that is, the reason or goal of a particular action. For example, say you help a younger sibling get ready for school because your mom is ill. What you are doing and why you are doing it are both good. Your action, therefore, is good and moral.

One's intention can involve a series of actions whose target is the same goal. Take a student who prepares a note card to help study for a test. Note taking seems like a good moral object. However, if the student is planning to use the note card to cheat on a test, the act is bad because it is motivated by the evil act of cheating.

We may have mixed motives in our actions. For example, you may offer to cut the lawn for your dad. Your first reason is to help him after his busy day at work, but you also want to put him in a better mood before he finds out that you failed your math test. This second reason is clearly a less than worthy motive.

Catholic morality teaches an important principle regarding intentions: *A good intention can never make an intrinsically evil action into a just one.* You may have seen this principle stated this way: "The end does not justify the means." Those actions that are not directed to the good of the human person can never be made good just because a person has a "good intention." For example, murder is always evil. Therefore, an abortion is always evil even though a woman may choose one so that she can stay in school and protect her reputation. Lying is contrary to the eighth commandment and always against truth. Thus, lying on an application to get a job is not justified. The motive—getting a job—is good. But the means—lying—is not.

Finally, an evil reason for doing something can turn a good act into a bad one. For example, suppose I buy you a present simply because I want you to lie for me. In this case, I am a phony. I am using you as a means to get me off the hook. My motive is evil, even though gift-giving is usually a good thing to do.

The third source of morality is the *circumstances* that surround an action. These are secondary factors that include the consequences of an action and its context, like who is involved and where, when, and how the action takes place.

The circumstances of one's acts can increase or reduce the evil or goodness. For example, stealing five dollars from a homeless man is much worse than stealing five dollars from a millionaire. Also note that the circumstances can never turn an evil act into a good one. Therefore, it is always wrong for us not to respond to a person in need, even though fear might reduce your blameworthiness for your lack of action. We must always do for others what we would have them do for us.

For our actions to be morally good, all three elements—the object (what I do), the intention (why I do it), and the circumstances surrounding it must all be good. Jesus is our best guide to forming a sensitive, loving conscience. By praying to him in the Holy Spirit, we can learn how to live a Christ-centered life. By staying close to Jesus in friendship and by asking "What would Jesus do?" we can learn how to distinguish between good and evil. In short, Jesus wants us to judge our actions against his Golden Rule: "Do to others whatever you would have them do to you" (Mt 7:12).

Also, we must look to the Magisterium of the Church for guidance (CCC, 2030–2040; 2044–2047; 2049–2051). The moral teachings of the Magisterium apply Christ's message to matters that affect our salvation and to issues involving our fundamental rights as human beings made in God's image. The pope and bishops draw their teachings from the Creed, the Lord's Prayer, the precepts of the natural law (see pages 207-208), the Ten Commandments, Jesus' Sermon on the Mount, and the moral instruction of the apostles.

The Church's moral teachings are Christ-given and help us to make good choices. The Church is like a mother who looks out for our welfare. Therefore, we must listen to and put into practice "the constitutions and decrees conveyed by the legitimate authority of the Church" (CCC, 2037).

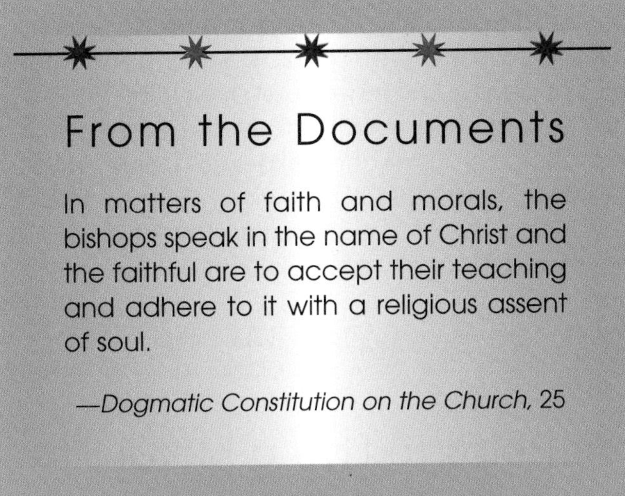

From the Documents

In matters of faith and morals, the bishops speak in the name of Christ and the faithful are to accept their teaching and adhere to it with a religious assent of soul.

—*Dogmatic Constitution on the Church,* 25

Follow Your Conscience

(*CCC,* 1790–1794; 1801).

From conscience formation, we must then do what it tells us is the good course of action. We must draw on the help of the Holy Spirit and eventually do what our conscience tells us is the right thing to do. "A human being must always obey the certain judgment of his conscience" (CCC, 1800).

After acting, our conscience can then help us judge whether or not we did the right thing. If we were sincere, prayed, acted as Jesus would, and paid attention to Church teaching, then we will have a clear conscience. As the proverb goes, "There is no pillow so soft as a clear conscience." Making wise and good decisions will help us become virtuous people. We will be forming good habits that will help us grow in holiness.

However, what if we make decisions against our conscience? If we violate our conscience, then we have sinned. Scripture tells us, "So for one who knows the right thing to do and does not do it, it is a sin" (Jas 4:17). Pangs of conscience that cause guilt can alert us to a bad decision.

Because we are human, we can make mistakes in our decisions. It is possible to have a conscience that is in error. Ignorance—lacking the information to choose the right course of action—can contribute to an erroneous conscience. Emotions can also affect our conscience, for example, anger or the strong craving for pleasure. Sometimes, we are not fully at fault for not knowing the right course of action. But at other times we are to blame because we made very little or no effort to discover the truth.

We can strengthen our conscience by making efforts to correct it if it is in error, by clearing up any doubts we might have by consulting competent people, by learning from our mistakes, and by avoiding those situations that have led us to sin before. In the last analysis, we form a good conscience by staying close to Christ and his love.

WritingAssignment

Write your resolution to the following dilemmas. Then identify and reflect on moral dilemmas you have faced.

- You agreed to go to the Homecoming Dance with a particular person. Two days later someone you really like asks you to go. What would you do? What should you do?
- A teacher falsely accuses you of cheating on an exam. You know that the person who was sitting next to you did in fact cheat. Moreover, you can prove that this person cheated. What would you do?
- Name two moral choices you made in the last week or so, one that was a good choice and one that you now recognize was an incorrect one. For each, tell how you made your choice and when you first knew it was good or bad. How did your conscience tell you that you had done the right thing? the wrong thing?

Discussion Questions

1. What will your plan for conscience formation entail?
2. Explain the principle "the end does not justify the means."
3. How is it possible to have a conscience that is in error?

ExplainingYourFaith

How do I know if I made the correct moral choice?

If your conscience has been well formed through the reading of Scripture, prayer, a study of Church teaching, an examination of conscience, and the assistance of the Holy Spirit, you can trust the urgings of your conscience to lead you to the correct choice. Making the right choice often leads to a sense of peace and inner quiet even if the choice has had consequences that were painful or difficult. On the other hand, when you make an incorrect choice, you will often experience guilt. In this case, guilt is a productive feeling. It reminds you of what you know to be right, and prompts you to seek forgiveness and to make amends.

Also, you know that some rules of morality apply to every decision that you make (e.g., the Golden Rule).

Virtues and Other Helps to Live a Moral Life

(*CCC,* 1803–1804; 1810–1834; 1839–1845)

The gifts and fruits of the Holy Spirit help us to live as Jesus did. The Holy Spirit also endows us with good habits known as virtues. The virtues help us control our passions and guide our actions according to faith and human reason. We can strengthen these virtues by receiving the sacraments and by praying to the Holy Spirit. The Holy Spirit also helps us to avoid vices. Vices are bad habits that incline us to do evil. They are the exact opposite of virtues. The principal vices, also known as the *capital sins* are pride, envy, anger, sloth, greed, gluttony, and lust.

The *theological virtues* provide the foundation for a life in Christ. They bring us in relationship to the Blessed Trinity who is their origin, motive, and object. The theological virtues are:

1. *Faith* makes it possible for us to believe in God and his revelation. Faith brings us into personal relationship with Jesus Christ and helps us believe his good news of salvation. Faith begins our life in union with the Blessed Trinity. As Christ's followers, we must profess and act on our faith, especially by serving others.
2. *Hope* implants in us a hunger for heaven and enables us to trust in God's promises for eternal life. Hope helps us to combat selfishness and strengthens us to cooperate with God's work of salvation. Jesus' Beatitudes inspire us to hope. Prayer strengthens the virtue of hope in our lives.
3. *Charity* makes it possible for us to love God above everything for his own sake. It enables us to love our neighbor as ourselves for the love of God. Charity is a share in the life of our God who is Love. It is the greatest of the virtues. Jesus commanded us to love others as he loved

us (Jn 15:12). This is the basic rule of **Christian morality**. When we obey the Lord, we are allowing God to live in us. This is what it means to live morally.

Christian morality—A life in Christ through responsible living that flows from our dignity as God's adopted children, made in his image, and from Christ's command to love.

Christ, through his Church, provides several other helps for making moral decisions. These involve varied expressions of the moral law, which are all interrelated. They are the eternal law (the source, in God, of all law), natural law, revealed law (comprising the Old Law and the New Law or Law of the Gospel), and civil and Church laws. More information follows.

Moral Law *(CCC, 1950–1953; 1975–1977)*

St. Thomas Aquinas defined the moral law as "a reasonable regulation issued by the proper authority for the common good." All law comes from the moral law of God's providence, that is, in his power, wisdom, and goodness.

Jesus Christ is the fullness and source of unity of the moral law. Three interconnected expressions of the moral law are:

1. the natural law;
2. revealed law, consisting of the Old Law and the Law of the gospel; and
3. civil and Church laws.

Expressions of Moral Law

(CCC, 1954–1960; 1978–1980)

St. Thomas Aquinas tells us that "the **natural law** is nothing other than the light of understanding placed in us by God; through it we know what we must do and what we must avoid. God has given this light or law at the creation" (quoted in CCC, 1955). By giving us a moral sense of right and wrong, God gives us a share in his own wisdom and goodness. The gift of human reason can discover the truth of natural law, for example, by discovering fundamental human rights and the duties that come from them.

natural law—God's plan for human living that is written in the very way he created things. Binding on all people at all times, it is the light of understanding that God puts in us so we can discover what is good and what is evil.

The beloved Pope John Paul II reigned for over twenty-six years from October 16, 1978 to his death on April 2, 2005.

The precepts of the natural law are unchanging, permanent, and universal, even though different cultures have applied them differently through the ages. Our ancestors in faith discovered that it is wrong to kill innocent people; the killing of innocents is still wrong today, even though some would try to justify it by using shaky arguments, for example, by attempting to justify practices like abortion.

Also, we could not live in peace without *civil laws* that flow from natural law. For example, chaos would result if we allowed people to take the property of others without their permission. If we permitted wholesale stealing, society would cease to function. The purpose of civil law is to apply the principles of the natural law to a particular society. For example, we have laws against shoplifting, burglary, and copyright violation—all trying to deter various kinds of stealing. Therefore, God revealed the precepts of the natural law so there would be no doubt whatsoever as to how we should act.

The Old Law of the Old Testament clearly states the precepts of the natural law and the truths that our own intellects are capable of discovering. God gave his Law to Moses because people had failed to discover it for themselves and often fell into sin. The Ten Commandments point out the kind of behavior we should both do and avoid. They reveal what is sinful and condemn it. They tell us what contradicts the love of God, neighbor, and self. This Old Law is good and holy, but it is not perfect. It does not give us the Holy Spirit and his graces that make it possible to live up to its commands. The Old Law only serves to prepare us for the Law of Christ and his gospel, a law of love written on the human heart.

Jesus Christ makes God's law perfect. Most perfectly revealed in the Sermon on the Mount, the New Law of Love is Christ's work. The Holy Spirit writes this law on our hearts, making it possible for us to imitate more closely our heavenly Father. Jesus' law of love does not list new rules for us to follow. Rather, it speaks to the attitudes and motives behind our actions. The Golden Rule (Mt 7:12) and Jesus' command to "love one another as I love you" (Jn 15:12) are excellent summaries of the New Law.

precepts of the Church—Basic rules that bind Catholics who belong to Christ's Body.

The Sermon on the Mount and other teachings from the apostles (found in Romans 12–15, 1 Corinthians 12–13, Colossians 3–4, and Ephesians 4–5) show that Christ's New Law is a law of love. The New Law is also a law of grace that helps us to obey it through faith and the sacramental graces. It is a law of freedom that opens our hearts to act as a child of God and a friend of Jesus Christ.

The New Law has several special virtues. These are the evangelical counsels of poverty, chastity, and obedience. These virtues help those who fully commit themselves to Christ to love more perfectly in their quest to become holy members of Christ's body.

Precepts of the Church

(*CCC*, 2041–2043; 2048)

Civil law applies the precepts of the natural law to various societies. In a similar way, Church law applies the precepts of the divine law to the Church which is trying to live a moral life. To live a moral life, we must also pray and celebrate the liturgy. Therefore, there are some important **precepts of the Church**, that is, minimum rules for Catholics to live as participating members of Christ's body. These minimum obligations help our spiritual growth. They are:

1. *You shall attend Mass on Sundays and on holy days of obligation and rest from servile labor.* Why? To celebrate our Lord's Resurrection, the joyful event of Salvation History and to observe the key liturgical feasts that honor the mysteries of our Lord, Blessed Mother, and the saints. Resting from work and activities on these days helps to keep these days holy.
2. *You shall confess your sins at least once a year.* Why? To prepare for the worthy reception of the Eucharist and to experience the work of conversion begun with Baptism.
3. *You shall receive the sacrament of Eucharist at least during the Easter season.* Why? To guarantee an absolute minimum reception of our dear Lord on a yearly basis, especially during the Easter season, the highlight of the Church's liturgical calendar.
4. *You shall observe the days of fasting and abstinence established by the Church.* Why? Jesus told us to do penance to prepare for worship, to purify our hearts, and to gain mastery over our instincts so we can grow in freedom.
5. *You shall help to provide for the needs of the Church.* Why? So the Church can continue its mission of proclaiming and celebrating the good news of Jesus.

Sin, Justification, and Grace

(*CCC*, 1846–1854; 1870–1873, 1987–2005; 2017–2024)

justification—The Holy Spirit's grace that cleanses us from our sins through faith in Jesus Christ and Baptism. It makes us right with God. Justification not only frees us from sin, but sanctifies us in the depth of our being.

We sin when we do not obey God's law of love and the dictates of our conscience. Sin offends against human reason, truth, and a good conscience. It violates love for God, neighbor, and self. It wounds our nature and disrupts the human family (see *CCC*, 1849).

God forgives our sins when we repent. God's mercy is known as **justification**. More precisely, justification is the grace of the Holy Spirit that cleanses us from our sins through faith in Jesus Christ and Baptism. Justification gives us God's own righteousness and unites us to the Lord's saving Passion. We need to be justified to live morally. Justification forgives our sins, helps us turn to the Lord, and gives us the theological virtues of faith, hope, and charity that make it possible for us to obey God's will and see him working in our lives.

Jesus' death on the cross brings about our justification. His great sacrifice gives us access to God's graces that are necessary for us to grow in holiness. By definition, grace is God's favor toward us. We cannot earn, nor do we deserve the gift of grace. The most important type of grace is *sanctifying grace* (from the Latin word *sanctus*, which means "holy"). It is also called *habitual grace* because it permanently disposes us to live like God. Conferred at Baptism, sanctifying grace makes us holy by adopting us into God's family and making us heirs of heaven.

Because grace is a gift, we can only accept it *freely*. God will never force his love on us. He has made us in such a way that we really do want to discover the truth and choose the good. Only God can satisfy these desires, which actually prepare us for our free response to his love. If we follow our hearts and respond to his inner promptings, our human freedom is made perfect and our search for truth and goodness is fulfilled.

Besides sanctifying grace, the Church names four other types of grace:

1. *actual grace*, God's special help to turn from sin or to help us act like Christ once we have turned;
2. *sacramental graces*, gifts that flow from particular sacraments;
3. *charisms*, special gifts the Holy Spirit bestows on individual Christians to help the Church grow; and
4. *graces of state*, God's special help for special ministers in the Church.

Discussion Questions

1. Which will be the only of the theological virtues necessary in heaven? Explain.
2. Explain how the precepts of natural law are unchanging.
3. Sum up Jesus' New Law of Love.
4. How can the precepts of the Church aid your spiritual growth?

Merit and the Vocation to Holiness

(*CCC*, 2006–2016; 2025–2029)

Merit is something we are owed because of our good deeds. It is a theological idea related to justification and grace. God does not really owe us anything because he has already given us all: our lives, the gift of salvation, and adoption into his family. But out of his great generosity and wisdom, God lets us share in his work of grace. God will reward us with heaven, but we must cooperate with the Holy Spirit's graces to live holy lives and therefore "merit" that reward. An important point to note: It is impossible to "earn" salvation; only God can save us through the gift of his justification. However, we must cooperate with this first grace, especially by loving God and other people as ourselves. The Holy Spirit makes it possible for us to merit certain blessings and graces for ourselves and others so we can grow in holiness on our journey to heaven.

Another amazing truth is that through prayer and following God's will we can also merit earthly goods like health and friendship, if this is in God's plan. All these gifts come through Jesus Christ, whose loving sacrifice has won us everything. To merit anything, we must let Christ live in us by power of the Holy Spirit and sanctifying grace. If Christ lives in us, then he and the Holy Spirit will make us holy. They will gain for us eternal life.

All of us are called to be holy, to be like our heavenly Father. We become holy by loving and imitating Jesus Christ our Savior. We strive to be holy because we want to be fully united to Jesus Christ. One of the surest ways to holiness is to pick up our cross and follow Jesus. The saints have taught us that works of self-denial and penance lead to holiness. The victory of heaven comes at the price of self-sacrificing love for the sake of Christ and others. The theological virtue of hope helps us continue to want to do good deeds for God. We pray and trust that God will give us the strength to serve and love him and others until our death so that we may "merit" our eternal reward.

Doing What Is Right

Test your knowledge of the principles of morality. For each case below, decide which principle applies and if sin would be involved if you followed one course of action rather than another. In the cases that involve sin, decide whether it would be mortal or venial sin.

Principles of Morality

1. Do good; avoid evil.
2. One may never do evil that good may result from it. ("A good end does not justify using evil means to attain it.")
3. Do unto others what you would have them do unto you.
4. Be the human being God intended you to be.

Cases

1. Most of your peers are picking on a classmate who is socially clumsy.
2. To get an edge on a job application, you are tempted to claim some work experience that you never had.
3. You know of a classmate who has completely plagiarized a term paper.

Discussion Questions

1. "God will never force his love on you." Tell what this statement means to you.
2. List some ways you can "pick up your cross" and die to selfishness.
3. Why doesn't God owe us justification?

4. A classmate you barely know has fallen off a bike alongside the road and you pass by.
5. Some friends want you to see a movie that your parents explicitly told you not to see.

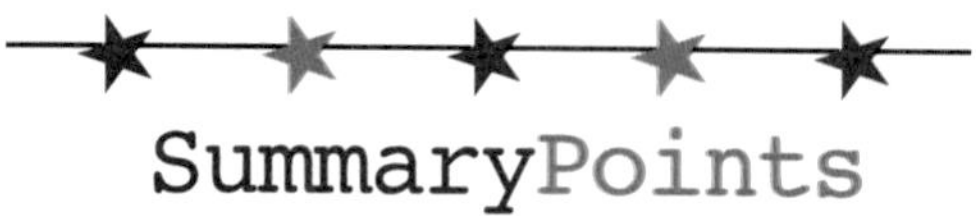

SummaryPoints

★ Though wounded by sin, we can think, choose, love, and act responsibly. The Holy Spirit lives in us and makes it possible for us to follow Jesus by doing good and avoiding evil.

★ The principle of subsidiarity holds that a larger social unit should not take over the functions of a smaller group if it can achieve for itself the common good.

★ Everyone is obligated to form continuously, and then follow, his or her conscience. Conscience is the judgment of reason that enables us to determine right and wrong. It operates before, during, and after we act. We sin when we do not follow our conscience.

★ Conscientious moral decision-making involves using our minds to discover the truth, imitating Jesus' teaching and example of loving and serving others, heeding the moral teachings of the Magisterium, putting into practice the theological and cardinal virtues, and growing in holiness according to the graces and helps (like the gifts and fruits of the Holy Spirit) that God gives to us.

★ Our conscience can be wrong because of factors like ignorance, emotions, peer pressure, total self-reliance, and loveless hearts. We have a lifelong duty to inform and reform our consciences.

★ The sources of every moral action are the object (what we do), the intention (why we do it), and the circumstances, which include the context and the consequences of our acts.

★ A good intention for an action cannot justify evil means used to attain it.

★ The virtues are good habits that help us choose the good and to act with ease and competence.

★ The theological virtues—faith, hope, and charity (love)—find their roots in God and turn us toward him.

★ God is the author of law, including the moral law, which guides us in responsible, Christian living.

★ We should avoid personal sin, both mortal and venial, because sin offends against God, human reason, truth, and a good conscience. It violates the love of God, neighbor, and self. The capital sins of pride, envy, anger, sloth, greed, and lust are vices or bad habits that lead us to commit mortal sin. If we sin, we should repent and return to God's friendship.

★ Justification, a work of the Holy Spirit, cleanses us of our sins through Baptism and faith in Christ. Flowing from grace, justification makes it possible for us to live a life in Christ. Sanctifying or habitual grace makes us holy because it is God's favor, the free and undeserved help he gives us to live as his adopted children.

★ Out of his unlimited goodness and generosity, God has won (merited) for us eternal life. God permits humans to cooperate with his gift of salvation, so our good works can earn merit for ourselves and others. But all is done through Jesus Christ, who is the source of all merit.

ReviewQuestions

1. What is the heart of Christian morality?
2. What does it mean to have a free will?
3. Explain the principle of subsidiarity.
4. What is the virtue of solidarity? How is it related to our social nature?

5. Define *conscience.*
6. How is a person's conscience formed?
7. List and briefly discuss the three sources of morality.
8. How can circumstances affect a person's blameworthiness for his or her actions?
9. Write the Golden Rule.
10. What is the role of the Magisterium in helping people make moral decisions?
11. Must a person always follow his or her conscience? Explain.
12. Explain how a conscience can be erroneous and what a person must do to correct it.
13. Name the theological virtues and cardinal virtues.
14. What are the theological virtues? Which is the most important? Why?
15. Define *law.* Why is natural law permanent and unchanging?
16. Where is the Old Law summarized? What is its purpose?
17. What is the New Law?
18. Name the precepts of the Church.
19. What does it mean to be justified?
20. What is sanctifying grace? List and briefly discuss other kinds of grace.

Applying What You Have Learned

1. Christopher News Notes. Read one of the newsletters that deal with living a Christ-like life from the Christopher Movement website. Prepare a report for class. Their homepage is: www.christophers.org
2. Make a list of ten "Teen Commandments," in other words, reasonable rules and guidelines for living in a family. For example, "Always call home when you will be more than a half-hour late." Share your list with your classmates. Combine all the lists into one class list. Make copies of the final list. Share it with your parents.
3. Evaluate ten radio and television advertisements aimed at teenagers. Discuss what message they are selling concerning a person's dignity and self-worth. Critique these messages considering the basic dignity of each person.

Prayer Reflection

The Prayer for Peace is attributed to St. Francis of Assisi. Pray that you can be an instrument of Christ's peace to all.

Prayer for Peace

Lord, make me an instrument of your peace.
Where there is hatred, let me sow love;
where there is injury, pardon;
where there is doubt, faith;
where there is despair, hope;
where there is darkness, light;
where there is sadness, joy.
O Divine Master, grant that I may not seek so much to be consoled as to console;
to be understood, as to understand,
to be loved, as to love.
For it is in giving that we receive,
it is in pardoning that we are pardoned,
and it is in dying that we are born to eternal life.

Devise a concrete plan for bringing peace to others over the course of the next week. Follow through on your plan.

You are the light of the world. A city set on a mountain cannot be hidden. Nor do they light a lamp and then put it under a bushel basket; it is set on a lampstand, where it gives light to all in the house. Just so, your light must shine before others, that they may see your good deeds and glorify your heavenly Father.

Matthew 5:14–16

Chapter 9 Outline

Unsung Heroes

Christian morality involves showing our love for God by loving others, especially the most needy.

Called to Happiness

The Beatitudes are a formula to help us love God and neighbor in a Christ-like way.

Love God: The First Three Commandments

The first three commandments show us how to love God with our whole heart, soul, strength, and mind.

Love Your Neighbor: The Fourth through Tenth Commandments

Commandments four through ten help us to love our neighbor as ourselves.

Chapter 9

Christian Moral Life: The Beatitudes and the Ten Commandments

Unsung Heroes

In his documentary novel *Hiroshima*, author John Hersey wrote about the aftermath of the atomic bomb dropped on that city at the end of World War II. Many helpless victims of the great blast found themselves trapped in caved-in buildings, unable to escape as raging fires spread.

Survivors of the initial shock waves jammed the streets and began fleeing to the countryside. Victims trapped in the collapsed buildings screamed out to those fleeing on the streets to rescue them, but most had only their own survival in mind and did not even hear the desperate cries for help.

Some others did hear the cries but did not help. They convinced themselves that the army, police, or the Japanese equivalent of the Red Cross would take care of the trapped victims. However, Hersey reports that a brave few of the fleeing refugees heard the cries, left the retreating crowd, and at extreme personal danger helped those trapped to escape. These were the unsung heroes of the great tragedy of the bomb that ushered in the atomic age.

Hiroshima Monument

John Hersey

Christians are called to be like these Japanese heroes. We must go beyond our own problems. We must hear the cry of those who need us. We must not wait for someone else to get involved. We must drop out of line and respond to the needs of others in our midst. This is Christian morality in action. We show our love for God by loving others, especially the most needy in our midst. If we do so, then we can indeed be worthy of the name *Christian*. Living the Beatitudes of Jesus and putting into practice the Ten Commandments are two sure paths to living a life in Christ.

Called to Happiness

(CCC, 1718–1724; 1728–1729)

What is the meaning of life? Our Catholic faith provides a great answer to this question: God created us to know, love, and serve him in this life and to be happy with him forever in the afterlife. God gave us a great gift by placing in us a deep hunger for happiness that only he can satisfy. He wants us to share in his divine nature, to partake in the vision of God, to enter into our Lord's joy. A word for happiness is *beatitude*.

For our part, we must accept the gift of happiness God freely gives to us by living upright, moral, and Christ-like lives so we are fully able to embrace God's love. We do so when we put into practice the teachings of Jesus in the Sermon on the Mount, obey the Ten Commandments, and follow the teachings of the apostles and the Magisterium. These all guide us on our road to eternal happiness. The Beatitudes lead the way.

The Beatitudes

(CCC, 1716–1717; 1725–1727)

Jesus shared the Beatitudes at the beginning of his Sermon on the Mount (see Mt 5:3–12). The Beatitudes are also found in the Sermon on the Plain in Luke 6:20–26. They complete the promises that God made to Abraham, the father of the Jewish faith. They show us how to fulfill our desire for happiness and teach us how we should live in order to reach our eternal destiny of union with him. The Beatitudes also explain how we should love God and neighbor in a Christ-like way.

The Beatitudes are summarized below.

Blessed are the poor in spirit, for theirs is the kingdom of heaven. Jesus associated with the poor, weak, and vulnerable. He wants us to do the same. Jesus does not praise the condition of material poverty. This is an evil. Rather, he wants us to recognize our spiritual poverty—that everything we are and everything we have are gifts from God. Your health, your intelligence, your friends, your life itself are all gifts from God. We thank God for these gifts by sharing what we have and what we are with others.

Blessed are they who mourn, for they shall be comforted. Jesus blesses those who mourn over injustices and evils committed against God and people in need. This beatitude leads us to empathize with children dying of starvation, innocent people experiencing the violence of abortion, murders, rape, and economic injustice. When our fellow humans succumb to drug addiction, misuse their sexuality, discriminate against those who are different, kill each other in senseless wars, then we should indeed mourn. Our hearts ache for the sins of the world, and for our own sins, too. But we should not lose heart, because Jesus promises that he will eventually console us.

Blessed are the meek, for they shall inherit the land. Humility is equated with meekness. Jesus demonstrated this virtue when he treated others with gentleness and compassion. He also forgave others when they hurt and taunted him. His heavenly Father also treats each of us with patience, forgiveness, and gentleness when we sin. We, too, should be patient with the weaknesses of others. We should work to solve disagreements with gentleness and good will and never give in to hate or violence.

Blessed are they who hunger and thirst for righteousness, for they shall be satisfied. St. Augustine noted that God made us with restless hearts that will not find happiness until we find God. In this Beatitude, Jesus blesses those who know that only God's righteousness can fulfill us. God made us so our hearts seek divine justice and a good relationship with him. Our hearts seek the holy God and the loving, forgiving friendship of Jesus Christ, our Savior. The Lord Jesus comes to us in the Eucharist to help us grow in holiness, to satisfy our spiritual hunger, and to join us so we can take him to others.

Blessed are the merciful, they will be shown mercy. When we pray the Our Father, we petition God to "forgive us our trespasses as we forgive those who trespass against us." God loves us beyond what we deserve. He proves this love by giving us his Son Jesus, who forgives our sins and makes it possible through the Holy Spirit and Baptism to become members of the divine family. In return, we should share with others the love, mercy, and forgiveness that we have been given. Our forgiveness of others, especially our enemies, is a sign to the world of a merciful God who loves everyone.

Blessed are the clean of heart, for they will see God. "Who is number one in your life?" is the question this Beatitude asks each of us. A person with a clean heart has a single-minded commitment to God. School, money, possessions, family, sports, friends, everything else should come after a total commitment to accomplish God's will.

Blessed are the peacemakers, for they will be called children of God. By definition, Christians are, and must be, peacemakers. Christians are to see others as brothers and sisters in the Lord. They will work hard to end strife that leads to violence.

Blessed are they who are persecuted for the sake of righteousness, for theirs is the kingdom of heaven. Suffering for faith in Jesus is a great sign of love for him. He himself suffered misunderstanding and abuse when he preached the truth. As a Christian, you are certain to meet ridicule and rejection sometime in your life. Many Christians in history have suffered martyrdom. But if we remain faithful to him, the Lord will reward us with eternal happiness in heaven. There is no greater reward.

Discussion Questions

1. How can living the Beatitudes bring happiness?
2. Which beatitude do you believe is most essential for the world to practice?
3. Why do you think Jesus' preaching of the Beatitudes in Matthew is set on a mountain, while in Luke it is set on a plain?

Love God: The First Three Commandments

Jesus taught that we should love the Lord our God with our whole heart, soul, strength, and mind (Lk 10:27). The first three commandments show us how to do so, that is, how to respond to a God who gave us life, his Son, and the gift of eternal life.

I. I, the Lord, Am Your God. You Shall Not Have Other Gods Besides Me.

(*CCC*, 2083; 2087-2094; 2101; 2103; 2111-2132)

I. The first commandment tells us to make God the top priority in our lives. How do we do this? One way of doing so is to practice the virtues of faith, hope, and charity. We practice our faith and hope when we show trust in God and his divine revelation, mercy, and promise of eternal life. We also demonstrate our faith when we worship God and share our faith with others. We exhibit charity when we love God, and our fellow humans, with our whole heart.

The theological virtues lead us to the moral virtues and to the *virtue of religion*. The virtue of religion helps us give to God what is his just due—that is, reverence, love, and worship. We have a duty to worship God both individually and socially. Civil law must protect the right of individuals and communities to worship God freely according to the dictates of their conscience.

The way to exercise the virtue of religion is through adoration, prayer, works of sacrifice, and keeping our promises and vows. When we adore

God, we are humble and thankful for all he has done for us. When we pray, we are lifting our minds and hearts to God in praise, thanksgiving, sorrow, petition, and intercession. Prayer also helps us keep God's commandments. When we join our works of sacrifice to Jesus' sacrifice on the cross, we make our lives pleasing to God. Finally, the virtue of religion makes it possible to keep the promises Catholics make at Baptism, Confirmation, Holy Orders, and Matrimony. The virtue of religion enables believers to keep their vows, that is, any special promises they made to God, especially the evangelical counsels (vows) of poverty, chastity, and obedience.

The first commandment counsels against sins against the virtue of faith like heresy (false teaching that denies a truth of the faith), **apostasy** (denial of Christ), and schism (a break in union with the pope by refusing to accept his authority to teach for Christ). The first commandment also teaches us to avoid sins against the virtue of hope. These include presumption, which says a person can save himself without God's help or without personal conversion, and **despair**, which occurs when a person believes that even God cannot or will not forgive a person his or her sins. The sin of despair is unjust to a God who is always faithful to his promises.

apostasy—The denial of Christ and repudiation of the Christian faith by a baptized Christian.

despair—Giving up hope in God's saving graces, his forgiveness of sins, and his promise of salvation.

Finally, sins against the virtue of love include refusing to accept God's love, ingratitude, and spiritual laziness. Outright hatred of God is the worst sin of all against a God of perfect love. The root of this sin is pride.

The first commandment condemns the worship of false gods and the following sins:

1. *Superstition* attributes magical powers to certain objects, acts, words, or external religious practices apart from proper interior dispositions, for example, of faith and humility.
2. ***Idolatry*** includes the worship of false gods, including the worship of many gods (polytheism). Today, idolatry includes not only cults that worship Satan, but also making a god out of things like money, prestige, sex, power, athletic ability, and so forth. Idolatry turns us away from the true God by taking a created good and making it a god.
3. *Divination* attempts to reveal what is hidden (occult). It involves calling on Satan or the demons, conjuring up the dead, consulting horoscopes and the stars (astrology) and mediums, reading palms, and playing with Ouija boards. These, and practices like **sorcery**, which tries to control hidden powers, show disrespect to God.
4. *Irreligion* disrespects God's loving care for us by tempting God in word or deed to manifest his goodness.
5. *Sacrilege* seriously disrespects (profanes) the sacraments and sacred things, places, or persons specially consecrated to God. Sacrilege is mortally sinful, especially when committed against Christ in the Eucharist.
6. *Simony* is the attempt to buy or sell spiritual things. This is wrong because God's graces are free gifts that can never be purchased or sold.

idolatry—Giving worship to something or someone other than the true God.

sorcery—Attempts to tame occult powers in order to use them to gain a supernatural power over others.

Putting the Ten Commandments into Practice

There are two versions of the Ten Commandments in the Old Testament: Exodus (20:2–17) and Deuteronomy (5:6–21). The first three commandments spell out what it means to love God; the last seven instruct us on love of neighbor.

Both Christ and the Church teach that the Ten Commandments are indeed *commandments,* not suggestions. God has written them on our hearts and he gives us the graces necessary to obey them. The Commandments teach truth. They tell us what we must do as humans who depend on God and live with one another. They protect basic human rights. They apply to all people in all places at all times.

Catholics must obey the commandments under the penalty of sin. All people have a serious duty to obey the Ten Commandments. Take some time to reread and memorize the Ten Commandments, listed below:

I. I, the Lord, am your God. You shall not have other gods besides me.

II. You shall not take the name of the Lord, your God, in vain.

III. Remember to keep holy the sabbath day.

IV. Honor your father and your mother.

V. You shall not kill.

VI. You shall not commit adultery.

VII. You shall not steal.

VIII. You shall not bear false witness against your neighbor.

IX. You shall not covet your neighbor's wife.

X. You shall not covet anything that belongs to your neighbor.

Reflect on how well you are living each of the following commandments and grade yourself honestly using a typical grading scale:
A (excellent) to **F (poor).**

____ I. God is the top priority in my life. Nothing else has my utmost loyalty—not my possessions, power over others, prestige, sex, etc.

____ II. I respect God's name and everything else that is holy.

____ III. I go to Mass every Sunday. I recreate my spirit through rest, healthful activities, and prayer on that day.

____ IV. I honor and obey my parents, respect my brothers and sisters, and show respect to other persons who hold authority over me.

____ V. I respect all life as a gift from God. I refrain from practices that would harm others or me. I show care for those who most need love.

____ VI. I respect my own sexuality and that of others. I refrain from doing anything that would bring shame to me as a child of God and temple of the Holy Spirit.

____ VII. I am honest in all my dealings, a person of integrity. I neither cheat nor steal.

____ VIII. My word is my honor. I always tell the truth. I do not spread gossip or ruin the reputations of others.

____ IX and X. I guard against lust. I am not envious of other people's good fortune. I am not jealous.

Writing Assignment

1. If God asked you to compose three additional commandments for the modern world, what would they be?
2. Rewrite the commandments in your own words. Turn all the negative statements into positive ones. Share your versions with your classmates.

7. *Atheism* denies that God exists. It has many forms. For example, *materialists* claim that something is real only if we can sense it. They deny the existence of spiritual realities like God and the human soul. *Humanists* make human beings their god and do not believe in God as the controlling source in our world. *Communists* look to economic laws and forces as the real basis of human freedom and claim that God is a fiction. All these forms of atheism are serious because they deny that the true God exists. However, a particular atheist may have diminished blameworthiness for this sin because of circumstances or intentions. For example, he or she may not have correctly heard about God and his love for mankind.
8. An *agnostic* claims that we can never be certain whether God exists or not. Agnostics do not outright deny God's existence like atheists, but they often live their lives as though God does not exist. Their refusal to take a stand is, in fact, a decision against God since they refuse to make any kind of a religious response to God.

Explaining Your Faith

Why do Catholics keep religious pictures, statues, and the like? Doesn't the first commandment outlaw the keeping of images?

Because the Son of God became a human being, the Church teaches that it is fitting for Christians to venerate icons (religious paintings, mosaics, and the like) and statues of Jesus, his Blessed Mother, and the angels and saints. Sacred images remind us of, and direct our attention to the persons they represent. But we should always remember that only God deserves adoration. In the Old Testament, Yahweh forbade the making of images because the Chosen People sometimes created and worshiped false idols.

Christians have special devotion to Mary and venerate her because she is the Mother of God and the Mother of the Church. We also venerate the saints, who inspire us and pray for us. However, veneration and special devotion are not the same as worship. To worship anyone other than God is idolatry.

II. You Shall Not Take the Name of the Lord, Your God, in Vain.

(*CCC*, 2142–2167)

When God revealed his name, Yahweh, to the Chosen People, he commanded that we honor his holy name through praise, reverence, and adoration. When we respect God's name, then we are honoring the holy and mysterious One behind the name. This is also true when we reverence the name of our Blessed Savior, Jesus Christ, and his Blessed Mother and the saints.

Our names are also holy. We have been called by Jesus and known by God from all eternity. We are baptized "in the name of the Father and of the Son and of the Holy Spirit." At that time, we also receive a baptismal name that often reminds us of a patron saint whose life can inspire us and who prays for us in heaven. Through Baptism, the Lord makes our name holy, marking us as his Christian disciples. Disciples have a wonderful way to pray throughout the day—by frequently praying the Sign of the Cross. This powerful prayer reminds us of our dignity. And it also tells us that we belong to a loving God whose graces make it possible for us to live up to the name *Christian*.

oath—A statement or promise that calls on God to be witness to it.

The second commandment outlaws any wrong use of God's name or the names of Jesus, Mary, or any saint. It teaches that we should keep our promises and vows and always be true to our word.

perjury—Lying under oath by asking God to witness a lie. This is a grave violation of the second commandment.

The taking of an **oath** should not be necessary for a Christian. Our word simply stated is enough to bind us. However, Jesus did not outlaw all oath-taking. Even St. Paul took oaths (see 2 Cor 1:23 and Gal 1:20.) For morally correct and serious reasons (for example, a legal trial), we may take an oath if we are doing so to serve justice. However, we may not take an oath if it requires us to support an institution that destroys human dignity or Christian unity. Church teaching holds that whenever we do take an oath we must keep it. **Perjury** is the name for lying under oath. Perjury seriously dishonors God's holy name by calling on God to witness to a lie.

blasphemy—Any thought, word, or act that expresses hatred or contempt for God, Christ, the Church, saints, or holy things.

Blasphemy also seriously violates the second commandment. Blasphemy involves using internal or external words of hate, defiance, or reproach against God, Jesus, the saints, sacred things, or the Church. Blasphemy also includes using God's name to hide a crime or to enslave, torture, or kill people. This sin is intrinsically evil and can never be justified, regardless of the circumstances or intention.

Swearing under oath is also serious business. If we do so deliberately with God as our witness, intending to break the oath, then we commit mortal sin. This kind of swearing makes God a witness to a lie.

The Catholic tradition distinguishes swearing, cursing, and vulgar language. By definition, *cursing* calls down evil on another person. It is forbidden by the second commandment. If the curse involves wishing serious harm on another, then it is a grave sin. Vulgar language involves using crude words ("bathroom talk"). It is immature, rather than sinful.

St. James knew the many problems caused by the human tongue when he wrote:

> For every kind of beast and bird, of reptile and sea creature, can be tamed and has been tamed by the human species, but no human being can tame the tongue. It is a restless evil, full of deadly poison. With it we bless the Lord and Father, and with it we curse human beings who are made in the likeness of God. From the same mouth come blessing and cursing. This need not be so, my brothers (Jas 3:7–10).

Writing Assignment

Spend a few minutes looking closely at a religious picture or statue at your home, school, or parish church. Write down, based on what you see, something about the person depicted in the artwork you have chosen.

St. Thomas More: A Man of Conscience and Principle

St. Thomas More is a famous example of a Catholic hero who refused to take an immoral oath. Thomas More was the Chancellor of England under King Henry VIII and a great and brilliant scholar. He was the author of the famous book *Utopia* (a word meaning "nowhere"), which outlined a society ruled by perfect justice. He wrote *Utopia* to protest the new economy of his age where the rich took advantage of the poor. In his own life, Thomas was a devoted family man who raised his family in a spirit of prayer and generosity to the poor.

Thomas ran into trouble with Henry VIII when the king wanted Thomas's support in making Henry head of the Church in England. In a celebrated dispute, the pope refused to annul Henry's marriage to Catherine of Aragon who had been unable to give a male heir. So Henry decided to take matters into his own hands. He declared himself the supreme authority of the church in England and forced the bishops to acknowledge him as such by taking an oath declaring their loyalty to him. Thomas More refused to do so because he knew this oath—the Act of Supremacy—would have denied the pope's authority over the Church. This would have been a denial of the pope's rightful authority as the vicar of Christ.

When Thomas refused the oath he also resigned his prestigious office, even though it meant that he and his family fell into poverty. King Henry then required all his subjects to take the Oath of Succession, recognizing the legitimacy of his heirs by his new wife, Anne Boleyn. Thomas More also refused to take that oath, because he knew it was clearly wrong, too. He was arrested and spent fifteen months in the feared Tower of London, deaf to the pleas of his family to reconsider his decision. To the end, Thomas would not violate his conscience:

> I do nobody any harm, I say none harm, I think none harm. And if this be not enough to keep a man alive, in good faith I long not to live.

Study the life and death of St. Thomas More. See:

www.apostles.com/thomasmore.html

III. Remember to Keep Holy the Sabbath Day.
(ccc, 2168-2188)

III.

The third commandment is related to two truths of the Old Testament: first, God "rested" after he completed the work of creation; second, God gave the Chosen People the sabbath day as a sign of the covenant that he made with them by rescuing them from slavery in Egypt. The Israelites understood that the purpose of this commandment was for them to praise God for his works of creation and to thank him for his saving works on their behalf.

God gives this commandment to all people for them to have a day of rest and re-creation. Jesus taught its true purpose, "The Sabbath was made for man, not man for the

Discussion Questions

1. What are some superstitions you have practiced?
2. Do you think it is sinful to read the daily astrology charts? Would it be sinful to take them seriously?
3. What are some ways that people your age search out spiritual meaning for their lives?
4. Give some examples of the "false gods" people worship today.
5. Would it be wrong for you to work on Sunday if you do not have to? Why or why not?

Sabbath" (Mk 2:27). It is most proper for humans to worship and thank God. We should acknowledge that we are totally dependent on our loving God for all that he has given to us. This day should serve as a break from work, especially for the poor and working class, and from the endless pursuit of money.

Jesus brought new meaning to the sabbath observance. Through his saving deeds, Jesus brought about a new creation, namely, eternal life for those who love him. The resurrection of Jesus took place on a Sunday, the first day of the week, the "eighth day" following the sabbath. We rightly call Sunday the "Lord's Day" and it is clearly distinguished from the sabbath. For Christians, the observance of the Lord's Day on Sunday replaces the sabbath. Since the time of the apostles, Christians have gathered on Sundays to obey Jesus' command to break bread in his name. On this day we worship, praise, and thank God for the gift of the Son and all the other divine blessings granted us. Sunday is the holy day that celebrates God's salvation through Jesus Christ.

Catholics are obliged to go to Mass on Sundays and holy days of obligation to express, celebrate, and deepen their unity in Christ. The Eucharist is the heart of Catholic life, an opportunity for us to acclaim to others that we belong to Christ and are members of his Body, the Church. The Eucharist gives us Christ's life and the strength and guidance of the Holy Spirit. Because the Eucharist is central to our life in Christ, participating in the Sunday Mass (and on holy days) is a serious obligation that we must fulfill under the penalty of sin, unless some critical reason like sickness excuses us. Catholics who willfully miss Mass are guilty of mortal sin.

The best way to make the Lord's day holy is to receive him in the Eucharist. We also make this day holy by staying away from unnecessary work and business activities. Relaxing activities, spending time with our families, reading, enjoying the outdoors, serving others in need, and doing anything that helps to refresh our minds, hearts, and spirits are all appropriate ways to make Sunday holy.

St. Paul

Love Your Neighbor: The Fourth through Tenth Commandments

Jesus taught that the way we express our love for God is that we love our neighbor as we love ourselves. And St. Paul taught,

> The commandments, "You shall not commit adultery; you shall not kill; you shall not steal; you shall not covet," and whatever other commandment there may be, are summed up in this saying, (namely) "You shall love your neighbor as yourself" (Rom 13:9).

The next subsections cover each of these commandments individually.

IV. Honor Your Father and Your Mother.

(*CCC*, 2197; 2201; 2204–2205; 2215; 2217–2219; 2222–2223; 2225; 2230; 2234; 2240, 2241)

The fourth commandment opens the second part of the Decalogue by stressing that charity begins at home. God created the family as the primary unit of society. It is a sacred community of love in which a husband and wife marry freely as equals to share their love and to participate with God in the procreation and education of children. The family is called the *domestic Church*, a community of faith, hope, and charity that teaches virtue, respect, and love. The family mirrors the love and unity of the Blessed Trinity.

The fourth commandment stresses several duties of parents. Parents must respect their children as persons with dignity. They must educate them, especially in the Catholic faith. They must provide them with a loving home where their children can experience warmth, love, respect, and forgiveness and where they can learn the meaning of service. Parents should encourage their children to respond to the Lord if he should call them to serve as a priest or in religious life, and they must respect the right of their adult children to choose a profession and marriage partner. Parents must at all times give their children unconditional love and affection and, in this way, serve as models of God's love.

The fourth commandment also requires certain behaviors from children. Children are to thank their parents for the gift of life. Children show their gratitude by respecting and honoring their parents throughout their lives. Furthermore, children should obey their parents as long as they live in their home. Adult children honor their parents by meeting their physical and spiritual needs when their aged parents are sick or lonely. Also, siblings are to treat each other with respect and love.

Respect and obedience due all proper Church and other authority figures (teachers, employers, police, leaders) is connected to the fourth commandment. In the civic order, this implies a moral obligation to pay taxes, exercise the right to vote, and serve the nation in its defense or some other way. Jesus himself taught, "Repay to Caesar what belongs to Caesar and to God what belongs to God" (Lk 20:25). St. Paul also instructed his readers to obey proper authorities (see Rom 13:1).

However, obedience to civil authority is not absolute. Governments must respect the God-given rights of individuals, parents, and families. For example, governments have the duty to recognize the parents' primary right to educate their children, according to their own convictions. When societal laws conflict with God's will or God's law, then we must obey God, even if this leads to personal suffering.

Today, when so many devalue the family and disrespect unborn human beings, a loving Christian family can be a shining beacon pointing to the presence of God in ordinary life.

V. You Shall Not Kill.

(*CCC*, 2258; 2263–2268; 2270–2298; 2307–2316)

The fifth commandment teaches respect for the sanctity of human life. God is the source

and final destiny of all human life. Therefore human life is sacred, from the first moment of conception until natural death. Every person has profound dignity because of being created in God's image and likeness.

We show respect for God's gift of life by eating healthy food, by getting proper exercise and rest, by challenging our minds to grow, and by avoiding harmful substances like drugs, alcohol, and tobacco. Taking care of ourselves physically, mentally, psychologically, and spiritually frees us to be persons for others. We respect life when we defend the rights of others so they may live with dignity. This is especially true when we defend the weak and helpless in our midst.

Any direct and intentional killing of a human being is a sinful violation of the fifth commandment. The Old Testament applies this to *murder*, that is, the deliberate killing of innocent human beings. Murder is the result of original sin. Anger and hate lead to mortal sin, including murder. Murder violates human dignity, God's holiness, and Jesus' teaching that we must love our neighbor as we love ourselves. Today we see how anger and revenge greatly threaten human dignity, for example in acts of kidnapping, hostage taking, and torture. *Terrorism* is an especially grave evil that results in the murder of countless innocent humans. It must be severely condemned.

The fifth commandment does *not* condemn killing in self-defense. Killing in self-defense is morally permitted as a last resort when a person is defending his or her own life against an unjust aggressor, or when someone responsible for another is protecting that person's life. In cases of legitimate self-defense, the intention is to save one's own life against an unjust aggressor. The killing of the assailant is not directly willed; it is only allowed. In a similar way, public authorities have both the right and duty to defend citizens against unjust aggressors, even if this might lead to the death penalty or to a defensive war.

In all cases, however, individuals and society *must* always use bloodless means to defend against unjust aggressors if at all possible. Consider for a moment that the reasons we punish criminals are to set right the disorder caused by the offense, to correct the offender, and to preserve public order and personal safety. The *death penalty* simply fails to achieve the first and second of these aims, and is only very rarely necessary to accomplish the third. It cannot "set right the disorder caused by the offense" as it does not undo the crime (e.g., if the criminal were a murderer, his or her death would not restore life to the victim), nor can it correct the offender since it ends his or her life. Public safety and order can be achieved in many ways without recourse to the death penalty. "The cases in which the execution of the offender is an absolute necessity are very rare, if not practically non-existent" (*CCC*, 2267) today. Therefore, the Church teaches that governments should use non-lethal means of punishment as an example of putting into practice Jesus' example of forgiving love. The death penalty may be permitted only "in cases of absolute necessity."

In a similar way, war must be reasonably avoided at all costs, because it involves great evil and injustice. We must always strive to be peacemakers. Peace is "the tranquility of order." It results when human dignity is respected, the goods of persons are safeguarded, and free communication among people takes place. "Peace is the work of justice and the effect of charity" (*CCC*, 2304).

However, the Church acknowledges the right of legitimate governments to participate in a just war of defense under these conditions:

1. the damage inflicted by the aggressor is lasting, grave, and certain;
2. it is truly a last resort after all other means to resolve the conflict have first been exhausted;
3. the prospects of success are serious; and
4. the use of arms will not produce evil graver than the evil to be eliminated (see *CCC*, 2309).

Once a nation goes to war, it must follow the moral law, for example, by protecting noncombatants and by using the minimum force necessary. It is for this reason that the American bishops teach that the use of nuclear and other weapons of mass destruction which cause grave harm to entire communities of people cannot be justified. Furthermore, the arms race and the selling of arms is sinful. Their cost seriously harms poor people, as it diverts valuable resources from assisting those in need to building up the tools of war. A Christian must always recall and live Jesus'

Beatitude, "Blessed are the peacemakers, for they will be called children of God" (Mt 5:9).

As covered above, the fifth commandment forbids several actions that directly and intentionally kill innocent people. It also forbids any action or failure to act that results in their indirect killing. The fifth commandment strictly outlaws the following:

1. *Direct **abortion***. Willed either as a means or an end, it is a grave violation of the fifth commandment. Human life must be respected and protected by law from the very first moment of conception. Everyone has a God-given right to life. This right does not have to be earned. Because abortion is such a serious attack on innocent life, the Church imposes the penalty of excommunication on those who cooperate in an abortion. The fifth commandment also outlaws as seriously wrong non-therapeutic genetic manipulation or medical

abortion—The direct and deliberate ending of a pregnancy by killing the unborn child. Direct abortion, willed either as a means or an end, gravely contradicts the moral law.

Suzanne Vitadamo (on the left), her mother Mary Schindler and father Bob Schindler grieve at the death of their sister and daughter, 41-year-old Terri Schindler Schiavo, the severly brain-damaged woman who passed away on March 31, 2005, thirteen days after a court ordered her feeding tube removed.

(Photo credit: Roberto Schmidt/AFP/Getty Images)

experimentation that treats the embryo as disposable biological material.

2. *Intentional euthanasia, which is murder.* This is true regardless of the form it takes (e.g., assisted suicide) or the motives for doing it (e.g., "to relieve pain"). A person does *not* commit the sin of **euthanasia** by refusing to use "extraordinary means" to keep oneself alive in the face of a terminal illness. A dying person must always use ordinary means (like taking in fluid) to sustain life; however he or she is not obligated to use "extraordinary" ones (like a heart transplant).
3. *Suicide,* gravely contradicts love of self. It also rejects God's rule over life and death and violates the virtues of justice, hope, and charity. Because of psychological problems, people who commit suicide may not be fully blameworthy for their actions. Their action is objectively wrong, but we commend their souls to the forgiveness of God and to our own prayers for their souls. As the *Catechism* consoles: "We should not despair of the eternal salvation of persons who have taken their own lives. By ways known to him alone, God can provide the opportunity for salutary repentance. The Church prays for people who have taken their own lives" (*CCC*, 2283).
4. *Scandal,* which is an attitude or act that helps lead others to commit evil, for example, encouraging someone to take illegal and harmful drugs. Scandal is a grave offense when it leads others to sin mortally. Scandal is especially serious when authority figures like parents or teachers mislead those given to their care.
5. *Immoral medical procedures,* which include medical experimentation that does not conform to the natural law, respect human dignity, involve informed consent, and promote public health and the common good. Procedures like bodily mutilations, amputations, and sterilizations are immoral unless they are done to benefit a person medically.

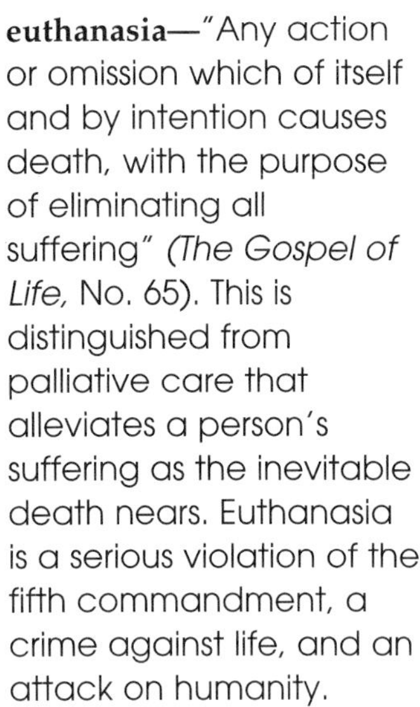

euthanasia—"Any action or omission which of itself and by intention causes death, with the purpose of eliminating all suffering" *(The Gospel of Life,* No. 65). This is distinguished from palliative care that alleviates a person's suffering as the inevitable death nears. Euthanasia is a serious violation of the fifth commandment, a crime against life, and an attack on humanity.

Explaining Your Faith

Why don't we have the right to choose how and when we die?

Life is one of God's greatest gifts. Our gratitude for that gift is best expressed by our efforts to preserve and care for life, both others' and our own. Euthanasia and suicide reject God's gift of life and take as our own the control over life that properly belongs to him alone.

Arguments for euthanasia and assisted suicide often focus on the intention to avoid or reduce the duration of suffering, helplessness, or degrading incapacity to care for oneself. Certainly working to reduce suffering is a moral good, but a greater moral principle is that one cannot do an evil act even for a good reason.

Also, it is important to reflect on our attitude to suffering. Suffering can be redemptive, as Jesus' suffering was on the cross. Suffering can also teach us to be more compassionate with others who suffer in a greater degree than we do.

Finally, death is not a right. Only God has absolute control over life and death. We do not have the right to claim death; death claims us.

VI. and IX. You Shall Not Commit Adultery. You Shall Not Covet Your Neighbor's Wife. (*CCC*, 2334; 2337; 2348–2359)

VI. and IX.

The sixth and ninth commandments teach us how to use our sexuality in accord with God's plan. God gave us the gift of human sexuality so married couples can share their love and cooperate with God in bringing forth new life. Both males and females are made in God's image and have equal dignity. These commandments direct us to exercise the virtues of chastity, purity, and modesty in order to live moral lives as God's precious children created with a beautiful sexual nature.

Chastity helps us integrate our sexuality with all aspects of who we are. Jesus is the perfect model of chastity. He calls everyone to live chastely according to their state in life. Therefore, married couples should be faithful to each other. Single people, those in religious and vowed life, and engaged couples should refrain from sexual relations. The virtue of chastity requires lifelong self-control. The Holy Spirit also helps us to be chaste. With the Spirit's help, works of self-sacrifice, prayer, and frequent

chastity—The moral virtue that enables persons to integrate their sexuality into their stations in life.

reception of the sacraments of Penance and Eucharist, we can use our sexual powers the way God intended.

The virtues of purity and **modesty** help us combat lust. Lust is the vice of a disordered craving for or enjoyment of sexual pleasure, apart from how God intended us to use our sexual powers. While sexual thoughts and desires are part of who we are as human beings, they can become evil when they control us or when we look at others as objects for self-gratification, and not as whole persons worthy of our respect.

The virtue of purity helps us in the struggle against lust by attuning our minds and hearts to God's holiness in all aspects of our lives. We gain purity when we cooperate with God's grace, for example, by refusing impure thoughts when they arise and by constantly praying for God's help. Purity requires modesty, a virtue that protects the mystery of persons and their love. Modesty refuses to unveil what should remain covered. This virtue requires patience, decency in the clothes we wear, and care and respectful attitudes when talking about sex. Modesty governs unhealthy curiosity and demands respect of persons. Today we live in a sex-saturated society. The virtue of modesty requires all people to work for wholesomeness in society, especially in the media which so often treat sex in unhealthy and even disgusting ways.

modesty—A fruit of the virtue of purity, it protects one's most intimate inner self, refusing to unveil what should remain covered.

Lust leads to the following sinful abuses of God's gift of sexuality. All of these are forbidden by the sixth and ninth commandments:

- *Masturbation* is deliberate stimulation of the sexual organs to gain sexual pleasure. Masturbation is wrong because God intended the pleasure associated with sexual activity for the commitment of a marriage union. Although any misuse of our sexual powers is sinful, we should be careful in judging whether serious sin has been committed. The Church teaches that inexperience, immaturity, habit, anxiety, or other psychological and social factors can lessen (or remove) a person's moral blameworthiness in this area (see *CCC*, 2352).
- *Fornication* is sexual intercourse engaged in by unmarried people. Fornication seeks pleasure without responsibility. It lacks the unconditional love that can only be found in the marriage of a totally committed couple.
- *Pornography* depersonalizes sex by putting something sacred on display for the sexual gratification of onlookers. It hurts the dignity of those who create, sell, and use it to arouse their passions.
- *Prostitution* debases those who sell their bodies. It is also a serious sin for those who pay prostitutes for sex.
- *Rape* is always a seriously, intrinsically evil act that is gravely unjust and unloving. Rape violates another's sexuality and attacks their human dignity. It is similar to two other abhorrent, inhuman acts that violate sexuality and human dignity: *incest* (sex acts performed by close relatives) and the *sexual abuse of children*.
- *Homosexual activity* contradicts God's intention of male-female bonding in a stable, permanent relationship of marriage. Homosexual acts differ from a homosexual orientation, that is, a predominant or

exclusive sexual attraction to someone of the same sex. The orientation is not sinful because people do not choose their orientation, heterosexual or homosexual. However, persons with homosexual desires must resist translating their desires into homosexual genital actions because these acts are seriously wrong. They contradict the purposes of God's gift of sexuality: unity between a husband and wife and openness to the transmission of human life. Like single people with a heterosexual orientation, Christ calls persons with a same-sex attraction to be chaste. Although homosexual acts are seriously wrong, prejudice and discrimination against those who have a homosexual orientation are unjust and wrong as well.

Christ calls us to live moral lives in the area of sexuality because he knows that a misuse of our sexual powers seriously hurts us spiritually, psychologically, and even physically. Jesus knows our human weakness. But he is also our Savior. This is why he extends his love and guidance to us through the Church and specifically through the graces the Holy Spirit gives us in the sacraments and prayer. If we give in to sexual temptations, we should not hate ourselves. Rather, we should remember our Lord's compassionate love and forgiveness, seek the sacrament of Penance, learn from our failures, and continue our commitment to be chaste.

Marriage and the Sixth and Ninth Commandments (CCC, 2360–2391; 2397–2400)

The sixth and ninth commandments support the institution of marriage. For example, they tell us that sexual intercourse, and all acts leading up to it, express the *total* commitment of love between a man and a woman who have given themselves to each other in marriage. This sexual sharing deepens and symbolizes their love. The husband and wife giving themselves totally to each other points to Christ's unconditional love for his body, the Church. A Christian marriage should be like God's permanent covenant of love and fidelity. A marriage should reflect the faithful love of our Lord. This love is unselfish; nothing can break it. Only death can end the lifelong covenant of love that is known as marriage.

Sexual intercourse in marriage has two purposes: *unitive,* that is, the bonding of husband and wife as lifelong partners; and *procreative,* that is, cooperating with God in bringing new life into the world. Therefore, the Church teaches that each act of sexual intercourse should be open to these two purposes of marriage: the sharing of life and mutual love. In planning their families, therefore, it follows that couples must use moral methods that are open both to love and to life.

For good reasons, couples may abstain from sexual relations or employ natural methods of regulating births (Natural Family Planning). These methods are in accord with God's will because they respect natural bodily functions and encourage tenderness and authentic communication. On the other hand, artificial means of birth control (e.g., contraceptive pills or devices like condoms) are unnatural and contrary to God's law. Sterilization, that is, making the sex organs unable to reproduce, is also wrong except when these organs are diseased and threaten a person's overall health and life.

Children are a gift of marriage. If couples experience difficulty having children, they may use moral methods of increasing fertility. However, techniques that involve third parties (for example donating sperm or eggs) are seriously wrong because they invade the exclusive marriage union of the husband and wife. Cloning of human beings is also a great evil because it directly contradicts God's plan for bringing forth new life from the loving union of husband and wife. A child is a gift from God, not an object or piece of property. We do not have an absolute right to a child. If couples cannot have children, they are encouraged to adopt. Or they can join their suffering to the cross of Christ and use their loving desires to serve others in creative and compassionate ways.

The following acts go against God's intention for marriage. They are seriously wrong.

adultery—Infidelity in marriage whereby a married person has sexual intercourse with someone who is not the person's spouse.

1. ***Adultery*** is a married person having sexual relations with someone who is not his or her spouse. It seriously destroys a couple's promise to remain faithful to each other through life. Adultery is unjust to one's spouse and children and also causes many problems for society.
2. *Divorce* is against Christ's commandment that marriage should last until death separates the couple. A true Christian marriage, in which consent was freely given, cannot be dissolved.
3. *Polygamy* (having several spouses), *incest* (engaging in sexual relations with close relatives), *sexual abuse of children and adolescents*, and *free union* (living together without exchanging marriage vows) are all serious violations of God's intent for marriage.

Commandment Issues

Complete the following assignments related to the commandments that teach us to live better lives for ourselves and others.

1. Research and report on the laws of your state regarding the death penalty. Are any efforts being made to change these laws?
2. Read the United States bishops' *Pastoral Plan for Pro-Life Activities.* Report on ways you can help to defend life. See: www.usccb.org/prolife/pastoralplan.htm
3. Interview a couple who has been married fifteen years or more. Record the qualities they believe are essential for a happy life together. Ask them to share practical ways a couple can improve the quality of their relationship as the marriage progresses.
4. Explain the teachings about sexual behavior in the following Scripture verses: 1 Thessalonians 4:1–8, 1 Corinthians 6:18–20, Ephesians 5:3–7, Colossians 3:5, Hebrews 13:4.

VII. and X. You Shall Not Steal. You Shall Not Covet Anything That Belongs to Your Neighbor.

(*CCC*, 2401–2144, 2450–2460, 2534–2540)

The seventh commandment teaches us to be good stewards of our material possessions. It stresses that God created the goods of creation for the benefit of everyone. We have the right to private property, but we must use that property responsibly. The related virtue of temperance teaches that we should not become too attached to our belongings. Also, the virtue of justice calls us to respect the property rights of others and to share our things, especially with those who are needy.

It is natural for us to want to own things that give us pleasure. This desire is morally acceptable as long as we are reasonable and do not unjustly crave the belongings of others. The tenth commandment teaches that when we covet the goods of others we might commit immoral acts outlawed by the seventh commandment, including theft, robbery, and fraud. Therefore, the tenth commandment outlaws greed, avarice, and envy. *Greed* tries to amass unlimited wealth. *Avarice* passionately seeks wealth and the power that comes from it. *Envy*, a capital sin, is a desire to have for oneself what another possesses, especially if one is willing to acquire it unjustly. Rather than rejoicing in another's good fortune, the envious person is angered or disappointed by it.

Avarice is an inordinate love of riches and the good things of life. Jesus Christ, to cure us of it, was born in extreme poverty, deprived of all comforts. He chose a mother who was poor. He willed to pass as the son of a humble workman.

—St. John Vianney

Jesus teaches that poverty of spirit is the way to combat the sinful attitudes of greed, envy, and avarice. In the last analysis, union with our God is the only way to satisfy our restless hearts. The problem with inordinately desiring wealth is that riches can become our god. Prayer to the Holy Spirit can help us resist the temptations of craving every material possession that promises happiness.

Disobedience against the seventh and tenth commandments are occasions of sin. These commandments are opposed to *theft*, that is, the taking of someone's property against his or her reasonable will. Also forbidden is the unjust taking and keeping of another's property. Examples of this include business fraud, paying of unjust wages, price fixing, corruption, shoddy work, tax evasion, forgery, expense account padding, wasteful practices, and vandalism. If one is guilty of any of these actions, he or she must make reparation. Commutative justice (see below) requires that stolen goods be returned.

The seventh commandment requires that we keep our promises and not break our contracts. Gambling does not violate the seventh commandment if it is done honestly and sparingly and does not lead to gambling addiction that can deprive others, like one's children, of the basic necessities of life. Enslaving people for profit and treating them as property to buy, sell, or exchange is a horrible offense to human dignity and freedom.

The seventh and tenth commandments strongly encourage justice for all people. Catholic teaching distinguishes between these types of justice:

1. *Commutative justice* regulates relations between individuals. It tells us that if we steal something, we should return it.
2. *Legal justice* concerns our duties as citizens and what we owe the government. For example, it requires that we pay taxes.
3. *Distributive justice* deals with the obligations the community has to its citizens according to their contributions and needs. An example would be to make sure that every child has access to an education.

In addition to these types of justice, there is *social justice*, which applies the teachings of Christ and the Church to the political, economic, and social orders. Entrusted with the gospel of Christ, the Church has spoken out on issues that affect our basic human rights and our salvation. Since the late nineteenth century, under the guidance of the Holy Spirit, the Church has developed its social teaching to interpret historical events in light of the gospel of Jesus Christ. This social teaching involves three elements: principles for reflection, criteria for judgment, and guidelines for action. These elements apply the gospel message to the systems, structures, and institutions of society because all human relationships take place within them. Respect for life is the overarching theme of Catholic social teaching.

The condemnation of any social, political, or economic system that is contrary to the dignity of the human person is a fundamental theme of Catholic social justice teaching. Therefore, the Church is against any government or political system that makes profit the *only* norm and ultimate goal of economic activity: "The disordered desire for money . . . causes . . . many conflicts which disturb the social order" (CCC, 2424). Political and economic ideologies or systems that make humans a mere means to profit include totalitarianism, atheism, communism, and unbridled capitalism. All these make money their god and dehumanize persons. All are morally unacceptable.

Catholic Social Teaching and the Seventh and Tenth Commandments

Catholic social teaching gives special emphasis to these four areas:

1. respect for creation,
2. economics,
3. solidarity among nations, and
4. love for the poor.

More details on each of these areas follows.

Stewardship

(*CCC*, 2415–2418; 2456–2457)

God gave humans dominion over all creation—the mineral, vegetable, and animal resources of our world. However, the book of Genesis teaches us that God expects us to be responsible stewards, that is, caretakers who will be respectful of God's world and will preserve its limited resources for future generations. Loving concern for the environment is essential for Christians because God intended these goods for *all* people in *all* generations.

People must be considerate of animals. Although it is morally acceptable to use animals

for food, clothing, and humane medical experiments for the benefit of humans, people must not cause animals needless suffering and death. Also, our love for animals must be reasonable. For example, if we spend so much on our pets that we neglect poor people, then human dignity will suffer.

Economic Justice

(*CCC*, 2426–2436; 2458–2460)

According to Catholic social teaching, the goods God created for everyone's benefit should in fact reach everyone in accordance with justice and with the help of charity. The purpose of the economy is to benefit both individuals and the human family. "The author, center, and goal of all economic and social life" is the human person (*CCC*, 2459). Therefore, a nation's economy exists for humans, not the other way around. Profit, power, or material goods cannot be its center. The basis for judging a just economy is this question: "What does the economy do *for* and *to* people, especially the poor and the weak?"

These fundamental truths of economic life teach us that work is both a right and a duty. We have the right to co-create with God to subdue the earth. Therefore, people should have access to a job that pays a just wage without discrimination based on sex, race, disability, and the like.

On the other hand, we have a duty to provide for our families by giving an honest day's work for an honest day's pay. Meaningful work also helps us fulfill our God-given duty to develop our talents, serve others, and grow in holiness by joining the toil of work to our Lord's sacrifice for us.

Solidarity and Preferential Love for the Poor

(*CCC*, 2437–2448; 2461–2463)

We are one human family. Therefore, nations blessed by God with wealth must express their solidarity with poorer nations. Rich

nations must help poorer nations develop their economies by:

- increasing direct aid;
- reforming international economic and financial institutions so poor nations can relate more favorably with rich nations;
- giving special aid to poor countries that are trying to work for growth and freedom,
- making special efforts to develop the farming efforts of poor nations, since so many of the world's poor people are peasants who work on farms, and since food production is a vital necessity to poorer nations whose governments lack funds to purchase food grown elsewhere;
- praying sincerely to be able to exercise our responsibility to poorer nations and their citizens.

For true reform to work, though, our world must have an "attitude adjustment" and make God our top priority. Only then will we recognize that material goods are meant to help us on our journey to him. Rediscovering God will also wake individuals and nations up to the truth that it is a grave evil to exploit the poor. Jesus himself identified with the poor and said that our judgment would be based on what we do to the "least" in our midst (see Mt 25:40, 45).

Jesus teaches us that we must give alms to the needy—that is, money, clothes, and other essentials necessary for life. This is a basic work of justice toward those who have less than we do. We must also put into practice corporal and spiritual works of mercy. These works of compassion help us identify with suffering people and are positive ways to relieve that suffering. The works of mercy are:

Corporal Works of Mercy

1. Feed the hungry.
2. Give drink to the thirsty.
3. Clothe the naked.
4. Visit the imprisoned.
5. Shelter the homeless.
6. Visit the sick.
7. Bury the dead.

Spiritual Works of Mercy

1. Counsel the doubtful.
2. Instruct the ignorant.
3. Admonish sinners.
4. Comfort the afflicted.
5. Forgive offenses.
6. Bear wrongs patiently.
7. Pray for the living and the dead.

VIII. You Shall Not Bear False Witness Against Your Neighbor.

(*CCC*, 2464–2492; 2504–2511)

VIII.

The eighth commandment teaches the value of truth-telling. Truth is a matter of justice. For Christians, being truthful is a great way to witness to Christ Jesus who is the Way, the Truth, and the Life. This commandment teaches us to stand up for the truth, something the martyrs did when they freely remained true to the Lord and his gospel.

If we honor truth, we will respect other people, their reputations, and their right to privacy. Honest people do not flatter or give false praise to others to win their approval. Nor do they gossip, brag about their accomplishments, or lie. Lying goes against God's gift of speech, which was given to us to tell the truth. Lying is mortally sinful when it causes grave harm to another. If we sin against the truth, we must repair any harm we have caused, especially if we have damaged someone's reputation. The eighth commandment calls us to avoid the following:

detraction— Without a legitimate reason, disclosing a person's faults to someone who did not know about them, thus causing unjust harm to that person's reputation.

calumny—Slander, that is, lies told about another person in order to harm his or her reputation and lead others to make false judgments about the person.

1. *False witness* in court and *perjury* (lying under oath), both of which violate justice. These are seriously wrong because they cause innocent people to suffer or to be unfairly punished.
2. *Rash judgment,* which is snap misjudgment about someone's moral culpability (blameworthiness). To counteract this irresponsible behavior, we should always try to put the most positive interpretation on another's thoughts, words, and deeds.
3. ***Detraction,*** which reveals the faults of someone else without a good reason. ***Calumny*** (spreading lies about someone) violates the virtue of truthfulness. These sins assault the honor of a person's reputation and therefore offend both justice and charity.

To tell the truth is important for followers of Jesus. However, people do not always have a right to know everything. At times, the prudent and loving thing to do is to remain silent or use discreet language; for example, to protect someone, to respect the common good, or to honor a reasonable right to privacy. A good example is that doctors and lawyers have the right to keep confidential secrets revealed to them unless grave harm would result from their silence. And public figures have a reasonable right to privacy from the glaring eyes of the media.

Judas Betrays Jesus

The eighth commandment also requires governments and entertainment industries to use the media responsibly and not for propaganda or to promote immoral behavior. People have a right to truthful information that comes from freedom, justice, and human solidarity. Truth is beautiful because it is real and reflected in God's creation and in Scripture. Human art (especially sacred art) can be a powerful tool to reveal God's truth, beauty, and love. It can inspire us to adore the Blessed Trinity, a God of truth and beauty.

Once there was a person who claimed to have the secret to good living. It turned out that the secret was really just two words she had taped to her bathroom mirror: "Yes, Lord!" By saying "yes" to the Lord, that is, by keeping the commandments, she found the secret to good living. Regarding moral living, never forget what Jesus said:

> If you keep my commandments, you will remain in my love, just as I have kept my Father's commandments and remain in his love. . . . You are my friends if you do what I command you (Jn 15:10, 14).

DiscussionQuestions

1. "It is better to let 1,000 guilty persons go free than to condemn to death an innocent person." Agree or disagree?
2. What support should the Church as a Christian community provide to teens who are contemplating abortion?

   What would or should you say to a friend who confides in you that she is thinking about an abortion? that she already had an abortion?
3. In light of all the evidence showing the high correlation between smoking and cancer, is it immoral to smoke? Why or why not?
4. What would our society define as immodest clothing for girls? for guys?

WritingAssignment

Write your responses to the following situations:

- *Star Athlete:* To impress his girlfriend, Brandon brags to her about his accomplishments in last week's football game. He also tears down the performance of a teammate to build himself up.

  What do you think is worse: bragging about your accomplishments or badmouthing another person's achievements? Explain.
- *Mental Health Day:* Your mother calls your school telling them you are sick, so you can stay home to finish a science project. You both call it a "mental health" day.

  Do you consider this lying? Why or why not?
- *Air Force Honor Code:* "I will not lie, cheat, or steal, nor will I tolerate anyone who does."

  Would this code work at your school? Why or why not?

SummaryPoints

★ The Ten Commandments (the Decalogue) proclaim God's Law and reveal his will. They are binding on all people, in all places, for all time. Jesus taught their true inner spirit when he taught the Law of Love. The Holy Spirit and his graces give us the strength to observe them.

★ God wills our eternal happiness. The Beatitudes teach us the attitudes of being and ways of acting that will help us achieve that happiness.

★ The first commandment requires us to worship the loving God who is the source of our life and all our gifts and talents. The theological virtues of faith, hope, and love help us honor our loving God.

★ The virtue of religion enables us to know and to love God. It expresses itself in adoration, prayer, sacrifice, and fidelity to our vows and promises.

★ The second commandment directs us to show reverence to God's name because God is holy.

★ The third commandment requires that we keep Sunday holy by celebrating the Eucharist, a serious obligation for Catholics, and by using the day for the refreshment of our spirit.

★ The fourth commandment teaches us to honor, respect, and show affection to and appreciation for our family members, especially our parents.

★ The fifth commandment teaches the sacredness of life, a precious gift of God that he alone can give or reclaim.

★ The sixth and ninth commands teach us to use the gift of our sexuality in accord with God's plan.

★ The seventh commandment forbids theft and commands justice and charity in the stewardship of material goods and respect for the integrity of creation.

★ The tenth commandment requires us to avoid the sins of greed, avarice, and envy. These lead to actions forbidden by the seventh commandment: theft, fraud, paying unjust wages, shoddy work, tax evasion, corrupt business practices, waste, forgery, destruction of private and public property, and so forth.

★ The Spirit-guided social justice doctrine of the Church includes principles for reflection, criteria for judgment, and guidelines for action. These apply the gospel to the political, economic, and social orders for the benefit of protecting human rights, the dignity of persons, and the salvation of souls.

★ The basis of the Catholic Church's social teaching is respect for the individual as another self. Therefore, in the area of economics, the human person, and not profit, must be its center and goal. Economic decision-makers must always ask, "What does the economy do *for* and *to* people, especially the poor?"

★ Global solidarity is a goal of social justice. Following Christ requires a special love and affection for the poor. Almsgiving and living the spiritual and corporal works of mercy are ways to help the poor.

★ By prohibiting false witness, the eighth commandment enjoins us to be people of truth. The eighth commandment forbids lying, that is, speaking a falsehood to deceive another who has a right to the truth.

ReviewQuestions

1. Name and explain each of the Beatitudes.
2. Name and explain each of the Ten Commandments.
3. How do each of the following violate the first commandment: heresy, apostasy, schism, presumption, despair, superstition, idolatry, divination, sacrilege, simony, and atheism?
4. How do each of the following violate the second commandment: perjury, blasphemy, swearing, and cursing?
5. Why is St. Thomas More known as a person of good conscience?
6. Besides going to Mass, how do Catholics keep Sunday holy?
7. List two ways parents and children should observe the values taught by the fourth commandment.
8. List and discuss five major violations of the fifth commandment that are common in our world today.
9. Under what conditions do governments have the right to inflict the death penalty? to go to war?
10. Why is it usually not necessary to inflict the death penalty in this day and age?

11. Define the virtues of chastity, purity, and modesty.
12. Explain the distinction between homosexual activity and homosexual orientation.
13. Define *greed, avarice,* and *envy.*
14. Distinguish between and among these forms of justice: *commutative, legal, distributive,* and *social.*
15. What does it mean to be a good steward?
16. Name and explain two key teachings concerning economic justice.
17. List two things nations could do to foster global solidarity.
18. Why must Christians have special love for the poor?
19. List the corporal and spiritual works of mercy.
20. List and discuss three ways people bear false witness.

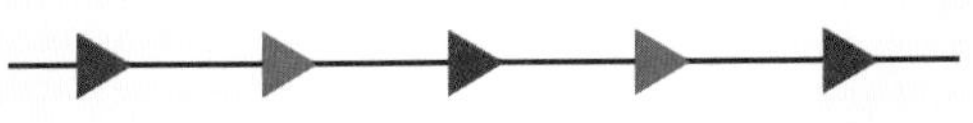

Applying What You Have Learned

1. Prepare a two-minute oral report on the morality of one of the topics discussed in this chapter. For example: astrology, divination, capital punishment, or atheism.
2. Create a practical list of Sunday activities that would be good ways for your family to observe the law of sabbath rest. Share it with your parents.
3. Prepare a report on a saint or modern Catholic who was concerned with justice or poor or suffering people. For example: St. Vincent de Paul, St. Louise de Marillac, St. John Baptist de LaSalle, St. Katherine Drexel, Dorothy Day, Jean Vanier, Pope John Paul II or Blessed Mother Teresa of Calcutta.
4. View justice topics at www.justicenet.org. Report on issues involving youth, criminal justice, or war and peace.
5. Report on an archived article from the Catholic online Social Justice magazine, *Salt of the Earth*: http://salt.claretianpubs.org/. Check articles on capital punishment, peace, and economic justice and the poor.
6. Research and report on some violations of human rights at one of these Internet sites: The Human Rights Web: www.hrweb.org Amnesty International: www.amnesty.org/

Prayer Reflection

A prayer by St. Richard of Chichester (popularized in the musical *Godspell*) stresses how important it is to love the Lord each day of our lives. One way we do that is by keeping his commandments and living a moral life.

Day by Day

Thank you, Lord Jesus Christ,
For all the benefits and blessings which you have given me
For all the pains and insults you have borne for me.
Merciful Friend, Brother and Redeemer,
May I know you more clearly,
Love you more dearly,
And follow you more nearly,
Day by day.

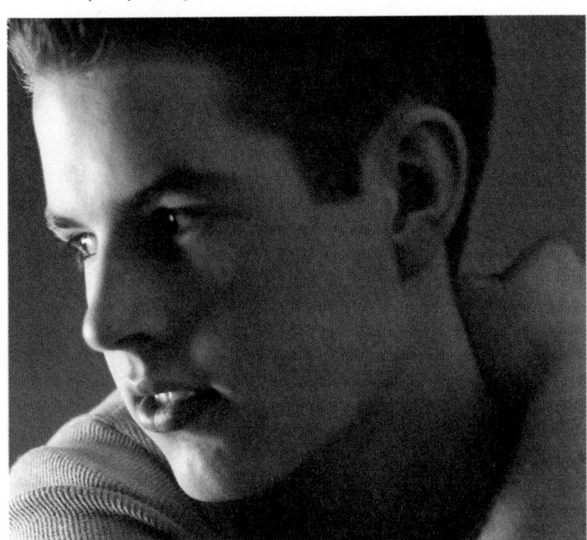

(Jesus) was praying in a certain place, and when he had finished, one of his disciples said to him, "Lord, teach us to pray just as John taught his disciples."

Luke 11:1

Chapter 10 Outline

Letters to God
It is important to always make time for prayer.

What Is Prayer?
Blessing, adoration, and praise, petition, and thanksgiving are among the types of "talking" prayers.

The Bible and Prayer
The Scriptures teach us to pray and are a source of prayer.

How to Pray
Getting started in prayer involves things like finding a place and time for pray, relaxing body and mind, and keeping a good attitude.

The Lord's Prayer (Our Father)
Jesus' taught us the Our Father. It is the prime Christian prayer.

Chapter 10

Prayer

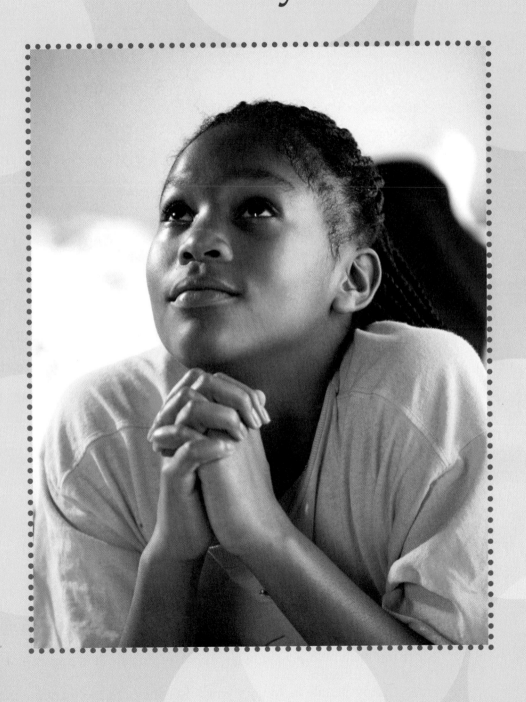

prayer—Conversation with God. Lifting of one's mind and heart to God or requesting good things from him. Joining one's thoughts and love to God in adoration and blessing, petition, intercession, thanksgiving, and praise.

Letters to God

"Prayer is a conversation between God and me."

This traditional definition of **prayer** was never taken more seriously than when a group of children composed "letters to God." Here is a sampling:

dear god,
thank you for my baby sister. but don't you remember? i asked for a puppy.
nicole

Dear God,
I think of you a lot, even when I'm not praying.
Do you think of me?
Joey

Dear God,
Did you mean for the hippopotamus to look like that? Or was it an accident. Just wondering.
Bobby

Dear God,
I was scared when it thundered so loud during the storm yesterday. But when it was all over, your rainbow came out. It was way cool.
Love, Annie

Dear God,
I read the Bible.
What does begat mean?
No one will tell me.
Love, Suzy

What is refreshing about these letters to God is how natural the children are in writing to God—a God whom they clearly love. We can all learn from the simple faith of children. Prayer should be something totally natural and part of our everyday lives. As food is to our bodies, prayer is to our souls. While food helps us live physically, it is prayer that helps us grow spiritually.

Many people in today's world say they are too busy for prayer. Yet they are never too busy to eat. If you are too busy for prayer, *you are too busy*! Is prayer part of your life?

Chapter 10 explores the functions and necessity of prayer, including these elements:

1. A Definition of Prayer
2. The Bible and Prayer
3. Ways to Pray
4. Prayer Expressions
5. The Lord's Prayer

What Is Prayer? *(CCC, 2558–2567; 2590; 2623–2649)*

Prayer is "the raising of one's mind and heart to God" (St. John Damascus). When we pray we consciously pay attention to God. We direct our thoughts to the loving God who calls us.

Prayer is also a loving conversation with God. A conversation has two parts: talking and listening. The *talking* part of prayer can include private prayers we say alone or public ones we say with others. Our prayers can be formal prayers, like the rosary, or spontaneous prayers said in our own words. They can be vocal, said out loud. Or they can be recited silently in our hearts, for example, while visiting our Lord in the Blessed Sacrament. The prayers we say include these types:

1. ***Blessing**, **adoration**, and **praise**.* We bless God because he first blesses us. We adore God because he is the Creator and we are his creations. Blessing and adoration lead to praise in which we sing to and glorify God because he is good, gracious, loving, and saving. God deserves our love, blessing, adoration, and praise for his own sake. When we praise God, the Holy Spirit is with us. The Spirit helps us to have faith in our Lord and brother Jesus Christ and to call God "Abba." True praise of God includes no selfish motive, because we take joy in our loving God alone. "I will praise you, Lord, with all my heart; I will declare all your wondrous deeds" (Ps 9:2).
2. ***Petition** (supplication).* When we petition God in prayer we are requesting favors. We ask God to give us what we need, especially the gift of the Holy Spirit who will help us live Christ-like lives. Prayers of petition include *contrition,* in which we humbly ask our merciful Father to forgive our sins, and prayers of ***intercession,*** in which we pray for others. Praying for others is an exercise of Christian mercy and love, especially when we pray for those who are in need and for our enemies.
3. *Thanksgiving.* God has given us so much: our very lives (including our health, families, talents, and so forth), the gift of Jesus and his salvation, and the gift of the Holy Spirit who lives in us. Thanking God in prayer shows that we owe him everything. He deserves our gratitude. The Psalmist tells us, "Give thanks to the LORD who is good, whose love endures forever!" (Ps 107:1). The Eucharist (a word which means "to give thanks") is a very special type of prayer of thanksgiving. In this supreme prayer, we bless, adore, praise, and thank God for all the blessings he has given to us. We express our sorrow, ask for forgiveness, and petition God for all the good things that we and others need to live our lives fully. When we receive Holy Communion our Lord Jesus lives in us and unites us to God and all our Christian brothers and sisters by the power of the Holy Spirit.

blessing—A prayer that invokes God's care on some person, place, thing, or undertaking.

adoration—Prayer that acknowledges that God is God—Creator, Savior, Sanctifier, Lord, and Master of all creation, the source of all blessings, and worthy of our total love and devotion.

praise—A form of prayer whereby we acknowledge God and his goodness and glorify him for who he is.

petition—A prayer in which we ask God for his help, or forgiveness, or for some good whether for ourselves or for others.

intercession—A prayer of petition for the sake of others.

In the *listening* part of prayer, we allow God to speak to us. He does so through our intellects, feelings, imaginations, wills, and memories. To hear God in prayer means we must still ourselves and be prepared to listen. Perhaps then we will discover God inspiring us with new ideas or images, calming our fears, strengthening our wills to do right, or healing bad memories that have been bothering us.

There are many definitions and descriptions of prayer. St. Thérèse of the Child Jesus defined prayer this way: "For me, prayer is a surge of the heart; it is a simple look turned toward heaven, it is a cry of recognition and of love, embracing both trial and joy." The *Catechism of the Catholic Church* defines prayer as "the living relationship of the children of God with their Father who is good beyond measure, with his Son Jesus Christ, and with the Holy Spirit" (CCC, 2565). God is our Father. Jesus is our Savior, our brother, and our friend. The Holy Spirit is our Helper. Prayer helps us discover who we really are as beloved children of our loving God. Prayer brings us into unity with our loving Triune God.

These definitions all tell us that in prayer we turn to God. We become aware of and how God lives in our hearts, how he invites us into fellowship with him, and how he is concerned about every aspect of our lives. St. Teresa of Avila said to imagine prayer as a journey with an invisible Friend who will always be with us. Like conversation with any of our friends, prayer will deepen our friendship with the Lord and give us the strength to live our life as God intended for us.

Discussion Questions

1. What is your definition of prayer?
2. What events or occasions in your life lead you to prayer?
3. Write about a time when prayer helped you.
4. How strong is your belief that God will answer your prayers? Explain.

Prayer in the New Testament

Read these four examples of prayer in the New Testament. Decide what type of prayer each represents: blessing, adoration, praise, petition, intercession, thanksgiving, or contrition.

Luke 18:1-5 ____________ Mark 10:46-49 ____________

Luke 1:46-55 ____________ John 11:41-42 ____________

The Bible and Prayer

(CCC, 2568-2606; 2617-2619; 2620; 2622)

The Bible is an essential source for defining prayer and reporting on how people pray. For example, the book of Genesis reveals how important faith is when we pray, a quality the patriarchs Abraham and Jacob exemplified in their dealings with Yahweh. The book of Exodus reveals prayer as a dialogue, a two-way conversation, but one that always starts with God. Moses prayed to God as a friend and learned from his prayer that God is just, loving, and faithful. Moses also represented many occasions of intercessory prayer by begging Yahweh to care for his people.

In addition, the Old Testament tells us how often religious leaders like Samuel, David, and Elijah taught prayer to the Chosen People and made the Temple in Jerusalem a special place for worshiping God. King David modeled in a special way the attitudes of submission, praise, and repentance that we need when we pray. So important was David's example as a person of prayer that he is credited with writing many of the Psalms. The Psalms express the longings of the human heart and look to the coming Messiah who alone could satisfy these longings. Because of their ability to express our deeply felt needs on both personal and communal levels, the Church reveres the Psalms as an essential part of its prayer life.

The greatest source for learning about prayer comes from Jesus himself, the perfect model of prayer. Prayer was essential to his life. For example, as a child, he was raised by his prayerful mother, Mary, and his foster-father, Joseph. As a pious Jew, he also learned to pray as his people did. He went to the synagogue. He attended the religious festivals in Jerusalem. As did most practicing Jews, Jesus probably memorized the Psalms and prayed them often. The New Testament includes many examples of the adult Jesus at prayer. For example, he prayed

1. in the desert before beginning his public preaching,
2. before choosing his apostles,
3. after performing miracles like the multiplication of the loaves and fishes, and
4. on the mountain at the time of his Transfiguration.

Jesus also prayed in the Garden before his arrest, asking to do God's will, even if it led to his death on the cross (see Lk 22:42).

Jesus prayed in many different ways, as we should, too. He *praised* the Father for revealing God's will to the humble and lowly (see Lk 10:21). He *thanked* God when he raised Lazarus from the dead (see Jn 11:41–42). He *petitioned* his heavenly Father to keep Peter from giving into temptation (see Lk 22:31–32). Chapter 17 of John's Gospel shares Jesus' great priestly prayer of *intercession*; Jesus asked his Father to keep his disciples in the truth. Most remarkably, Jesus also prayed for us that "they may all be one, as you, Father, are in me and I in you, that they also may be in us" (Jn 17:21). A great example of Jesus at prayer took place at his crucifixion. He prayed for all sinners, and forgave his persecutors. His final words are a prayerful act of trust in his heavenly Father: "Father, into your hands I commend my spirit" (Lk 23:46).

Mary, the Mother of God, is also an inspiration for prayer. She showed two great qualities in her prayer life: faith and humility. Mary demonstrated faith when she accepted the angel Gabriel's news that she was to become the Mother of God. She trusted God to work through her; yet she did not fully understand how: "Behold, I am the handmaid of the Lord. May it be done to me according to your word"

Writing Assignment

1. Compose a short prayer using this traditional format:

- Opening address, calling God by name.
- Praise
- Thanksgiving
- Petition

Raising Lazarus from the dead

(Lk 1:38). Because of her trust in God, she helped bring the Word of God into humanity. Mary's great prayer, the Magnificat, also reveals her humility. She rightly credited God for all the goodness that happened to her and through her. "The Mighty One has done great things for me, and holy is his name" (Lk 1:49). Her Magnificat teaches the Church to show humble gratitude to God, who is the source of all our blessings.

Mary's appearances throughout the New Testament are accompanied by prayer. For example, when she went to help her cousin Elizabeth, she sang joyfully of God's goodness. She, like Joseph, went to the great religious feasts at the Temple. Like most mothers, she also taught her child Jesus to pray and instilled in him a love for the prayers and scriptures of the Chosen People. Finally, after Jesus ascended to heaven, Mary waited in the Upper Room on Pentecost Sunday when the Holy Spirit came in all his power (Acts 1:14).

The examples of Jesus and Mary have much to teach us. If prayer was important to the Son of God and to his sinless Mother, then how much more important should it be to us? Prayer is essential for being a Christian.

ExplainingYourFaith

Do Catholics worship Mary and the saints?

No. Catholics worship and adore God alone, as taught by the first commandment. Worship of any other person or thing would be idolatry, a sin against the first commandment. Catholics do honor, venerate, and respect Mary as the Mother of God, the Queen of All Saints.

Sometimes people who are not Catholic, and even Catholics themselves, will get the wrong idea when they hear that Catholics "pray to" the saints. Remembering that prayer is, first of all, a conversation may help. Catholics do talk with the saints. We ask for their prayers—that they will talk to God on our behalf—just like we ask our living friends to pray for us when we are in need.

WritingAssignment

1. Read the psalms listed below (or ones of your choice). Then write one of the psalms in your own words.

Psalm 8: The glory of God and the dignity of human beings

Psalm 23: The Lord is my shepherd

Psalm 28: A cry for help

Psalm 46: God is on our side

Psalm 51: A prayer for forgiveness

Psalm 63: Longing for God

Psalm 104: Praise God the Creator

Psalm 150: Praise the Lord

2. Read these passages that depict times that Jesus prayed alone. Write your answers to the questions that follow:

Luke 4:1–11 Mark 1:35–37 Luke 6:12–13

Luke 5:15–16 Matthew 14:13–33 Mark 14:32–42

What kinds of things are happening when Jesus goes off to pray?

When do you like to be alone and pray?

How to Pray

(*CCC*, 2650–2698; 2720; 2725–2758)

The Holy Spirit teaches the Church how to pray primarily through the living Tradition of the Church and through the sacred Scriptures that we hear at liturgies and meditate on afterward. The Holy Spirit also gives us the theological virtues to help us pray. Through these virtues, the Holy Spirit teaches us that we can pray always. God is always present to us and the Spirit lives in us. Christ stands beside us. We can and should pray often.

Getting Started in Prayer

Hopefully, you have already learned many things about prayer from your parents, teachers, priests, and others who have made prayer an important part of their lives. Throughout the history of the Church, the saints have taught different ways to approach

God in prayer. They share many points in common on how to get started. Here are some basics:

- ★ *Place.* You can pray anywhere, but it is good to find a special place where you can slow down, relax, and focus your attention. Many have found their bedrooms, the school chapel or parish Church, or the outdoors to be good places for prayer.
- ★ *Time.* You can pray at any time of the day. However, it is good to get in the habit of choosing a special time each day to pray. Good times to pray include when rising in the morning or before going to bed, as a break between homework assignments, before and after meals, during a free period at school, and so forth. Catholics also pray each Sunday when they go to Mass.
- ★ *Relax body and mind.* It is hard to pray if you are tense or distracted. Prayer requires both alertness and relaxation. Breathing exercises that help you drain away the cares of the day and comfortable body posture—like sitting upright in a chair, lying on the floor, or kneeling—can help you to concentrate when you pray.
- ★ *Good Attitude.* To pray we must be open to God. Begin your prayer time by recalling that God is present, that he loves you immensely, and that he has given you many gifts, including the gift of life. Approach God with a humble heart. Remember that God has invited us to spend time with him in prayer. Therefore, you can trust that the Lord will be with us and will answer our heartfelt desire to be with him.
- ★ *Keep at it.* It can be difficult to pray regularly. You may be lazy or tired. Also, Satan will tempt humans in many ways to ignore their time for prayer. Even if you are faithful in your prayer, sometimes you may feel that God is not listening to you. Added to this are the distractions that always seem to come along, making it difficult to focus and hear the Lord in the depth of our hearts. To persevere with prayer, you must keep the faith that God always hears you, even if you do not "feel" anything. When things seem to be going poorly, pray for the Holy Spirit to come to you.

  Distractions in prayer caused by a wandering mind, an overactive imagination, or external noises are normal. One way to deal with them is to gaze at a crucifix, holy picture or icon, or a lit candle to help keep your attention on God. Another good technique is to recite repeatedly a prayer-word or phrase like "Abba," "Savior," or "Jesus help me." This practice can "distract you from the distractions" and refocus your attention on the Lord. Always remember this truth: the Lord is very pleased with your efforts. Trying to pray is itself a prayer. God appreciates any and all efforts you make at prayer.

We should address our prayers to the Father, our loving Abba who is the source of our life. We should also pray to Jesus and invoke his blessed name often. For example, we can pray the famous Jesus Prayer: "Lord Jesus Christ, Son of God, have mercy on me, a sinner." We should also invoke the help of the Holy Spirit, the interior teacher of Christian prayer.

Discussion Questions

1. What does it mean to "praise God"?
2. Which example from Jesus' life is your favorite model of prayer?
3. Who is someone who has been a model of prayer to you? How so?

Through the ages, Catholics have also found it valuable to pray in union with our Blessed Mother, who shows us how to cooperate with the graces of the Holy Spirit and how to live a Christ-like life. The Hail Mary is special because it praises God for his goodness shown to Mary and petitions our Blessed Mother to pray for us to her beloved Son.

Prayer Expressions (CCC, 2700–2719; 2721–2724)

Christian prayer comes from the heart. Prayer expresses itself in these ways:

1. *Vocal prayer.* Prayers can be said mentally or out loud. When you express your feelings in words you are doing what Jesus himself did when he taught the Our Father. When you pray with fellow Christians, you strengthen your spiritual relationships with them.
2. *Meditation.* In **meditation**, you actively use your thoughts, emotions, imaginations, and desires to think about God's presence in the world and in your life. Meditation helps you to "tune into God," to gain a greater knowledge and love of the Lord so you can serve him better. Saints like Teresa of Avila and Ignatius of Loyola used the gospels to help them meditate. Besides following their example, you can also meditate on the writings of the saints, world events, and the action of God in your own life.
3. *Mental prayer.* This type of prayer typically centers on Jesus. In mental prayer, you converse with Jesus or reflect on one of the mysteries of his life, for example, his passion and crucifixion. Sometimes mental prayer can lead to **contemplation**, a form of silent, wordless prayer in which you simply rest in the presence of our all-loving God. St. John Vianney told of a simple peasant who described contemplative prayer. The peasant sat daily in front of our Blessed Lord present in the tabernacle. "I look at him and he looks at me." When praying this way, you can empty your mind of thoughts and images and simply allow the divine presence to penetrate your being. You do not have to do anything at all.

meditation—A form of prayer where the mind and imagination focus on Christ or some truth of divine revelation with the purpose of applying the lessons we learn to our lives.

contemplation—Wordless prayer whereby a person's mind and heart rest in God's goodness and majesty.

Meditating on Scripture

Use the following steps to help you meditate using Scripture.

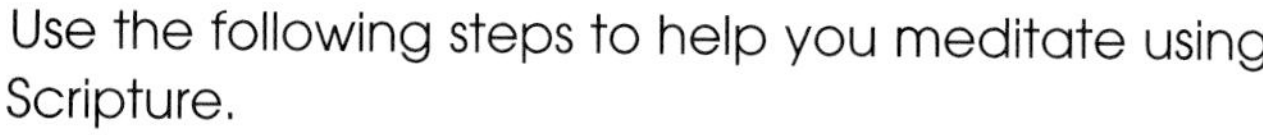

Prepare

1. Find a quiet place to pray, a place where you will not be disturbed.
2. Choose one of the passages from the list below. Find it in your bible and mark the place so that it will be ready for you to read when the time comes.
3. Set a mood for prayer by calming your body. Let the cares of the day drain away. Breathe slowly. Relax your body so your mind can focus on the meditation. Sit with your spine straight, hands on your lap, with your eyes closed.

4. Now consciously realize that God is present to you. Focus on a crucifix or an icon of Jesus. Ask the Holy Spirit to guide you during your time of prayer. Now you are ready to begin your meditation.

Meditation

Select one of the passages from the list below. Read it slowly and reflectively.

Events from Jesus' Life

The Young Jesus (Lk 2:41–50)
Temptation in the Desert (Mt 4:1–11)
Call of the First Apostles (Lk 5:1–11)
Calming of the Storm (Mk 4:35–41)
Woman in Simon's house (Lk 7:36–50)
Sermon on the Mount (Mt 5–7—worth several meditations)
Miracle of Cana (Jn 2:1–12)
"Who Do People Say I Am?" (Mt 16:13–17)
Curing of the Blind Man of Jericho (Lk 18:35–43)
Feeding of the 5,000 (Jn 6:1–13)
Jesus and Zaccheus (Lk 19:1–10)
Raising of Lazarus (Jn 11:1–44)
Rich Young Man (Mt 19:16–22)
Washing the Apostles' Feet (Jn 13:1–17)
Gethsemane (Lk 22:39–46)
Jesus' Crucifixion (Lk 23:32–48)
Disciples on the Road to Emmaus (Lk 24:13–35)

Parables

Laborers in the Vineyard (Mt 20:1–16)
Merciless Official (Mt 18:21–35)
Rich Man and Lazarus (Lk 16:19–31)
Good Samaritan (Lk 10:25–37)
Good Shepherd (Jn 10:1–21)
Prodigal Son (Lk 15:11–32)
Treasure and the Pearl (Mt 13:44–46)

1. Observe. Put yourself imaginatively into the passage. Picture what is taking place. What do you see? smell? feel? taste? hear? What is Jesus like? What is Jesus saying? What do his words mean? How does he look? What does he reveal about God? How does this story affect others? What does this story say to you? Do you identify with one of the characters in the story?

Discussion Questions

1. Where is a good place for you to pray?
2. When is a good time for you to pray?
3. What is a good prayer position for you?
4. How do you approach God in prayer?
5. What is the best way for you to handle distractions in prayer?

2. Meditate. What is the theme of the passage (for example, God's love for the sinner)? Pause periodically to talk intimately to the Lord. Let him speak to you through the reading. Turn to God and respond to his presence to you. Share with the Lord your deepest thoughts and feelings. Turn over to him your cares and needs. Praise God for his goodness. Ask God to forgive your sins and failings. If distractions come your way, return to the scripture passage. Take your time and enjoy these moments with the Lord.
3. Listen. Ask yourself, "What is the Lord saying *to me*? What message is there in this biblical passage for my life?"
4. Conclude. Thank God for being present to you. Make a resolution to do something concrete as a result of your meditation. For example, perhaps you will try to be more patient with people during the coming day.

Writing Assignment

Read the two versions of the Our Father in Luke 11:2–4 and Matthew 6: 9–13. Write about the similarities and differences between these two versions of the Lord's Prayer.

The Lord's Prayer (Our Father) (CCC, 2759–2865)

The Lord's Prayer is the prime Christian prayer, what the Church Father Tertullian called "the summary of the whole gospel." From the earliest centuries until today, the Church has prayed the Lord's Prayer in its liturgical celebrations, especially the Eucharist. It is central to a Christian's daily prayer.

The Lord's Prayer appears in the gospels of both Luke and Matthew. Luke's version, probably the older of the two, has only five petitions. Matthew's version, which has seven petitions, is more familiar because the Church prays it in its liturgies. The added conclusion to the prayer at Mass—"For the kingdom, the power and the glory are yours, now and forever and ever"—is called a *doxology* (prayer of praise). It comes from the *Didache*, a first-century catechetical manual, and the *Apostolic Constitutions*. This doxology repeats in praise and thanksgiving the first three petitions to God the Father: the glorification of God's name, the coming of the kingdom, and the power of God's saving will.

Matthew's gospel reports that Jesus taught the Lord's Prayer in the Sermon on the Mount (Mt 5–7). In this famous sermon, Jesus instructed his followers on the Christian way of life, including how to pray. Jesus told us to pray humbly and not to babble on. He gave us the Our Father as the prototypical prayer that relies totally on God.

Luke's context for Jesus' teaching the Lord's Prayer differs from Matthew's. In his version, the apostles approached Jesus one day while he was praying by himself. They asked him to teach them how to pray. Jesus then instructed them to say the Lord's Prayer. Because of his instructions, Jesus' disciples can dare address God as *Abba* ("Daddy" or "Dear Father"). The Lord's Prayer identifies us as *Christians*. Because it was so special, the early Christians only learned it after they were baptized.

Meaning of the Our Father

The Our Father consists of seven petitions. The first three glorify God; the last four take our needs to our loving Father. A discussion of the parts of the Lord's Prayer follows.

Our Father

Jesus invites us to call God Abba, to address the almighty God intimately, securely, and with childlike trust. Jesus teaches us that God is good, gracious, and absolutely loving.

Calling God *Father* contains two very important truths. First, Jesus' Father is our Father too. We should humbly trust Abba to care for our needs. Second, since God is *our* Father, we are brothers and sisters to all people. Every person is intimately related to us. If we believe what Jesus teaches us by this prayer, we will commit ourselves to understand, love, and respond to *everyone* who comes into our lives.

Who art in heaven

"In heaven" refers to God's way of being, his majesty. It does not refer to a place. Christians affirm that through Jesus, God lives in the hearts of the just. When we address our heavenly Father, we are professing that we are God's people who are in union with Christ in heaven. At the same time, we await the day when our heavenly reward will be fully ours.

Hallowed be thy name

Our individual names remind us of our uniqueness. In the ancient world, a person's name typically stood for the person. For example, Jesus wanted Simon bar Jonah to be the leader of the apostles; therefore, he renamed him *Peter* which means "Rock"; describing Peter's role as the Church's foundation. Your name, too, has special meaning. For example, Christopher means "Christ bearer"; Carol means "joyful song."

When we "hallow" God's name, we pray that everyone on earth will regard God as holy (as he is in heaven). God is the source of all holiness. We make God's name holy when we believe in God's love and act on it by taking on the identity of our Savior, Jesus Christ. When we live up to the name *Christian*, others will come to know and praise God because they can see God's image in us.

Thy kingdom come; thy will be done on earth as it is in heaven

With the coming of Jesus Christ, God's rule has broken into our world. God's kingship or reign is one of peace, justice, truth, community, and mutual love. Jesus has inaugurated this reign by preaching the gospel to the poor, freeing captives, and healing and saving everyone.

God's kingdom will be fully established only at the end of time, but we are to live, experience, and work for it right now. When we pray "thy kingdom come," we petition primarily for Christ's return, the final coming of God's kingdom. Then there will be full righteousness, peace, and joy.

When we pray for the coming of this kingdom, we must join Jesus in his work, which primarily entails loving others and responding to the needs of our least brothers and sisters.

Give us this day our daily bread

Bread is a source of sustenance for life. When we "break bread" with others we share fellowship and company with them. When we pray for our daily bread we are really praying for:

Discussion Questions

1. How do you make God's name holy by living a Christ-like life?
2. Who needs your forgiveness? What can you do to make clear your forgiveness to this person?
3. What are you doing right now to build up your spiritual strength to better resist any temptation that might come your way?
4. What is the greatest temptation facing you? facing teens today? facing our world?

1. physical life—food, shelter, clothing;
2. psychological life—friendship, love, companionship; and
3. spiritual life—the Word of God accepted in faith and the Body of Christ we receive in Holy Communion.

When we pray for *our* daily bread, we ask for our needs as well as the needs of all people. The Lord's Prayer challenges us to share with others, especially the less fortunate. The parables of the Last Judgment (Mt 25:31–46) and Lazarus (Lk 16:19–31) likewise teach us that God's children *must* share their material goods with the poor. These parables also warn that God will punish those who are selfish and do not share their goods with the less fortunate.

The word "daily" in the original Aramaic spoken by Jesus may also have meant something similar to "for tomorrow, today." Therefore, when we pray for our daily bread, we are also asking God for the fullness of the material and spiritual blessings that will be ours in heaven. We dare to ask our Father to give us a taste of these gifts even today.

And forgive us our trespasses as we forgive those who trespass against us

It is difficult both to forgive and to ask for forgiveness. When we ask God for forgiveness, we are honestly admitting that we are sinners who need God's saving love. We acknowledge that we need the Spirit who will enable us to repent of our selfishness and turn to a more loving life of service. We confess in humility that we need Jesus' help on our journey to the Father.

But we must also forgive others. Jesus connects God's forgiveness of us to our forgiveness of others. Scripture teaches that it is impossible to love the God we cannot see if we cannot love the brother or sister we do see (1 Jn 4:20). God's forgiving love should become flesh in our lives as we extend forgiveness to others. When we forgive those who have hurt us, we are sharing love and understanding, thus encouraging others to respond to us in love. The Lord's Prayer calls us to action: to forgive as we have been forgiven.

And lead us not into temptation

This petition asks God to keep us off the path that leads to sin. It also asks God to help us to be faithful to the end of our lives when we struggle with death, our final test.

Following Jesus requires picking up the cross of suffering. This petition asks for God's strength to overcome any difficulties that might steer us away from a Christian life of service. We also ask for the help of the Holy Spirit to gift us with fortitude, watchfulness, perseverance, and a discerning heart that can distinguish between trials that strengthen us spiritually and temptations that lead to sin and death.

But deliver us from evil. Amen.

In union with the saints, we ask God to manifest the victory Christ has already won over Satan. We pray that the Father will deliver us from Satan's snares, and the temptations of a sensuous, materialistic, violent,

Prayer Reflection

Read Matthew 6:25–34. Enter into the scene the Lord describes—God cares for the birds and adorns the fields with beautiful flowers. Reflect on what the Lord says about *you*. After praying over this passage, write your responses to the following questions:

1. What are things that cause you worry and anxiety?
2. Analyze the things you worry about from the viewpoint of eternity. How valid is your concern when seen from the vantage point of five years from now? ten? after you have died?

and godless society. We beg God to spare us from the evil of accidents, illness, and natural disasters. We pray that God will give us strength to stop our own participation in unjust and evil practices like prejudice. We pray that no situation arises that might tempt us to deny our loving Creator. Finally, we pray with the Holy Spirit and all God's people for the second coming of the Lord. On that glorious day, all humanity will be forever free of the snares of the Evil One.

We end our prayer with "Amen," a word that means, "So be it." We should say Amen with enthusiasm because it means we are making the "Lord's Prayer" our prayer, too.

SummaryPoints

★ Prayer is the lifting of one's mind and heart to God. It is a loving conversation with God.

★ The types of prayer are *blessing, adoration, and praise; petition* (which includes prayers of contrition and intercession); and *thanksgiving*. The Eucharist is a privileged prayer for Catholics and exemplifies many types of prayer.

★ In the listening part of prayer, God can speak to us through our intellects, wills, imaginations, memories, and feelings.

★ The Old Testament images prayer as walking with God and tells us of the importance of faith when we pray.

★ The Psalms are a rich treasury of prayer for both Jews and Christians.

★ Our greatest source of learning about prayer comes from Jesus. He prayed often and taught us to pray with a pure heart and a right attitude of trust in his heavenly Father.

★ We can learn prayer, too, from the Blessed Mother. Her faith and obedience to God's will show us the proper attitudes to have in prayer.

★ It is always good to choose a special place and time to pray, making sure we relax both body and mind. We must persist in our prayer and never give up.

★ The various prayer expressions include *vocal prayer, meditation* ("tuning into God"), and *mental prayer*, including *contemplation*.

★ The Lord's Prayer is the perfect Christian prayer, "the summary of the whole gospel." Found in both Matthew and Luke's gospel, it was taught to us by Jesus himself.

★ In the Lord's Prayer, we praise our loving Father and petition that his kingdom may come and his will be done. We also ask God to give us what we need for life, to forgive our sins, and to save us from the path that leads to sin and the snares of the evil one.

ReviewQuestions

1. Define prayer.
2. Explain what true praise of God entails.
3. What does it mean to petition God?
4. How did St. Thérèse of Lisieux define prayer?
5. Why are *contrition* and *intercessory* prayer considered forms of petition?
6. What is the Church's special prayer of thanksgiving?
7. How can God speak to us in the listening part of prayer?
8. Discuss three things we can learn about prayer from the Old Testament.
9. What were some of the ways that Jesus prayed?
10. How is Mary an inspiration for prayer?
11. List five things Jesus taught us about prayer.
12. What are two ways the Holy Spirit teaches the Church to pray?
13. How would you advise a beginner to get started in prayer?

14. What does having a good attitude have to do with being effective at prayer?
15. What is a strategy for persevering at prayer when tempted to do otherwise?
16. What is the difference between meditation and mental prayer?
17. Define *contemplation.*
18. Where in the New Testament do we find the Lord's Prayer?
19. What did Tertullian call the Lord's Prayer?
20. Briefly discuss the meaning of each phrase of the Lord's Prayer.

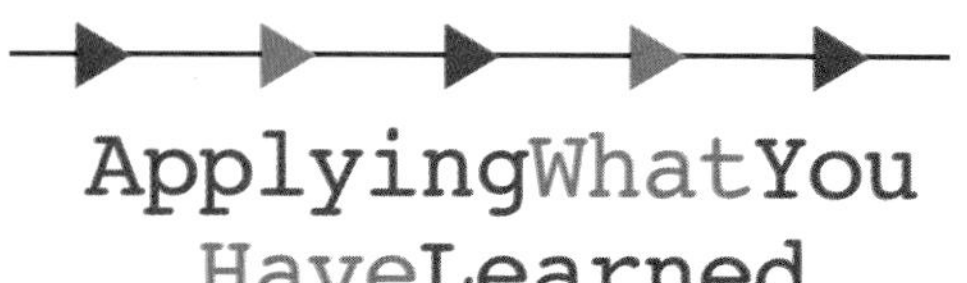

Applying What You Have Learned

1. Read and summarize the following three Lucan parables on prayer: Friend at Midnight (Lk 11:5–13), Persistent Widow (Lk 18:1–8), Pharisee and Tax Collector (Lk 18:9–14). What major point is Jesus is making in each of these parables? Compose your own contemporary version of one of these parables. Share with your classmates.
2. Browse some websites devoted to prayer. Read some of the prayers. Write your own. Or, write a report on something interesting you found or tried by way of prayer.
   Prayer:
   http://landru.i-link-2.net/shnyves/prayer.html
   Catholic Prayers:
   www.webdesk.com/catholic/prayers/index.html
   Introduction to Daily Prayer:
   www.cptryon.org/prayer/day.html
   Catholic Life and Prayers:
   www.catholic.org/clife/prayers/
3. Create your own visuals to illustrate the Lord's Prayer. Make a PowerPoint® presentation, a video with background music, or a collage for posting in your classroom.
4. Analyze the main phrases of the Hail Mary using the model used to analyze the Our Father on pages 252–255. After the discussion of each phrase, pose questions to yourself for personal growth.

Prayer Reflection

The Memorare is a great prayer to our Blessed Mother as our intercessor. It has been part of Catholic tradition for centuries. In it we humbly acknowledge our sinfulness and honestly ask for Mary's motherly help before her Son.

Memorare

Remember, O most gracious Virgin Mary,
that never was it known
that anyone who fled to your protection,
implored your help,
or sought your intercession was left unaided.
Inspired by this confidence,
I fly unto you,
O Virgin of virgins, my mother,
To you I come, before you I stand,
sinful and sorrowful.
O Mother of the Word incarnate,
despise not my petitions,
but in your mercy hear and answer me. Amen.

Which line of the prayer is most inspiring to you? Why?

Appendix: Catholic Handbook for Faith

A. BELIEFS

Who Is Catholic?

A summary of what it means to be a Catholic includes the following points. A Catholic . . .

★ is a Christian who belongs to a family of faith that shares Jesus' vision and responds to his presence in our midst.

★ loves each member of his or her family of faith and uses his or her unique talents to contribute to it in a positive way.

★ believes in God, who is our loving Father.

★ acknowledges the divinity of Jesus Christ, God's Son, our Lord and Savior.

★ believes in the Holy Spirit and the Spirit's powerful presence in the Church and in the world.

★ uses the many gifts of the Spirit, including the gift of faith that enables us to accept Jesus into his or her life; the gift of hope that helps us to trust the Lord and his word; and the gift of charity that empowers us to love as Christ has loved us.

★ attempts to live in harmony with Jesus' teaching by loving God above all things; by loving one's neighbor as oneself; by forgiving enemies; and by showing special care to the poor, lonely, and the outcast.

★ works for peace and justice, thus helping the Lord promote the spread of his reign on earth as it is in heaven.

★ celebrates the Paschal mystery by living a sacramental life.

★ recognizes the need for forgiveness through the celebration of the sacrament of Penance.

★ greatly values the Eucharist as a special sign of God's nourishing love, a way to encounter the living Lord Jesus and, therefore, fully participates in Mass every Sunday and holy day of obligation

★ prays because regular prayer deepens one's friendship with the Lord.

★ cherishes the Bible, the word of God, and reads it regularly.

★ acknowledges the role of the Christ-appointed official teachers in the Church whose role it is to teach, to sanctify, and to govern.

★ seeks guidance from the Magisterium in forming one's conscience on moral issues.

★ serves others by imitating Jesus who washed the feet of his disciples and commanded us to do the same.

★ has a universal vision that is open to all people and to truth in Jesus Christ.

★ courageously proclaims the gospel, thus publicly acknowledging Jesus Christ and his Church, even if this leads to ridicule and suffering.

★ has special devotion to Mary—the Mother of God and the Mother of the Church—and esteems the saints as models of how to live the Christian life.

★ is profoundly respectful of the dignity of all human beings and promotes human rights from "womb to tomb," taking special care to protect helpless unborn human life.

This list could go on. What would you add? But never forget the essentials: A Catholic belongs to Jesus Christ; to his Body, the Church; and to the world that God created and loves. A Catholic must celebrate the good news he or she is privileged to know by proclaiming it in word and deed:

God so loved the world that he gave his only Son, so that everyone who believes in him might not perish but might have eternal life (Jn 3:16).

Apostles' Creed

I believe in God, the Father almighty,
Creator of heaven and earth.

I believe in Jesus Christ, his only son, our Lord.
He was conceived by the power of the Holy Spirit,
and born of the Virgin Mary.
He suffered under Pontius Pilate,
was crucified, died, and was buried.
He descended into hell.
On the third day he rose again.
He ascended into heaven,
and is seated at the right hand of the Father.
He will come again to judge the living and the dead.

I believe in the Holy Spirit,
the holy catholic Church,
the communion of saints,
the forgiveness of sins,
the resurrection of the body,
and the life everlasting. Amen.

Nicene Creed

We believe in one God,
the Father, the Almighty,
maker of heaven and earth,
of all that is seen and unseen.
We believe in one Lord, Jesus Christ,
the only Son of God,
eternally begotten of the Father,
God from God, Light from Light,
true God from true God,
begotten, not made, one in Being with the Father.
Through him all things were made.
For us men and for our salvation he came down from heaven:
by the power of the Holy Spirit
he was born of the Virgin Mary, and became man.
For our sake he was crucified under Pontius Pilate;
he suffered, died, and was buried.
On the third day he rose again in fulfillment of the Scriptures;
he ascended into heaven and is seated at the right hand of the Father.
He will come again in glory to judge the living and the dead,
and his kingdom will have no end.
We believe in the Holy Spirit, the Lord, the giver of life,
who proceeds from the Father and the Son.
With the Father and the Son he is worshiped and glorified.
He has spoken through the Prophets.
We believe in one holy catholic and apostolic Church.
We acknowledge one baptism for the forgiveness of sins.
We look for the resurrection of the dead,
and the life of the world to come.
Amen.

Gifts of the Holy Spirit

1. Wisdom
2. Understanding
3. Counsel
4. Fortitude
5. Knowledge
6. Piety
7. Fear of the Lord

Fruits of the Holy Spirit

1. Charity
2. Joy
3. Peace
4. Patience
5. Kindness
6. Goodness
7. Generosity
8. Gentleness
9. Faithfulness
10. Modesty
11. Self-control
12. Chastity

The Symbol of Chalcedon

Following therefore the holy Fathers, we unanimously teach to confess one and the same Son, our Lord Jesus Christ, the same perfect in divinity and perfect in humanity, the same truly God and truly man composed of rational soul and body, the same one in being *(homoousios)* with the Father as to the divinity and one in being with us as to the humanity, like unto us in all things but sin (cf. Heb 4:15). The same was begotten from the Father before the ages as to the divinity and in the later days for us and our salvation was born as to his humanity from Mary the Virgin Mother of God.

We confess that one and the same Lord Jesus Christ, the only-begotten Son, must be acknowledged in two natures, without confusion or change, without division or separation. The distinction between the natures was never abolished by their union but rather the character proper to each of the two natures was preserved as they came together in one person *(prosôpon)* and one hypostasis. He is not split or divided into two persons, but he is one and the same only-begotten, God the Word, the Lord Jesus Christ, as formerly the prophets and later Jesus Christ himself have taught us about him and as has been handed down to us by the Symbol of the Fathers.

From the General Council of Chalcedon (451)

B. GOD AND JESUS CHRIST

Attributes of God

St. Thomas Aquinas named nine attributes that tell us some things about God's nature. They are:

1. *God is eternal.* He has no beginning and no end. Or, to put it another way, God always was, always is, and always will be.
2. *God is unique.* God is the designer of a one and only world. Even the people he creates are one of a kind.
3. *God is infinite and omnipotent.* This reminds us of a lesson we learned early in life: God sees everything. There are no limits to God. Omnipotence is a word that refers to God's supreme power and authority over all of creation.
4. *God is omnipresent.* God is not limited to space. He is everywhere. You can never be away from God.
5. *God contains all things.* All of creation is under God's care and jurisdiction.
6. *God is immutable.* God does not evolve. God does not change. God is the same God now as he always was and always will be.
7. *God is pure spirit.* Though God has been described with human attributes, God is not a material creation. God's image cannot be made. God is a pure spirit who cannot be divided into parts. God is simple, but complex.
8. *God is alive.* We believe in a living God, a God who acts in the lives of people. Most concretely, he came to this world in the incarnate form of Jesus Christ.
9. *God is holy.* God is pure goodness. God is pure love.

The Holy Trinity

The Trinity is the mystery of one God in three persons—Father, Son, and Holy Spirit. The mystery is impossible for human minds to understand. Some of the Church dogmas, or beliefs, can help:

★ *The Trinity is One.* There are not three Gods, but one God in three persons. Each one of them—Father, Son, and Holy Spirit—is God whole and entire.

★ *The three persons are distinct from one another.* For example, the Father is not the Son, nor is the Son the Holy Spirit. Rather, the Father is Creator, the Son is begotten of the Father, and the Holy Spirit proceeds from the Father and Son.

★ *The divine persons are related to one another.* Though they are related to one another, the three persons have one nature or substance.

St. John Damascus used two analogies to describe the doctrine of the Blessed Trinity.

Think of the Father as a root,
of the Son as a branch,
and of the Spirit as a fruit,
for the substance of these is one.

The Father is a sun
with the Son as rays
and the Holy Spirit as heat.

Read the *Catechism of the Catholic Church* (232–260) on the Holy Trinity.

Faith in One God

There are several implications for those who love God and believe in him with their entire heart and soul (see *CCC* 222–227):

★ It means knowing God's greatness and majesty.
★ It means living in thanksgiving.
★ It means knowing the unity and dignity of all people.
★ It means making good use of created things.
★ It means trust God in every circumstance.

Famous Quotations about Jesus Christ

Christ did submit himself unto the elements, unto cold and heat, hunger and thirst . . .concealing his power and despoiling himself thereof in the likeness of man, in order that he might teach us weak and wretched mortals with what patience we ought to bear tribulation.

Blessed Angela of Foligno

Christ with me, Christ before me
Christ behind me, Christ in me,
Christ beneath me, Christ above me,
Christ on my right, Christ on my left,
Christ where I lie, Christ where I sit,
Christ where I arise,
Christ in the heart of everyone who
thinks of me,
Christ in the mouth of everyone who
speaks of me,
Christ in every eye that sees me,
Christ in every ear that hears me,
Salvation is of the Lord,
Salvation is of Christ,
May your salvation, Lord be ever
with us.

from the breastplate of St. Patrick

Oh, if all were to know how beautiful Jesus is, how amiable he is! They would all die of love.

St. Gemma Galgani

About Jesus Christ and the Church, I simply know they're just one thing, and we should not complicate the matter.

St. Joan of Arc

Judaism's Belief in One God

Like Catholics, Jews are monotheistic, that is, they believe in one God. Jews believe that God reveals himself in the Torah, through the prophets, in the life of the Jewish people, and through the history of the Jews. The key event of Jewish history is the Exodus, when God freed the Jewish nation from slavery in Egypt. This pivotal event is recounted every year during the seven-day festival known as Passover, celebrated around the time of Easter.

Jews believe that the covenant God established with Abraham and the Sinai covenant require Israel to adore and serve God always, and to observe his Law. In turn, they believe God will remain faithful to them and treat the members of the Jewish nation as special.

Jews believe that God is eternal, almighty, all-knowing, present everywhere, and loving of his creation. In prayer, God is addressed as *Adonai* (Lord). Jews use God's name respectfully and avoid saying the name revealed to Moses—Yahweh—because it is so holy. Jewish faith is summed up in a prayer pious Jews recite every day, the *Shema:*

> Hear, O Israel! The LORD is our God, the LORD alone! Therefore, you shall love the LORD, your God, with all your heart, and with all your soul, and with all your strength (Dt 6:4–5).

Jews differ on how God will fulfill his covenant with them, how God's kingdom will be established, and on the nature of the final judgment. For example, some Jews believe the concept of a Messiah refers to an individual person; others think of it in terms of the community of God's people or the development of historical events; still others believe God himself will intervene directly into human history.

The Catholic Church encourages utmost respect for the Jewish faith. For example, at the Second Vatican Council, Church fathers wrote:

> This sacred Synod . . . recalls the spiritual bond linking the people of the New Covenant with Abraham's stock. . . .
>
> The Church, therefore, cannot forget that she received the revelation of the Old Testament through the people whom God in his inexpressible mercy deigned to establish the Ancient Covenant. . . .
>
> The Church recalls too that from the Jewish people sprang the apostles, her foundation stones and pillars, as well as most of the early disciples who proclaimed Christ to the world. . . .
>
> The Jews still remain most dear to God because of their fathers, for He does not repent of the gifts He makes nor of the calls He issues (*Declaration on the Relationship of the Church to Non-Christian Religions,* No. 4).

C. SCRIPTURE AND TRADITION

Canon of the Bible

There are seventy-three books in the canon of the Bible, that is, the official list of books the Church accepts as divinely inspired writings: forty-six Old Testament books and twenty-seven New Testament books. Protestant Bibles do not include seven Old

Testament books on its list (1 and 2 Maccabees, Judith, Tobit, Baruch, Sirach, and the Wisdom of Solomon). Why the difference? Catholics rely on the version of the Bible that the earliest Christians used, the *Septuagint*. This was the first Greek translation of the Hebrew scriptures begun in the third century BC. Protestants, on the other hand, rely on an official list of Hebrew scriptures compiled in the Holy Land by Jewish scholars at the end of the first century AD. Today, most Protestant Bibles print the disputed books in a separate section at the back of the Bible called the *Apocrypha*.

The twenty-seven books of the New Testament are divided into three categories: the gospels, the letters written to local Christian communities or individuals, and the letters intended for the entire Church. The heart of the New Testament, in fact all of Scripture, is the gospels. The New Testament is central to our knowledge of Jesus Christ. He is the focus of all Scripture.

There are forty-six books in the Old Testament canon. The Old Testament is the foundation for God's self-revelation in Christ. Christians honor the Old Testament as God's word. It contains the writings of prophets and other inspired authors who recorded God's teaching to the Chosen People and his interaction in their history. For example, the Old Testament recounts how God delivered the Jews from Egypt (the Exodus), led them to the Promised Land, formed them into a nation under his care, and taught them in knowledge and worship.

The stories, prayers, sacred histories, and other writings of the Old Testament reveal what God is like and tell much about human nature, too. In brief, the Chosen People sinned repeatedly by turning their backs on their loving God; they were weak and easily tempted away from God. Yahweh, on the other hand, *always* remained faithful. He promised to send a Messiah to humanity.

Listed below are the categories and books of the Old Testament and the New Testament:

The Old Testament

The Pentateuch

Genesis	Gn
Exodus	Ex
Leviticus	Lv
Numbers	Nm
Deuteronomy	Dt

The Historical Books

Joshua	Jos
Judges	Jgs
Ruth	Ru
1 Samuel	1 Sm
2 Samuel	2 Sm
1 Kings	1 Kgs
2 Kings	2 Kgs
1 Chronicles	1 Chr
2 Chronicles	2 Chr
Ezra	Ezr
Nehemiah	Neh
Tobit	Tb
Judith	Jdt
Esther	Est
1 Maccabees	1 Mc
2 Maccabees	2 Mc

The Wisdom Books

Job	Jb
Psalms	Ps(s)
Proverbs	Prv
Ecclesiastes	Eccl
Song of Songs	Sg
Wisdom	Wis
Sirach	Sir

The Prophetic Books

Isaiah	Is
Jeremiah	Jer
Lamentations	Lam
Baruch	Bar
Ezekiel	Ez
Daniel	Dn
Hosea	Hos
Joel	Jl
Amos	Am
Obadiah	Ob
Jonah	Jon
Micah	Mi
Nahum	Na
Habakkuk	Hb

Zephaniah	Zep
Haggai	Hg
Zechariah	Zec
Malachi	Mal

The New Testament

The Gospels

Matthew	Mt
Mark	Mk
Luke	Lk
John	Jn
Acts of the Apostles	Acts

The New Testament Letters

Romans	Rom
1 Corinthians	1 Cor
2 Corinthians	2 Cor
Galatians	Gal
Ephesians	Eph
Philippians	Phil
Colossians	Col
1 Thessalonians	1 Thes
2 Thessalonians	2 Thes
1 Timothy	1 Tm
2 Timothy	2 Tm
Titus	Ti
Philemon	Phlm
Hebrews	Heb

The Catholic Letters

James	Jas
1 Peter	1 Pt
2 Peter	2 Pt
1 John	1 Jn
2 John	2 Jn
3 John	3 Jn
Jude	Jude
Revelation	Rv

How to Locate a Scripture Passage

Example: 2 Tm 3:16–17

1. *Determine the name of the book.*

   The abbreviation "2 Tm" stands for the second book of Timothy.

2. *Determine whether the book is in the Old Testament or New Testament.*

   The second book of Timothy is one of the Catholic letters in the New Testament.

3. *Locate the chapter where the passage occurs.*

   The first number before the colon—"3"—indicates the chapter. Chapters in the Bible are set off by the larger numbers that divide a book.

4. Locate the verses of the passage.

   The numbers after the colon indicate the verses referred to. In this case, verses 16 and 17 of chapter 3.

5. Read the passage.

   For example: "All scripture is inspired by God and is useful for teaching, for refutation, for correction, and for training in righteousness, so that one who belongs to God may be competent, equipped for every good work."

Timeline of Church History

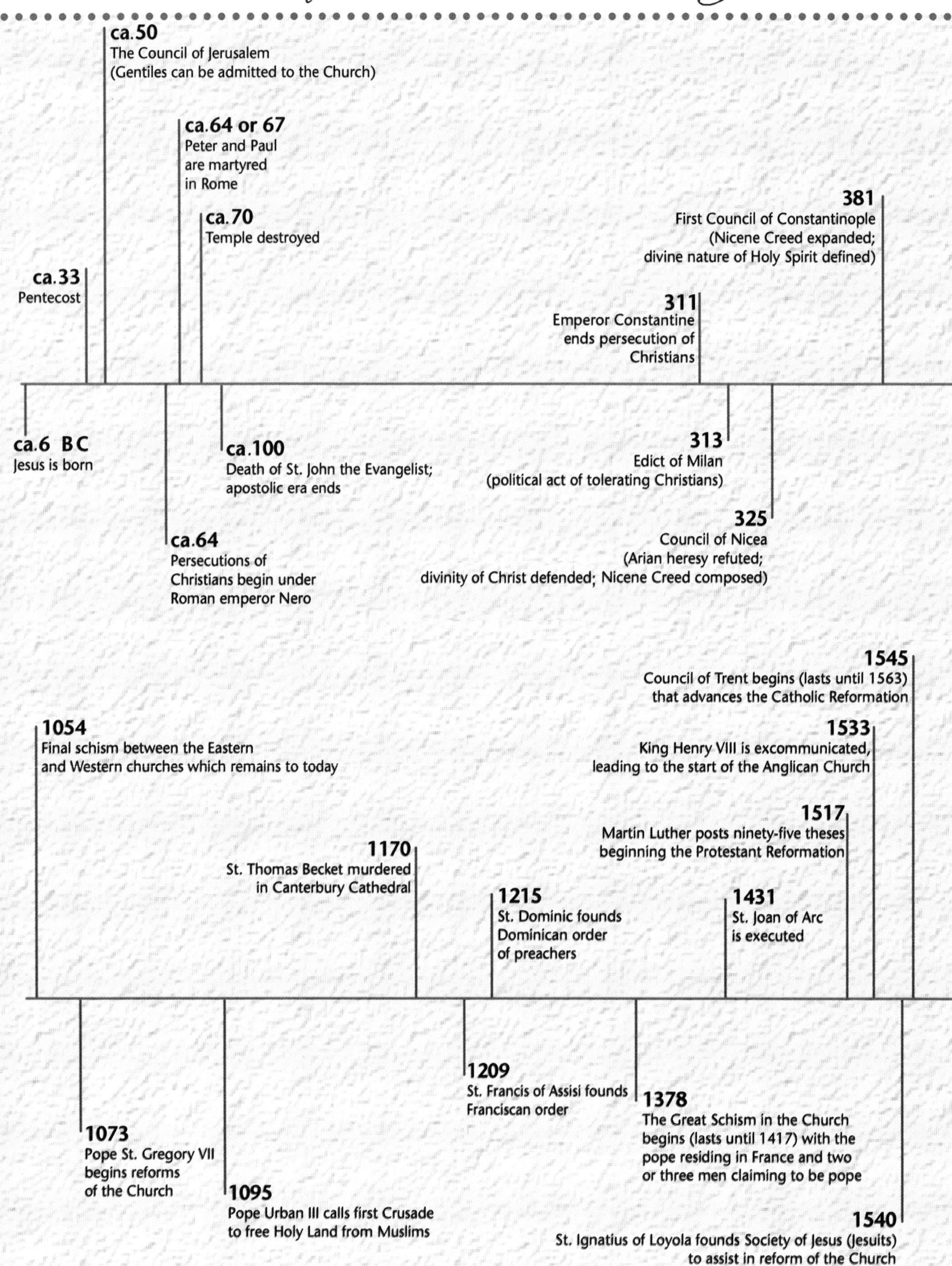
ca.6 BC
Jesus is born
ca.33
Pentecost
ca.50
The Council of Jerusalem
(Gentiles can be admitted to the Church)
ca.64
Persecutions of Christians begin under Roman emperor Nero
ca.64 or 67
Peter and Paul are martyred in Rome
ca.70
Temple destroyed
ca.100
Death of St. John the Evangelist; apostolic era ends
311
Emperor Constantine ends persecution of Christians
313
Edict of Milan
(political act of tolerating Christians)
325
Council of Nicea
(Arian heresy refuted; divinity of Christ defended; Nicene Creed composed)
381
First Council of Constantinople
(Nicene Creed expanded; divine nature of Holy Spirit defined)
1054
Final schism between the Eastern and Western churches which remains to today
1073
Pope St. Gregory VII begins reforms of the Church
1095
Pope Urban III calls first Crusade to free Holy Land from Muslims
1170
St. Thomas Becket murdered in Canterbury Cathedral
1209
St. Francis of Assisi founds Franciscan order
1215
St. Dominic founds Dominican order of preachers
1378
The Great Schism in the Church begins (lasts until 1417) with the pope residing in France and two or three men claiming to be pope
1431
St. Joan of Arc is executed
1517
Martin Luther posts ninety-five theses beginning the Protestant Reformation
1533
King Henry VIII is excommunicated, leading to the start of the Anglican Church
1540
St. Ignatius of Loyola founds Society of Jesus (Jesuits) to assist in reform of the Church
1545
Council of Trent begins (lasts until 1563) that advances the Catholic Reformation

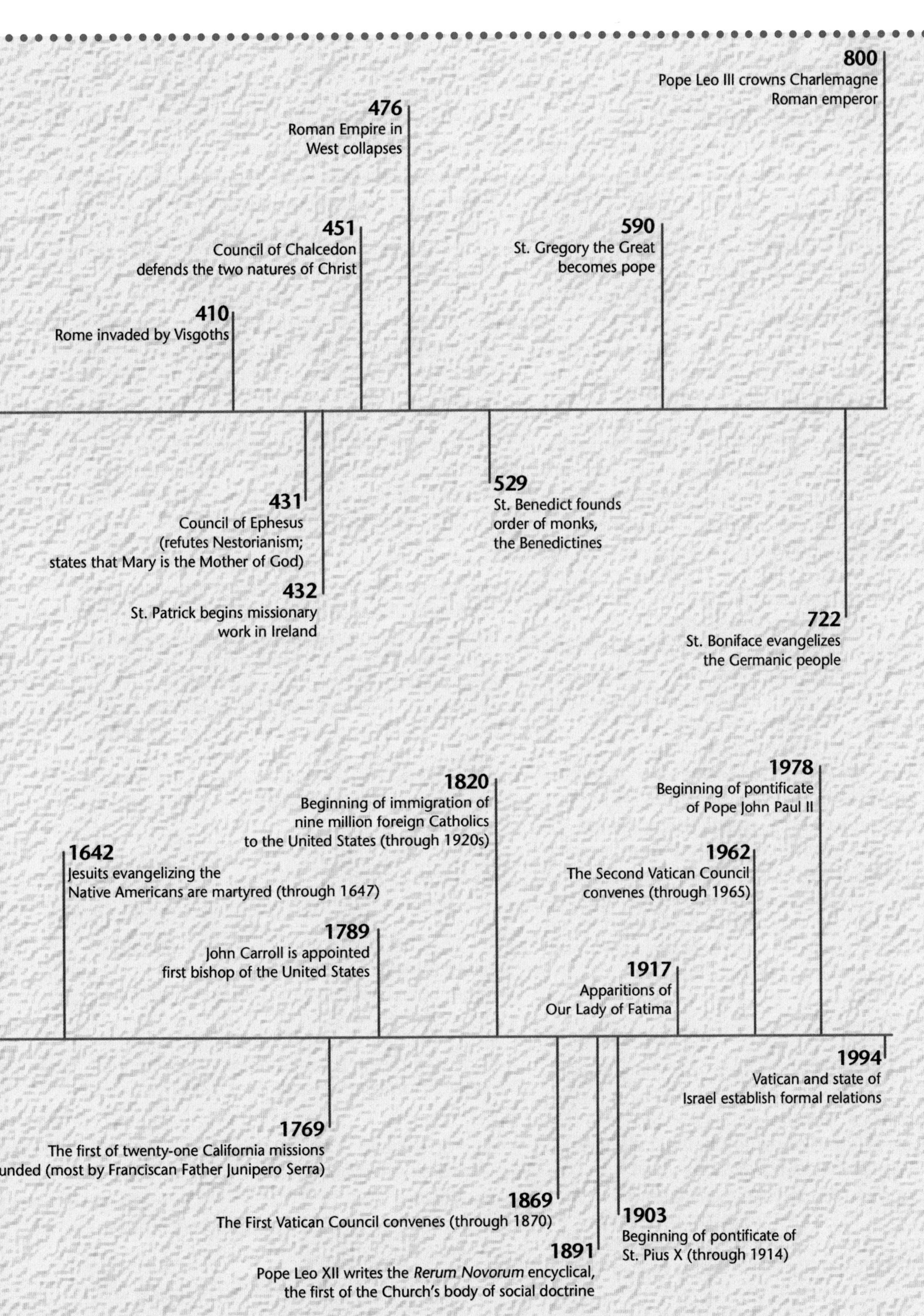

410
Rome invaded by Visgoths
431
Council of Ephesus
(refutes Nestorianism;
states that Mary is the Mother of God)
432
St. Patrick begins missionary
work in Ireland
451
Council of Chalcedon
defends the two natures of Christ
476
Roman Empire in
West collapses
529
St. Benedict founds
order of monks,
the Benedictines
590
St. Gregory the Great
becomes pope
722
St. Boniface evangelizes
the Germanic people
800
Pope Leo III crowns Charlemagne
Roman emperor
1642
Jesuits evangelizing the
Native Americans are martyred (through 1647)
1769
The first of twenty-one California missions
ounded (most by Franciscan Father Junipero Serra)
1789
John Carroll is appointed
first bishop of the United States
1820
Beginning of immigration of
nine million foreign Catholics
to the United States (through 1920s)
1869
The First Vatican Council convenes (through 1870)
1891
Pope Leo XII writes the *Rerum Novorum* encyclical,
the first of the Church's body of social doctrine
1903
Beginning of pontificate of
St. Pius X (through 1914)
1917
Apparitions of
Our Lady of Fatima
1962
The Second Vatican Council
convenes (through 1965)
1978
Beginning of pontificate
of Pope John Paul II
1994
Vatican and state of
Israel establish formal relations

D. CHURCH

Marks of the Church

1. *The Church is one.* The Church remains one because of its source: the unity in the Trinity of the Father, Son, and Spirit in one God. The Church's unity can never be broken and lost because this foundation is itself unbreakable.
2. *The Church is holy.* The Church is holy because Jesus, the founder of the Church, is holy and he joined the Church to himself as his body and gave the Church the gift of the Holy Spirit. Together, Christ and the Church make up the "whole Christ" (*Christus totus* in Latin).
3. *The Church is catholic.* The Church is catholic ("universal" or "for everyone") in two ways. First, it is Catholic because Christ is present in the Church in the fullness of his body, with the fullness of the means of salvation, the fullness of faith, sacraments, and the ordained ministry that comes from the Apostles. The Church is also catholic because it takes its message of salvation to all people.
4. *The Church is apostolic.* The Church's apostolic mission comes from Jesus: "Go, therefore, and make disciples of all nations" (Mt 28:19). The Church remains apostolic because it still teaches the same things the apostles taught. Also, the Church is led by leaders who are successors to the apostles and who help to guide us until Jesus returns.

The Pope

The bishop of Rome has carried the title "pope" since the ninth century. Pope means "papa" or "father." St. Peter was the first bishop of Rome and, hence, the first pope. He was commissioned directly by Jesus:

> And so I say to you, you are Peter, and upon this rock I will build my church, and the gates of the netherworld shall not prevail against it. I will give you the keys to the kingdom of heaven. Whatever you bind on earth shall be bound in heaven; and whatever you loose on earth shall be loosed in heaven (Mt 16:18–19).

Because Peter was the first bishop of Rome, the succeeding bishops of Rome have had primacy in the Church. The entire succession of popes since St. Peter can be traced directly to the apostle.

The pope is in communion with the bishops of the world as part of the Magisterium, which is the Church's teaching authority. The pope can also define doctrine in faith or morals for the Church. When he does so, he is infallible and cannot be in error.

The pope is elected by the College of Cardinals by a two-thirds majority vote in secret balloting. If a pope is not elected after 30 votes, a new pope can be chosen by an absolute majority—that is half the votes plus one. Cardinals under the age of eighty are eligible to vote. If the necessary majority is not achieved the ballots are burned in a small stove inside the conclave chambers along with straw that makes dark smoke. The sign of dark smoke announces to the crowds waiting outside St. Peter's Basilica that a new pope has not been chosen. When a new pope has been voted in with the necessary majority, the ballots are burned without the straw, producing white smoke signifying the election of a pope.

Recent Popes

Since 1900 and through the pontificate of Pope Benedict XVI, there were ten Popes. Pope John Paul II was the first non-Italian pope since Dutchman Pope Adrian VI (1522–1523). The popes since the twentieth century through Pope Benedict XVI with their original names, place of origin, and years as pope:

- ★ Pope Leo XIII (Giocchino Pecci): Carpineto, Italy, February 20, 1878–July 20, 1903.
- ★ Pope St. Pius X (Giuseppe Sarto): Riese, Italy, August 4, 1903–August 20, 1914.

(continued on page 268)

The Apostles and Their Emblems

St. Andrew

Tradition holds that Andrew was crucified on a bent cross, called a saltire.

St. Bartholomew

Bartholomew was flayed alive before being crucified. He was then beheaded.

St. James the Greater

James the Greater, the brother of John, was beheaded by Herod Agrippa. It is the only death of an apostle mentioned in Scripture (Acts 12:2). The shell indicates James' missionary work by sea in Spain. The sword is of martyrdom.

St. James the Less

James the Less is traditionally known as the first bishop of Jerusalem. The saw for his emblem is connected with the tradition of his body being sawed into pieces after he was pushed from the pinnacle of the Temple.

St. John the Evangelist

John was the first bishop of Ephesus. He is the only apostle believed to have died a natural death, in spite of many attempts to murder him by his enemies. One attempt included his miraculous survival of drinking a poisoned drink.

St. Jude

Some traditions have Jude and St. Peter martyred together. It is thought that he traveled throughout the Roman Empire with Peter.

St. Matthew

Matthew's shield depicts three purses reflecting his original occupation as tax collector.

St. Matthias

Matthias was the apostle chosen by lot to replace Judas. Tradition holds that Matthias was stoned to death and then beheaded with an ax.

St. Peter

Simon Peter was the brother of Andrew. The first bishop of Rome, Peter was crucified under Nero, asking to be hung upside down because he felt unworthy to die as Jesus did. The keys represent Jesus' giving to Peter the keys to the kingdom of heaven.

St. Philip

Philip may have been bound to a cross and stoned to death. The two loaves of bread at the side of the cross refer to Philip's comment to Jesus about the possibility of feeding the multitudes of people (Jn 6:7).

St. Simon

The book with fish depicts Simon as a "fisher of men" who preached the gospel. He was also known as Simon the Zealot.

St. Thomas

Thomas is thought to have been a missionary in India, where he is thought to have built a church. Hence, the carpenter's square. He may have died by arrows and stones. It is then thought that he had a lance run through his body.

- ★ Pope Benedict XV (Giacomo della Chiesa): Genoa, Italy, September 3, 1914–January 22, 1922.
- ★ Pope Pius XI (Achille Ratti): Desio, Italy, February 6, 1922–February 10, 1939.
- ★ Pope Pius XII (Eugenio Pacelli): Rome, Italy, March 2, 1939–October 9, 1958.
- ★ Pope John XXIII (Angelo Giuseppe Roncalli), Sotto il Monte, Italy, October 28, 1958–June 3, 1963.
- ★ Pope Paul VI (Giovanni Battista Montini): Concessio, Italy, June 21, 1963–August 6, 1978.
- ★ Pope John Paul I (Albino Luciani): Forno di Canale, Italy, August 26, 1978–September 28, 1978.
- ★ Pope John Paul II (Karol Wojtyla): Wadowice, Poland, October 16, 1978–April 2, 2005.
- ★ Pope Benedict XVI (Joseph Ratzinger): Marktl am Inn, Germany, April 19, 2005-

Pope Benedict XVI

Fathers of the Church

Church Fathers, or Fathers of the Church, is a traditional title that was given to theologians of the first eight centuries whose teachings made a lasting mark on the Church. The Church Fathers developed a significant amount of doctrine which has great authority in the Church. The Church Fathers are named as either Latin Fathers (West) or Greek Fathers (East). Among the greatest Fathers of the Church are:

Latin Fathers	**Greek Fathers**
St. Ambrose	St. John Chrysostom
St. Augustine	St. Basil the Great
St. Jerome	St. Gregory of Nazianzen
St. Gregory the Great	St. Athanasius

Doctors of the Church

The Doctors of the Church are men and women honored by the Church for their writings, preaching, and holiness. Originally the Doctors of the Church were considered to be Church Fathers Augustine, Ambrose, Jerome, and Gregory the Great, but others were added over the centuries. St. Teresa of Avila was the first woman Doctor (1970). St. Catherine of Siena was named a Doctor of the Church the same year. The list of Doctors of the Church:

NAME	LIFE SPAN	DESIGNATION
St. Athanasius	296–373	1568 by Pius V
St. Ephraem the Syrian	306–373	1920 by Benedict XV
St. Hilary of Poitiers	315–367	1851 by Pius IX
St. Cyril of Jerusalem	315–386	1882 by Leo XIII
St. Gregory of Nazianzus	325–389	1568 by Pius V
St. Basil the Great	329–379	1568 by Pius V
St. Ambrose	339–397	1295 by Boniface VIII
St. John Chrysostom	347–407	1568 by Pius V
St. Jerome	347–419	1295 by Boniface XIII
St. Augustine	354–430	1295 by Boniface XIII
St. Cyril of Alexandria	376–444	1882 by Leo XIII
St. Peter Chrysologous	400–450	1729 by Benedict XIII
St. Leo the Great	400–461	1754 by Benedict XIV
St. Gregory the Great	540–604	1295 by Boniface XIII
St. Isidore of Seville	560–636	1722 by Innocent XIII
St. John of Damascus	645–749	1890 by Leo XIII
St. Bede the Venerable	672–735	1899 by Leo XIII
St. Peter Damian	1007–1072	1828 by Leo XII
St. Anselm	1033–1109	1720 by Clement XI
St. Bernard of Clairvaux	1090–1153	1830 by Pius VIII
St. Anthony of Padua	1195–1231	1946 by Pius XII
St. Albert the Great	1206–1280	1931 by Pius XI
St. Bonaventure	1221–1274	1588 by Sixtus V
St. Thomas Aquinas	1226–1274	1567 by Pius V
St. Catherine of Siena	1347–1380	1970 by Paul VI
St. Teresa of Avila	1515–1582	1970 by Paul VI
St. Peter Canisius	1521–1597	1925 by Pius XI
St. John of the Cross	1542–1591	1926 by Pius XI
St. Robert Bellarmine	1542–1621	1931 by Pius XI
St. Lawrence of Brindisi	1559–1619	1959 by John XXIII
St. Francis de Sales	1567–1622	1871 by Pius IX
St. Alphonsus Ligouri	1696–1787	1871 by Pius IX
St. Thérèse of Lisieux	1873–1897	1997 by John Paul II

Ecumenical Councils

An ecumenical council is a worldwide assembly of bishops under direction of the pope. There have been twenty-one ecumenical councils, the most recent being the Second Vatican Council (1962–1965). A complete list of the Church's ecumenical councils with the years each met:

Nicaea I	325
Constantinople I	381
Ephesus	431
Chalcedon	451
Constantinople II	553

Constantinople III	680
Nicaea II	787
Constantiople IV	869–870
Lateran I	1123
Lateran II	1139
Lateran III	1179
Lateran IV	1215
Lyons I	1245
Lyons II	1274
Vienne	1311–1312
Constance	1414–1418
Florence	1431–1445
Lateran V	1512–1517
Trent	1545–1563
Vatican Council I	1869–1870
Vatican Council II	1962–1965

E. MORALITY

The Ten Commandments

The Ten Commandments are a main source for Christian morality. The Ten Commandments were revealed by God to Moses. Jesus, himself, acknowledged them. He told the rich young man, "If you wish to enter into the life, keep the commandments" (Mt 19:17). Since the time of St. Augustine (fourth century) the Ten Commandments have been used as a source for teaching baptismal candidates. See chapter 9 for more information.

I. I, the Lord am your God: you shall not have other gods besides me.

II. You shall not take the name of the Lord, your God, in vain.

III. Remember to keep holy the Sabbath day.

IV. Honor your father and your mother.

V. You shall not kill.

VI. You shall not commit adultery.

VII. You shall not steal.

VIII. You shall not bear false witness against your neighbor.

IX. You shall not covet your neighbor's wife.

X. You shall not covet your neighbor's goods.

The Beatitudes

The word *beatitude* means "supreme happiness." Jesus preached the Beatitudes in his Sermon on the Mount. They are:

Blessed are the poor in spirit, for theirs is the kingdom of God.

Blessed are they who mourn, for they will be comforted.

Blessed are the meek, for they will inherit the land.

Blessed are they who hunger and thirst for righteousness, for they will be satisfied.

Blessed are the merciful, for they will be shown mercy.

Blessed are the clean of heart, for they will see God.

Blessed are the peacemakers, for they will be called children of God.

Blessed are they who are persecuted for the sake of righteousness, for theirs is the kingdom of heaven.

Cardinal Virtues

Virtues—habits that help in leading a moral life—that are acquired by human effort are known as moral or human virtues. Four of these are called the cardinal virtues because they form the hinge that connect all the others. They are:

★ Prudence ★ Fortitude
★ Justice ★ Temperance

Theological Virtues

The theological virtues are the foundation for moral life. They are related directly to God.

★ Faith ★ Hope ★ Love

Corporal (Bodily) Works of Mercy

★ Feed the hungry.
★ Give drink to the thirsty.
★ Clothe the naked.
★ Visit the imprisoned.
★ Shelter the homeless.
★ Visit the sick.
★ Bury the dead.

Spiritual Works of Mercy

★ Counsel the doubtful.
★ Instruct the ignorant.
★ Admonish sinners.
★ Comfort the afflicted.
★ Forgive offenses.
★ Bear wrongs patiently.
★ Pray for the living and the dead.

Precepts of the Church

1. You shall attend Mass on Sundays and on holy days of obligation and rest from servile labor.
2. You shall confess your sins once a year.
3. You shall receive the sacrament of Eucharist at least during the Easter season.
4. You shall observe the days of fasting and abstinence established by the Church.
5. You shall help to provide for the needs of the Church.

In addition, Catholics have the duty to support the Church with gifts of their time and talents and with monetary gifts.

Catholic Social Teaching: Major Themes

The 1998 document *Sharing Catholic Social Teaching: Challenges and Directions—Reflections of the U.S. Catholic Bishops* highlighted seven principles of the Church's social teaching. They are:

1. Life and dignity of the human person
2. Call to family, community, and participation
3. Rights and responsibilities
4. Option for the poor and vulnerable
5. The dignity of work and the rights of workers
6. Solidarity
7. Care for God's creation

Sin

Sin is an offense against God.

Mortal sin is the most serious kind of sin. Mortal sin destroys or kills a person's relationship with God. To be a mortal sin, three conditions must exist:

★ The moral object must be of grave or serious matter. Grave matter is specified in the Ten Commandments (e.g., do not kill, do not commit adultery, do not steal, etc.).
★ The person must have full knowledge of the gravity of the sinful action.
★ The person must completely consent to the action. It must be a personal choice.

Venial sin is less serious sin. Examples of venial sins are petty jealousy, disobedience, and "borrowing" a small amount of money from a parent without the intention of repaying it. Venial sins, when unrepented, can lead a person to commit mortal sins.

Vices are bad habits linked to sins. The seven capital vices are pride, avarice, envy, wrath, lust, gluttony, and sloth.

F. LITURGY & SACRAMENTS

Church Year

The cycle of seasons and feasts that Catholics celebrate is called the Church Year or Liturgical Year. The Church Year is divided into six main parts: Advent, Christmas, Lent, Triduum, Easter, and Ordinary Time.

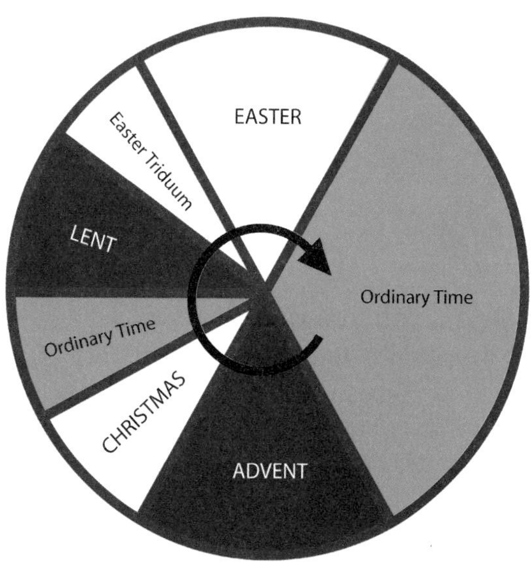

Holy Days of Obligation in the United States

- ★ Immaculate Conception of Mary
  December 8
- ★ Christmas
  December 25
- ★ Solemnity of Mary, Mother of God
  January 1
- ★ Ascension of the Lord
  Forty days after Easter
- ★ Assumption of Mary
  August 15
- ★ All Saints Day
  November 1

The Seven Sacraments

1. Baptism
2. Confirmation
3. Eucharist
4. Penance and Reconciliation
5. Anointing of the Sick
6. Holy Orders
7. Matrimony

How to Go to Confession

1. Spend some time examining your conscience. Consider your actions and attitudes in each area of your life (e.g., faith, family, school/work, social life, relationships). Ask yourself, "Is this area of my life pleasing to God? What needs to be reconciled with God? with others? with myself?
2. Sincerely tell God that you are sorry for your sins. Ask God for forgiveness and for the grace you will need to change what needs changing in your life. Promise God that you will try to live according to his will for you.
3. Approach the area for confession. Wait an appropriate distance until it is your turn.
4. Make the Sign of the Cross with the priest. He may say: "May God, who has enlightened every heart, help you to know your sins and trust his mercy." You reply: "Amen."
5. Confess your sins to the priest. Simply and directly talk to him about the areas of sinfulness in your life that need God's healing touch.
6. The priest will ask you to pray an act of contrition. Pray an Act of Contrition you have committed to memory. Or, saying something in your own words, like: "Dear God, I am sorry for my sins. I ask for your forgiveness and I promise to do better in the future."

7. The priest will talk to you about your life, encourage you to be more faithful to God in the future, and help you decide what to do to make up for your sins—your penance.
8. The priest will then extend his hands over your head and pray the Church's official prayer of absolution:

    God, the Father of mercies, through the death and resurrection of his Son, has reconciled the world to himself and sent the Holy Spirit among us for the forgiveness of sins; through the ministry of the Church may God give you pardon and peace, and I absolve you from your sins in the name of the Father, and of the Son, and of the Holy Spirit.

    You respond: "Amen."
9. The priest will wish you peace. Thank him and leave.
10. Go to a quiet place in church and pray your prayer of penance. Then spend some time quietly thanking God for the gift of forgiveness.

Order of Mass

There are two main parts of the Mass, the Liturgy of the Word and the Liturgy of the Eucharist. The complete order of Mass:

The Introductory Rites

The Entrance
Greeting of the Altar and of the People Gathered
The Act of Penitence
The *Kyrie Eleison*
The *Gloria*
The Collect (Opening Prayer)

The Liturgy of the Word

Silence
The Biblical Readings (the reading of the Gospel is the high point of the Liturgy of the Word)
The Responsorial Psalm
The Homily
The Profession of Faith (Creed)
The Prayer of the Faithful

The Liturgy of the Eucharist

The Preparation of the Gifts
The Prayer over the Offerings
The Eucharistic Prayer
The Communion Rite
The Lord's Prayer
The Rite of Peace
The Fraction (Breaking of the Bread)
Communion
Prayer after Communion

The Concluding Rites

Communion Regulations

To receive Holy Communion properly, a person must be in the state of grace (free from mortal sin), have the right intention (only for the purpose of pleasing God), and observe the Communion fast.

The fast means that a person may not eat anything or drink any liquid (other than water) one hour before the reception of Communion. There are exceptions made to this fast only for the sick and aged.

Three Degrees of the Sacrament of Orders

There are three degrees of the sacrament of Holy Orders: the ministries of bishop, priest, and deacon.

The bishop receives the fullness of the sacrament of Orders. He is the successor to the apostles. When he celebrates the sacraments, the bishop is given the grace to act in the person of Christ who is the head of the body of the Church.

Priests are ordained as co-workers of the bishop. They too are configured to Christ so that they may act in his person during the sacraments of Eucharist, Baptism, and the Anointing of the Sick. They may bless marriages in the name of Christ and, under the authority of the bishop, share in Christ's ministry of forgiveness in the sacrament of Penance and Reconciliation.

Deacons are ordained for service and are configured to Christ the servant. Deacons are ordained to help and serve the priests and bishops in their work. While bishops and priests are configured to Christ to act as the head of Christ's body, deacons are configured to Christ in order to serve as he served. Deacons may baptize, preach the Gospel and homily, and bless marriages.

G. MARY AND THE SAINTS

Mother of God

Mary, the mother of Jesus, is the closest human to cooperate with her Son's work of redemption. For this reason, the Church holds her in a special place. Of her many titles, the most significant is that she is the Mother of God.

The Church teaches several truths about Mary.

First, she was conceived immaculately. This means from the very first moment of her existence she was without sin and "full of grace." This belief is called the Immaculate Conception. The feast of the Immaculate Conception is celebrated on December 8.

Second, Mary was ever-virgin. She was a virgin before, in, and after the birth of Jesus. As his mother, she cared for him in infancy and raised him to adulthood with the help of her husband, Joseph. She witnessed Jesus' preaching and ministry, was at the foot of his cross at his crucifixion, and present with the apostles as they awaited the coming of the Holy Spirit at Pentecost.

Third, at the time of her death, Mary was assumed body and soul into heaven. This dogma was proclaimed as a matter of faith by Pope Pius XII in 1950. The feast of the Assumption is celebrated on August 15.

The Church has always been devoted to the Blessed Virgin. This devotion is different than that given to God—Father, Son, and Holy Spirit. Rather, the Church is devoted to Mary as her first disciple, the Queen of all Saints, and her own Mother. Quoting the fathers of the Second Vatican Council:

> In the meantime the Mother of Jesus, in the glory which she possesses in body and soul in heaven, is the image and the beginning of the Church as it is to be perfected in the world to come. Likewise she shines forth on earth, until the day of the Lord shall come, a sign of certain hope and comfort to the pilgrim People of God (*Lumen Gentium,* 68).

Marian Feasts Throughout the Year

January 1	Solemnity of Mary, Mother of God
March 25	Annunciation of the Lord
May 31	Visitation
August 15	Assumption
August 22	Queenship of Mary
September 8	Birth of Mary
September 15	Our Lady of Sorrows
October 7	Our Lady of the Rosary
November 21	Presentation of Mary
December 8	Immaculate Conception
December 12	Our Lady of Guadalupe

Canonization of Saints

Saints are those who are in glory with God in heaven. *Canonization* refers to a solemn declaration by the Pope that a person who either died a martyr or who lived an exemplary Christian life is in heaven and may be honored and imitated by all Christians. The canonization process first involves a process of beatification that includes a thorough investigation of the person's life and certification of miracles that can be attributed to the candidate's intercession.

The first official canonization of the universal Church on record was St. Ulrich of Augsburg by Pope John XV in 993.

Some non-Catholics criticize Catholics for "praying to saints." Catholics *honor* saints for their holy lives but we do not pray to them as if they were God. We ask the saints to pray with us and for us as part of the Church in glory. We can ask them to do this because we know that their lives have been spent in close communion with God. We also ask the saints for their friendship so that we can follow the example they have left for us.

Patron Saints

A patron is a saint who is designated for places (nations, regions, dioceses) or organizations. Many saints have also become patrons of jobs, professional groups, and intercessors for special needs. Listed below are patron saints for several nations and some special patrons:

PATRONS OF PLACES

Americas	Our Lady of Guadalupe, St. Rose of Lima
Argentina	Our Lady of Lujan
Australia	Our Lady Help of Christians
Canada	St. Joseph, St. Anne
China	St. Joseph
England	St. George
Finland	St. Henry
France	Our Lady of the Assumption, St. Joan of Arc, St. Thérèse of Lisieux
Germany	St. Boniface
India	Our Lady of the Assumption
Ireland	St. Patrick, St. Brigid, St. Columba
Italy	St. Francis of Assisi, St. Catherine of Siena
Japan	St. Peter
Mexico	Our Lady of Guadalupe
New Zealand	Our Lady Help of Christians
Poland	St. Casmir, St. Stanislaus, Our Lady of Czestochowa
Russia	St. Andrew, St. Nicholas of Myra, St. Thérèse of Lisieux
Scotland	St. Andrew, St. Columba
Spain	St. James, St. Teresa of Avila
United States	Immaculate Conception

SPECIAL PATRONS

Accountants	St. Matthew
Actors	St. Genesius
Animals	St. Francis of Assisi
Athletes	St. Sebastian
Beggars	St. Martin of Tours
Boy Scouts	St. George
Dentists	St. Apollonia
Farmers	St. Isidore
Grocers	St. Michael
Journalists	St. Francis de Sales
Maids	St. Zita
Motorcyclists	Our Lady of Grace
Painters	St. Luke
Pawnbrokers	St. Nicholas
Police Officers	St. Michael
Priests	St. John Vianney
Scientists	St. Albert
Tailors	St. Homobonus
Teachers	St. Gregory the Great, St. John Baptist de la Salle
Wine Merchants	St. Amand

H. DEVOTIONS

The Mysteries of the Rosary

JOYFUL MYSTERIES

1. The Annunciation
2. The Visitation
3. The Nativity

4. The Presentation in the Temple
5. The Finding of Jesus in the Temple

Mysteries of Light

1. Jesus' Baptism in the Jordan River
2. Jesus' Self-manifestation at the Wedding of Cana
3. The Proclamation of the Kingdom of God and Jesus' Call to Conversion
4. The Transfiguration
5. The Institution of the Eucharist at the Last Supper

Sorrowful Mysteries

1. The Agony in the Garden
2. The Scourging at the Pillar
3. The Crowning with Thorns
4. The Carrying of the Cross
5. The Crucifixion

Glorious Mysteries

1. The Resurrection
2. The Ascension
3. The Descent of the Holy Spirit
4. The Assumption of Mary
5. The Crowning of Mary as the Queen of Heaven and Earth

How to Pray the Rosary

Opening

1. Begin on the crucifix and pray the Apostles' Creed.
2. On the first bead, pray the Our Father.
3. On the next three beads, pray the Hail Mary. (Some people meditate on the virtues of faith, hope, and charity on these beads.)
4. On the fifth bead, pray the Glory Be.

The Body

Each decade (set of ten beads) is organized as follows:

1. On the larger bead that comes before each set of ten, announce the mystery to be prayed (see above) and pray one Our Father.
2. On each of the ten smaller beads, pray one Hail Mary while meditating on the mystery.
3. Pray one Glory Be at the end of the decade. (There is no bead for the Glory Be.)

Conclusion

Pray the following prayer at the end of the rosary:

Hail, Holy Queen

Hail, holy Queen, Mother of Mercy,
our life, our sweetness, and our hope.
To thee do we cry,
poor banished children of Eve.
To thee do we send up our sighs,
mourning and weeping in the valley of tears.
Turn then, most gracious advocate,
thine eyes of mercy toward us;
and after this our exile,
show unto us the blessed fruit of thy womb, Jesus.
O clement, O loving, O sweet Virgin Mary.
Pray for us, O holy Mother of God,
that we may be made worthy of the promises of Christ.
Amen.

Stations of the Cross

The stations of the cross is a devotion and also a sacramental. (A sacramental is a sacred object, blessing, or devotion.) The stations of the cross are individual pictures or symbols hung on the interior walls of most Catholic churches depicting fourteen steps along Jesus' way of the cross. Praying the stations means meditating on each of the following scenes:

1. Jesus is condemned to death.
2. Jesus takes up his cross.
3. Jesus falls the first time.
4. Jesus meets his mother.
5. Simon of Cyrene helps Jesus carry his cross.

6. Veronica wipes the face of Jesus.
7. Jesus falls the second time.
8. Jesus consoles the women of Jerusalem.
9. Jesus falls the third time.
10. Jesus is stripped of his garments.
11. Jesus is nailed to the cross.
12. Jesus dies on the cross.
13. Jesus is taken down from the cross.
14. Jesus is laid in the tomb.

Some churches also include a fifteenth station, the resurrection of the Lord.

Novenas

The novena consists of the recitation of certain prayers over a period of nine days. The symbolism of nine days refers to the time Mary and the apostles spent in prayer between Jesus' ascension into heaven and Pentecost.

Many novenas are dedicated to Mary or to a saint with the faith and hope that she or he will intercede for the one making the novena. Novenas to St. Jude, St. Anthony, Our Lady of Perpetual Help, and Our Lady of Lourdes remain popular in the Church today.

Liturgy of the Hours

The Liturgy of the Hours is part of the official, public prayer of the Church. Along with the celebration of the sacraments, the recitation of the Liturgy of the Hours, or Divine Office (office means "duty" or "obligation"), allows for constant praise and thanksgiving to God throughout the day and night.

The Liturgy of Hours consists of five major divisions:

1. An hour of readings
2. Morning praises
3. Midday prayers
4. Vespers (evening prayers)
5. Compline (a short night prayer)

Scriptural prayer, especially the psalms, is at the heart of the liturgy of the hours. Each day follows a separate pattern of prayer with themes closely tied in with the liturgical year and feasts of the saints.

The Divine Praises

These praises are traditionally recited after the benediction of the Blessed Sacrament.

Blessed be God.
Blessed be his holy name.
Blessed be Jesus Christ, true God and true man.
Blessed be the name of Jesus.
Blessed be his most Sacred Heart.
Blessed be his most Precious Blood.
Blessed be Jesus in the most holy sacrament of the altar.
Blessed be the Holy Spirit, the Paraclete.
Blessed be the great Mother of God, Mary most holy.
Blessed be her holy and Immaculate Conception.
Blessed be her glorious Assumption.
Blessed be the name of Mary, Virgin and Mother.
Blessed be St. Joseph, her most chaste spouse.
Blessed be God in his angels and his saints.

I. PRAYERS

Sign of the Cross

In the name of the Father,
and of the Son,
and of the Holy Spirit. Amen.

Our Father

Our Father
who art in heaven,
hallowed be thy name.
Thy kingdom come;
thy will be done on earth as it is in heaven.
Give us this day our daily bread
and forgive us our trespasses
as we forgive those who trespass against us.
And lead us not into temptation,
but deliver us from evil.
Amen.

Glory Be

Glory be to the Father
and to the Son
and to the Holy Spirit,
as it was in the beginning,
is now,
and ever shall be,
world without end. Amen.

Hail Mary

Hail Mary, full of grace,
the Lord is with thee.
Blessed art thou among women
and blessed is the fruit of thy womb, Jesus.
Holy Mary, Mother of God,
pray for us sinners now
and at the hour of our death. Amen.

Memorare

Remember, O most gracious Virgin Mary,
that never was it known
that anyone who fled to your protection,
implored your help,
or sought your intercession was left unaided.
Inspired by this confidence,
I fly unto you,
O virgin of virgins, my mother,
To you I come, before you I stand,
sinful and sorrowful.
O Mother of the word incarnate,
despise not my petitions,
but in your mercy hear and answer me. Amen.

Hail, Holy Queen

Hail, holy Queen, Mother of Mercy,
our life, our sweetness and our hope!
To you do we cry,
poor banished children of Eve;
to you do we send up our sighs,
mourning and weeping in this valley of tears.
Turn then, O most gracious advocate,
your eyes of mercy toward us,
and after this exile,
show us the blessed fruit of your womb, Jesus.
O clement, O loving, O sweet Virgin Mary.

V. Pray for us, O holy mother of God.

R. that we may be made worthy of the promises of Christ. Amen.

The Angelus

V. The angel spoke God's message to Mary.

R. And she conceived by the Holy Spirit.
Hail Mary . . .

V. Behold the handmaid of the Lord.

R. May it be done unto me according to your word.
Hail Mary . . .

V. And the Word was made flesh.

R. And dwelled among us.
Hail Mary . . .

V. Pray for us, O holy mother of God.

R. That we may be made worthy of the promises of Christ.

Let us pray: We beseech you, O Lord, to pour out your grace into our hearts. By the message of an angel we have learned of the incarnation of Christ, your son; lead us by his passion and cross, to the glory of the resurrection. Through the same Christ our Lord. Amen.

Regina Caeli

Queen of heaven, rejoice, alleluia.
The Son you merited to bear, alleluia,
has risen as he said, alleluia.
Pray to God for us, alleluia.

V. Rejoice and be glad, O Virgin Mary, alleluia.

R. For the Lord has truly risen, alleluia.

Let us pray.

God of life, you have given joy to the world by the resurrection of your son, our Lord Jesus Christ. Through the prayers of his mother, the Virgin Mary, bring us to the happiness of eternal life. We ask this through Christ our Lord. Amen.

Grace at Meals

Before Meals

Bless us, O Lord,
and these your gifts,
which we are about to receive from
your bounty,
through Christ our Lord. Amen.

After Meals

We give you thanks, almighty God,
for these and all the gifts
which we have received
from your goodness
through Christ our Lord. Amen.

Guardian Angel Prayer

Angel of God, my guardian dear,
to whom God's love entrust me here,
ever this day be at my side, to light
and guard, to rule and guide. Amen.

Prayer for the Faithful Departed

Eternal rest grant unto them, O Lord.

R: And let perpetual light shine upon them.

May their souls and the souls of all faithful departed,
through the mercy of God, rest in peace.

R: Amen.

Morning Offering

O Jesus, through the immaculate heart of Mary, I offer you my prayers, works, joys, and sufferings of this day in union with the holy sacrifice of the Mass throughout the world. I offer them for all the intentions of your Sacred Heart: the salvation of souls, reparation for sin, the reunion of all Christians. I offer them for the intentions of our bishops and all members of the apostleship of prayer and in particular for those recommended by your Holy Father this month. Amen.

Act of Faith

O God,
I firmly believe all the truths that you
have revealed
and that you teach us through your
Church,
for you are truth itself
and can neither deceive nor be
deceived.
Amen.

Act of Hope

O God,
I hope with complete trust that you will give me,
through the merits of Jesus Christ, all necessary grace in this world
and everlasting life in the world to come,
for this is what you have promised
and you always keep your promises.
Amen.

Act of Love

O my God, I love you above all things, with my whole heart and soul, because you are all good and worthy of all my love. I love my neighbor as myself for the love of you. I forgive all who have injured me, and I ask pardon of all whom I have injured. Amen.

Prayer for Peace (St. Francis of Assisi)

Lord, make me an instrument of your peace.
Where there is hatred, let me sow love;
where there is injury, pardon;
where there is doubt, faith;
where there is despair, hope;
where there is darkness, light;
where there is sadness, joy.
O Divine Master,
grant that I may not seek so much to be consoled as to console;
to be understood, as to understand,
to be loved, as to love.
For it is in giving that we receive,
it is in pardoning that we are pardoned,
and it is in dying that we are born to eternal life.

Notes

1. Liraz Publishing Co., *The 30 Best Inspiring Anecdotes of All Time*, 2003, www.liraz.com/Anecdote.htm (06 April 2005).
2. The Graduate Center of the City University of New York, *American Religious Identification Survey*, 2001, www.gc.cuny.edu/studies/key_findings.htm (06 April 2005).
3. "Definition of the Faith" from the Council of Chalcedon found in *Decrees of the Ecumenical Councils*, ed. Norman P. Tanner, n.d., www.piar.hu/councils/ecum04.htm (09 April 2005).
4. Wildway.org, "Wakan Tanka: 'The Ten Thousand Things Are One,'" www.wildway.org/voice_wakan.php (15 February 2005)
5. Found at www.worldprayers.org/ (08 April 2005).
6. Originally found at Soul to Spirit website, www.soultospirit.com/teachers/quotes/catholic_saints.aspfrancis.
7. Ibid.
8. Adapted story "The Bishop's Gift" from an anonymous author, Afterhours Inspiration Stories, 2001,http://inspirationalstories.com/3/310.html (08 April 2005).
9. From *Pastoral Care of the Sick: Rites of Anointing and Viaticum*, International Committee on English in the Liturgy, Inc., 1982.

Glossary

Abba—An Aramaic term of endearment meaning "Daddy." Jesus used this word to teach that God is a loving Father.

abortion—The direct and deliberate ending of a pregnancy by killing the unborn child. Direct abortion, willed either as a means or an end, gravely contradicts the moral law.

absolution—The prayer by which a priest, by the power given to the Church by Christ Jesus, pardons a repentant sinner in the sacrament of Penance.

adoration—Prayer that acknowledges that God is God—Creator, Savior, Sanctifier, Lord, and Master of all creation, the source of all blessings, and worthy of our total love and devotion.

adultery—Infidelity in marriage whereby a married person has sexual intercourse with someone who is not the person's spouse.

Advent—The four-week season in the liturgical year that prepares for the coming of our Savior on Christmas.

agnostics—People who claim that God's existence cannot be known.

Amen—A Hebrew word for "truly" or "it is so," thus signifying agreement with what has been said. New Testament and liturgical prayers, creeds, and other Christian prayers end with "Amen" to show belief in what has just been said.

annulment—An official Church declaration that what appeared to be a Christian marriage never existed in the first place.

Anointing of the Sick—A sacrament of healing, administered by a priest to a baptized person, in which the Lord extends his loving, healing touch through the Church to those who are seriously ill or dying.

apostasy—The denial of Christ and repudiation of the Christian faith by a baptized Christian.

apostle—"One sent" to be Christ's ambassador, to continue his work. In its widest sense, the term refers to all of Christ's disciples whose mission is to preach his gospel in word and deed. Originally, it referred to the Twelve whom Jesus chose to help him in his earthly ministry. The successors of the twelve apostles are the bishops.

Assumption—The Church dogma that teaches that the Blessed Mother, because of her unique role in her Son's Resurrection, was taken directly to heaven when her earthly life was over. The feast of the Assumption on August 15 is a holy day of obligation.

atheist—A person who denies the existence of God.

avarice—An inordinate passion for riches and the power that comes with them.

beatific vision—Seeing God "face-to-face" in heaven, the source of our eternal happiness; final union with the Triune God for all eternity.

Bible—The inspired word of God; the written record of revelation.

bishop—A successor to the apostles who governs the local Church in a given diocese and governs the worldwide Church in union with the pope and the college of bishops. A bishop receives the fullness of the sacrament of Holy Orders.

blasphemy—Any thought, word, or act that expresses hatred or contempt for God, Christ, the Church, saints, or holy things.

Blessed Trinity—The central dogma of the Christian faith that there are three divine Persons—Father, Son, and Holy Spirit—in one God.

blessing—A prayer that invokes God's care on some person, place, thing, or undertaking.

calumny—Slander, that is, lies told about another person in order to harm his or her reputation and lead others to make false judgments about the person.

canon law—The official body of rules (canons) that provides for good order in the Catholic Church.

capital sins—Sins that are the root of other sins and vices. There are seven capital sins: pride, covetousness, envy, anger, gluttony, lust, and sloth.

cardinal virtues—The "hinge" virtues from which all other virtues come. They are prudence, justice, fortitude, and temperance.

catechesis—A process of "education in the faith" for young people and adults with the view of making them disciples of Jesus Christ.

Catechism of the Catholic Church—A compendium of Catholic doctrine on faith and morals published in 1992 that serves Catholics as "a sure norm for teaching the faith" and "an authentic reference text."

catechumen—An unbaptized person who is preparing to receive all of the sacraments of Christian initiation.

Catholic—From a Greek word meaning "universal" or "general." The Catholic Church is the Christian community that is one, holy, apostolic, and catholic—that is, open to all people everywhere at all times and that preaches the fullness of God's revelation in Jesus Christ.

celibacy—The state of being unmarried that priests and other religious choose in order to dedicate their lives totally to Jesus Christ and God's People.

charism—A special gift of the Holy Spirit that helps us build up the Church, Christ's body. Some of these gifts are the ability to express wisdom and knowledge, healing, prophecy, and discernment of spirits (1 Cor 12:4-11).

chastity—The moral virtue that enables persons to integrate their sexuality into their stations in life.

Chrism—Blessed by the bishop, this perfumed oil is used for anointing in the sacraments of Baptism, Confirmation, and Holy Orders. It represents the gift of the Holy Spirit.

Christ—A title for Jesus meaning "the anointed one." In Greek, the word Christos translated the Hebrew Messiah.

Christian morality—A life in Christ through responsible living that flows from our dignity as God's adopted children, made in his image, and from Christ's command to love.

Church—The Body of Christ, that is, the community of God's people who profess faith in the risen Lord Jesus and love and serve others under the guidance of the Holy Spirit. The Roman Catholic Church is guided by the pope and his bishops.

common good—The sum total of social conditions that allow people to reach their fulfillment more fully and more easily.

communion of saints—The unity in Christ of all those he has redeemed—the Church on earth, in heaven, and in purgatory.

concupiscence—An inclination to commit sin that can be found in human desires and appetites as a result of original sin.

contemplation—Wordless prayer whereby a person's mind and heart rest in God's goodness and majesty.

contrition—Heartfelt sorrow and aversion for sins committed along with the intention of sinning no more. Contrition is the most important act of penitents, necessary for receiving the sacrament of Penance.

covenant—The open-ended contract of love between God and human beings. Jesus' death and resurrection sealed God's new covenant of love for all time. Testament translates to covenant.

deism—The belief that God did create the universe but that he takes no further interest in it.

despair—Giving up hope in God's saving graces, his forgiveness of sins, and his promise of salvation.

detraction— Without a legitimate reason, disclosing a person's faults to someone who did not know about them, thus causing unjust harm to that person's reputation.

diaconate—The third degree in the hierarchy of Holy Orders. The diaconate is not a degree of the ministerial priesthood. Deacons are ordained ministers who assist bishops and priests in the celebration of liturgy, distribute communion, witness and bless marriages, proclaim and preach the Gospel, celebrate funerals and perform various ministries of Christian charity all under the authority of their bishop.

divine missions of the Blessed Trinity—The special roles in salvation history attributed to each member of the Trinity: the Father is the Creator, the Son is the Savior, and the Holy Spirit is the Sanctifier. The whole plan of salvation is the common work of the three divine Persons who possess one and the same nature.

divine providence—God's loving and watchful guidance over his creatures on their way to their final goal and perfection.

Doctor of the Church—A Church writer of great learning and holiness whose works the Church has highly recommended for studying and living the faith.

dogma—A central truth of revelation that Catholics are obliged to believe.

ecumenical council—A worldwide, official assembly of the bishops under the direction of the pope. There have been twenty-one ecumenical councils, the most recent being the Second Vatican Council (1962–1965).

ecumenism—The movement, inspired and led by the Holy Spirit, that seeks the union of all Christian religions and eventually the unity of all peoples throughout the world.

epiclesis—The prayer that petitions God to send the Holy Spirit to transform the bread and wine offered at the Eucharistic liturgy into the body and blood of Jesus Christ. This term also applies to the prayer said in every sacrament that asks for the sanctifying power of the Holy Spirit.

Epiphany—The feast that celebrates the mystery of Christ's manifestation as the Savior of the world.

eschatology—A study of and teaching about the "last things" (death, judgment, heaven, hell, purgatory, the Second Coming of Christ, and the resurrection of the body).

essential rite—That portion of the liturgical celebration of a sacrament that is strictly necessary in order for the sacrament to be valid.

euthanasia—"Any action or omission which of itself and by intention causes death, with the purpose of eliminating all suffering" (The Gospel of Life, No. 65). This is distinguished from palliative care that alleviates a person's suffering as the inevitable death nears. Euthanasia is a serious violation of the fifth commandment, a crime against life, and an attack on humanity.

evangelical counsels—Vows of personal poverty, chastity understood as lifelong celibacy, and obedience to the demands of the community being joined which are professed by those entering the consecrated life.

evangelists—The four evangelists refers to the authors of the four gospels: Matthew, Mark, Luke, and John. The word evangelist means "one who proclaims in word and deed the good news of Jesus Christ."

evangelization—To bring the good news of Jesus Christ to others.

fruits of the Holy Spirit—Perfections that result from living in union with the Holy Spirit.

gifts of the Holy Spirit—An outpouring of God's gifts that enable us to live a Christian life. The traditional gifts of the Holy Spirit are wisdom, understanding, knowledge, counsel (right judgment), fortitude (courage), piety (reverence), and fear of the Lord (wonder and awe).

gospel—A term meaning "good news." The term refers to 1) Jesus' own preaching; 2) the preaching about Jesus the Savior (Jesus Christ is the good news proclaimed by the Church); and 3) the four Spirit-inspired written versions of the good news—the gospels of Matthew, Mark, Luke, and John.

grace—God's gift of friendship and life that enables us to share his life and love.

Great Schism—A major break between the churches of the West (centered in Rome) and the East (centered in the Greek city of Constantinople). The Roman Church had added the expression "and the Son" to the article of the Nicene Creed, referring to the Holy Spirit ("he proceeds from the Father and the Son), without seeking approval from a Church-wide council of bishops.

heaven—A perfect life of supreme happiness with God and the communion of saints for all eternity.

hell—Eternal separation from God that results from a person dying after freely and deliberately choosing to act against God's will (that is, not repenting of mortal sin).

heresy—An obstinate denial after Baptism to believe a truth that must be believed with divine and Catholic faith, or an obstinate doubt about such truth.

hierarchy—The official, sacred leadership in the Church made up of the Church's ordained ministers—bishops, priests, and deacons. The symbol of unity and authority in the Church is the pope, the Bishop of Rome, who is the successor of St. Peter.

icons—Religious images or paintings that are traditional among many Eastern Christians.

idolatry—Giving worship to something or someone other than the true God.

Immaculate Conception—The Church dogma that holds that the Blessed Mother, by a special grace from God and by virtue of her Son's merits, was preserved immune from all stain of original sin from the very first moment of her human existence. This feast is celebrated on December 8, a holy day of obligation.

immanence—A trait of God which refers to God's intimate union with and total presence to his creation.

Incarnation—The dogma that God's eternal Son assumed a human nature and became man in Jesus Christ to save us from our sins. (The term literally means "taking on human flesh.")

infallibility—A gift of the Spirit whereby the pope and bishops are preserved from error when proclaiming a doctrine related to Christian faith or morals.

intercession—A prayer of petition for the sake of others.

justification—The Holy Spirit's grace that cleanses us from our sins through faith in Jesus Christ and Baptism. It makes us right with God. Justification not only frees us from sin, but sanctifies us in the depth of our being.

kingdom of God—The reign of God proclaimed by Jesus and begun in his life, death, and resurrection. It refers to the process of God reconciling and renewing all things through his Son, to the fact of his will being done on earth as it is in heaven.

laity—All the members of the Church who have been initiated into the Church through Baptism and who are not ordained (the clergy) or in consecrated life. The laity participate in Jesus' prophetic, priestly, and kingly ministries.

last (general) judgment—Jesus Christ's judgment of the living and the dead on the last day when he comes to fully establish God's kingdom fully.

Lent—A season of intensified prayer, fasting, and almsgiving in preparation of Christ's resurrection and our redemption at Easter. The season begins on Ash Wednesday and continues to Holy Thursday, a period of forty weekdays and six Sundays.

liturgy—The official public worship of the Church. The sacraments and the Divine Office constitute the Church's liturgy. The Mass is the most important liturgical celebration.

Magisterium—The official teaching authority of the Church. The Lord bestowed the right and power to teach in his name on Peter and the apostles and their successors. The Magisterium is the bishops in communion with the successor of Peter, the Bishop of Rome (pope).

marks of the Church—Four essential signs or characteristics of Christ's Church that mark it as his true Church. The Church is one, holy, catholic, and apostolic.

meditation—A form of prayer where the mind and imagination focus on Christ or some truth of divine revelation with the purpose of applying the lessons we learn to our lives.

modesty—A fruit of the virtue of purity, it protects one's most intimate inner self, refusing to unveil what should remain covered.

monotheistic—Religions that believe that there is only one God. Christianity, Judaism, and Islam are the three great monotheistic world religions.

mortal sin—A serious violation of God's law of love that results in the loss of God's life (sanctifying grace) in the soul of the sinner. To commit mortal sin there must be grave matter, full knowledge of the evil done, and full consent of the will.

mystery—A reality filled with God's invisible presence. This term applies to the Blessed Trinity's plan of salvation in Jesus Christ, the Church which is his body, and the sacraments.

natural law—God's plan for human living that is written in the very way he created things. Binding on all people at all times, it is the light of understanding that God puts in us so we can discover what is good and what is evil.

neophytes—Those newly received into the Church through the sacraments of initiation at the Easter vigil.

oath—A statement or promise that calls on God to be witness to it.

original holiness and justice—The state of man and woman before sin. "From their friendship with God flowed the happiness of their existence in paradise" (CCC, 384).

original sin—The fallen state of human nature into which all generations of people are born. Christ Jesus came to save us from original sin.

parable—A favorite teaching device of Jesus in which he told a short story with a striking, memorable comparison that taught a religious message, usually about some aspect of God's kingdom.

Paraclete—Another name for the Holy Spirit that means advocate, defender, or consoler.

Parousia—The second coming of Christ when the Lord will judge the living and the dead.

particular judgment—The individual's judgment immediately after death, when Christ will rule on one's eternal destiny to be spent in heaven (after purification in purgatory, if needed) or in hell.

Paschal mystery—The saving love of God most fully revealed in the life and especially the passion, death, resurrection, and glorious ascension of his Son Jesus Christ.

passions—Our emotional response to the good or evil we encounter.

perjury—Lying under oath by asking God to witness a lie. This is a grave violation of the second commandment.

petition—A prayer in which we ask God for his help, or forgiveness, or for some good whether for ourselves or for others.

polygamy—Having more than one wife at the same time. It distorts the unity of marriage between a man and a woman and offends the dignity of women.

polytheistic—Religions that believe in multiple gods and goddesses. The ancient Greeks and Romans were polytheistic as is the Hindu faith.

praise—A form of prayer whereby we acknowledge God and his goodness and glorify him for who he is.

prayer—Conversation with God. Lifting of one's mind and heart to God or requesting good things from him. Joining one's thoughts and love to God in adoration and blessing, petition, intercession, thanksgiving, and praise.

precepts of the Church—Basic rules that bind Catholics who belong to Christ's Body.

presbyters—Priests or members of the order of priesthood who are coworkers with the bishop and servant to God's people, especially in celebrating the Eucharist.

Protestant—A baptized Christian who believes in Christ but who does not accept all the teachings of the Catholic Church. Protestant communities first came into existence during the Reformation in the sixteenth century.

purgatory—The state of purification that takes place after death for those who need to be made clean and holy before meeting the all-holy God in heaven.

religion—The relationship between God and humans that results in a body of beliefs and a set of practices: creed, cult, and code. Religion expresses itself in worship and service to God and by extension to all people and all creation.

resurrection of the body—The Christian belief that when Christ comes again he will reunite the bodies of every human with their souls.

sacrament—An outward (visible) sign of an invisible grace. An "efficacious" symbol that brings about the spiritual reality to which it points. This term applies to Christ Jesus, the great sign of God's love for us; to the Church, his continuing presence in our world; and to the seven sacraments.

sacrament of Holy Orders—The sacrament of apostolic ministry at the service of communion whereby Christ, though the Church, ordains men through the laying on of hands. It includes three degrees: episcopate, presbyterate, and diaconate. Those who exercise these orders are bishops, priests, and deacons.

sacrament of Matrimony—A Sacrament at the Service of Communion in which Christ binds a man and woman into a permanent covenant of love and life and bestows his graces on them to help them live as a community and as a loving family, if he blesses them with children.

sacrament of Penance—A Sacrament of Healing, also known as reconciliation or confession, through which Christ extends his forgiveness to sinners, bringing about reconciliation with God and the Church. Its essential elements consist of the acts of the penitent (contrition, confession of sins, and satisfaction) and the prayer of absolution of the priest.

sacramental character—A lasting effect of Baptism, Confirmation, and Holy Orders that seals and configures the recipient to Christ in a special way. Baptism makes us a child of God; Confirmation makes us a witness of Jesus Christ; Holy Orders permanently designates a man as a bishop, priest, or deacon. These sacraments can be received only once.

sacramentals—Sacred signs (for example, objects, places, and actions) that resemble the sacraments. Through the prayers of the Church, spiritual effects are signified and obtained.

Sacred Tradition—The living transmission of the Church's gospel message found in the Church's teaching, life, and worship. It is faithfully preserved, handed on, and interpreted by the Church's Magisterium.

saint—A "holy one" of God who lives in union with God through the grace of Jesus Christ and the power of the Holy Spirit and whom God rewards with eternal life in heaven.

salvation—God's forgiveness of sins, accomplished through the mercy of Jesus Christ, resulting in the restoration of friendship with God.

sanctifying grace—The grace, or gift of God's friendship, that heals fallen human nature and gives us a share in the divine life of the Blessed Trinity. A habitual, supernatural gift, it makes us perfect, holy, and Christlike (CCC, 1999).

sin—An offense against God through a violation of truth, reason, and conscience.

society—Any community of human beings that unites them in a common purpose.

social justice doctrine—The teachings of the Magisterium that pertain to the ways in which societies function to promote the common good.

solidarity—A Christian virtue of charity and friendship whereby material and spiritual goods are shared among members of the human family.

sorcery—Attempts to tame occult powers in order to use them to gain a supernatural power over others.

sources of morality—The three basic elements of every action: the moral object (what we do), the intention (our motive), and the circumstances (context and consequences). All three elements must be good for a proposed action to be good. In addition, some moral objects (like murder and adultery) are always evil and can never be justified. Also, a good intention can never justify an evil act.

subsidiarity—A principle of Catholic social justice that holds that a community of a higher order should not interfere in the internal life of a community of a lower order, depriving it of its functions.

theological virtues—Three important virtues bestowed on us at baptism which relate us to God: faith (belief in and personal knowledge of God) hope (trust in God's salvation and his bestowal of the graces needed to attain it) and charity (love of God and love of neighbor).

theophany—An appearance or manifestation of God to humans.

transcendence—A trait of God that refers to God's total otherness and being infinitely beyond and independent of creation.

transubstantiation—The term used to describe what happens at the consecration of the bread and wine at Mass when their entire substance is turned into the entire substance of the Body and Blood of Christ, even though the appearances of bread and wine remain. The Eucharistic presence of Christ begins at the moment of consecration and endures as long as the Eucharistic species subsist.

Triduum—The three-day long liturgy that is the Church's most solemn celebration of the Paschal mystery. It begins with the Mass of the Lord's Supper on Holy Thursday, continues through the Good Friday service, and ends on Holy Saturday with the conclusion of the Easter vigil. Although it takes place over three days, the Triduum is considered one single liturgy.

venial sin—Actual sin that weakens and wounds our relationship with God, but does not destroy divine life in our souls.

viaticum—Holy Communion received by dying persons to help them pass over to God in the afterlife.

vices—Bad habits or dispositions (like pride) that turn us from the good and incline us to commit evil.

virgin birth—A Church dogma that teaches that Jesus was conceived through the Virgin Mary by the power of the Holy Spirit without the cooperation of a human father.

virtues—Firm attitudes, stable dispositions, habitual perfections of intellect and will that govern our actions, order our passions, and guide our conduct according to reason and faith (CCC, 1804).

Yahweh—The sacred Hebrew name for God which means "I am who am," " I am," or "I am who I am."

Index

P

R

S

T